Realism and the Audiovisual Media

Also by Lúcia Nagib

WERNER HERZOG: Film as Reality

AROUND THE JAPANESE NOUVELLE VAGUE

BORN OF THE ASHES: The Auteur and the Individual in Oshima's Films

THE BRAZILIAN FILM REVIVAL: Interviews with 90 Filmmakers of the 90s

BRAZIL ON SCREEN: Cinema Novo, New Cinema, Utopia

THE NEW BRAZILIAN CINEMA (*edited collection*)

OZU (*edited collection*)

MASTER MIZOGUCHI (*edited collection*)

WORLD CINEMA AND THE ETHICS OF REALISM (*forthcoming*)

Realism and the Audiovisual Media

Edited by
Lúcia Nagib
and
Cecília Mello

palgrave
macmillan

First published 2009 by
PALGRAVE MACMILLAN

Palgrave Macmillan in the UK is an imprint of Macmillan Publishers Limited, registered in England, company number 785998, of Houndmills, Basingstoke, Hampshire RG21 6XS.

Palgrave Macmillan in the US is a division of St Martin's Press LLC, 175 Fifth Avenue, New York, NY 10010.

Palgrave Macmillan is the global academic imprint of the above companies and has companies and representatives throughout the world.

Palgrave® and Macmillan® are registered trademarks in the United States, the United Kingdom, Europe and other countries

ISBN-13: 978-0-230-57722-0   hardback

This book is printed on paper suitable for recycling and made from fully managed and sustained forest sources. Logging, pulping and manufacturing processes are expected to conform to the environmental regulations of the country of origin.

A catalogue record for this book is available from the British Library.

A catalog record for this book is available from the Library of Congress.

10 9 8 7 6 5 4 3 2 1
18 17 16 15 14 13 12 11 10 09

Printed and bound in Great Britain by
CPI Antony Rowe, Chippenham and Eastbourne

Contents

List of Illustrations

Notes on Contributors

Louis Bayman is an Arts and Humanities Research Council (AHRC)-funded Ph.D. candidate at King's College London. His research focuses on melodrama in post-war Italian cinema, including its realist and operatic aspects.

Mary Ann Doane is George Hazard Crooker Professor of Modern Culture and Media at Brown University. She is the author of *The Emergence of Cinematic Time: Modernity, Contingency, the Archive* (Harvard University Press, 2002), *Femmes Fatales: Feminism, Film Theory, Psychoanalysis* (Routledge, 1991) and *The Desire to Desire: The Woman's Film of the 1940s* (Indiana University Press, 1987). She has published a wide range of articles on feminist film theory, sound in the cinema, psychoanalytic theory, television, and sexual and racial difference in film. Currently, she is researching the use of the close-up in film practice and theory.

Thomas Elsaesser is Professor of Film and Visual Culture at the University of Amsterdam. His book publications include, among others, *New German Cinema: A History* (1989), *Early Cinema: Space Frame Narrative* (1990), *Fassbinder's Germany* (1996), *A Second Life: German Cinema's First Decades* (1996), *Cinema Futures* (1998, with Kay Hoffmann), *Weimar Cinema and After* (2000), *Metropolis* (2001), *Filmgeschichte und frühes Kino* (2002), *Kino der Kaiserzeit* (2002, with Michael Wedel), *Studying Contemporary Film* (2003, with Warren Buckland), *Harun Farocki – Working on the Sightlines* (2004), *European Cinema: Face to Face with Hollywood* (2005), *Terror und Trauma: die Gewalt des Vergangen in der BRD* (2007) and *Filmtheorie: zur Einführung* (2007, with Malte Hagener).

Armida de la Garza joined the Department of Hispanic and Latin American Studies at the University of Nottingham, UK, in 2004. Since 2005 she has been teaching in the Nottingham Ningbo Campus, China. Her research interests centre on film and its relation to cultural identity, especially national identity, as well as on the links between documentary and diaspora. She is the author of the book *Mexico on Film* (2006) and is currently working on a collaborative research project entitled *Transnational Cinema in Globalising Societies: Asia and Latin America*.

Leighton Grist is a senior lecturer in Media and Film Studies at the University of Winchester, where he is Programme Director for the MA in Film Studies. The writer of numerous articles published in edited collections and journals, his output has included work on classical and post-classical Hollywood, genre and matters pertaining to film theory, psychoanalysis and gender. He is the author of *The Films of Martin Scorsese, 1963–77: Authorship* *and Context* (Macmillan/St Martin's Press, 2000), and is currently working on a follow-up volume.

Beth Johnson is a lecturer in Media and Film Studies at Liverpool Hope University. She has completed her Arts and Humanities Research Council (AHRC)-funded Ph.D. research on avant-garde real-sex film and literature, entitled *Ocularcentric [Re]vision*, at Lancaster University, in 2007. Her research interests include avant-garde cinema, the European aesthetic, the extreme scene, modernity and spectatorship. She is the author of various academic and commercial publications, including 'Masochism and the Mother, Pedagogy and Perversion' (*Angelaki: Journal of Theoretical Humanities*, forthcoming, Routledge, Nov 2009), 'Sex, Psychoanalysis and Sublimation in Dexter' (forthcoming in *Dexter: Cutting Edge Television*, IB Tauris, 2009) and reviews for *Screen* journal. She is currently developing a monograph based upon 'body spectacle' in the films of Catherine Breillat.

Jacob Leigh teaches at Royal Holloway, University of London, in the Media Arts Department, where he is responsible for the following courses: Film Aesthetics, Documentary, Hitchcock and Point of View, and Hollywood Star Performances. His research interests include film style, film narrative, film interpretation and evaluation. His publications include *The Cinema of Ken Loach* and *Reading Rohmer*, published in *Close-Up* 02. He is currently writing *The Cinema of Eric Rohmer* for Wallflower Press.

Cecília Mello is FAPESP Postdoctoral Fellow in the Film Department, University of São Paulo. In 2006 she completed her Ph.D. in Film Studies at Birkbeck College, University of London, fully funded by the Brazilian Ministry of Education, under the supervision of Laura Mulvey. Her thesis *Everyday Voices: The Demotic Impulse in English Post-war Film and Television* focuses on issues of realism in English film. Her publications include 'Open Arms and Crowed Rooms: The 6th Shanghai International Film Festival' (*Framework*, Spring 2003) and 'I Don't Owe You Anything: The Smiths and Kitchen-sink Cinema' (forthcoming in *Why Pamper Life's Complexities: Essays on The Smiths*, Manchester University Press, 2010).

Diane Myers has specialized as a producer/director in access-driven observational documentaries and currently leads the BA Broadcasting programme within the Institute of Communications Studies at the University of Leeds. Her research interests include media law and ethics, and her programme credits include 'Partners in Crime', a Channel 4 series which secured first-time access to every agency in the criminal justice system, and 'Nobody's Child' which opened Channel 4's Adoption Season and won the Royal Television Society Award for Best Educational Campaign. She is an executive committee member of the Centre for Practice Based Research in the Arts and a member of the Communications Ethics Theme Team (IDEA CETL) at the University of Leeds.

Lúcia Nagib is Centenary Professor of World Cinemas and Director of the Centre for World Cinemas, University of Leeds. Her major research subjects are cinematic realism, new waves and contemporary new cinemas. She is the author of the books *Werner Herzog: Film as Reality* (Estação Liberdade), *Around the Japanese Nouvelle Vague* (Editora da Unicamp), *Born of the Ashes: The Auteur and the Individual in Oshima's Films* (Edusp), *The Brazilian Film Revival: Interviews with 90 Filmmakers of the 90s* (Editora 34) and *Brazil on Screen: Cinema Novo, New Cinema, Utopia* (IB Tauris). She is the editor of *The New Brazilian Cinema* (IB Tauris), *Ozu* (Marco Zero) and *Master Mizoguchi* (Navegar). Her book *World Cinema and the Ethics of Realism* is forthcoming with Continuum.

Davina Quinlivan is a Ph.D. candidate in the Film Studies department at King's College. Her research project explores the breathing body in the cinema of David Cronenberg, Atom Egoyan and Lars von Trier. She has two articles forthcoming, a paper on Marina de Van's *In My Skin* in an edited volume entitled *Shame and Guilt* (Oxford: Peter Lang, Modern French Identities Series) and an experimental essay on installation spaces, video art and the 'emotional geographies' of Giuliana Bruno in a book on new feminist practices and aesthetics. She has also written for the peer-reviewed online filmsalon *www.film-philosophy.com*.

Ming-yeh T. Rawnsley joined the University of Leeds in 2007, where she lectures on Chinese-language films. Before this, she was the Head of Chinese Studies and Head of the Institute of Asia-Pacific Studies, University of Nottingham in Ningbo, China, between August 2005 and January 2007. She publishes widely in both Chinese and English languages on media, culture and literature. Her recent English publications include *Political Communications in Greater China* (co-edited with Gary Rawnsley, 2003) and *Critical Security, Democratisation and Television in Taiwan* (with Gary Rawnsley, 2001). She is currently working on a monograph, *Culture and Social Change in Taiwan: Society, Cinema and Theatre*, to be published by RoutledgeCurzon.

Anna Backman Rogers is a Ph.D. candidate at the University of Edinburgh. Her research area is crisis, ritual and liminality in the cinema of Sofia Coppola, Jim Jarmusch and Gus Van Sant, using the writings of Gilles Deleuze, Arnold Van Gennep and Victor Turner as a thematic and aesthetic approach.

João Moreira Salles is a documentary filmmaker. In 1985 he wrote the screenplay for the documentary series *Japan, a Journey in Time*. In 1987 he directed *China, The Empire of the Centre* and wrote the screenplay for *Krajberg, the Poet of the Remains*. Two years later he directed the television series *America* and the documentary *Poetry is One or Two Lines and behind It a Huge Landscape* about poet Ana Cristina César. In 1990 he directed *Blues*. For cable channel GNT, he directed the documentary *Jorge Amado* and the series *Football*, co-directed by Arthur Fontes. Together with Katia Lund, he directed *News of a Personal War* in 1999. In 2000 he directed *The Valley* and *Santa Cruz: Holy Cross*, both made in collaboration with journalist Marcos Sá Corrêa. In 2002, he directed *Nelson Freire*, his first documentary for cinema. In 2004, he launched *Intermissions*, a behind-the-scenes look at the election of Luiz Inácio Lula da Silva, the President of Brazil. In 2007 he directed *Santiago*.

Marc Silberman is Professor of German and Director of the Centre for German and European Studies at the University of Wisconsin-Madison. His research and teaching focus on three related fields: the history of German cinema, Bertolt Brecht and the tradition of political theatre, and East German literature and culture. He authored *German Cinema: Texts in Context* (Wayne State UP, 1995) and has edited 20 additional volumes or special journal issues, most recently 'The Art of Hearing' (*Monatshefte* 98.2 / 2006) and 'Cold-War German Cinema' (*Film History* 18.1 / 2006). In addition, he edited the *Brecht Yearbook* from 1990–5 and is active as a translator, including *Brecht on Film and Radio* (Methuen 2000).

Vlad Strukov is Lecturer in Russian and World Cinemas at the University of Leeds. His publications on Russian film, animation, mass media and national identity have appeared in various journals, including 'Russia's Internet Media Policies: Open Space and Ideological Closure' (*Post-Soviet Russian Media: Conflicting Signals*, edited by B. Beumers, S. Hutchings and N. Rulyova, London: Routledge, 2008), 'Virtualization of Space and Self in Tarkovsky's *Solaris* (1972)' (*Tarkovsky*, edited by N. Dunn. London: Black Dog Publishing, 2008) and 'The Return of Gods: Andrei Zviagintsev's *Vozvrascheniie* [*The Return*]' (*Slavic and East European Journal*, USA, Volume 51, No. 2; June 2007). He is a new media curator and the founding editor of *Static*, an international online journal of culture supported by the Tate and The Institute of Contemporary Arts. He is the editor of *Russian Cyber Space* journal. He is currently researching digital and web-induced arts, space and authorship.

Ismail Xavier is Professor of Film at the University of São Paulo. He is the author, among other books, of *Allegories of Underdevelopment: Aesthetics and Politics in Modern Brazilian Cinema* (London/Minneapolis, University of Minnesota Press, 1997), *O olhar e a cena: Hollywood, melodrama, Cinema Novo, Nelson Rodrigues* (São Paulo, CosacNaify, 2003) and *Sertão mar – Glauber Rocha e a estética da fome* (São Paulo, CosacNaify, 2007, 3rd edition). He has contributed to *Brazilian Cinema*, edited by Randal Johnson & Robert Stam (New York, Columbia University Press, 1995), *The New Brazilian Cinema*, edited by Lúcia Nagib (London, IB Tauris, 2003) and *A Companion to Film Theory*, edited by Toby Miller and Robert Stam (Oxford, Blackwell Publishing, 1999).

Acknowledgements

The editors would like to thank, in the first place, the British Academy, for having contributed substantial funds to the conference 'Realism and the Audiovisual Media', held by the Centre for World Cinemas at the University of Leeds, in December 2007. Many of the chapters included in this book originated at this conference. Thanks are also due to the Leeds School of Modern Languages and Cultures (SMLC) and its director, Mark Williams, as well as the Louis le Prince Centre for Cinema, Photography and Television and its previous and current directors, Graham Roberts and Simon Popple, whose financial, intellectual and practical support were instrumental to the success of the conference. We are also thankful to the SMLC for extending its funding to this book. The Centre for World Cinemas staff and students, and Paddy Power in particular, gave us invaluable help and organisational backing. We are greatly indebted to those who granted us free use of pictures in this book: Kim Ki-duk; Kramsie Productions Ltd; Praesens-Film, Zurich; HBO®; Andrew Repasky McElhinney; Trust Films; Emily Watson; BBC; Ken Loach; Kazuo Hara, Sachiko Kobayashi and Shisso Production; VideoFilmes; and Producciones Anhelo, S.A. de C.V. Thanks to Sarah Metcalf, Soh-youn Kim and Dudley Andrew, we were able to resolve some thorny copyright issues. Christopher White contributed excellent copy-editing work. Our appreciation also goes to Christabel Scaife, our brilliant editor at Palgrave Macmillan. Finally, our love goes to Stephen Shennan and João Lemos, our unfailing companions.

Introduction

At the origin of this book are two recent phenomena: on the one hand, the return of realist tendencies and practices in world cinema and television; on the other, the 'rehabilitation' of realism in film and media theory. This book undertakes an in-depth – though by no means exhaustive – investigation of these phenomena, querying their origins, relations, divergences and intersections from a variety of perspectives.

The trend widely perceived as world cinema's 'realist revival' finds its beginning in a *post*-postmodern era, kick-started in the mid-1990s by movements such as Dogma 95 in Denmark, whose uncompromising realist project was famously expressed in a manifesto in the form of a 'Vow of Chastity'. Such movements, as pointed out by Anne Jerslev (2002, pp. 7–8), signalled the end of irony and intertextuality, and the re-establishment of moving image's ties with objective reality. Just a few years earlier, Godard had launched a typical postmodern take on realism with *Germany Year 90 Nine Zero* (*Allemagne 90 neuf zéro*, 1991), bringing history and cinema back to a 'new zero' in reunified Germany by evoking, through a humorous pun, Rossellini's neorealist milestone *Germany Year Zero* (*Germania anno zero*, 1947). Postmodern cinema was thereafter consecrated through the pastiche style of the likes of Quentin Tarantino and David Lynch, and replicated across the globe. The early 1990s postmodern style has, however, long ceased to inflect the ways in which art cinema evolves – Lynch himself has been exploring the borderline between realism and fantasy in his digital experiments, such as *Inland Empire* (2006). Instead it has been appropriated by, and confined to, commercial productions, stretching from Hollywood to Korea and Hong Kong, which, in lieu of narrative, rely almost exclusively on the multiplication of attractions and special effects.

On the other hand, if the new cinemas that popped up across the world from the mid-1990s, in Denmark, Brazil, Argentina, Mexico, Lithuania, Russia and many other countries, are clear evidence of a 'return to the Real' – to resort to Zizek's Lacanian vocabulary – it is no less true that the historical chain of realist film cycles has never really been disrupted (Elsaesser, in this volume, actually defines world cinema of all times by its higher degree of realism, as opposed to Hollywood). Since Italian neorealism, new waves, partly or entirely committed to revelatory realism, have emerged in France, Japan, Britain and India from the late 1950s, in Eastern Europe and Latin America in the 1960s, and in Germany in the 1960s–70s. When from the mid-1980s storytelling, together with history and reality itself, were brought under suspicion with the collapse of the socialist utopia, realism continued to thrive, in minimalist form in Iran (Kiarostami, Makhmalbaf), as 'observational realism' (Rawnsley, in this volume) in Taiwan (Hou Hsiao-hsien, Edward Yang, Tsai Ming-liang), then in epic dimensions with Zhang Yimou and Chen Kaige's early historical films, in China.

What seems to be the real novelty about the current world cinema trend is its obstinate adherence to realism when all odds would point to its succumbing to the virtual lures of the digital. Instead, digital technology has been more often than not resorted to as a facilitator of the recording of real locations and characters, as well as a means to expand the application of techniques traditionally identified with realism, such as the long take so cherished by Bazin. The most notable example here is Sokurov's *Russian Ark* (*Russkiy kovcheg*, 2002), a feature film shot entirely in a single take straight onto hard-disk (see Strukov's chapter). Sokurov's tour de force, at least as a premise, would fulfil Bazin's most extravagant dreams of spatial continuity, which, as we know, was for him an indispensable realist requirement. There is, of course, the question of whether digital manipulation inevitably effaces the indexical trace from the moving image and its accompanying sound, and we will return to this later. Let us for the moment retain the fact that, be it on digital, super-16mm or 35mm, the long take, combined with real locations and characters, has become a recurrent feature in the works of contemporary world cinema's most creative directors, including names such as Tsai Ming-liang (Taiwan/Malaysia), Carlos Reygadas (Mexico), Béla Tarr (Hungary), Apichatpong Weerasethakul (Thailand), Jia Zhang-ke (China) and Manoel de Oliveira (Portugal). Despite the often specialized audiences this production attracts, it nonetheless signals a much wider reception trend as reflected in the documentary boom in recent years, which has allowed the genre to break away from its restricted distribution niche and go on to win festivals such as Cannes and become box-office hits across the globe, as Michael Moore's case well illustrates. The same applies to television, whose programming profile has radically changed in the past decade, to respond to the huge – and often baffling – popularity of reality shows.

Realism rehabilitated

The question of realism permeates audiovisual media at all levels. In the first place, as recording media, they entertain an unmediated (or 'ontological' or 'indexical') relation with objective reality, as opposed to other mimetic or representational arts (Kracauer, 1997; Bazin, 1967; Wollen, 1998; Cavell, 1979). On the perceptual level, they also benefit from a surplus of resemblance with the phenomenological world because of their unique combination of movement and time, something that has been referred to as an 'impression of reality' (Metz, 1974; Baudry, 1986). On the other hand, and regardless of their recording prerogatives, audiovisual media can affect spectators through a 'reality effect' by means of graphic representations able to cause physical and emotional impact even when resulting from animation or computer-generated images and sound (Black, 2002). Film practices are often deemed 'realist' when they operate on the confluence between cinema and news media in general, and television in particular, so as to share their immediacy and direct access to reality (see Mello's and Xavier's chapters). Film currents and movements, in their turn, have often resorted to realism as style, in order to reveal concealed or unknown political, social, psychological or mystical dimensions of reality, such as French poetic realism in the 1930s, Italian neorealism in the 1940s and the various cycles of new waves and new cinemas we have listed above. Finally, in the realm of genre, disputable though the category of generic realism may be in fiction film (see Bayman's chapter on melodrama and realism), it is certainly the issue at stake when it comes to documentary-making both for cinema and television, including the ethical implications of dealing with, manipulating and representing reality (see Salles's and Myers's chapters). By surveying the current state of the realist issue in theory and practice, this book intends to address as many of these layers as possible, including hitherto little-explored perspectives, such as the ways in which cinematic scale effects a sense of the real and the unreal (Doane) and film as the production of reality (Nagib).

Identified as it is with the very nature of cinema, realism has underpinned film theory from its inception, from Béla Balázs and Jean Epstein in the 1920s to Umberto Barbaro in the 1930s–40s, and in particular after World War II with Siegfried Kracauer's and most notably André Bazin's realist theories. Based on a study dating back to 1945, Bazin published in 1958 his foundational essay 'The Ontology of the Photographic Image', according to which film, more than any other plastic arts, is destined to realism from birth owing to its photographic basis, which enables a transfer of 'the reality from the thing to its reproduction' (Bazin, 1967, p. 14). In 1960, and unaware of Bazin's work, Kracauer, in his book *Theory of Film – The Redemption of Physical Reality*, embraced the same principle by asserting that film, as a photographic medium, is not only uniquely equipped to record and reveal physical reality, but depends on and gravitates around it (Kracauer, 1997, p. 28). Film's ontology has since become the focus of a number of approaches (Cavell, 1979, Perez, 1998 and many others, as comprehensively reviewed in Leigh's chapter, apropos of Rohmer). The most influential of these has no doubt been Wollen's 1969 essay 'The Semiology of Cinema', in which Bazin's ontology is identified with the indexical sign, in Peirce's terms, for stressing 'the existential bond between sign and object' (Wollen, [1969] 1998, p. 86). Wollen's point was certainly not to defend realism as style, as Bazin had done, but to celebrate Godard's self-reflexive cinema as an expression of 'Peirce's perfect sign', given that it allegedly presented 'an equal amalgam of the symbolic, the iconic and the indexical', that is to say 'conceptual meaning, pictorial beauty and documentary truth' (Wollen, 1998, p. 106). However, it was Wollen's concept of indexicality that remained central to film theory as it captured the essence of Bazin's insight into film's relation with the real while disengaging it from its transcendental and religious resonances.

However, adherence to realist theories experienced a decline for more than a decade from the late 1960s, as they became associated with 'narrative closure', 'bourgeois ideology' and the so-called Hollywood classical cinema. Bazin was the first to fall victim to this turn, which started at home in the pages of *Positif* and the very *Cahiers du Cinéma* he co-founded and masterminded in the 1950s (Andrew, 2005, pp. xx–xxi), as well as in newly created Marxist journals, such as *Cinéthique*. Eisenstein and Vertov's montage cinemas, previously banished by Bazin in the name of spatio-temporal integrity as provided by depth of field and the sequence-shot, regained centre stage. In an article whose fragmentary form emulates the discontinuity they were defending in cinema, Sylvie Pierre, Jean Narboni and Jacques Rivette declared that Eisensteinian montage was 'the only way to make a non-reactionary cinema, as opposed to a cinema of absorption, of representation' (Pierre, Narboni and Rivette, 1969, p. 25; see also Xavier, 2005, p. 146). Psychoanalytic, structuralist and semiotic approaches, meanwhile, gave rise to the apparatus theory (Baudry, 1986) as the phenomenon of the spectator's regression to the mirror phase, as defined by Lacan (Metz, 1982). Thus realism in cinema, with its positive connotation of a window on the world, gave way to an 'illusion' or 'impression' of reality, in the negative sense of an ideology-tinged discourse.

This French phase began to fade in 1973 (Andrew, 2005, p. xxii), but re-emerged in Britain in the journal *Screen*, where, inspired by Barthes, Metz, Althusser, Freud, Lacan and Brecht, an 'anti-realist' theory was developed through the 1970s in the form of a prescriptive programme aimed at deconstructing subjective identification as produced by classical cinema's illusionist narratives. The impact of '*Screen* theory', as it became known (see Elsaesser and Doane in this volume), and in particular Laura Mulvey's revolutionary feminist take (Mulvey, [1976] 1989), was enormous and continues to reverberate up to this day. To clear current film studies of the *Screen* legacy would require the demolition of film theory as a whole, as was, in fact, proposed by Bordwell and Carroll in their double-bill introduction to the book *Post-Theory* (1996), drawing on cognitivism. It must be noted, however, that *Screen*'s dismissal of Bazin's ideas together with realism as a whole required a considerable amount of distortion and convoluted thought. Stephen Heath, for example, denounced the 'dramatic' quality of what Bazin deemed, in neorealism, the 'reality of space', resulting from the combination of the long take and deep focus; but he then added that the Bazinian thought might also 'show the possibilities of the long take away from an absorbed dramatic space' (Heath, [1976] 1986, pp. 396–7).

Colin MacCabe, in his turn, was unambiguous in his dismissal of realism as a bourgeois genre in the cinema. He started by comparing it to the 19th century realist novel on the basis of a narrative discourse that 'allows reality to appear and denies its own status as articulation' (MacCabe, 1974, p. 9). His next move was to place neorealism on an equal footing to Hollywood so as to reject both:

> Whether we look to Hollywood, where realism is purchased at almost any price, or to the Italian neorealist cinema, we find that the struggle is to represent reality as effectively as possible; in both cinemas the possibility as such of the representational relation is taken for granted.
>
> (MacCabe, [1976] 1986, p. 180)

Because of his defence of the latter, Bazin was accused of rendering a 'characterization of realism ... centrally concerned with a transparency of form which is reduplicated within Hollywood filmic practice' (MacCabe, [1976] 1986, p. 180). Needless to say, the lumping together of such disparate terms as the 19th century novel, Hollywood classical cinema, Italian neorealism and Bazin's realist theory did little service to the understanding of any of them. It nevertheless became a popular formula, responsible for a great deal of confusion within realism scholarship up to this day, despite successive revisions by former *Screen* critics themselves. One of them, Christopher Williams, has recently argued:

> There are at least four other kinds of real and realism: emotional, pragmatic, philosophical and scientific, as well as the artistic kind, of which the 19th century realist novel may well be a subset. Film is not dominated by the forms of the 19th century novel. It draws on a wider range of sources and inputs.
>
> (Williams, 2000, p. 207)

Film theory has since moved away from the debate around transparency versus opacity, illusionism versus alienation, visual pleasure versus critical spectatorship, realism versus anti-realism. MacCabe is nowadays an admirer of Bazin's ontology and expresses regret that '[Bazin's] Catholic humanism and realist aesthetic had banished him from the theoretical reading lists of the 60s and 70s' (1997, p. 73). In the process, Barthes, who with Brecht had been constantly held in opposition to him, has been the subject of a re-evaluation which unveils their affinities. Laura Mulvey, for example, suggests:

> This precise mixture, the religious and the realist, drew Bazin to Rossellini and also formed the backdrop to [Barthes'] thoughts on the photograph. In *Camera Lucida*, questions of religion, magic and the supernatural do figure, more surprisingly, alongside an uncompromising insistence on the index.
>
> (Mulvey, 2006, p. 54)

Bazin specialist Dudley Andrew strikes a similar note, when commenting on the French critic's growing popularity in recent years:

> Beyond the university, the broader culture that bubbles into journals and now into websites has been awash with fresh feeling for Bazin's value and values. Is this due to the popularity of Roland Barthes' beautiful and final dirge, the 1980 *La Chambre claire*, a book that replays (without, however, citing) so many of Bazin's ideas and metaphors?
>
> (Andrew, 2005, p. xxiii)

Along the same lines, would it not make sense to question the opposition between Bazin and Brecht, as representatives respectively of realism and anti-realism? For one thing, Brecht's epic theatre was nothing but a realist method, one concerned with the reality of the medium, rather than that of the fable, as explained by Silberman in his chapter. And so was Bazin's, with his emphasis on showing rather than representing, on actors rather than characters, on the contingent rather than narrative, and even on cinema's 'impure' nature which included the theatrical as one of its realist constituents. Bazin's stress on ambiguity and openness, as opposed to an idea of totality often attributed to him, has been the subject of re-evaluations within the framework of a modernist project (see Trotter, 2006; and Grist's chapter) which is perfectly applicable to recent phenomena.

As we write this introduction, conferences and events worldwide are marking the 50th anniversary of Bazin's precocious death at a mere 40 years of age. This volume is no less a tribute to the world's most important thinker of cinematic realism, as he is referred to in 8 out of 17 chapters, one of them entirely devoted to him.

The index, the digital and the body

Since the early 1990s, and very much in keeping with world cinema's realist turn, the psychoanalytic and post-structuralist theories that had inspired *Screen* critics have been the object of successive revisions. Shaviro ([1993] 2006) refocused the question of cinematic pleasure by rejecting the Lacanian model of spectatorial regression and passive identification, emphasizing instead the active and corporeal element of the film experience. The Brechtian approach to estrangement and distanciation, as propagated by realism critics, was questioned by cognitivists such as Murray Smith, who pointed out that 'emotion is integrated with perception, attention, and cognition, not implacably opposed to any of them' (Smith, 1996, p. 133). Ivone Margulies resorted to Bazin to formulate her concept of 'corporeal cinema' based on re-enactments of real events (Margulies, 2002). Psychoanalytic approaches have meanwhile reinvented themselves on the basis of Lacan's concept of the Real, as applied to film (McGowan, 2007; Zizek, 2002; Peucker, 2007).

Once the ban on realism was lifted, the index became so identified with cinema itself that the emergence of the digital suddenly seemed to pose a death threat to it. Miriam Hansen was quick to raise the alarm in her introduction to a 1997 edition of *Theory of Film*, Kracauer's much battered (see Andrew, 1976) and nearly forgotten defence of cinema's redemptive realism. 'What *Theory of Film* can offer us today', she wrote, 'is not a theory of film in general, but a theory of a particular type of film experience, and of cinema as the aesthetic matrix of a particular historical experience' (Hansen, 1997, p. x). The reason for framing cinema within a limited historical period was that, in Hansen's view, current cinematic practices had ceased to function exclusively on the basis of photographic traces and indexical contingency:

> Digital technologies such as computer enhancement, imaging, and editing have shifted the balance increasingly toward the postproduction phase. Not only can 'mistakes' made during shooting be 'corrected' and recorded effects be maximized, but on the very level of production live-action images and sounds can be generated independently of any referent in the outside world.
>
> (Hansen, 1997, p. viii)

Commenting on Hansen's assessment of Kracauer on the basis of the index, as well as on Willemen's notion of cinephilia, Mary Ann Doane then suggested:

> [a] certain nostalgia for cinema precedes its death. One doesn't – and can't – love the televisual or the digital in quite the same way. It is as though the object of theory were to delineate more precisely the contours of an object at the moment of its historical demise.
>
> (Doane, 2002, p. 85)

David Rodowick, in his turn, saw the introduction of the digital technology and its challenge to cinema's photographic basis as an ideal opportunity to relaunch Bazin's question: What is cinema? (2007, p. 9). For Rodowick, a film such as *Russian Ark* cannot be characterized as an uninterrupted sequence and not even as a 'film', given that it was subjected to extensive postproduction manipulation (Rodowick, 2007, pp. 164–9).

But we are now turning away from the debate on realism, which is by no means restricted to the question of indexicality. Bazin himself had always welcomed technological innovations in the realm of the audiovisual media, as in his view they all pointed towards a single direction: the enhancement of realism. Bazin is also behind current film theory's most influential figure, Gilles Deleuze, whose monumental work on cinema, *L'Image movement* and *L'Image temps*, published as early as 1983 and 1985 respectively, is still triggering innovative approaches to the audiovisual media. Deleuze pays allegiance to Bazin, in the first place, by adopting his view of neorealism as the dividing line between classical and modern cinemas, corresponding respectively to the 'movement-image' and the 'time-image' (Deleuze, 1989); and, secondly, by drawing on Bergson's notion of duration as the defining element of the modern, as Bazin had done in his defence of the long take. One of Deleuze's many novelties, however, resides in his displacing the focus from the level of the real to that of the 'mental' and the 'sensory-motor'. This move has proliferated in film scholarship in ideas such as the 'haptic', which concerns touch and draws on Deleuze's assumption that 'memory is embodied in the senses' (Marks, 2000, p. xiv). In the process of recovering the physicality of spectatorial experience, phenomenological approaches to film other than Bazin's have equally regained a pre-eminent status in studies such as Vivian Sobchack's, who draws on Merleau-Ponty to 'demonstrate how the very nature of our embodied existence "in the flesh" lays the concrete foundations for a materialist – rather than idealist – understanding of aesthetics and ethics' (Sobchack, 2004, p. 3; see also Quinlivan's chapter).

In current audiovisual scholarship, Kracauer, Barthes, Bazin, Deleuze and Merleau-Ponty seem to be part of a happy family, generating approaches not at all averse to pleasure, emotion and sensation, as was largely the case with the *Screen* generation. Film theory has been re-energized with a whole set of new concepts, all of which concern in varying degrees the physicality of the audiovisual experience. If audiovisual interbreeding across national borders had already resulted in 'hybrid', 'intercultural', 'transnational' and 'accented' works, they now become visceral, carnal, corporeal, sensate; in short, more real (and realist) than ever.

Keeping a safe distance from dogmas, prescriptive theories and master narratives, this book opens up to a gamut of mutually complementary and questioning approaches to realism, reality and the real with relation to the audiovisual media. Driven by the perception that this question necessitates, more than ever, a theoretical reassessment, we have devoted Part I to 'Theorizing Realism'. Chapter 1, by Thomas Elsaesser, interweaves the book's two main strands by looking at world cinema in the light of recent theoretical developments. Here, realism is understood as a defining element of world cinema of all times, a tendency, however, that is becoming increasingly infused with fantasy and magic in current filmmaking, bringing into question terms such as 'evidence', 'authenticity' and spectatorial presence, as illustrated by the films of Korean Kim Ki-duk.

Marking his centrality as a reference in the book, Bazin is the subject of Chapter 2, in which Leighton Grist argues that Bazin's take on matters of ambiguity, phenomenology, the materiality of cinematic representation and even faith would seem to imply much less realism than modernism. Unpacking the connotations of such issues, and building on recent revaluations of Bazin's work, Grist investigates how Bazin is currently regarded and positioned within the academy, and queries whether his ideas could have been historically misrepresented and misplaced.

In Chapter 3, a close analysis of Brecht's collaborative film *Kuhle Wampe* (Slatan Dudow, 1932), as well as his book-length essay *The Threepenny Lawsuit*, gives Brecht specialist and translator Marc Silberman the opportunity to re-evaluate a question central to the *Screen* theory of the 1970s, which drew on Brecht as a touchstone for anti-illusionistic, constructivist approaches to reality as opposed to traditional notions of realism. Silberman returns to some of Brecht's writings on the media from the early 1930s, including his radio essays and his reflections on the status of the cinema as a new art, in order to redefine and situate his realist method.

An indispensable reflection concerns Italian neorealism, given its importance both in film history and as originator of realist theories. Louis Bayman's approach in Chapter 4 tackles the aesthetic conundrum posed by the concurrence of melodrama and realism in the Italian school. Contrary to most views, Bayman sees this relationship as complementary rather than oppositional, thus proposing a new theoretical take on it.

Closing this part, Mary Ann Doane, in Chapter 5, drives the question of realism away from traditional approaches hinging on the indexicality of the photographic image and sound or generic conventions that produce an effect of the 'real'. Instead, she formulates the problem of scale and its relation to a sense of either the real or the unreal. She argues that, amid the euphoria of the digital and a whole host of new technologies of representation – high-definition television, video, mobile phone photography, virtual reality – scale has re-emerged as one of the primary markers of cinematic specificity. Thus, she proposes to investigate the ways in which screen size and its corresponding scale, as well as the scale of the shot, have figured in the negotiation of the human body's relation to space in modernity.

Triggered as it has been by new developments in current cinematic practices, the book devotes Part II to 'new realisms' in world cinema, with four case studies stemming from different parts of the globe. Techniques traditionally seen as realist, such as the long take, location shooting and real characters, come again into play, though greatly complicated by experimentations with time reversals, the dissolution of the diegetic space and digital manipulation. As Anna Backman Rogers argues, in Chapter 6, Gus Van Sant's *Elephant* (2003) contains elements that seemingly pertain to realist filmmaking techniques as described by Bazin (the preservation of real time through long takes, the presence of non-actors, the film as a representation of actual events). However, these are subverted to uncanny effect so that it is the realism of the experience of trauma and its aftershock that is shown, thus blurring actual and virtual representations. Ming-yeh Rawnsley, in Chapter 7, expounds on the notion of 'observational realism', a turn towards reality that, as in previous new waves, had characterized the New Taiwan Cinema of the 1980s, but unlike them continues to bear fruit up to this day in the work of directors such as Hou Hsiao-hsien and the long-take champion Tsai Ming-liang. Armida de la Garza strikes a different note, in Chapter 8, by approaching realism through an audience perspective. In her analysis of Alfonso Cuarón's highly successful *Y tu mamá también*, she questions the extent to which realism served colonizing ends when used to investigate the 'truth' of the Other. Realism, cinema and nation, she argues, are inextricably linked and equally strained under the current decline of the Enlightenment paradigm. This part closes with an analysis of Sokurov's long-take tour de force, *Russian Ark*, by Vlad Strukov in Chapter 9. Here, an attempt is made to demonstrate a complex (and sometimes paradoxical) relationship between mimetic art and the possibilities put forward by new digital forms of film production.

'The Realism of the Medium', as Part III is called, takes its starting point from Metz's old notion that the 'impression of reality' carries with it the reality of the film's movement when it is projected (Metz, 1974). However, beyond the 'cinematic apparatus', we have considered, as constituents of the 'medium', the physicality of filming devices, actors and locations, as well as the bodily sensations experienced by spectators through viewing and listening. Beth Johnson, in Chapter 10, explores an extreme example of the reality of the medium in her detailed analysis of Andrew McElhinney's experimental film *Georges Bataille's Story of the Eye* (2004). She argues that the film's self-reflexive (anti-) narrative draws attention to both the medium of film, as an artificial and mediated representation, and the mode of production – a digital video aesthetic that attempts to convey an experience of authenticity. She then questions the effects of real sex on screen and 'cuming' on the camera, proposing that such acts draw attention not only to the real act of viewing but also to the camera itself and the means of viewing the real. Another aspect of physical filmmaking and viewing experience is explored by Davina Quinlivan in Chapter 11, in her analysis of *Breaking the Waves* (Lars von Trier, 1996), seen as a radical expression of Dogma 95 realist aesthetic. Drawing on Irigaray's feminist philosophy she proceeds to unveil a hyperrealist dimension, the breathing body, which for her encapsulates both an index of a real, lived corporeality and, by contrast, the symbolic, the realm of the fantastic and the unreal.

In Chapter 12, Jacob Leigh looks at the work of Eric Rohmer as a key director within the tradition of cinematic realism. For Leigh, in acknowledging the importance of film's ontological connection to reality, Rohmer follows the insights of his former editor at *Cahiers du Cinéma*, André Bazin. To explain the way Rohmer incorporates his understanding of the medium of film into his method of writing and directing, the chapter undertakes a comprehensive theoretical survey of the ways ontology has been understood, including its relation to narrative transparency, verisimilitude and scepticism. Chapter 13 closes this part with an approach to television through the analysis of Ken Loach's *Up the Junction*. Cecília Mello here argues that the film, partly made on 16mm and aired on BBC1 in 1965, both incorporates and negates elements of post-war realist traditions in English cinema, a production that perhaps needed television finally to incorporate the subversion of film language pioneered a few years earlier by various new waves across the world.

Closing the volume, Part IV is devoted to 'Documentary, Television and the Ethics of Representation'. Here, not only questions of genre are contemplated, but also the 'production' of the real through filmmaking, the frictions between documenting and narrating, the filmmaker's dilemma between showing and staging, and television's dubious plays with fact and truth. Lúcia Nagib, in Chapter 14, turns to Japan to focus on the outrageous director Kazuo Hara and his producer and collaborator Sachiko Kobayashi. She argues that their films, commonly defined as 'documentaries' on the basis of their use of real characters and locations, have actually extended the frontiers of the genre to hitherto unknown realms. They testify to an auteurist realist project based on physicality pushed to the 'extreme' as a means to go beyond realism as style and turn the act of filmmaking into producing, as well as reproducing, reality. The examination of the conflicting authorial subjectivities at work within each film leads to the evaluation of the ethical imperative – as well as consequences – of Hara and Kobayashi's unique project.

In Chapter 15, Ismail Xavier focuses on Eduardo Coutinho's *The Mighty Spirit* (*Santo forte*, 1999) and *Master Building* (*Edifício Master*, 2002) as well as on José Padilha and Felipe Lacerda's *Bus 174* (*Ônibus 174*, 2002), to define two different documentary responses to changes in the Brazilian public sphere caused by the hegemony of television as a producer of social identities and regulator of political voices. Xavier argues that these films develop a new kind of audiovisual counter-discourse concerned with the unveiling of personal and social experiences reduced to clichés in current media representations. In his turn, documentarist João Moreira Salles, in Chapter 16, defines the blurring of boundaries between fiction and non-fiction as the very nature of the documentary genre. For him, documentary-making is nothing but a constant exercise of accepting or rejecting chance, narration and fiction, an arduous task that has more often than not failed to resolve documentary's identity problem.

The book closes with a study of the ways in which contemporary television comes to grips with reality. In Chapter 17, Diane Myers argues that the boundaries between game show and documentary, reality and artifice, are becoming increasingly blurred. The insatiable hunger for reality has spawned a new breed of development producer, anxious to push the boundaries of taste and decency in an effort to secure absolute victory in the ratings war. By examining the power play in the elements of the factual production process, Myers suggests the ways in which television might develop in the future.

The depth and breadth of the concepts and case studies about realism encompassed in this book are thus considerable, although this line of enquiry could certainly be extended to other audiovisual media, such as the Internet, which infinitely multiply screens and avenues and possibilities for screen studies. But this is precisely the point of this volume: the hope that its message will be received, discussed and expanded by others.

Lúcia Nagib
Cecília Mello

References

Andrew, Dudley (1976), *The Major Film Theories: An Introduction.* New York: Oxford University Press.

Andrew, Dudley (2005), 'Foreword to the 2004 Edition', in André Bazin, *What Is Cinema?*, vol 2, pp. xi–xxvi.

Barthes, Roland (1982), *Camera Lucida.* London: Vintage.

Bazin, André (1967), *What Is Cinema?*, vol 1, ed. and trans. by Hugh Gray. Berkeley/Los Angeles/London: University of California Press.

Bazin, André (2005), *What Is Cinema?*, vol 2, ed. and trans. by Hugh Gray. Berkeley/Los Angeles/London: University of California Press.

Baudry, Jean-Louis (1986), 'Ideological Effects of the Basic Cinematographic Apparatus'; 'The Apparatus: Metapsychological Approaches to the Impression of Reality in Cinema', in Philip Rosen (ed.), *Narrative, Apparatus, Ideology: A Film Theory Reader.* New York: Columbia University Press, pp. 286–318.

Bazin, André (1997), *Bazin at Work: Major Essays & Reviews from the Forties & Fifties,* ed. by Bert Cardullo, trans. by Alain Piette and Bert Cardullo. New York: Routledge.

Black, Joel (2002), *The Reality Effect: Film Culture and the Graphic Imperative.* New York: Routledge.

Bordwell, David (1996), 'Contemporary Film Studies and the Vicissitudes of Grand Theory', in David Bordwell and Noël Carroll (eds), *Post-Theory: Reconstructing Film Studies.* Madison: The University of Wisconsin Press.

Carroll, Noël (1996), 'Prospects for Film Theory: A Personal Assessment', in David Bordwell and Noël Carroll (eds), *Post-Theory: Reconstructing Film Studies.* Madison: The University of Wisconsin Press.

Cavell, Stanley (1979), *The World Viewed: Reflections on the Ontology of Film.* Cambridge, MA/London: Harvard University Press.

Deleuze, Gilles (1986), *Cinema 1: The Movement-Image.* London/New York: Continuum.

Deleuze, Gilles (1989), *Cinema 2: The Time-Image.* London: Athlone.

Doane, Mary Ann (2002), 'The Object of Theory', in Ivone Margulies (ed.), *Rites of Realism: Essays on Corporeal Cinema.* Durham/London: Duke University Press, pp. 80–9.

Hansen, Miriam (1997), 'Introduction', in Siegfried Kracauer, pp. vii–xlv.

Jerslev, Anne (2002), 'Introduction', in A. Jerslev (ed.), *Realism and 'Reality' in Film and Media.* Copenhagen: Museum Tusculanum Press/University of Copenhagen.

Kracauer, Siegfried (1997), *Theory of Film: The Redemption of Physical Reality.* Princeton: Princeton University Press.

MacCabe, Colin (1974), 'Realism and the Cinema: Notes on Some Brechtian Theses', in *Screen*, 15(2), Summer, pp. 7–27.

MacCabe, Colin (1986), 'Theory and Film: Principles of Realism and Pleasure', in Philip Rosen (ed.), *Narrative, Apparatus, Ideology: A Film Theory Reader.* New York: Columbia University Press, pp. 179–97.

MacCabe, Colin (1997), 'Barthes and Bazin: The Ontology of the Image', in Jean-Michel Rabaté (ed.), *Writing the Image After Roland Barthes*. Philadelphia: University of Pennsylvania Press.

Marks, Laura U. (2000), *The Skin of the Film: Intercultural Cinema, Embodiment, and the Senses*. Durham/London: Duke University Press.

McGowan, Todd (2007), *The Real Gaze: Film Theory after Lacan*. New York: State University of New York Press.

Metz, Christian (1974), *Film Language: A Semiotics of the Cinema*. New York: Oxford University Press.

Metz, Christian (1982), *Psychoanalysis and Cinema: The Imaginary Signifier*. London/Basingstoke: Macmillan.

Mulvey, Laura (1989), *Visual and Other Pleasures*. Basingstoke/London: Macmillan.

Mulvey, Laura (2006), *Death 24x a Second: Stillness and the Moving Image*. London: Reaktion.

Narboni, Jean, Pierre, Sylvie and Rivette, Jacques (1969), 'Questions théoriques', in *Cahiers du Cinéma*, 210(3), March, pp. 16–35.

Peucker, Brigitte (2007), *The Material Image: Art and the Real in Film*. Stanford: Stanford University Press.

Perez, Gilberto (1998), *The Material Ghost: Films and Their Medium*. Baltimore/London: The Johns Hopkins University Press.

Rodowick, D. N. (2007), *The Virtual Life of Film*. Cambridge, MA/London: Harvard University Press.

Shaviro, Steven (2006), *The Cinematic Body*. Minneapolis/London: University of Minnesota Press.

Smith, Murray (1996), 'The Logic and Legacy of Brechtianism', in David Bordwell and Noël Carroll (eds), *Post-Theory: Reconstructing Film Studies*. Madison: The University of Wisconsin Press.

Sobchack, Vivian (2004), *Carnal Thoughts: Embodiment and Moving Image Culture*. Berkeley/Los Angeles/London: University of California Press.

Trotter, David (2007), *Cinema and Modernism*. Malden: Blackwell.

Xavier, Ismail (2005), *O discurso cinematográfico: a opacidade e a transparência*. São Paulo: Paz e Terra.

Wollen, Peter (1998), *Signs and Meaning in the Cinema*. London: BFI.

Zizek, Slavoj (2002), *Welcome to the Desert of the Real*. London: Verso.

Part I Theorizing Realism

1
World Cinema: Realism, Evidence, Presence

Thomas Elsaesser

Realism and world cinema

European art/auteur cinema (and by extension, world cinema) has always defined itself against Hollywood on the basis of its greater realism. Whether one thinks of Italian neorealism, the French *nouvelle vague's* semi-documentary *cinéma vérité*, or Ingmar Bergman's clinically probing psychological realism: our notions of non-Hollywood filmmaking are generally tied to some version of a realist aesthetics. Denmark's Dogma movement or the New Iranian Cinema, for instance, were hailed as welcome returns to the precepts of neorealism, and many other emerging national cinemas, notably from Africa, Latin America, and parts of Asia, are fêted at festivals for their quasi-documentary, ethnographic engagement with the slow rhythms of the everyday, with the lives of ordinary people, with the disappearing natural environment, the wasted desolation of the shanty towns and urban slums, or the ennui and anomie of the newly affluent Asian middle classes.

If I had to give a quick definition of who I consider to be typical of world cinema directors, it would be that

- they are integral to the transnational film festival circuit, focused notably on Cannes and Berlin, but now also on Toronto and Pusan. Typical names over the past two generations are Ousmane Sembène (from Senegal), Youssef Chahine (Egypt), Souleymane Cissé (Mali), Lino Broka (Philippines), Abbas Kiarostami (Iran), Mira Nair (India), Hou Hsiao-hsien (Taiwan), Wong Kar-wai (Hong Kong), Apichatpong Weerasethakul (Thai, of *Tropical Malady* – *Sud Pralad*, 2004 – fame), Tsai Ming-liang (*Vive l'amour*, 1994), Nuri Bilge Ceylan (Turkey), Carlos Reygadas (Mexico), or Josué Méndez (Peru) – who follow on from Satyajit Ray and Akira Kurosawa.
- some are either self-taught, or they left their country, in order to go to film school or art school in Paris, London, New York, Chicago, or Los Angeles,

before returning 'home', not unlike an earlier European generation: Volker Schlöndorff, Johan van der Keuken, Theo Angelopoulos, who all went to film school in Paris in the 1950s.

- as a result, they often have an ambiguous relation both to their indigenous film culture and the national film industry: they tend to be resented, isolated, go unrecognized, or are accused of making films for the gaze of the Western 'other'.
- finally, the current generation of world cinema directors use digital video by choice as much as by necessity, and their films manifest the inherent specifics of digital media, as well as thematize the challenges to photographic realism.

It would be interesting to make the implications of such a definition fully explicit: perhaps one can surmise that historical distinctions between national cinema, international art cinema, and world cinema can be drawn along these lines and across these markers, while the *aesthetics* of world cinema, however we finally agree to define the latter term, have less to do with national provenance or geopolitical location, but come together around theoretical issues in what is clearly a global context.

Thus, although stylistic choices such as static shots, fixed frames, deep focus, and the long take – traditional markers of a realist aesthetics – are still much in evidence, they are put to different uses in the films of Michael Haneke, Abbas Kiarostami, or Hou Hsiao-hsien. Likewise, materialist critiques of photographic realism no longer aspire to Brecht's realism as distanciation, to counter 'illusionism' and 'identification', nor do they emulate the political agitprop realism of 'third cinema' practice of the 1970s. Instead, where such a foregrounding of the different media that construct cinematic representations is in evidence, for instance when the technologies of mechanical reproductions (television sets, video recorders, digital cameras, photographs, etc.) are featured, they tend to be infused with fantasy and magic, nurtured from ghost stories and spectral apparitions, or they function as the very evidence of the real, rather than as its betrayal or loss. The impersonal 'thing' or apparatus taking my picture, or capturing an event, is a better guarantee of my existence, according to this new realism, than the unmediated face-to-face, likely to give rise to misunderstandings. Another notable feature are narratives that play with indeterminate or non-linear temporalities and privilege memory over chronology. Invariably they make sense/perception a major issue; however, not so much as deceptive, illusory or unreliable (the old postmodern paradigm), but by extending perception beyond the visual register, in order to expose or engage the body as a total perceptual surface, while deploying other senses/ perceptions – notably touch and hearing – as at least equally relevant to the cinematic experience.

The ontological turn

A preliminary hypothesis imposes itself: to address realism in world cinema, today, would, by this analysis, also mean engaging with what has been termed the 'ontological turn', the return of the real, the presence and agency of 'things'. On the agenda is a new materiality, a new concern and respect for reference in the visual media, after half a century of mourning the loss of the real and complaining about or celebrating simulacra, copies without originals, mediality and mediatization. In the thematic conjunction of world cinema and realism, I therefore propose to approach films and filmmakers who partake in the increasing realization – nowadays less a discovery than a truism – that in the cinema, we can no longer trust our eyes, if ever we could. This means that if we speak of an ontological turn, it will refer to a post-photographic ontology. For regardless of whether defined as independent cinema, international art cinema, new national cinema, or festival auteur cinema, 'world cinema' in my sense shares the general scepticism towards ontological versions of photographic realism: ontology mark one, if you like. This ontological realism is forever – and not always fairly – identified with André Bazin and his notion that the cinema is unique among the representational arts by virtue of the existential bond it has with the phenomenal world; what later came to be known as the indexicality (in Bazin: the ontology) of the photographic image. But, well before digitization seemingly did away with the material 'ground' for this indexicality of the optic–chemical imprint or trace, ontological realism had already been challenged, critiqued, and denounced as an ideological fiction.

These critiques have been typical of what one might call the epistemological version of film theory: that is, their critique of 'naïve' realism, such as it was undertaken by *Screen* theory in the 1970s. Its deconstruction of Bazinian realism as a reality effect masking a subject effect was based on the notion that both the cinema's apparatus and mainstream narrative practice precluded it from generating objective knowledge about the world. Instead, a film was only able to produce 'subjects': that is, reproduce the state of miscognition and self-alienation deemed typical of gendered subjectivity in our Western societies. Whether arguing in the name of alienation, anti-illusionism or rupture (as in Brechtian theories of realism), or denouncing the society of the spectacle, as Guy Debord and Jean Baudrillard have done, the assumption underlying all epistemic critiques of realism is that there is such a thing as 'correct representation', or at least that 'reality' can be distinguished from 'illusion' and that a 'truth' can be meaningfully opposed to 'mere appearance'. So-called apparatus theory in film studies was deeply implicated in these epistemological positions, hoping to produce a 'materialist' cinema immune to the reign of appearances, and it was in turn criticized for it, often by an even more radical epistemic scepticism.

This epistemic scepticism took two seemingly antagonistic, but to my mind related, forms: one was a cognitivist critique, which held that cinematic representations are ultimately no different from perceptions of any other (audio)visual field, and that cognitive processes of matching, sampling, comparing, and assigning sense to raw perceptual data were what determined how we understand filmic images, or make use of them, in relation to our goals and intentions. The other critique of ontological realism came from cultural or social constructivism, which holds that all representations are culturally coded: that is, they do not reflect any external, inherent, or 'transcendent' realities, but are contingent on convention, human perception, history, and social experience. Within constructivism, race, gender, class, but also personal identity and subjectivity, are (social) constructs, appearing natural and self-evident to those who accept their boundaries, or who benefit from the hierarchies they imply, thereby overlooking the extent to which they are an invention, an artefact or the result of power relations operating within a particular culture or society.

On the other hand, one particular version of this scepticism, also associated with *Screen* theory – that is a combination of semiotics, psychoanalysis, and feminism – nonetheless maintained, albeit implicitly, that the cinema was a mimetic art, whose central metaphor was not the window on the world, typical of ontological realism, but the mirror, typical of the negative epistemology of miscognition. As such, the cinema, in different ways, would still be seen as conforming to the subject–object split typical of the Cartesian world picture. Whether cinema as mirror or cinema as window, both inherit from the Renaissance perspectival projection the assumption of the upright forward orientation of the human visual field, but which in pictorial representation is delimited by a frame, allowing for a certain range of options with respect to the place and position of the spectator vis-à-vis the painted, photographic, or cinematic image. This monocular central perspective, as present in cinematic space, notably invests off-screen space, and its folding back into on-screen space, with a special constitutive power, that of suture. Cultural constructivism, on the other hand, subscribed to no such view of suture, tending more towards a critique of 'representations' and treating films as 'texts' whose meanings can be resisted or negotiated by appropriate reading strategies.

The ontological turn, with which I began – now perhaps best called ontology mark two, or post-epistemological ontology – would maintain that all these paradigms are in doubt, not only those relying on psychoanalysis or its arch-enemy, cognitivism. The new realist ontology would, on the one hand, be in tune with overcoming postmodernism, as already alluded to; but, it would also be dissatisfied with constructivism, of which it would present itself as an implicit critique or an explicit turning away. More specifically, with respect to window and mirror (the key metaphors of epistemic film theory), the post-epistemological ontology would therefore be one that also breaks with the Cartesian subject–object split, abandoning or redefining notions of subjectivity, consciousness, identity in the way these have hitherto been used and understood. By extension, it does not mourn the so-called loss of indexicality of the photographic image.

One can argue, for instance, that the Deleuzian intervention in film studies is precisely this: to cut the Gordian knot by no longer speaking of subjectivity, representation, consciousness, or the gaze, and instead of the sensory–motor schema, the 'brain is the screen', intensities, becomings, and 'pure optical (or acoustic) situations'. Although many of Deleuze's followers tend to mix concepts from phenomenology (which include subjectivity, consciousness, intentionality) with those of Deleuze (which are, strictly speaking, not always compatible), the very popularity of Deleuze in film studies betokens to the need to overcome constructivism. To this extent Deleuzians partake in the 'ontological turn', even if they might not always be aware of it. What is so attractive about Deleuze is not only that he talks about all the things that contemporary audiences (and indeed, filmmakers) seem to be interested in: affect, time, the virtual, and the actual. He does so with a vocabulary that slides easily between metaphor and concept – his famous 'toolbox' – allowing for a degree of indeterminacy and instrumentalization in the application of his insights or formulations, which befits thinking in a time of flux and transition. But, above all, Deleuze is almost irresistible in the way he jolts one's thinking quite generally, and his unshakeable conviction that there is a way out of the deadlocks around truth and appearance, that there is light at the end of the modernist/postmodernist epistemological tunnel.

Nonetheless, I shall resist the temptation of 'becoming Deleuzian', and instead try another way of understanding the current conjuncture, as it impacts the social sciences, philosophy, art history, and media theory. The outcome of the critique of constructivism is that we know there must be such a thing as a material reality, and something given, or 'hard-wired' in our human make-up. On the other hand, we know there are conventions and human constraints on our perception, indeed on our ways of knowing and being: that is, on our epistemological horizon.

Narrowing this horizon and focussing on the cinema, one can note two tendencies. On the one hand, the new realism, if expressing the recognition that not everything is constructed, finds its manifestation in the humanities in general, but especially in film studies around a revival of interest and re-investment in 'the body', 'the senses', skin, tactility, touch, and the haptic, to which corresponds in philosophy and evolutionary neuroscience the idea of the 'embodied mind'. On the other hand, the legacy of constructivism has been, first, to open up categories of the in-between: giving us terms like 'hybridity', 'creolization', 'entanglement'. However, there is also the notion, already implicit at the outset in the constructivist project of cultural studies, to put the emphasis less on the limits of social determinations or the positioning of subjects, and instead concentrate on the spaces of positive appropriation, on 'play' and especially on 'performativity', a term that has had a most remarkable career in the humanities over the past two decades. In other words, rather than seeing human beings as victims of the constraints imposed by constructed identities or representations, why not see them as empowering factors? Put more strongly: is it possible to build on constructivism what one might call a form of 'contractualism'? That is, the notion that what allows one to cope with social constructions both in real life and in visual representations are in each case not only hidden power structures, but also openly negotiated conventions, usually well understood, such as the codes of verisimilitude applicable to individual genres, or institutional markers that tell us what horizon of expectations to assume? Empowerment in this sense might be the tacit or explicit understanding that an audience is neither master nor dupe, but that spectators are partners in negotiated conventions, which make the social field, or indeed the visual field, into an arena where contracts can be entered, where there are conditions and conditionality, specifying what are the rules of the game, or indicating that a re-negotiation of the rules of the game is required.

Perspective, perception, posthumous presences

However, one can take a somewhat more prescriptive stance, and put forward a more specific agenda of what is at stake in the ontological turn. Once one understands it not so much as a radical break with, but as a response to, the dilemmas of constructivism, the new realism will not be confused with positivism. Instead, it can be seen as informing the poetics of filmmakers as well as the perspective of theorists. Out of potentially many different issues, which – as we saw – seem to be affected by the 'ontological turn' (or perhaps more cautiously, the 'ontological unrest'), I want to select three areas for further comment, which I think are relevant to our topic.

First, as already hinted, the ontological turn is confirmation that our visual culture is in the process not only of putting into crisis, but definitely bidding farewell to, the monocular central perspective mode of visual representation, as inherited from Leon Battista Alberti's 1435 treatise on painting, of which easel painting and the classic cinema experience of the projected image are the most familiar but also most sophisticated manifestations. I am not talking about the critique of perspective as manifested in the various modernist subversions of painting, starting with Cézanne's landscapes, Picasso and Braque's cubist collages, Duchamp's 'Nude Descending a Staircase' mimicking chronophotography, and Malevich and the Suprematists' flat canvases of white squares, or black or red wedges of primary colour: maintaining the space, site, and form of painting, but evacuating its function as windows or representational planes. Rather, I mean the 'fading' or 'supercession' of perspective as symbolic form, in Erwin Panofsky's phrase, as a culturally dominant, implicit reference point, guiding not just this or that artistic practice, or this or that aspect of visuality, visual culture, and looking, but breaking with and re-orienting an entire episteme of representation of knowing as seeing. This is what we usually mean by Cartesian world picture, and by extension, the way of perceiving and thus knowing the world 'out there', while placing oneself as subject 'in here'. Obviously, this is no news to the hard sciences or to philosophy. However, now it seems the shift in our visual culture has come about not by the usual means of intellectual critique, or by teaching it to children at school (for example, that the Earth is round and not flat), but almost by itself, as a matter of habit more than fact, almost out of laziness and convenience, one might say, and of course with a little help from technology and our favourite gadgets, such as iPods, mobile phones, and other hand-held devices.

Secondly, the 'new realism' tends to engage a point of view and identify a portal or entry point that no longer takes for granted the centrality of the human agent, her position in Euclidean space, and her sense-perceptions as reference base or normative default value. Instead, characters' actions, narrative spaces, and dramatic situations challenge the spectator's 'suspension of disbelief', by featuring protagonists whose view of the world is different, that is, marked by limits placed on their physical or mental faculties: restrictions, which, however, turn out to be enabling conditions in some other register. I am thinking of characters who suffer from, or display certain 'conditions', such as schizophrenia, amnesia, paralysis, who are pathologically violent, or traumatically mute, who are blind, possess extrasensory faculties, or give themselves over to obsessions, whose sense of taste or of smell is hyper-developed, who think they can make themselves invisible, or can time-travel, or who are recovering from a mortal illness or not recovering from trauma – films such as Michael Winterbottom's *Nine Songs* (2004), Werner Herzog's *Grizzly Man* (2005), Guillermo Del Toro's *Pan's Labyrinth* (*El laberinto del fauno*, 2006), Peter Weir's *Fearless* (1993), Jane Campion's *The Piano* (1993), Tom Tykwer's *Perfume* (2006), Alejando Amenábar's *The Sea Inside* (*Mar adentro*, 2004), Claire Denis' *The Intruder* (*L'Intrus*, 2004), Julio Medem's *Earth* (*Tierra*, 1996), Catherine Breillat's *For My Sister* (*A ma soeur!*,2001), Park Chan-wook's *Old Boy* (2003), Lynn Ramsay's *Morvern Callar* (2002), Wong Kar-wai's *2046* (2004), Julian Schnabel's *The Diving Bell and the Butterfly* (*Le Scaphandre et le papillon*, 2007).

The world, perceived through these at once restricted and enlarged sensibilities, manifests itself as having special properties. Relations of size are different, distance and proximity take on equally dangerous features, temporal registers no longer line up, terrible or miraculous things can happen. Repetitions, retracings of steps and bodily re-enactments are what guarantee a modicum of identity or a sense of self-presence.

Thirdly – and probably connected to the second point – the new realism or ontological unrest favours what I have elsewhere called post-mortem protagonists: that is, protagonists where it is not clear to either themselves or the audience whether they are still alive or dead, whether they inhabit another realm altogether or have come back from the dead. This group of films includes not only world cinema of festival authors or independents, but can also be found among the Hollywood output, very often by foreign directors working either temporally or permanently there. This includes virtually the entire oeuvre of M. Night Shyamalan and Alejando Amenábar, films like *The Sixth Sense* (1999) or *The Others* (2001), the films of Christopher Nolan (*Memento*, 2000; *Insomnia*, 2002; *The Prestige*, 2006), Richard Kelly's *Donnie Darko* (2001), but also, I would argue, Aki Kaurismäki's *The Man without a Past* (*Mies vailla menneisyyttä*, 2002), Fatih Akin's *Head On* (*Gegen die Wand*, 2004) and very many others.

What is typical of these films is that objects, spaces, houses take on a particular kind of presence or agency, referring us to the conventions of the horror film. However, instead of working towards fright and terror, they aim to produce at first perceptual insecurity but then develop a more directly ontological doubt, as we are obliged to make a kind of cognitive switch or radical retroactive readjustment of our most fundamental assumptions about the diegetic world as a coherent time–space continuum, as well as becoming intensely aware of our own presence as spectators, as in the opening of Michael Haneke's *Hidden* (*Caché*, 2005). Equally characteristic of many of these films is that a special kind of understanding or 'contract' exists between the main protagonists (and is extended to the spectator) about accepting as given or 'normal' what on the face of it is psychologically aberrant or impossible according to the laws of physics. And thus they (and we) enter into a kind of mutually confirming 'as-if' mode, which may at first look like a solipsistic game, but which turns out to be the very condition of keeping the world 'real' or 'consistent'. Indeed, in some cases, it 'saves' the world (as in *Donnie Darko*) thanks to what one could call 'embodied self-perception through the perception of another', but what Robert Pfaller (2000) might call interpassivity: the delegation or 'outsourcing' of my pleasures, my doubts, my affective life, my beliefs, or my self-presence to someone else, who not so much 'lives' in my place, but through whom I can once more take possession of myself, or believe in myself, beyond all the epistemological scepticism that radical constructivism of the kind discussed above, but also hardcore cognitivism, inevitably entails.

At the same time, there is no way back to assuming that 'evidence' can be based on ocular verification ('to see is to know'). Not so much because the physical world is per se unknowable, but because people are opaque to each other, and thus intersubjectivity poses special epistemic challenges. Watching characters in the 'new realism' mode is like watching other people have a headache: there is no way I can have positive evidence, other than reading signs for minds. Classical movies assume a transparency between introspection and action, or that there is a direct path from perception to mind and from mind to action, which in turn allows one to infer from this action the corresponding state of mind, with the spectator's translation of 'evidence' into 'belief' as the facilitating link. However, the realism of the movies I am referring to is more akin to the philosophical (Wittgensteinian) problem about the fundamental unknowability of other minds. 'Evidence' would then be an inferential relation to an outward sign: indexical not as trace, but as symptom, in the semantics of an agreed language of 'pain' (that is screwing up one's face). But what if someone with a headache does not screw up their face, and simply says: 'I couldn't come to work because of a splitting head-ache?' We then have to take the other 'on trust', but against the background of 'no trust'. When it comes to the cinema, this opens up two options, related to what I have termed 'ontology mark one' and 'ontology mark two'. Ontology mark one – say, along the lines of Deleuze's 'belief in the world' (Deleuze, 1989, p. 179) or Stanley Cavell's 'trust in the world' (Cavell, 1979, p. 85) – would derive from the unknowability or inaccessibility of other minds the argument that the cinema is ontologically privileged, because it always already is a mind externalized. It therefore can give us trust in the world and liberate us from the anxiety of scepticism, thanks either to the presence of the contingently real through photographic indexicality (Cavell) or by redefining the cinema as 'mind and matter' (Deleuze). My own argument – ontology mark two – would be that such trust has to be a function of scepticism, has to involve a leap across an abyss (precisely such an ontological switch as we get in *The Others*, *Donnie Darko*, *Hidden*). Such a cinema of realism would amount to a step in the dark (a Pascalian definition of faith, if you like), or would be a version of the famous Prisoner's Dilemma, where your own self-interest becomes a function of someone else's faith in you.

Interestingly enough, one of the inventors of this type of game theory, the mathematician John Nash, is the hero of a film in the style of those about characters with aberrant perceptual powers made for Hollywood by foreigners: Ron Howard's *A Beautiful Mind* (2001). In his case, one might say, that he had so much faith in himself, that he needed to delegate it to another, whose existence he once more believed in, even though for others this person did not exist, but also did not have to exist. This means that, for John Nash and his mathematical imagination, the grounds for evidence and belief were co-extensive with each other, because many mathematicians 'see' things that ordinary mortals do not. For instance, the mathematician Benoit Mandelbrot 'saw' fractals when nobody else did, and he needed the imaging power of the modern computer to make fractals visible to the rest of the world. For a mathematician, 'knowing' and 'seeing' deal with the real, but not necessarily on the basis of the phenomenal or the material: where we see chaos, they see patterns; where we see forms, they see equations. This is perhaps what is meant by mathematically modelling the world.

I think it would also be possible to take Deleuze's famous distinction between the movement-image and the time-image, and rewrite it according to the schema I am outlining here. Whereas, as indicated, films that function according to the sensory–motor schema rely on a direct link between perception, mentation, affect, and action, from which we as spectators construe the characters' inner lives, in the time-image, as Deleuze points out, it is not the characters' actions that give us a clue to their inner life, but 'things': objects, landscape, and the materialized passage or duration of time itself. Similarly, the aberrant psychologies, the productive pathologies, and sensory deprivations in the films I mentioned, as well as the post-mortem situations the characters so often find themselves in, would be the narrative strategies or motivational devices that seek consciousness and subjectivity not in the recesses of the self, but by trying to disembody it, externalize it, void it even, and then relocate it in the world of things, of spaces, and the space of the 'other'. This in turn can include the self-as-other, the out-of-body experience, or moments when the eye becomes a hand (haptic vision), or the hand becomes an eye (a feature typical of digital cinema, with its tactile, extremely close-range imaging). Yet, unlike the Bazinian ontology, where such a faith in the 'disclosure' of the world was a given, in the new ontology of realism any trust, faith, or belief needs to be contractually secured: this is both the lesson of constructivism and its overcoming, or *Aufhebung*. In other words, ontology mark two would require a new 'social contract' that is itself not ontologically grounded.

The new realism and the space in front: Kim Ki-duk

In order to test this proposition, I want to return to the *transformations of perspective* as symbolic form and examine, focused on a specific filmmaker and film, what this means for the spectator-positions available in contemporary world cinema. The first point to note is that forward projection and the delimited frame have certainly not gone away, but – I would argue – they are now embedded within another symbolic form, as one of its special cases. I hesitate to give a definite name to this new symbolic form or even call it a symbolic form (because it functions, in my scheme of things, as an ontology); rather than oppose it to perspective as such, by calling it 'flatness' (as in modernist painting) or cubist multi-perspectival (or panoptic) projection, the salient features of perspective to contrast it with would be infinity, so that the new ontology is characterized by 'ubiquity', here defined as the felt presence of pure space. And within ubiquity, as potential omni-presence, perspective has survived, but in paradoxical ways: on the one side, it can be the mark of paranoia (for instance, in the films of Michael Haneke, where framing and reframing become the director's way of exerting total control both over his characters and the audience); but it can also emerge as a crucial element in the construction of a new kind of cinematic space, in which frontal staging seems to assign to the spectator a different role and function. This latter point can be illustrated with examples taken from a 2004 film by

Kim Ki-duk, called *Bin jip*, meaning 'empty houses', but better known in the West as *3 Iron*, after the size of a particular golf club.

Kim Ki-duk is a South Korean filmmaker, to whom apply most of the characteristics initially outlined as typical for a world cinema director. He is largely self-taught, went to Paris for two years, came to prominence through festivals, notably Venice and Berlin, and is extremely controversial in his native country, where he is seen, confusingly, as too violent, exploitative, and destructive and as too Western, artsy, and esoteric. He has made 13 films in just over ten years, but even the 'Pope' of Asian Cinema, Tony Rayns, has denounced Kim Ki-duk as a fraud with limited talent, calling his European admirers 'stooges', while nonetheless leaving open the possibility that he might be a 'Korean Fassbinder' (Rayns, 2004, pp. 50–1). Be that as it may, *Time* (*Shi gan*, 2006), *Breath* (*Soom*, 2007), *Samaritan Girl* (*Samaria*, 2004), and above all *Bin jip* seem to me the sort of films that not only prove how sometimes failure can be more interesting than success, but demonstrate the limits of the categories of auteur or of national cinema when a director sets out to rethink the cinema as if he was inventing it, coming up with something both symptomatic and exemplary.

At first sight, many of Kim Ki-duk's films are 'boy meets girl' stories, or tales of doomed romantic love, which he complicates by having a third person interfere – often enough an older man, a father figure, a patriarchal husband, or other representative of authority and the law. Yet rather than develop an Oedipal tale of rivalry and eventual defeat, these triangular relationships follow a different and, in many ways, much more perverse logic of substitution and exchange. In *Samaritan Girl*, for instance, two teenage girls in need of money for a trip to Europe decide to go into casual prostitution, one setting the other up with clients, while keeping a lookout for the police. But when the one prostituting herself jumps out of a window to escape arrest and accidentally kills herself, the other seeks out all the clients her friend had sex with, sleeps with them and secretly returns the money. Meanwhile, her father, discovering what his daughter is doing, also visits the clients, but this time to shame them in front of their families, for having sex with minors, even killing one of them in a fit of rage, an act for which he knows he will end his life in jail. A double circuit of exchange is opened up, where the daughter tries to redeem herself by re-enacting the offensive act, in the hope of undoing what has been done, while the father takes revenge, negating the daughter's self-sacrifice, but in the process ends up sacrificing himself. Central to the film is thus a father–daughter relationship, where monstrously displaced incestuous desires drive the narrative, only finally to allow a face-to-face between father and daughter, which comes too late, but which would not have been possible without the mutual burden of transferred guilt.

As a story, *Bin jip* is similarly perverse, and offers an even more preposterous but equally apt resolution through 'poetic justice' to the impossible face-to-face. A young fast-food delivery man on a motorbike devises a trick to identify homes and houses, temporarily vacated by their owners, in order not to steal or vandalize, but to live the occupants' lives, wash their clothes, repair their broken appliances and water their plants. In one of the houses, he is himself silently observed by a battered housewife, with whom he bonds, and who eventually leaves her abusive husband to join the boy on his strange and strangely silent house-minding rounds. Eventually they are caught, and the young man goes to prison, where he trains himself to become invisible. Released, he visits the house of the wife and haunts it like a ghost, sensed but not seen by the husband, yet fully present to the wife at first in the mirror, then as a shadow, and across the back of her unsuspecting husband (Figure 1.1).

No doubt there are any number of interpretations of this strange tale, perhaps even an old Chinese or Korean ghost story, from which the central idea is taken. There is certainly the accusation, made by Tony Rayns, that Kim Ki-duk 'shamelessly plagiarized Tsai Ming-liang's *Vive l'amour*' (Rayns, 2004, pp. 50–1), but what is intriguing is the extent to which *Bin jip* responds to, and indeed expands on, the idea of ubiquity (and its corollary, invisible presence) to produce a new concept of cinematic indexicality and evidence, while 'educating' the spectator into another mode of 'being present'.

I will indicate briefly some of the ways in which the film instantiates, almost to the point of literalizing them, features I have identified with the new post-epistemological ontology of realism. First of all, there is a hero with a sensory restriction: throughout the film, he does not utter a single word, as if the deprivation of speech at once focuses and intensifies the body's other perceptual resources and faculties. Second, the film is constructed around

Figure 1.1   The hero of *3 Iron*, sensed but not seen by the husband, yet fully present to the wife. Reproduced with kind permission from Kim Ki-duk.

an architecture of looks, where the act of looking is emphasized by placing the face in a narrow aperture: a barely opened door, the edge of a screen, or a glance around the corner of a wall or door-frame. Yet time and again this gazing corresponds to what I earlier called 'embodied self-perception through the perception of another': that is, it is a form of looking that can bear or even valorize the fact of being looked at while looking, to the point of wanting this look, as an enabling fiction. Thus, the circulation of looks between the young man and the wife does not conform to the classic paradigm, where an exhibitionist look counters a voyeuristic one. At the same time, this architecture finds its point of most intense contact not in the direct face-to-face, but, as we see at the end, it requires the unseeing, impeding, and yet enabling presence of a third, in order to stabilize itself, however fleetingly.

Such a feeling of only existing when another is present is very well theorized, but also philosophically validated by Bishop Berkeley's reversal of Descartes '*cogito ergo sum*' into '*esse est percipi*'. But the 'being seen' in this case extends from being seen by persons to being seen by objects: a little like the behaviour of tourists, when they take a picture of themselves at the spot they visit, in order to assure themselves of really having been there. This is me, and the presence of Notre Dame or the Eiffel Tower is my witness: the object world becomes the witness to my presence, rather than the other way round. And this is precisely what the young man does, obsessively, systematically: he takes pictures of himself in front of other pictures in the houses he enters, assuring himself of his presence like a tourist, but also literally 'inserting himself' into an already constituted picture, usually of the owners of the house when they pose as a wedded couple (Figure 1.2).

Figure 1.2 Taking a photograph in front of a photograph, in *3 Iron*: Index, trace, or proof of existence? Reproduced with kind permission from Kim Ki-duk.

Yet, by the status it gives to these photographs, *Bin jip* is at its most enigmatic, as well as most theoretically prescient: photographs play a complex
role, both within the story and as emblems. Narratively, because the wife
is also a model, whose posed picture they find in one of the houses, which
belongs to a photographer. As emblems, because the snaps the young
man takes of himself act as an index, a proof of existence, less by fixing
a particular space, nor even a particular time, but because they serve more
like a mask, a cast or imprint, rather than a representation. It is as if he slips
into the photographs as a second skin, a notion made explicit when he lays
out for the wife, after a particular violent and harrowing encounter with her
husband, a set of clothes into which she 'enters': at once a space and a self-
image, after her previous one having been 'shattered' or destroyed.

A clue to the ontological significance of this gesture can be found in the
way the young man initially ascertains that the houses he enters are unoc-
cupied: he sticks a takeaway restaurant flyer on the door and, if it has not
been removed after 24 hours, he picks the lock to gain entrance. In other
words, while he enters a physical space, he identifies this space purely by
a time index, the undisturbed flyer, rather than by any other marker (of
class, wealth, size, or beauty). In this sense, the borrowed space represents
in fact borrowed – or stolen – time, as if his aim was not to inhabit space,
but through space, to occupy or immerse himself in time. And inside this
time, what does he do? He lets the everyday take over, almost in the manner
of André Bazin's description of a maid making coffee in de Sica's *Umberto D*
(1952) (Bazin, 1972, pp. 79–82): he scrubs shoes, repairs a set of scales, glues
a broken appliance, sprays the plants. In other words, he lets pure *durée*
take over, but always on condition that it is 'time out of time', as it were,
suspended in the dead-ends of someone else's absence, and thus it is a neorealism 'virtualized'; put even more directly, it becomes a necro-realism, in
that the reality of his presence in the house is a condition of, and confirms,
his being a ghost, an apparition. Space is the medium of the real only in the
sense that it can trap and thus index time, when the camera (or the body)
no longer indexes space. The empty house and the whole manner of gaining
entry become a veritable light-chamber, as if both literalizing and allegoriz-
ing, and thus strangely perverting, Roland Barthes's *chambre claire*, or *camera
lucida* of photography (Barthes, 1982), re-inventing it for the digital age.

Finally, what is striking about the manner in which he takes the photographs is their frontality, the way the hand with the digital camera extends
into ours, the viewer's, space, as if to invite us either to hold the camera or
see ourselves in the camera's screen, like a mirror, or *mise-en-abyme*. This
hand–eye correlation is further highlighted in the scene in the prison,
where he paints an eye onto his palm, before becoming invisible by always
occupying the guard's own shadow space.

As if to drive home the lesson, not about the play of light and shadows, as
in photography, but of the new distribution of the visible and the invisible,

Figure 1.3   3 Iron: Between the real and the virtual, in the imaginary line of flight of a tethered golf-ball. Reproduced with kind permission from Kim Ki-duk.

which no longer coincides with presence and absence, *Bin jip* narrates an extended parable around golf balls. These golf balls are alternately hyperreal (they do real, physical damage and can even kill) and virtual – as in the prison scene, where its sound is present but its image is absent, or when he practices in the park, and a passer-by inadvertently ducks to avoid being hit, when there is no ball. It is as if the scenes ask a crucial question about the relation of the visible to what is present, precisely the question that ubiquity raises: how can I position myself in relation to a world where the real becomes virtual, and where the virtual can have real consequences? A similar distribution of the visible and the sensible is enacted by the wife, when she systematically places herself in the imaginary line of flight of the tethered golf-ball, complementing but also exceeding the more obvious feminist point being made, when she literally puts herself between her husband and her lover, united as the men are by their obsession with golf (Figure 1.3).

Acts of presence for a new way of being in the world

If one can accept that there has been an 'ontological turn' in film theory, and that it forms the philosophical basis for a new realism, then my more specific argument has been that 'ubiquity' is its ontological ground, but also its point of 'failure' so to speak, because ubiquity in this sense signifies the very absence of ground. Several consequences flow from this. First, ubiquity implies (as the human response to an unrepresentable and unlocalizable sense of presence) a *spatialization of time*, which manifests itself in seemingly compulsive behaviour, comparable to the response to trauma – a compulsion to repeat, an obsessive return to the same scenes, staging such 'returns' as a way to give a bodily envelope, to add an imprint to the 'evidence' of presence.

Secondly, because this ubiquity is not tied to a human other, in fact it suspends the existence of an 'other', its forms of embodiment are in themselves problematic–enigmatic. It can manifest itself in non-sentient objects or 'things', and these things enter the realm of presence in seemingly contradictory forms: as effigies (imprints, sculptures, photographs, fetish-objects, or even stones, as in *Spring, Summer, Autumn, Winter ... and Spring – Bom yeoreum gaeul gyeoul geurigo bom*, another Kim Ki-duk film, from 2003) and as apparitions (ghosts, revenants, post-mortem creatures). Together, the effigy (as index) and the apparition (as material–immaterial presence) would constitute a modality of *evidence* in this new ontology. An example are the final scenes of *Bin jip*, when the wife, during the young man's time in jail, revisits the houses when the owners are back, making tactile contact with the objects they shared. Once he is out of prison, he follows her and does the same, but invisibly, 'haunting' the houses by his felt but immaterial presence.

Thirdly, the ghostly visitations of the houses have much in common, thanks to the handheld camera, with the moving 'subjective' Steadicam shots notorious from horror movies. But they are here extended into a generalized frontality. The story's premise about how to enter houses allegorizes the seemingly perverse desire to make oneself an empty signifier or a 'blur', and yet to leave traces in the perceptual field of the other. To this corresponds, on the side of the spectator, a similarly generalized frontality: protagonist and spectator become each other's other, but not on the analogy of the mirror, and instead performing more like guests at a ceremony, whose *acte de présence* 'authenticates' the evidentiary status of the event. Each is the perfect extension of the other's projected existence, suggesting that the film is also a parable about training or re-calibrating the spectator as agent and the agent as spectator.

This new spectator clearly responds to the changing viewing habits of our audiovisual culture, where watching a film has become infinitely more varied an activity. To the different sites, screens, and platforms of movie theatre, video screen, DVD, monitor, or handheld device correspond different roles: voyeur, witness, participant, player, user, pro-sumer; and different stances: placing oneself face to face with an image, or 'inhabiting' it, instrumentalizing it, or identifying with it. In this context, *frontal staging* – the limit case of 'classical' cinema – now re-emerges as the default value, just as it had been in early cinema. The space in front (first person): whether as an analogy to a first-person shooter sitting in front of a computer screen, or re-invested with narrative potential, as in Michael Haneke's films, now serves to remind us of the 'basics' of cinematic space harking back to the frontality of early cinema, such as Edwin Porter's cowboy shooting directly at the viewer in *The Great Train Robbery* (1903) or D.W. Griffith's use of frontal staging in, for instance, *A Corner in Wheat* (1909).

Yet the 'new spectator' re-training and re-calibrating her perceptual registers does not merely react to technological change or to the greater choices of viewing practices on offer. The contract thus being enacted has a philosophical dimension, whose common denominator, I have been arguing, is a post-epistemological concept of realism, accepting the groundless ground of representation, as well as an ontology, based on the (new) conditions of visibility and presence that include invisibility and virtual presence. These conditions have to be negotiated case-by-case, across trust and belief, rather than by presuming reference and ocular verification. In this respect the new ontological realism inherits the scepticism of the epistemological view of cinema, but without basing itself either on truth-claims for its 'visible evidence', or on scepticism for its ideological critique. Such a concept of cinematic realism responds to the unknowability of 'other minds', but also 'shows some respect' for this otherness. This is a challenge, but also a chance for a new way of 'being in the world' – and thus as good a description as any for some of the expectations, beyond all normative framings, that can attach themselves to the idea of 'world cinema' today.

References

Barthes, Roland (1982), *Camera Lucida*. New York: Hill & Wang.
Bazin, André (1972), '*Umberto D*: A Great Work', in André Bazin (ed.), *What is Cinema*, vol 2. Berkeley/Los Angeles/London: University of California Press, pp. 79–82.
Cavell, Stanley (1979), *The World Viewed: Reflections on the Ontology of Film*. Cambridge, MA: Harvard University Press.
Deleuze, Gilles (1989), *Cinema 2: The Time Image*. Minneapolis: Minnesota University Press.
Pfaller, Robert (2000), *Interpassivität. Studien über delegiertes Genießen*. Vienna and New York: Springer.
Rayns, Tony (2004), 'Sexual Terrorism: The Strange Case of Kim Ki-duk', in *Film Comment* 40 (6), November/December, pp. 50–1.

2
Whither Realism? Bazin Reconsidered

Leighton Grist

Towards the end of the film *Germany, Year Zero* (*Germania anno zero*, Roberto Rossellini, 1947), the film's young protagonist, Edmund (Edmund Meschke), who, following comments made by his former teacher – the Nazi and implied paedophile, Henning (Erich Gühne) – has poisoned his ailing father (Ernst Pittschau), is shown walking through bomb-ruined Berlin. During the sequence he has his attempts at joining a game of football with some other children rebuffed, then his attention drawn to a priest playing an organ in a damaged church. After stepping and hopping between some debris and dents in the road, he finally sits, upset, upon a kerb.

Germany, Year Zero has been considered critically to be an exemplary instance of Italian neorealist cinema, as the noted sequence would appear to demonstrate. Situated within a narrative that carries, ideologically, a distinct anti-fascist weighting, it likewise exhibits the use of location shooting, natural lighting, deep-focus cinematography and comparatively long takes; the central presence of a non-professional performer; and the representation of then-present, lower-order actuality. As such, it might be seen in terms of representation to display what Raymond Williams has described as the 'defining characteristics' of realism in general: 'the secular, the contemporary and the socially extended' (Williams, 1977, pp. 63, 65). However, the sequence also conveys a sense of something else, of something uncertain and incommensurate, that – complemented by the interpolation of snatches of the film's score, which are variously dramatic, plangent and foreboding – approaches, almost literally, Sigmund Freud's concept of the uncanny (Freud, 1919).

Rossellini and *Germany, Year Zero* were, in turn, among the directors and films championed by critic-cum-theorist André Bazin. Bazin has been acknowledged as being one of the most significant and influential persons to engage with cinema: 'the single thinker', according to Peter Matthews, 'most responsible for bestowing on cinema the prestige both of an artform and of an object of knowledge' (Matthews, 1999, p. 22) and the source of, according to Dudley Andrew, 'what many consider to be the most brilliant, subtle, and consequential body of writing the cinema engendered in its first century' (Andrew, 1997, p. 73). Philip Rosen correspondingly opined in 1987 that it was writing that, despite Bazin's death in 1958, 'remained required reading for anyone with a serious interest in cinema' (Rosen, 1987, p. 8), a situation that – given the continued metadiscursive explication of Bazin's output, of which this paper is obviously an example – can be seen to have sustained since. Further, although Bazin is famous as being the co-founder, with Jacques Doniol-Valcroze, of the magazine *Cahiers du Cinéma*, his critical and theoretical importance and reputation predominantly rests on his arguments about cinema as a medium innately attuned to the representation of the real, with his work being considered central to the realist tradition of classical film theory (Andrew, 1976, pp. 134–78).

Nevertheless, the contours and ramifications of Bazin's position respecting cinema and reality have been subject to shifting and contrasting elucidation; in two articles published during 2007 alone, Bazin's work is described as, on one hand, 'an articulate and powerful defence of cinematic realism' (DiIorio, 2007, p. 27) and, on the other, 'an investment in surrealism' (Lowenstein, 2007, p. 54).[1] The argument pursued by this paper will seek to mediate the poles implied by these latter perspectives and, as it attempts to place Bazin's conception of cinematic realism epistemologically, effectively render manifest that which has been barely latent in a good deal of writing on his ideas. As it centres largely upon matters of form and history, it will also propose a provisional explanation of why Bazin's writing sustains as a focus of what seems to be ever-increasing critical and theoretical fascination, reference and enquiry.

Bazin, realism, modernism

The principal tenets and emphases of Bazin's conception and discussion of the relationship between cinema and reality, and, concordantly, of cinematic realism, have become long familiar within film studies. There is, for example, his belief that cinema and its technological and aesthetic forerunner, photography, have, as Matthews states, a 'privileged relationship with the real', and thus, reciprocally, 'a special obligation towards reality' (Matthews, 1999, p. 23); his associated proposition that photography and cinema are 'discoveries that satisfy, once and for all and in its very essence, our obsession with realism' (Bazin, 1945, p. 12); and his embrace of developments that potentially brought cinema nearer to reality, be they sound, colour, widescreen or even 3-D. Complementing such is his excoriating of montage and expressionism and his extolling of the stylistic virtues of the long take and, especially, deep-focus cinematography, which, according to Bazin, 'brings the spectator into a relation with the image closer to that which he enjoys with reality', and of which he notes 'it is correct to say that, independently of the contents of the image, its structure is more realistic' (Bazin, 1958, p. 35), and his lauding of the Italian neorealist cinema that can be regarded as both shaping and vindicating his opinions. However, there is also, more problematically, from a materialist perspective, in the essay 'The Ontology of the Photographic Image', Bazin's contention that the photographic image 'is the object itself', '*is* the model' of which 'it is the reproduction' (Bazin, 1945, p. 14).[2] Extended to cinema, moreover, his argument sets films as being 'no longer content to preserve the object, enshrouded as it were in an instant', but 'the image of things' as becoming instead 'likewise the image of their duration, change mummified as it were' (Bazin, 1945, pp. 14–15).[3]

Yet should one read Bazin with any degree of attention, seeming contradictions emerge within his writing's apparent realist emphasis. Thus for Bazin, whereas montage 'by its very nature rules out ambiguity of expression', deep-focus cinematography also, beneficially, 'reintroduced ambiguity into the structure of the image if not of necessity' then 'at least as a possibility' (Bazin, 1958, p. 36). Correspondingly, its use in one of Bazin's filmic touch-stones, *Citizen Kane* (Orson Welles, 1941), sees the 'uncertainty in which we find ourselves as to the spiritual key or the interpretation we should put on the film' as 'built into the very design of the image' (Bazin, 1958, p. 36). He similarly asserts, apropos of neorealism, that it 'tends to give back to the cinema a sense of the ambiguity of reality' (Bazin, 1958, p. 37). This stress on ambiguity and uncertainty jars somewhat with other notions of realism. Consider, for instance, what Terry Lovell declares as 'the first principle of realism': 'that there exists an objective and independent social world, which can be known' (Lovell, 1983, p. 23). Another film discussed by Bazin, *Bicycle Thieves* (*Ladri di biciclette*, Vittorio De Sica, 1948), can be seen to invite analysis in terms of Marxist theorist Georg Lukács's concept of narrative realism. The film centres upon a working-class protagonist, Antonio (Lamberto Maggiorani), who obtains and then faces losing a precious job upon the theft of the bicycle necessary for his employment. In turn, through the experiences of this character – who, in the course of the narrative, interacts with various and contrasting social forces – it can be seen to clarify, to evoke Lukács, the totality of the represented social reality, to provide an understanding of the determinant factors impacting upon a particular historical conjuncture (Lukács, 1936a, 1936b). However, although Bazin posits analogously that the film is informed by a critical 'social message', that 'in the world where this workman lives, the poor must steal from each other in order to survive', the focus of his account of *Bicycle Thieves* is on how it treats each of its incidents 'according to its phenomenological integrity': 'The events are not necessarily signs of something, of a truth of which we are to be convinced, they all carry their own weight, their complete uniqueness, that ambiguity that character-izes any fact' (Bazin, 1949b, pp. 51–2).

Further, discussing Rossellini, Bazin avers that neorealism 'contrasts with the realist aesthetics that preceded it', that it 'by definition rejects analysis, whether political, moral, psychological, logical, or social, of the characters and their actions', and rather 'looks on reality as a whole, not incomprehensible, certainly, but inseparably one' (Bazin, 1955b, p. 97). Regarding this, we might return to the described sequence from *Germany, Year Zero* and its transmission of a manifest, unsettling indeterminacy. Writing on the sequence, closely following which Edmund commits suicide, Bazin notes that the close-ups of the character that 'punctuate' it 'never show us anything other than a worried, pensive, perhaps frightened face', and concludes that 'the signs of play and the signs of death may be the same on a child's face, at least for those of us who cannot penetrate its mystery' (Bazin, 1949a, pp. 123–4) (Figure 2.1). Such captivation by the equivocal, by the indeterminate, moreover, tends to imply an engagement with and advocacy of not so much realism as modernism. This is particularly the case for a film in which, according to Colin MacCabe, as he outlines his concept of the classic realist text, 'the reading subject finds himself without a position from which the film can be regarded' (MacCabe, 1974, p. 19). That is, instead of 'providing us with knowledge', with a dominant discourse through which, as MacCabe argues of the classic realist text, we can gauge the film, *Germany, Year Zero* 'provides us with various settings' (MacCabe, 1974, p. 19). It is, in addition, perhaps more than coincidental that the shot showing Edmund and other people standing at intervals listening to the priest's organ playing suggests less realism per se than the stylized representation of the likes of, say, the paintings of Giorgio de Chirico (Figure 2.2). Similarly, if *Citizen Kane* is for Bazin 'the most significant' single indication of what he perceived as 'a vast stirring of the geological bed of cinema' (Bazin, 1958, p. 37), then it is also – with, in Peter Wollen's words, 'its complex pattern of nesting, overlapping and conflicting narratives' (1975, p. 50) – widely considered a modernist text.[4]

Figure 2.1 Germany, Year Zero: 'the signs of play and the signs of death may be the same on a child's face, at least for those of us who cannot penetrate its mystery'. Permission by Kramsie Productions Ltd.

Figure 2.2   Germany, Year Zero: de Chirico shapes. Kramsie Productions Ltd.

Concordantly, although Bazin's critical emphasis on films that convey ambiguity and uncertainty might be read as placing them in conformity with a broad realist aspiration, that of, as Williams puts it, 'a commitment to describing real events and showing things as they actually exist' (Williams, 1988, p. 59), not only does his work privilege numerous films and filmmakers – like Rossellini and Welles, or Jean Renoir, or Robert Bresson – that can be aligned with modernism, but, epistemologically, it partakes less of the post-Enlightenment positivism that imbues most realism than of an embrace of contingency and the indefinite that bespeaks the modernist. Witness Bazin's assertion that a neorealist film has meaning 'to the extent that it permits our awareness to move from one fact to another, from one fragment of reality to the next' (Bazin, 1955b, p. 99), or his declaring that cinema's 'profound vocation' is 'to show before it expresses' and that its 'ultimate aim' should be 'not so much to mean as to reveal' (Bazin, 1953, pp. 90–1). The modernist reference of Bazin's writing is, besides, tacitly admitted within it. Apart from the particular films and filmmakers that it often qualitatively upholds, the arguments that it makes, or its proselytizing in the name of 'the originality of the postwar cinema as compared with that of 1938' (Bazin, 1958, p. 29), its approbatory points of reference are not infrequently the examples of modernist novelists such as John Dos Passos, André Malraux, James Joyce and William Faulkner. Correspondingly, 'not the least of the merits' of neorealism was that it was 'able to find the truly cinematic equivalent for the most important literary revolution of our time' (Bazin, 1948, p. 40).[5]

Strangely, writing about Bazin has inclined both to acknowledge and to disavow the seemingly pressing epistemological connotations of his output. Thus Andrew, possibly Bazin's most ardent academic advocate, can state in a recently published piece that Bazin had 'the fortune to observe cinema during the transition from its classic to its modern phase', and that 'the cinema of his time found itself in tune with and contributing to a modern – that is, a postwar, largely existentialist – sense of ordered disorder' (Andrew, 2005, pp. xviii–xix), yet shy away from drawing the near unavoidable conclusion. True, in the same piece Andrew does describe Bazin as having 'scouted out and grasped an idea of cinematic modernism' (Andrew, 2005, p. xxiv), but he does so only within the context of summarizing an argument advanced by Serge Daney. Andrew's mention of existentialism further brings us to the phenomenology that shapes Bazin's work, to which existentialism can be regarded to stand as philosophically adjacent. A body of thought that, in characteristic modernist fashion, is attuned to the irreducibility of existence, phenomenology – simplifying – emphasizes the ineffability of phenomena, positing that such are the sole material of insight, with underlying realities and causes being unfathomable. Hence Bazin's proclaiming of neorealism itself 'a phenomenology': 'Neorealism knows only immanence. It is from appearance only, the simple appearance of beings and of the world, that it knows how to deduce the ideas that it unearths' (Bazin, 1951, pp. 64–5).

What is thereby deduced, moreover, is, as propounded by Bazin, invariably of a transcendental, supra-rational order. For example, in discussing the director Federico Fellini, whom he situates but with difficulty within neorealism, Bazin opines that the filmmaker's work, through its 'interest in appearances', which goes 'beyond' the 'boundaries of realism', evokes an 'identification with the supernatural', 'expresses the hidden accord which things maintain with an invisible counterpart of which they are, so to speak, merely the adumbration' (Bazin, 1957b, p. 88).[6] As much can in turn be considered in terms of the intimation of the numinous that reverberates throughout Bazin's writing. With Bazin someone who could term expressionism 'heresy' (Bazin, 1948, p. 26), this is usually referred to his Catholicism, and more particularly to the influence of the Catholic French Personalist movement, a grouping that in addition declared, pointedly, an affinity with existentialism (Gray, 1971, pp. 2–5). However, this also accords with the way in which numerous modernist artefacts, movements and positions can be regarded to stage the return of the Enlightenment repressed; consider, once more, the adduced sequence from *Germany, Year Zero* and its implication of the uncanny, which, as previously suggested, invites relation, through Freud's aetiology of the effect, to the awakening of animistic beliefs that in 'civilized people' are 'in a state of having been (to a greater or lesser extent) *surmounted*' (Freud, 1919, p. 372). The same modernist tendency may also shed a sidelight on Bazin's assertion that the photographic image is what it reproduces. On one level conceivably a rhetorical provocation, on another it constitutes, again, a typically modernist metaphysical gesture, which is equally made within the context of Bazin's declaration of 'the irrational power of the photograph to bear away our faith' (Bazin, 1945, p. 14).

Surreality, materiality

Noteworthy, likewise, are Bazin's remarks in the same essay on the categorically modernist mode that is surrealism. For the surrealist, according to Bazin, 'the logical distinction between what is imaginary and what is real tends to disappear' (Bazin, 1945, p. 15). Accordingly, photography 'ranks high in the order of surrealist creativity because it produces an image that is a reality of nature, namely, an hallucination that is also a fact' (Bazin, 1945, p. 16). However, the last sentence of 'The Ontology of the Photographic Image' would appear to take things in a completely different direction: 'On the other hand, of course, cinema is also a language' (Bazin, 1945, p. 16). This is, besides, reflective of a concern with the fact of cinema as a signifying system that recurs across Bazin's writing. Examples are his postulating, with respect to neorealism, that 'realism in art can only be achieved in one way – through artifice', or that some 'measure of reality must always be sacrificed in the effort of achieving it' (Bazin, 1948, pp. 26, 30); the title of the article 'The Evolution of the *Language* of Cinema' (emphasis added), or his related contention that 'the decade from 1940 to 1950 marks a decisive step forward in the development of the language of the film' (Bazin, 1958, p. 38); his declaration that the relation of cinema to reality is that of an 'asymptote' (Bazin, 1952, p. 82), a line that approaches a curve but reaches it only at infinity; or his assertion that 'in the perfect aesthetic illusion of reality there is no more cinema' (Bazin, 1949b, p. 60). Not that this removes us from the modernist orbit. On the contrary, it suggests another aspect, certainly, of modernist aesthetic epistemology, that in which the contingency of what is represented is complemented by an emphasis on the contingency, the materiality of the means of representation.

Neither is modernism, in its representational embodiments, anti-realist. Rather, it works reflexively to foreground the act of representation of reality simultaneous to that reality being itself represented. This in addition prompts a revisiting of the polar descriptions of Bazin's work cited earlier in this paper. For although Bazin's manifest modernist affiliation distances that work from realism itself, this does not make it – despite his affirmatory comments in 'The Ontology of the Photographic Image' – surrealist, not least as surrealism's materialist, psychical emphasis contrasts significantly with the spiritual bent of Bazin's ideas.[7] Even so, within his writing there is yet set out a model of cinematic practice that is not only suggestively modernist, but tacitly materialist. Bazin proposes cinema as comprising a dialectical interplay of reality and abstraction, of subject matter and its stylistic transformation – although he critically privileges those syntheses in which style and technique subordinate themselves before subject, in which the 'abstraction that is necessary to art' emerges, 'paradoxically', 'from what is most concrete in the image' (Bazin, 1953, p. 88). Moreover, 'the degree of relationship between technique and subject matter depends in part on the personality of the director' (Bazin, 1955a, p. 114); extending which, Bazin, in an evident contradiction of his assertion that the photographic image 'is formed automatically, without the creative intervention of man' (Bazin, 1945, p. 13), installs within his schema the familiar modernist figure of the individual, innovative artist, of the auteur, even though he distinguishes, consonantly, and with due spiritual inference, between 'those directors who put their faith in the image and those who put their faith in reality' (Bazin, 1958, p. 24).

Indeed, in the essay 'In Defense of Rossellini', Bazin goes as far as to state: 'Neorealism as such does not exist. There are only neorealist directors' (Bazin, 1955b, p. 99). Yet if this bears testimony to his investment in the figure of the auteur, then it reciprocally implies certain, indicative tensions regarding his ascription of neorealism – and, possibly, of realism as a whole – that is besides suggested by his stretching of the notion to encompass not just the films of the likes of Rossellini, De Sica and Luchino Visconti, but those of Michelangelo Antonioni and Fellini. Thus the strain that is apparent when Bazin writes about Fellini, as he moves from somewhat exaggeratedly asserting that it 'is absurd, preposterous even, to deny him a place among the neorealists' to noting, in the very next paragraph, that Fellini 'goes even so far' within the 'neorealist aesthetic' that 'he goes all the way through it and finds himself on the other side' (Bazin, 1957b, p. 87).[8]

La politique des auteurs, the *nouvelle vague,* modernity

Through his association with *Cahiers du Cinéma*, which was first published in 1951, Bazin has been considered the presiding spirit of *la politique des auteurs* that dominated the magazine for the rest of the 1950s, this despite his seeking to distance himself from its excesses in the essay 'La Politique des Auteurs', from within the pages of *Cahiers du Cinéma* itself. The essay confronts the 'aesthetic personality cult' that he perceived as being latent within *la politique des auteurs* with a call for a consideration of the contextual factors – 'the social determinism, the historical combination of circumstances, and the technical background' – that shape an auteur's output and reflect an emphasis that runs throughout Bazin's writing. Nevertheless, his censures remain at the level of 'a family quarrel' (Bazin, 1957a, pp. 152, 142, 138).[9] Further, given that several of the critics involved in propagating *la politique des auteurs* went on to become filmmakers within the *nouvelle vague*, Bazin is 'also often regarded as the father' of the same (Matthews, 1999, p. 24). However, his influence – which is frequently asserted, but rarely interrogated – can be seen to extend beyond that of personal guidance, although this is far from negligible, particularly with respect to François Truffaut, to whom he became more or less a surrogate parent. The *nouvelle vague* is arguably the modernist film movement par excellence. Moreover, as it differently incorporates, among other elements, location shooting, self-consciously long takes, natural lighting, jump-cuts, handheld camerawork, improvisation and cinematic allusion, and hence combines naturalism with stylization, the aleatory with the formally and contextually reflexive, so it can be considered an extrapolation upon the preferred concept of cinema that is implicit to Bazin's writing.

The *nouvelle vague* mediates, in terms of representation, an emerging, belated French modernity, a context within and in relation to which we need to situate Bazin's own modernist postulations. Correctly situating Bazin's arguments critically and epistemologically has, in turn, ramifications beyond those of academic precision, of correcting their long-standing misrepresentation and misplacement. Recasting Bazin's concerns as modernist tacitly lends them the same symptomatic resonance as that of the films through which they are chiefly addressed. Further, if this sets Bazin's writing as part of a closed past, then it also places that writing as an appropriately nuanced attempt at reflecting upon the cinematic engagement with a contingent, complex reality, the likes of which can be seen to have been eroded, epistemologically, by the advent of postmodernism, and, technologically, by the movement from analogue to digital modes of image capture and construction.

Certainly, the parallels made in 'The Ontology of the Photographic Image' between photography and, respectively, 'the molding of death masks' and 'a fingerprint' (Bazin, 1945, pp. 12n.,15) would suggest that for Bazin photography – and cinema – is, to evoke Charles Sanders Peirce, strongly indexical.[10] Positioning Bazin's work within the larger context of modernity, Rosen submits that 'Bazin's arguments constitute ideas whose time had come' (Rosen, 1987, p. 29). In a like fashion, although the seemingly sustained interest in Bazin's arguments might be regarded to imply a certain, itself modernist, nostalgia, a yearning for, as Fredric Jameson notes, 'a past beyond all but aesthetic retrieval' (Jameson, 1984, p. 66), it can also be conceived as invoking an historical and epistemological discontent with both the increasing solipsism and affectlessness of the contemporary audiovisual media and the way in which those media have been contemporaneously addressed critically and theoretically. As such, Bazin, to cite Rosen, 'may point us towards something we wish to explore in ways different from him' (Rosen, 1987, p. 29), not least ideologically, but it is nevertheless maybe where the value of the continued discussion of his work presently lies.

Notes

1. Adam Lowenstein is not the first critic to align Bazin's work with surrealism; see, for instance, Ray (1998, pp. 71–3).
2. To state the problem implicit to Bazin's position succinctly, one can cite Jean Mitry, who, in a tacit rejoinder to Bazin, observes that 'what is involved in the film is not so much the object itself but an aspect of the object, an *image*' (Mitry, 1990, p. 44).

3. For detailed consideration of Bazin's work in relation to what he himself terms the 'mummy complex' (Bazin, 1945, p. 9), see Rosen (1987) and Falkenberg (1987).
4. Wollen's 1975 essay discusses *Citizen Kane* as well explicitly in relation to Bazin's account of the film.
5. In his biography of Bazin, Andrew states that during the years of World War II, Bazin began 'specializing in literary theory' and hoped 'to compose a theory of the novel' (Andrew, 1978, p. 50).
6. Not that phenomenology need partake of such spiritual implication. Hence Mitry states, from within the sphere of phenomenology, and once more contra Bazin: 'In the cinema, the immanent finds expression in a *certain transcendence* but not in the "transcendental"' (Mitry, 1990, p. 45).
7. This notwithstanding, Andrew points out that Bazin was for a short time in the early 1940s 'a fanatic surrealist' (Andrew, 1978, p. 58). Further, Lowenstein bases his argument regarding Bazin and surrealism almost entirely upon Bazin's brief discussion of surrealism in 'The Ontology of the Photographic Image'; see Lowenstein (2007, pp. 56–9).
8. For Bazin's debatably no less forced argument about *Chronicle of a Love* (*Cronaca di un amore*, Michelangelo Antonioni, 1950) as an example of neorealism, see Bazin (1951, p. 66).
9. 'La Politique des Auteurs' was initially published in *Cahiers du Cinéma*, 70 (April 1957).
10. For a discussion of Peirce's work, see Wollen (1972, pp. 120–4).

References

Andrew, Dudley (1976), *The Major Film Theories: An Introduction.* London/Oxford/New York: Oxford University Press.

Andrew, Dudley (1978), *André Bazin.* New York: Oxford University Press.

Andrew, Dudley (1997), 'André Bazin's "Evolution"', in Peter Lehman (ed.) *Defining Cinema.* London: Athlone, pp. 73–94.

Andrew, Dudley (2005), 'Foreword to the 2004 Edition', in André Bazin, *What is Cinema?*, vol 2, trans. by Hugh Gray. Berkeley/Los Angeles/London: University of California Press, pp. xi–xxvi.

Bazin, André (1945/1967), 'The Ontology of the Photographic Image', in *What is Cinema?*, vol 1, trans. by Hugh Gray. Berkeley/Los Angeles/London: University of California Press, pp. 9–16.

Bazin, André (1948/1971), 'An Aesthetic of Reality: Neorealism (Cinematic Realism and the Italian School of the Liberation)', in *What is Cinema?*, vol 2, trans. by Hugh Gray. Berkeley/Los Angeles/London: University of California Press, pp. 16–40.

Bazin, André (1949a/1997), '*Germany, Year Zero*', in Bazin *at Work: Major Essays & Reviews from the Forties & Fifties*, ed. by Bert Cardullo, trans. by Alain Piette and Bert Cardullo. New York/London: Routledge, pp. 121–4.

Bazin, André (1949b/1971), '*Bicycle Thief*', in *What is Cinema?*, vol 2, trans. by Hugh Gray. Berkeley/Los Angeles/London: University of California Press, pp. 47–60.

Bazin, André (1951/1971), 'De Sica: Metteur en Scène', in *What is Cinema?*, vol 2, trans. by Hugh Gray. Berkeley/Los Angeles/London: University of California Press, pp. 61–78.

Bazin, André (1952/1971), '*Umberto D*: A Great Work', *in What is Cinema?*, vol 2, trans. by Hugh Gray. Berkeley/Los Angeles/London: University of California Press, pp. 79–82

Bazin, André (1953/1997), 'Will CinemaScope Save the Film Industry?', in *Bazin at Work: Major Essays & Reviews from the Forties & Fifties*, ed. by Bert Cardullo, trans. by Alain Piette and Bert Cardullo. New York/London: Routledge, pp. 77–92.

Bazin, André (1955a/1997), '*La Strada*', in *Bazin at Work: Major Essays & Reviews from the Forties & Fifties*, ed. by Bert Cardullo, trans. by Alain Piette and Bert Cardullo. New York/London: Routledge, pp. 113–20.

Bazin, André (1955b/1971), 'In Defense of Rossellini', in *What is Cinema?*, vol 2, trans. by Hugh Gray. Berkeley/Los Angeles/London: University of California Press, pp. 93–101.

Bazin, André (1957a/1968), 'La Politique des Auteurs', translator not cited, in Peter Graham (ed.), *The New Wave*. London: Secker & Warburg, pp. 137–55.

Bazin, André (1957b/1971) '*Cabiria*: The Voyage to the End of Neorealism', in *What is Cinema?*, vol 2, trans. by Hugh Gray. Berkeley/Los Angeles/London: University of California Press, pp. 83–92.

Bazin, André (1958/1967) 'The Evolution of the Language of Cinema', in *What is Cinema?*, vol 1, trans. by Hugh Gray. Berkeley/Los Angeles/London: University of California Press, pp. 23–40.

DiIorio, Sam (2007), 'Total Cinema: *Chronique d'un été* and the End of Bazinian Film Theory', in *Screen*, 48(1), pp. 25–43.

Falkenberg, Pamela (1987), '"The Text! The Text!": André Bazin's Mummy Complex, Psychoanalysis and the Cinema', in *Wide Angle*, 9(4), pp. 35–55.

Freud, Sigmund (1919/1990), 'The "Uncanny"', trans. by J. Strachey, in Albert Dickson (ed.), *Art and Literature*. Harmondsworth: Penguin, pp. 335–76.

Gray, Hugh (1971), 'Translator's Introduction', in André Bazin, *What is Cinema?*, vol 2, trans. by Hugh Gray. Berkeley/Los Angeles/London: University of California Press, pp. 1–15.

Jameson, Fredric (1984), 'Postmodernism, or the Cultural Logic of Late Capitalism', in *New Left Review*, 146, pp. 53–92.

Lovell, Terry (1983), *Pictures of Reality: Aesthetics, Politics, Pleasure*. London: British Film Institute.

Lowenstein, Adam (2007), 'The Surrealism of the Photographic Image: Bazin, Barthes, and the Digital *Sweet Hereafter*', in *Cinema Journal*, 46(3), pp. 54–82.

Lukács, Georg (1936a/1970), 'Art and Objective Truth', in *Writer and Critic and Other Essays*, ed. and trans by Arthur D. Kahn. London: Merlin Press, pp. 25–60.

Lukács, Georg (1936b/1970), 'Narrate or Describe?', in *Writer and Critic and Other Essays*, ed. by Arthur D. Kahn. London: Merlin Press, pp. 110–48.

MacCabe, Colin (1974), 'Realism and the Cinema: Notes on Some Brechtian Theses', in *Screen*, 15(2), pp. 7–27.

Matthews, Peter (1999), 'Divining the Real', in *Sight and Sound*, 9(8), pp. 22–5.

Mitry, Jean (1990/1998), *The Aesthetics and Psychology of the Cinema*, trans. by Christopher King. London: Athlone.

Ray, Robert B. (1998), 'Impressionism, Surrealism, and Film Theory: Path Dependence, or How a Tradition in Film Theory Gets Lost', in John Hill and Pamela Church Gibson (eds), *The Oxford Guide to Film Studies*. Oxford: Oxford University Press, pp. 67–76.

Rosen, Philip (1987), 'History of Image, Image of History: Subject and Ontology in Bazin', in *Wide Angle*, 9(4), pp. 7–34.

Williams, Raymond (1977), 'A Lecture on Realism', in *Screen*, 18(1), pp. 61–74.

Williams, Raymond (1988), *Keywords: A Vocabulary of Culture and Society*, revised and expanded edition. London: Fontana.

Wollen, Peter (1972), *Signs and Meaning in the Cinema*, 3rd edition. London: Secker & Warburg.

Wollen, Peter (1975/1982), 'Introduction to *Citizen Kane*', in *Readings and Writings: Semiotic Counter-Strategies*. London: Verso, pp. 49–61.

3
Brecht, Realism and the Media

Marc Silberman

Bertolt Brecht was born in 1898 in Augsburg, southern Germany. He died of a heart attack in East Berlin, in the German Democratic Republic, in 1956. The 1928 musical *The Threepenny Opera*, based on John Gay's eighteenth-century parody of high opera in the style of Handel, was a collaboration between Brecht, Elisabeth Hauptmann and composer Kurt Weill that became the most successful stage performance of the Weimar Republic, translated into numerous languages and produced all over the world. With the Nazi accession to power in March 1933, Brecht went into exile, his books were burned in Germany and his German citizenship was revoked.

Brecht authored a considerable oeuvre that was published in a 30-volume German edition during the 1990s: ten of those contain his plays, five his collected poetry, another five his collected prose (short stories, novels and two entire volumes of his film scripts, screenplays and film exposés); five additional volumes comprise his critical writings and essays, two volumes contain diaries and journals, and three volumes his selected letters (Brecht, 1988–2000). In 2010 the first of 13 volumes of Brecht's notebooks is to appear as a supplement to the 30 volumes (Brecht, 2010). This was a prodigious writer. As a young man in Germany's Weimar Republic of the 1920s, he was considered variously to be a gadfly, an annoyance or a shooting star. Today he is considered a towering, canonical figure, with all the ambiguity that the term conveys about authority and weightiness. In any case, he is a major twentieth-century German dramatist, an important contributor to avant-garde theatre theory and practices, as well as a remarkable lyric poet.

In regards to Brecht and realism: he considered 'Realism' to be a nineteenth-century style based on the illusion that a work of art can mirror or reproduce reality. He, on the contrary, saw reality as a construction, and art's function to make visible how our perception of reality is constructed. Thus, when Brecht uses the word 'realism', that is, when he is not referring to a past epoch of cultural history, he is pointing to the internal, structural coherence of a work of art. But beware: coherence does not mean totality, completeness or unity for Brecht. His aesthetics of distanciation, interruption and open forms suggests a realism marked by the fragmentation, alienation and crisis of subjectivity we associate with modernity and modernist cultures. In short, Brechtian realism is related not to formal criteria of verisimilitude and authenticity, but rather to an aesthetic process or set of artistic practices that expose the way things change by abstracting from reality.

Brecht and media may be a less visible side of this writer's productivity. Although it is generally known that Georg Wilhelm Pabst directed the 1931 version of *The Threepenny Opera* (*Die Dreigroschenoper*), a remarkable, early German sound film, it is less well known that Brecht himself wrote a script for the adaptation, which Pabst did not use, and that Brecht and Weill then sued the production company. Brecht's collaboration on the 1932 film *Kuhle Wampe oder: Wem gehört die Welt?* (Slatan Dudow), which was censored before its release and then banned less than a year later by the Nazis, has been documented; and that Brecht shared screen credits on Fritz Lang's 1943 feature *Hangmen Also Die*, one of Hollywood's classic anti-Nazi films, has also not escaped attention. However, that Brecht wrote more than 40 other film treatments – some elaborately worked out – but none of which were realized during his lifetime, is a well-kept secret, at least to those who do not have access to the German edition of his works. Furthermore, there is no question about his enthusiasm for the movies. His diary and journal entries, as well as reminiscences of friends and acquaintances, testify to frequent excursions to the movies going back to at least 1919. Finally, Brecht's interest in film comprises only one dimension of his work in various media, including – beyond theatre and opera – radio broadcasting, gramophone recording, photography, fine arts, ballet and book printing. Indeed, we might best understand his entire artistic career as an ongoing and explicit experiment in how to reach an audience by using the specific advantages of different media. The fact that his 'experiments' often did not succeed led him to reflect repeatedly on the possibilities and limits of such undertakings.

This, then, is the framework of my thoughts on 'Brecht, Realism, and the Media'. I want to examine some central concepts Brecht developed, especially during that most fertile time of his career between 1928 and 1933, concepts that have had a decisive impact on certain kinds of filmmaking, notably on what we call the radical or counter-cinema emerging during and after the 1960s in the European New Waves, in the New Latin American Cinema and among feminist filmmakers. In fact, I think a case can be made that anyone who is concerned with the politics of visual representation will eventually encounter in Brecht a fruitful but not a simplistic thinker about realism and the media. On the other hand, I want to emphasize at the outset that Brecht never produced an aesthetic theory or a systematic media critique. As an experimenter, he was more interested in the challenges presented by the changing demands of technology and history. His interest in the cinema, as well as in other media, was to make the familiar strange so that the audience sees the principles governing reality and learns how to manipulate them.

Brecht goes to the movies

Brecht's enthusiasm for the movies in the early 1920s had two sources. First, he saw them as a popular form of entertainment whose sensationalism, suspense, grotesque humour and documentary quality appealed to a broad public, a public he too wished to reach. Second, the movie industry represented a challenge to prevailing forms of high-culture production and reception, a development that the young iconoclast Brecht appreciated. This led him to author three well constructed screenplays in a matter of several months between 1921 and 1922: 'The Mystery of the Jamaica Bar', 'The Jewel Eater' and 'Three in the Tower' (Brecht, 2000, pp. 49–128). The main motivation for this sudden flurry of activity seems to have been financial need, but the romantic adventures also deal with themes and figures typical of his early poems and plays. Brecht adapted here genre conventions of the silent cinema but transformed the metaphysical soul-searching and melodrama of the expressionist period with humour and irony. Of course, the screenplays are only preliminary sketches of films that never materialized, but they do demonstrate principles that would continue to interest Brecht in other media as well: episodic structure, aspects of rupture and distanciation, and a strong story line.

When Brecht's theatre career began to prosper in 1923 with stage productions in Berlin and Munich, his active interest in the cinema waned. More substantial for understanding the role of the new medium in his thinking were his occasional reflections *on* the cinema. A fruitful stimulus, for example, was the discovery of Charlie Chaplin.[1] The first Chaplin film he saw in 1921 – the 1914 *Face on the Barroom Floor* – led him to comment on the actor's simplicity and directness, which struck Brecht because the deadpan, unsentimental earnestness elicited constant laughter from the audience in the cinema (see the journal entry from 29 October 1921 in Brecht, 1988–2000, vol 29, pp. 256–7). Chaplin's non-psychological acting contrasted with the introspective habits of German actors on stage and screen, and it became a major factor in the economy of expression that Brecht would develop later. After viewing Chaplin's *Goldrush* in 1926, he returned to this simplicity as a quality of the film structure itself and drew an explicit comparison with the possibilities of stage dramaturgy ('Less Certainty!!!', 1926, in Brecht, 2000, pp. 5–6). Because the film as a new medium was not burdened with the techniques that had developed over centuries in the theatre, its power, Brecht proposed, was in the simple documentation of reality.

Additional evidence for Brecht's sophisticated understanding of the cinema comes from another direction entirely. In his highly accomplished short story 'The Monster' (written in 1928), Brecht creates a fictional narrative about the difficulty of filming a historically inspired scene realistically (Brecht, 1998, pp. 107–11). Set in a 1920s Soviet film studio, the story involves a film crew preparing to shoot a pogrom scene in which a ruthless Russian governor, the monster of the title, signs the execution order for a group of Jews, here played by two actors who themselves were authentic victims of a pogrom before the 1917 revolution. An old man who is standing around the set is allowed to try the role of governor because his bearing and physique seem to resemble him to a T. The attentive reader quickly surmises that he is indeed the historical governor, now impoverished and trying to earn some money as a studio extra. All the others, however, prefer the effect produced by the film star engaged for the role, who is better able to convey the idea of monstrosity with his expressive acting. In other words, Brecht constructs the narrative situation around the issue of representation: what is the value of authenticity for representing reality? How does the effect of artistic representation conceal the governor's real, actual monstrosity vis-à-vis the Jewish victims? The story's ironic structure of three run-throughs of the scene punctuated with commentaries by the film director poses the question, then, as to how the film viewer might distinguish the real from the acted; that is, someone who plays himself from someone who plays a role. The narrator's closing statement refers to what would become Brecht's major concern during the next years – how to render the natural or familiar problematic: 'It had been shown yet again that mere physical resemblance to a killer means nothing, and that it takes art to convey an authentically monstrous impression' (Brecht, 1998, p. 111).[2]

The centrality of the film medium for Brecht can be most clearly ascertained in the traces it left in his theatre work during the 1920s. The disruptive, episodic construction of his plays – what he came to refer to as Epic Theatre – recalls the shot-by-shot development of the early film scripts. The use of projected titles in his stagings is a technique adapted from the silent movies. The exaggerated expressivity of expressionist acting on stage and in the cinema provoked Brecht to devise a new acting style he would later call 'gestic acting'. His 'behaviourist' approach to dramatic characterization derived from an inductive method of observing events and attitudes related to the documentary quality of film images. Beyond these formal aspects, however, he was also beginning to understand by the late 1920s that the cinema was changing the way people perceived reality. The introduction of new media technology, including radio broadcasting, which went live in Germany in 1924, was affecting not only artistic production but also audience expectations and habits. Brecht's experience with the filming of *The Threepenny Opera* provided him just the occasion to examine the implications of these changes.

The *Threepenny* complex

Brecht was unusual among German artists and cultural critics of the Weimar Republic in that he did not fear the entertainment industry. On the contrary, he sought out opportunities to use its mechanisms as a weapon against conservative and progressive intellectuals alike who clung to traditional art forms. Nothing illustrates this practice better than the fate of *The Threepenny*

Opera in its metamorphosis from the most successful stage production of the Weimar Republic, to the scenario called 'The Bruise' he was commissioned to write for the commercial film adaptation of the musical, to the actual film directed by G.W. Pabst. Accompanying these creative stages were the court trial initiated by Brecht and composer Kurt Weill against the film production company for copyright infringement and the book-length essay about the trial called *The Threepenny Lawsuit*, Brecht's most incisive and sustained reflection on the conditions of cultural production under capitalism.

As I mentioned, the legendary success of *The Threepenny Opera* in 1928 had launched Brecht's international theatre career. Based on the popularity of Weill's music and the provocative but cynical decadence of the play's characters, the Nero-Film company bought the adaptation rights, which included a proviso that Brecht and a team of collaborators would write the film scenario. Though the agreement gave Brecht the right to demand changes if the final cut did not follow his scenario, it also obliged him to follow the original play's text both in style and content. Yet two years after he had written the original *Threepenny Opera*, Brecht's views had changed, and when it became clear that his scenario differed in essential ways from the play, Nero-Film, under pressure to begin the shoot on deadline, sought some kind of accommodation with Brecht. When that failed, the production began with a new, different script – and Brecht went to court.

The bone of contention was the text of 'The Bruise', Brecht's *Threepenny* film scenario, which compared with the play is definitely a cinematic treatment but also substantially changed in its thrust (see 'The Bruise – A Threepenny Film', in Brecht, 2000, pp. 131–44). Not only had Brecht's own views about capitalist society become more radical through his study of Marxism, but also the turn to didacticism in his 'learning plays' (*Lehrstücke*) was increasingly at odds with the mix of politics and entertainment that characterized the original play. Moreover, the two years since the play had been written witnessed the market crash and a worldwide depression, creating a politically more polarized context than was the case in 1928. I cannot summarize here the plot of either the musical or the film scenario, but let me say that the film adaptation basically took from the play the characters and the setting in order to construct a much more radical image of class struggle among competing beggars, gangsters and small-time entrepreneurs. Brecht and his collaborators not only revamped the story to sharpen the political message but also took into account the cinematic medium for which they were writing. As in his earlier film scripts, he integrated conventions of the American gangster and romance film genres. And just as the musical *The Threepenny Opera* 'quoted' traditional theatre dramaturgy in order to undermine or parody its conventions, so too does 'The Bruise': not the head gangster but his wife is the boss; a bank break-in is staged as a peaceful buy-out; a classical chase sequence does not lead to closure but to a higher level of corporate corruption, and so on. Moreover, the scenario calls for striking parallel montage sequences that crosscut simultaneous actions, for example, when the head gangster disappears into a brothel and his newly-wed wife proceeds to buy a bank to protect their ill-gotten profits.

Because Nero-Film was interested in cashing in on the *Threepenny* stage hit, Brecht's revision did not serve their ends of remaking the original. Cinephiles and Pabst specialists have celebrated the resulting film as one of his masterpieces, whereas Brecht scholars have largely regarded it as a betrayal of the Brecht/Weill original.[3] In fact, the film version of *The Threepenny Opera*, which was shot in late 1930, and opened in Berlin in February 1931 as an impressive example of early German sound film technology, undoubtedly contributed to the play's international fame as well as to Brecht's, even though it contradicted the most elementary aesthetic aspects of the original play's structure: separation of the elements, distanciation and the anti-illusionist foregrounding of stage mechanics. Instead, Pabst used his well-honed atmospheric cinematography to create the backdrop of the London docks for a romance, and his signature style of editing on movement or with dissolves smoothed over any sense of epic disruption. Consequently Brecht's political satire became an amorous adventure, and Weill's songs were turned into hum-along melodies rather than biting commentaries. Brecht and Weill filed suit against Nero-Film, however, not because the company had rejected their scenario but rather to regain the film adaptation rights for their musical *The Threepenny Opera*. On the grounds that the film production company had not fulfilled its contractual obligation of 'protecting' the integrity of the work, they threatened the entire investment of the production company with a court injunction to stop the shoot. The trial lasted four days in October 1930 and generated an unusually large press response owing both to Brecht's own notoriety and the fact that the case had a signal function. It touched on the sensitive question of competition between the cinema and the theatre, and on the speculative issue of artists' rights to control their ideas in the new mass media.

Brecht must have been pleased with the fact that he lost his lawsuit, for if he had won, he would have had to recognize that the capitalist system was *not* following its own rules. The book-length essay on the lawsuit represents Brecht's analysis of how this system functions, exposing the intersection of power, false ideas and art. As such it sought to confirm Brecht's political victory by unmasking the justice of the liberal state as the justice of the ruling class that is willing to violate its own legal system in order to protect its financial interests. Although the lawsuit against the film production company was the point of departure, the text of the essay neither documents the trial nor raises the issues of cinematic adaptation surrounding his scenario or, for that matter, Pabst's film. Rather, Brecht plays the role of the naïve artist who goes to court to defend the inviolability of intellectual property guaranteed by the liberal, democratic Weimar constitution. There he discovers that in fact the validity of individual ownership is measured against economic consequences, for in the case of the cinema the economic risk is so great that the profit motive in producing the commodity (the film) is deemed more important than the right of the poet to his immaterial property (the ideas). In short, Brecht shows that, contrary to what many artists would like to believe, the work of art, like other commodities, is subject to market forces. *The Threepenny Lawsuit* is a brilliant demonstration of the implications of this insight.

Divided into five unequal sections, the essay comprises a montage of press reports about the trial, excerpts from contracts, lawyers' explanations, reports on discussions and polemical analyses. Brecht spells out in a brief introduction that his purpose was to 'stage' his own experience in the film industry as an object of critical regard in order to make visible the difference between the actual practices and the ideas of how culture, law and public opinion function. In one section he investigates the consequences of the lawsuit's possible resolutions, only to conclude, as the court did, that the artist's 'ideal' – that is, the belief that contractual law protects ideas – is false. Like all property rights, they can be purchased by capital. This was, in effect, the actual outcome of Brecht's trial, and the echo registered in the press excerpts indicate that from this perspective Brecht's action corroborated traditional and even left-wing attitudes about the incompatibility of art and commerce. If he had stopped here, he would have achieved at least one important concession from the court: the public admission that the tradition of the law, oriented exclusively towards notions of individual creativity, was incompatible with the capitalist mode of production based on collective activity, as in the domain of film production.

However, Brecht proceeds a step further. He argues that art can neither reject nor simply avoid the new mass media as 'bad' because the technologically most progressive media define the standard for all other arts, including traditional forms of poetry and drama. This is an issue not merely of collective forms of production but also of audience reception. The fact that traditional forms of art still dominate the cinema, for example, by filming the stage play *The Threepenny Opera*, results from an obsolete ideology of individualism needed for the functioning of production in a historically specific phase of capitalism. Yet the addressees of the work of art perceive reality differently: that is, they read novels and they go to the theatre knowing how the mass media represent reality. Brecht takes aim here in his own technologically sophisticated environment not only at the still widespread adherence to Romantic aesthetics with its cult of the genius, as well as the insistence on the aura of originality; he is also criticizing an approach to reality based on introspective psychology and anthropomorphism. His turn to behaviourist psychology and materialist philosophy in the late 1920s drew his attention to the process of 'looking from the outside'. He began to explore in the theatre, for example, the literal notion that a gesture is the physical, visible expression or externalization of an inner attitude, *not* the expression of an emotion. Later he would theorize this as the concept of Gestus, the expression of real behaviour and real attitudes to which language, ideas and emotions conform. From this perspective the inner attitude is not 'objectified' in an external gesture, but rather it orients itself towards outside reality. This allows Brecht to focus on inter-subjectivity because attitudes, ways of speaking, gestures and facial expressions all have a demonstrative quality: they are socially and historically contingent types of behaviour that one sees from the outside (Silberman, 2006, pp. 318–35).

In this context let me point to a note Brecht attached to his scenario 'The Bruise': 'the camera searches for motives, it is a sociologist' (Brecht, 2000, p. 135, n. 12). The camera becomes here the ideal instrument for 'looking from the outside'; the camera as sociologist allows the film-maker to construct each sequence with distinct cinematographic techniques and a visual rhythm dictated by external action. Brecht's critique of mimesis and illusionism in the theatre transfers here to the cinematic medium where the goal cannot be the duplication of external reality, as if it is there, waiting to be reproduced. In a famous passage in *The Threepenny Lawsuit*, Brecht uses still photography to make a similar point about reality:

> The situation has become so complicated because the simple 'reproduc-tion of reality' says less than ever about that reality. A photograph of the Krupp works or the AEG[4] reveals almost nothing about these institutions. Reality as such has slipped into the domain of the functional. The reifi-cation of human relations, the factory, for example, no longer discloses those relations. So there is indeed 'something to construct', something 'artificial', 'invented'. Hence, there is in fact a need for art. But the old concept of art, derived from experience, is obsolete.
>
> (Brecht, 2000, pp. 164–5)

Visible surfaces, the very content of visual images, no longer communicate the structural conditions of capitalism. For that the dramatist, the film-maker, the photographer must find a new approach to reality.

Constructing reality in *Kuhle Wampe*

In *The Threepenny Lawsuit* Brecht stages an original and fundamental critique of the outmoded, idealist understanding of art that today con-tinues to dominate aesthetic judgment. He recognized the revolutionary nature of the capitalist process of commodity circulation that was chang-ing the entire system of artistic production and reception, and at the same time he greeted capitalism's self-destructive power that promised to release transformative cultural energies, like those that fed his own lawsuit. If this represents Brecht's most sophisticated contribution to media theory, then the 1932 film *Kuhle Wampe* can be considered his most important legacy in film history, the only example of his practical work that came close to realizing the idea of de-individualizing (aesthetic) production in the cinema. Not only the film's planning and shooting, but also its themes and structure, integrate the collective experience with new ways of representing reality. In contrast to Pabst's *Threepenny Opera* adaptation, *Kuhle Wampe* fell outside the boundaries of commercial film production. It can be considered more pertinently within the context of ambitious efforts during the 1920s to develop in Germany an independent, non-commercial cinema aimed at serving the political and entertainment needs of the organized working classes.

Early in 1931 the Bulgarian Slatan Dudow approached the Prometheus-Film company with a film sketch co-authored by Brecht and him about the problem of unemployment in a working-class family. Indeed the film's title *Kuhle Wampe* refers to a summer campsite on the periphery of Berlin that by 1932 had become a popular tent city for working-class families evicted from their homes. Prometheus-Film was founded in 1926 in loose conjunction with the German Communist party as a distribution outlet for the new, revolutionary Soviet films by Sergei Eisenstein, Dziga Vertov and Vsevolod Pudovkin; gradually it had become interested in producing original films for the working-class audience as well. The introduction of sound technology, however, coupled with the effects of the Depression, seriously undermined the existence of an alternative, leftist cultural institution such as Prometheus-Film. Despite financial uncertainties, the company accepted the collaborative project suggested by Dudow, but in fact *Kuhle Wampe* was the last Prometheus production and its only sound film before it collapsed in 1932. The collective structure that came together around Brecht and Dudow resulted in part from these less than ideal production conditions but also reflected a self-conscious attempt to counteract the hierarchical studio arrangements in the commercial movie industry.

Dudow brought in novelist Ernst Ottwalt to help with the script because of the latter's intimate knowledge of the working-class environment. The composer Hanns Eisler also joined the team, contributing his experience writing modernist film music and popular workers' songs. Some of the actors were well known in the workers' theatre movement, and the appearance of the leading agitprop theatre group 'The Red Megaphone' "as well as the participation of thousands of enthusiasts organized in workers" sports clubs for the film's finale' brought an unusual degree of visibility and public attention to the collective project (Figure 3.1). Indeed, the successful completion of the shooting was a significant public event in Brecht's sense because it had brought together several leading intellectuals of the Left with workers' organizations in a creative process.

Kuhle Wampe's story presents a loose sequence of episodes and events divided into three sections. The exposition, in section one, introduces the Bönike family and its disintegration under the pressure of unemployment (the son commits suicide). Section two follows the complications of family life: eviction, the daughter's pregnancy, the parents' pressure on her to

Figure 3.1   Kuhle Wampe: The agitprop theatre group 'Red Megaphone' performs at the workers festival in the last part of the film. Permission by Praesens-Film, Zurich.

marry her lover. Section three suggests a resolution to the young couple's quandary (she has an abortion) and an alternative to the parents' resignation in the face of impoverishment when the lovers reunite at the workers' sports festival. The film problematizes, in other words, an issue that was proving to be a fertile ground for the Nazis as well. In the period of political and economic crisis characterizing the last years of the Weimar Republic, the instability of the working class, caused by unemployment and impoverishment, made it particularly susceptible to petty bourgeois ideologies of social harmony and classless statism proposed by the National Socialists. *Kuhle Wampe* addressed this issue not so much to clarify the causes but to show the powerlessness effected by the desire to escape from politics altogether. Furthermore, an alternative was portrayed in athletic competitions as an allegory for solidarity and strength in the class struggle.

Beyond its thematic and political distinction, *Kuhle Wampe* introduced a new structural approach that was influenced by the Soviet cinema. Although Soviet films had been widely distributed in Germany since 1926, their innovative film narration had less impact on the German cinema than on literature and the dramatic arts. The Prometheus-Film productions, for example, stressed their proletarian content as a 'class conscious' alternative to the dominant cinema, but the films' narrative and visual structure tended to imitate popular melodramas of the major studios at the expense of formal innovation. Brecht had met and corresponded with Soviet intellectuals in these years; clearly the montage principles of the Soviet cinema reveal parallel considerations to his own explorations in the Epic Theatre. What Brecht found congenial was the constructivist principle of cinematic montage, premised on the idea of interruption and collision. This type of montage editing brings together images or shots that do not 'fit' and insist on being 'read' by the spectator. In *Kuhle Wampe*, for example, the filmmakers' attention focused on the organization of the images within the cinematic frame (the documentary quality of the image) as well as between frames (the disjointed quality of montage). This explains why the camera work itself is relatively restrained, when compared to the expressivity of earlier Weimar cinematography or to Pabst's style in the *Threepenny Opera* film.

On the other hand, Dudow and Brecht integrated from the Soviet cinema an awareness of narrative punctuation that they exploited to the fullest. The opening sequence is a paradigmatic example.[5] It opens not with an establishing shot but with a collage of quick takes from dynamically contrasting camera angles, localizing the action geographically in Berlin (the Brandenburg Gate), in a working-class quarter of the city (shots of a factory and tenements) and temporally during the Depression (a sequence of newspaper headlines indicate the steep rise in unemployment figures). The initial printed title ('One Unemployed Worker Less') and the overture-like music cue the spectator to the film's structural pattern: the narration has been assembled to solicit the spectator's active role in a cognitive process beyond mere watching. The montage of static, discontinuous images suggests not the reproduction of reality but its construction; and the stress on the documentary aspect of each shot has an almost fine-arts, photographic quality rather than a dramatic or narrative quality. Moreover, the sequence reveals a striking economy of images indicating quickly and efficiently location, urban space and economic crisis.

Brecht saw his work on the film *Kuhle Wampe* as a theoretical and practical contribution to the development of a notion of realism that breaks with mimesis (that is, with the idea that representation reproduces or mirrors reality). Here realism becomes an approach that produces knowledge *about* reality in specific historical conditions. The film's second sequence, often referred to as the bike race, illustrates this principle: the unemployed gather on a street corner, waiting for the newspaper boy to deliver the 'help wanted ads'. The newspapers are torn from his hands, with practiced eyes the unemployed glance through the ads, and then the bike race begins. In fact, this is a race for work, conveyed through the rhythmic montage of wheels accompanied by Hanns Eisler's pulsating music and creating a kind of condensation of human desperation into speed and repetition. Increasingly the sequence of images describes a pattern of circularity as a metaphor for the hopelessness of the job search: the wheels turning, the feet pumping bike pedals, the ever-quicker turnaround at factory gates (Figure 3.2). Brecht's comment on the function of the camera as a sociologist – 'the camera searches for motives, it is a sociologist' – comes to life in this sequence with the focus on external action; here we see a 'gestic camera' that interrupts the representation of reality in order to cite

Figure 3.2   Kuhle Wampe: The bike race in the second sequence conveys desperation through the montage of images of speed, repetition and circularity. Permission by Praesens-Film, Zurich.

and repeat discrete elements. In fact, one could summarize the mounting frustration conveyed by the sequence in the Gestus (gesture) of the young man who crumples up the newspaper and throws it away in the final shot. For Brecht such a Gestus articulates the moment when we – as viewers – recognize ourselves in the film's reality and at the same time see ourselves being confronted with reality as a construct. If it functions properly, this is the moment when we cease to be in agreement with ourselves, the moment when we become able to agree (or disagree) with the historical reality around us and then begin to consider how to change it.

If the bike race is constructed around the dynamics of movement, this movement leads inexorably to the suicide of the young man in the film's third scene. Returning home from the unsuccessful job search, the young boy must listen to the criticism of his equally unemployed father and worried mother. Having finished lunch, they all leave, and he sits alone at the table, while the camera cuts to a hand-stitched banner hanging on the kitchen wall with the homily: 'Don't blame the morn that brings hardship and work. It's wonderful to care for those one loves.' The ironical, even cynical commentary on a dysfunctional family introduces the suicide itself. We see how the young, unemployed worker calmly but deliberately reacts to an accumulation of episodes showing impoverishment, his parents' platitudes, his isolation and the indifference of those around him. The detail shot showing the young man removing his watch and placing it on a table before jumping out the window to his death becomes especially significant in this context: we do not see the expression of an inner emotion but the conscious performance of that inner emotion qua affect. The camera movement towards and focus on the gesture of removing the watch produces that inner emotion of desperation and deliberation for us to see. The scene also includes distinctive elements of montage: the use of the printed text mentioned above, ruptures or breaks in continuity, commentary spoken by one of the characters front-face to the camera, all of which invite the viewer to put together the parts to make meaning. Typical of the Brechtian approach to realism, this is an open structure, not based on audience identification and catharsis but on the construction of a dynamic relation of contradiction between continuity and discontinuity. Furthermore, these first scenes taken together (the film's first section) do not propose an answer to this young man's desperation but rather appeal to the viewer to recognize the conditions that produce this suicide.

Kuhle Wampe is an exceptional example of how to link questions of representation, social change and the subject who will effect that change as suggested by Brecht in *The Threepenny Lawsuit*. This didactic quality is most pronounced in the film's last section where family and personal problems are subordinated to the collective spirit of the workers' sports festival. The film culminates in a final scene that transfers the lesson of solidarity from the sports events to a political discussion, from image to word. Pressed into a subway car is a socio-political cross-section of the city's inhabitants, each of whom comments on a newspaper report that the Brazilian government had burned millions of pounds of coffee to protect the falling commodity price. The quick, polemical argument, mirrored by fast cuts from one face to another, climaxes in the question: 'who will change the world?' Speaking face-front to the camera in a direct challenge to the spectator, one of the young female workers responds with the answer: 'those who don't like it' (Figure 3.3).

The film's reception indicates the consequences of the filmmakers' untraditional approach. The conditions under which the film was conceived and produced – always with an eye to the eventuality of censorship problems and to its precarious financial backing – necessitated compromises at every level of its realization. This meant that the complicated filmic structure had to camouflage further its agitational thrust behind the relatively harmless allegory of sports and racing and the appeal of the youthful participants. Nonetheless, the film ran successfully but briefly until it fell victim to the elimination of the left-wing public sphere with the onset of National Socialism in March 1933. Its impact, therefore, as a model for a politically motivated revolutionary cinema and as an alternative to studio conventions was in fact negligible until a younger generation rediscovered the film in the 1960s.

Brecht spent seven years in exile in the USA during the 1940s, most of them in Los Angeles because of the large community of German émigré artists there and because of what he saw as potential contacts to the movie industry in Hollywood. He was encouraged by reports that German screenwriters actually enjoyed a good reputation in the industry, and during

Figure 3.3   Kuhle Wampe: At the end of the film a young woman answers the question: 'Who will change the world?' while speaking face-front to the camera: 'Those who don't like it!' Permission by Praesens-Film, Zurich.

these years he rubbed shoulders with many of the most important studio personalities. Yet, obviously, Brecht in no way fit the pattern of Hollywood filmmaking. He held its formula writing in contempt, criticized its immense waste and shared none of its sensitivity to serious criticism. He still considered the script to be a literary text, whereas Hollywood practice had already broken it down into a series of separate responsibilities (the idea, treatment, scenario, script, shooting script and so on). Furthermore, his notion of collective production did not fit the studio model of movie industry specialization and rationalization. Neither his aesthetics nor his temperament prepared him for the conditions in Hollywood. On the other hand, Brecht never lost his fascination with American movies, as the many entries in his *Journals* about screenings from these years indicate (Brecht, 1993). That he mentioned or actually brought to paper at least 50 film projects evidences his determination to break into the industry, especially because of the fact that his hopes were hardly fulfilled.

Brecht, who consistently and knowingly sought unconventional solutions for his cinematic projects, could not have been surprised by his lack of success in Hollywood. Called with other motion picture personalities before the House Committee on Un-American Activities (HUAC) on 30 October 1947, he could state with a clear conscience, but not without irony: 'I am not a film writer, and I am not aware of any influence I have had on the film industry, either politically or artistically.'[6] Brecht left the United States for Europe immediately after this hearing, and ultimately settled in East Berlin where the government provided him with money and support to form his own theatre, known as the Berliner Ensemble. This was the opportunity at last to produce plays under congenial conditions, to continue the theatre experiments broken off in 1933 and to see his own plays come to life in the context for which they were written. It is even more surprising, then, that he found any time for the film projects that continued to preoccupy him until he died in 1956. Ironically, though, even under the socialist regime in East Germany, Brecht found himself once again confronted with the limitations of an industrially and ideologically conservative apparatus at the newly established state film studios, not to mention the state-controlled radio broadcasting networks.

This broad overview of Brecht's practical and critical interventions in the cinema during a period of 35 years demonstrates his important role in defining sites of conflict and contestation in the new mass media. At a crucial point in his artistic development, he perceived that the power relations in the institutions of cultural production and reception determine the product, the work of art. This fundamental insight led him to formulate an experimental approach that was produced by institutional realities but that also produces reality, all the while observing the practice of this 'production' itself.

The various representational innovations he devised in the theatre and transferred to the cinema were attempts to foreground this complex activity. The goal was to demonstrate the historicity of any specific moment in order to empower the audience to change it. Although Brecht's understanding of the relation of representation to power and social change is still germane, his experimental method suggests that the anti-illusionistic techniques of distanciation and disruption are dependent on the respective context in which they operate. In short, it is necessary to reinvent constantly new ways of seeing that are themselves to be problematized as means of perception. Brecht offers no abstract answers for the media apparatus, but he does model a self-reflexive practice of media representation that is aware of its function, its historicity and its inherent social and economic interests. In the post-modern age of simulations, it is worthwhile to reconsider Brecht's questions about representation and the construction of reality.

Notes

1. Owing to American export regulations during and after World War I, there was a 5–6 year lag in distribution of American films in Germany at this time.
2. 'The Monster' was inspired by Josef von Sternberg's Hollywood feature *The Last Command*, produced in 1928 and starring the German émigré actor Emil Jannings, who won the first acting Oscar for this very role of the governor!
3. The British Film Institute distributes a double DVD with both the German (*Die Dreigroschenoper*) and French (*L'Opéra de quat' sous*) sound versions of Pabst's film.
4. The Krupp works was a major weapons company, and AEG was a prominent electrical company in Germany.

5. See the digitally restored version of *Kuhle Wampe* on DVD produced by the DEFA Film Library, University of Massachusetts Amherst, 2008 (www.umass.edu/defa).
6. For the German version of his statement before the House Un-American Activities Committee, see Brecht, *Werke*, 23, pp. 19–61 (for this passage, 61, line 13–15).

References

Brecht, Bertolt (1988–2000), *Werke*, Werner Hecht, Jan Knopf, Werner Mittenzwei, Klaus-Detlef Müller (eds.). Frankfurt am Main: Suhrkamp, 30 volumes plus index volume.

Brecht, Bertolt (2010), *Notizbücher 7 (1927–1930)*, Peter Villwock (ed). Forthcoming Frankfurt am Main: Suhrkamp.

Brecht, Bertolt (2000), *Brecht on Film and Radio*, ed. and trans. by Marc Silberman. London: Methuen.

Brecht, Bertolt (1998), *Collected Stories*, John Willett and Ralph Manheim (eds). London: Methuen.

Brecht, Bertolt (1993), *Journals 1934–1955*, John Willett and Ralph Manheim (eds). London: Methuen.

Silberman, Marc (2006), 'Brecht's Gestus: Staging Contradictions', in Jürgen Hillesheim (ed.), *The Young Mr. Brecht*, The Brecht Yearbook 31. Pittsburgh: International Brecht Society, pp. 318–35.

4
Melodrama as Realism in Italian Neorealism

Louis Bayman

Italian neorealism is a foundational realist cinema movement, but one that has posed a conundrum for realist criticism because it is pervaded throughout by melodrama. Because aesthetic theory (and common sense) defines realism and melodrama against each other, the relationship between melodrama and realism in neorealist films has never been considered beyond opposition. Yet in Italian neorealism, melodrama and realism interact and at times even combine. I argue that examining this interaction is crucial to understanding neorealism fully, and suggest that the continual recurrence of melodrama and realism together necessitates a reconceptualization of aesthetic theory.

Realism is not simply that which is 'realistic', nor is it one single set of properties, but rather a claim (open to argument and dependent on the conventions an audience is used to) that a particular artwork reaches closer to an important, otherwise neglected, aspect of reality. Realism then is not a fixed attribute, but a relationship between text, reality and audience that changes as does the culture in which it operates. One constant has, however, emerged: that realism is defined against melodrama. Whatever differences separate the relationship between art and reality in the conceptions of Lukács, Brecht or Bazin, one thing theory agrees upon is that realist aims exclude melodrama. Why then have the two forms, melodrama and realism, so much shared history? Why do they continually recur at the centre of the same artworks? Do melodrama and realism have to be antithetical, or can they be mutually reinforcing and illuminating?

Melodrama and realism: A historical relationship

Realism and melodrama share many important aspects. In the historical analysis provided by Christine Gledhill (1987, pp. 14–33), they emerged in the eighteenth century distinguished from tragedy principally by their popular nature. Both melodrama and realism use a social typing of wicked landlords/aristocrats/moneylenders against the virtuous poor. Authenticity is key to both, with realism seeking to illuminate society's motive forces, and melodrama focusing on innocence tormented by wicked dissimulators. The drama of both emerges from the confrontation of passionate emotions marked as primal with external restrictions.

Raymond Williams's stipulations for the historical origins of realism apply equally to the simultaneously emerging form of melodrama (1976). Firstly, they are socially extended, moving from tragedy's portrayal of kings and demigods to the 'people' (a nebulous entity, a construct of bourgeois hegemony which broader masses can feel part of). By the end of the eighteenth century, British drama was consciously adopting what Williams calls the realist intention of extending the action socially to characters without high rank. The dramatic purpose of this social extension is summed up in an important phrase that Williams picks up on, to 'let not your equals move your pity less' (Williams, 1976, p. 63). It is worthwhile noting how moving the pity of the audience gives prominence to feeling in realism, which as I shall detail below is sometimes artificially separated from melodrama's focus on emotion. Secondly, according to Williams, realism moves the action to a contemporary setting, which, thirdly, is secular, with the understanding of tragic action in human terms seen as a 'sentimentalization' of tragedy (Williams, 1976, p. 64), again, placing sentiment centrally. Finally, realism has a moral lesson that the audience can apply to their own lives. These factors – social extension, contemporary setting, secular terms and personal morality – can be seen as a historical shift in the function of art that encompasses both melodrama and realism.

Despite this historical affinity, criticism usually separates realism from melodrama. Gledhill reviews the trend in British and American criticism and journalism in the late nineteenth century to consider realism as displaying the repression and rationalism thought of as refined masculine values, distinguished from the perceived feminine and populist characteristics of melodramatic sentimentality. These critics disavowed melodrama for its excessive emotionality and use of cliché, which was thought to preclude the rational understanding that, Gledhill claims, is the aim of realism (1992, pp. 113–7). Although the class and gender bias is now outmoded (and, as can be seen in the persistence of melodrama in late Victorian art, the repudiation of melodrama was always partial and inconsistent), Gledhill maintains that the principal aim of realism is the psychological comprehension of causes based on dialogue, character analysis and naturalism, and that the primacy melodrama gives to emotionally charged effects counterbalances this realist aim (Gledhill, 1992, pp. 137–41).

Yet, broadly speaking, melodrama, in cinema, is simply the pathos of the expressive elevation of fundamentally ordinary feelings, whereas realism is a recognizable attempt to bring representation closer to extra-filmic reality. Fruitful lines of enquiry can emerge if we examine the compatibility of these aims in a culture in which the relationships between melodrama and realism, stylization and naturalism, or thought and feeling are different to those in Victorian Britain. Can the dominance of melodrama in neorealism, particularly striking at its most celebrated moments, be satisfactorily treated just as an annoyance (Overbey, 1978, p. 11), a peculiarly Italian cultural excess (Bazin, 2004, p. 55) or an example of commercial artifice that realism consciously pastiches so as to criticize (Marcus, 1986, p. 87)? Does comprehension of causality through psychological motivation suffice as an overarching definition of realism, or is it simply one particular manifestation of realism especially important to the Victorian literary and theatrical realists, on whose work Gledhill bases her claim? Are there examples in which emotional contrivance aids, rather than deters, a closer identification with reality?

Melodrama and Italian realism

Contemporaneously with the late Victorian anxiety over melodramatic emotionality, Italian drama was developing forms that incorporated realism and social engagement into melodrama. Verist operas, such as *Rustic Chivalry* (*Cavalleria rusticana*, Pietro Mascagni, 1890) and *Clowns* (*Pagliacci*, Ruggero Leoncavallo, 1892), were considered realist because of the sensational occurrences, popular locales and folk art that it brought to the stage. On the operatic stage, a vivid intensity of presentation can unite the realism of environment and subject matter with theatrical stylization. The early days of cinematic narrative, with the silent Neapolitan tradition of *Assunta Spina* (Francesca Bertini and Gustavo Serena, 1915), *Lost in the Dark* (*Sperduti nel buio*, Nino Martoglio, 1914) and the films of Elvira Notari, absorbed from the opera libretto a forcefulness of melodramatic expressivity. The realism of their settings of urban landscape heightens the dramatic desperation of their poor and persecuted protagonists.

This is one important heritage from which neorealism emerged, with its realism deriving not primarily from the need of psychological comprehension but from the desire to show (see Lovell, 1980, for a discussion of the importance of showing to realism). Neorealist director Alberto Lattuada offers a clear statement of this principle:

> We are in rags? Let's show everyone our rags. We are defeated? Let's look at our disasters. How much are we obligated to the mafia? To hypocritical bigotry? To conformity, to irresponsibility, to bad breeding? Let's pay all our debts with a ferocious love of honesty and the world will participate, moved by this great contest with the truth.
>
> (cited in Marcus, 1986, p. 27)

It is my contention that this 'showing', the driving force of realist representation, is frequently expressed in neorealism through melodrama. However, although the presence of melodrama in neorealism has been much noted, this is not how it has previously been understood. David Overbey expresses a common sentiment by wanting to 'put aside' the 'turgid melodrama' (Overbey, 1978, p. 11) of neorealism. In part, this displays a not uncommon critical difficulty with realism as found in forms enjoyable for the popular masses. Overbey's own viewpoint oscillates from allowing that the realism of Neapolitan fairytales resides in the dream 'to wear clothes like a princess' (Overbey, 1978, p. 15), to castigating neorealism as a disguise for melodrama and *verismo*'s objectivity as an excuse for 'shop-girl fantasies' (Overbey, 1978, p. 18). Neorealism, a movement that aimed to bring cinema closer to the lives of the people, emerged from, engaged with and transformed popular forms.

In the canon that is seen as heralding neorealism, realism emerges from melodrama. *Four Steps Amongst the Clouds* (*Quattro passi fra le nuvole*, Alessandro Blasetti, 1942) sets its story within a frame of the urban mundane of the ordinary daily routine of a travelling salesman Paolo (Gino Cervi). A chance meeting with an unmarried pregnant woman leads him to become embroiled for a day in her homecoming to her traditional rural family, before he returns to the dissatisfactions of his city life. The realist frame of dull urbanity allows one to feel more strongly the family melodrama of the pastoral daydream that interrupts it (showing a rural existence that is itself dependent on notions of the natural authenticity of peasant life). *The Children Are Watching Us* (*I bambini ci guardano*, Vittorio De Sica, 1944), an early collaboration between Vittorio De Sica and Cesare Zavattini, is a melodrama whose bleak view of parental responsibility implied a critique of the faltering fascist regime. *Ossessione* (Luchino Visconti, 1942), the film that allowed those critics most vociferously calling for a new realism in the pages of the journal *Cinema* to put their ideas into effect (see Alicata and De Santis, 1978, and De Santis, 1978), used the open environment in dramatic contrast to the oppressively enclosed space of the domestic melodrama.[1] In the film, based on James M. Cain's *The Postman Always Rings Twice*, the wife (Clara Calamai) of a petrol station owner starts an affair with a drifter (Massimo Girotti), and together they plot to murder the owner. The melodramatic sensibility in *Ossessione* is built out of the barely repressed desire seen through the sweaty realism of the scandalously frank bodily intimacy between the cheating couple, the corporeality of their continual gestures expressing the heat and their physical yearnings with a cloying sensual materiality. In each of these three important precursors to neorealism, an expressive whole is formed in which realism and melodrama grow out of each other.

After these precursors, neorealism began to emerge fully from the experience of the years of war and occupation, the reality of which it sought to document. For the early, and in particular Italian, critics, it was realist predominantly through its subject matter. This subject matter sought to confront the social problems that blighted post-war Italy in dramatic narratives that took a position of sympathy with the popular, leftwing upsurge that dismantled fascism. This *impegno* (engagement) was part of the great democratic social change in Italy after 20 years of fascist censorship. The revelatory power of the sudden ability to openly discuss momentous and previously unmentionable topics encouraged a faith in the early critics of neorealism for film style to retreat and subject matter to come to the fore (Chiarini, 1978a and 1978b).

A less engaged but more sophisticated aesthetic appreciation came from the French of the *Cahiers du Cinéma*, led by André Bazin. For Bazin (2004), an innovative use of location shooting, long takes, episodic narratives and non-professional actors endowed neorealist subject matter with a new aesthetic realism. This often rough-and-ready aesthetic achieved what Bazin considered to be the goal of cinema, which has a scientific (because photographic) capacity to make the spontaneity and ambiguity of reality appear.

Melodrama in Italian neorealism

Although it is found much more frequently than episodic narrative or non-professional actors, melodrama was treated by both Italian and French critics as foreign to the aims of neorealism. Examples are Bazin's comments on *Pact with the Devil* (*Il patto col diavolo*, Luigi Chiarini, 1949), a 'melodrama [which] took visible pains to find a contemporary alibi' and *In the Name of the Law* (*In nome della legge*, Pietro Germi, 1949) which 'although well done on some accounts ... cannot escape similar criticisms' (Bazin, 2004, p. 48). Giulio Castello elucidates the general feeling that melodrama deflects neorealism from its mission when he lists the films *Tragic Pursuit* (*Caccia tragica*, Giuseppe De Santis, 1947), *Lost Youth* (*Gioventù perduta*, Pietro Germi, 1947), *No Stealing* (*Proibito rubare*, Luigi Comencini, 1948), *The Bandit* (*Il bandito*, Alberto Lattuada, 1946), *Without Pity* (*Senza pietà*, Alberto Lattuada, 1948) and *Flight into France* (*Fuga in Francia*, Mario Soldati, 1948) as works that 'signal the phase of neorealism's "popularization", inserting more or less garish novelistic and melodramatic elements into the sincerity of the investigation' [my translation] (Castello, 1956, p. 19).

Neorealist films themselves sometimes use melodrama to join in on a radical critique of certain forms of the genre. The German occupiers and their collaborators in both *Rome, Open City* (*Roma, città aperta*, Roberto Rossellini, 1945) and *The Sun Also Rises* (*Il sole sorge ancora*, Aldo Vergano, 1946) belong to a decadent and affected culture, as does the bourgeois landlady (Lina Gennari) in *Umberto D.* (Vittorio De Sica, 1952). They play out their narratives of dissimulation and extreme emotional conflict within studio sets of elaborately furnished salons, using histrionic acting and artificial lighting. Silvana (Silvana Mangano) in *Bitter Rice* (*Riso amaro*, Giuseppe De Santis, 1948) is tempted to betray class solidarity in part through her addiction to the superficial romances she reads in the photo-story magazines (*fotoromanzi*, precursors to television soap opera) (Marcus, 1986, p. 87). This decadent, affected melodrama is linked by neorealism with the socially reactionary (and, incidentally, to femininity).[2]

However, this is only one type of melodrama alongside others, and is more a critique of artificiality than of melodrama per se. In *Roma, città aperta*, when the children escape from the blast of a bomb they plant, the light and sound effects, the dramatic music and Pina's (Anna Magnani) anxious walk towards the window clutching at her clothes are melodramatic effects. Peter Brooks's definition of melodrama is that it is a structure of feeling, relying on a wealth of energy that violently erupts to create an excess of expression (1985). The Resistance struggle, in this film, is melodramatically structured as such an eruption of repressed emotional force from the underground of the realist representation of the city environment. If the representation of Resistance and the city, key to the film's realism, draw on this melodramatic structure of feeling, how can melodrama be opposed to realism?

Nineteenth century European realism sought to reveal the sentiments that animate people, which naturalist theorists aimed to discover through the artist's dispassionate observation. The naturalist aim to reach truth by recreating the surface details of reality suggests a highly questionable belief that fiction can be a tool to collect empirical evidence along positivist paradigms, achieving 'scientific investigation, experimental reasoning' (French naturalist Zola, cited in Marcus, 1986, p. 8) for a 'science of the heart' (Italian *verist* Verga, cited in Marcus, 1986, p. 12). Yet realism makes contact with reality through art, which, rather than being a tool of scientific measurement, necessitates creative treatment. For Hungarian critic Georg Lukács, the artist must not describe, but narrate (1970). Lukacsian realism goes beyond surface detail, moving from recognition towards revelation[3] of the greater truth of the underlying motive forces of history (Lukács, 1971, p. 57). Where these historical debates are relevant for neorealism is how the greater truth of both the sentiments that animate people and their historical basis can occur through melodrama.

Paisan (*Paisà*, 1946), Rossellini's follow up to *Roma, città aperta*, dramatizes the occupation of Italy by German and Allied troops through six episodes following the allied advance up Italy. The third episode, set in Rome, begins with a voiceover detailing the progress of the soldiers, over a four-minute montage of newsreel footage showing devastated buildings, then Germans leaving Rome and the allied soldiers arriving amid street celebrations. Six months pass, from summer to winter, and the allied forces have established their command as occupying forces, while Rome is a place of poverty and social discord as the war slowly grinds on in the north.

One of the characters, the prostitute Francesca, is played by Maria Michi, who had also played Marina, the woman who melodramatically betrays the Resistance through her drug addiction, which leads her to liaise with the Germans, in *Città aperta*. In *Paisà*, after fleeing a fight in a bar, Francesca picks up a drunken GI called Fred (Gar Moore). In bed, he recalls how different things were when he arrived, describing an encounter with a young woman – who, unbeknownst to him, is Francesca herself – hopeful with the possibilities of peace. This memory recalls the lost exuberance that greeted the liberation, and Francesca's turn to prostitution becomes representative of how a nation's hope gave way to a desperate struggle to survive. Realizing who he is, Francesca leaves her address and a meeting time as he sleeps, in the possibility of recapturing their thwarted romance. Billeted at a checkpoint later in the day, he throws away her address, telling his comrade it is 'nothing, just the address of a whore'.

Although often dismissed as old-fashioned for its sentimental melodramatic coincidences (Bondanella, 1993, p. 76), the melodrama of this central episode is woven within the realism to show how personal dramas are determined by history. The first shot of the bar Francesca is in repeats the high angle track of the newsreels it follows, linking Francesca to the crowds to establish her typicality and making her story one of the coincidental encounters and missed opportunities that form part of everyday life in the contemporary mass city. Fred's memories are prompted by the repeated question of whether Francesca as a hopeful woman or as a prostitute is 'a girl like all the others', her representativeness, and the melodrama, lying in the trajectory from one to the other.

The poignancy of this episode captures a historic shift from hope to disillusionment. The historical events, newsreel footage and everyday typicality act to incorporate human dramas in the gears of history, the motivating emotional forces of which are felt through the melodrama. Thus the most melodramatic of episodes in this canonical neorealist work illuminates the dialectic between the individual and social change. Its effect at the centre of the film's structure confers an effect of historical movement on the film as a whole within the northwards geographical advance of its episodes. We can thus suggest this episode as the kind of narrative that led Elio Vittorini, communist novelist and intellectual, to state that literary melodrama reached that goal of Lukacsian realism, a 'greater truth' (*una realtà maggiore*) (Vittorini quoted in Tinazzi and Zancan, 1983, p. 26).

Thus to consider melodrama in neorealism solely as a pastiche of affected bourgeois stylization is a misunderstanding of the dramatic function of realism. Such judgements fail to appreciate how melodrama often works. Neorealism does not condemn unrepressed emotion, but insists on its authenticity when given a working-class foundation. Neorealism uses melodrama to make more intense and more vivid the desperation of the popular masses, under subjection to material circumstance (vividness is described as a central trait of neorealism by Morlion, 1978, p. 121). Melodrama helps neorealism assert that the genuine pathos of social restrictions and important moral questions are found in ordinary people's lives. However, although melodrama and realism can share aspects of emotion, reality and subject matter, what of the formally precise but more delicate interaction of realist and melodramatic aesthetics?

Neorealism as popular genre: *Il bandito*

The differentiation of realism from melodrama as made by Gledhill is one of epistemology: realism seeks to subject the world to rational understanding whereas melodrama, drawing on Peter Brooks, renders it 'morally legible' (Brooks, 1985, p. 42). *Il bandito* offers an example of how neorealist aesthetics blur these realist and melodramatic epistemologies into each other. Directed by Alberto Lattuada – who has somewhat disappeared from current scholarship despite being mentioned by contemporaries alongside Rossellini, Visconti and De Sica – it tells the story of Ernesto, a prisoner of war returning after the war to his native Turin. Played by pre-war star Amedeo Nazzari, he is hungry for both the steak and the female company he lacked during his incarceration, but finds at the start of the film that his apartment block has been bombed to rubble, his mother has died and his sister disappeared.

Two scenes, each forming a moment of revelation in *Il bandito*, demonstrate the incorporation of melodrama into realist revelation, and of realism into melodramatic climax. Shown in long shot and long take walking through the city streets, Ernesto passes a street fire, continues on to his old housing block, and the rubble that it has become is revealed to him and the audience with a quick pan that then slowly lingers along the remains of the destroyed structure of the devastated block, completing an almost 360-degree turn to alight back on Ernesto's disappointed face. Bazin described this scene as exemplary of realism. The single shot allows the revelation to unfurl apparently by accident, the spectator identifying with Ernesto's viewpoint and then, surprisingly, shifting perspective to objectively view his horrified expression. In one shot, the spontaneity of reality is revealed before the spectator's eyes at different speeds as it does before the protagonist (Bazin, 2004, p. 32), the quintessential neorealist searcher adrift in the postwar world he discovers.

Formally, this scene is echoed later. Having searched in vain for work and had his first incursion into the world of vice and sexuality (personified by Anna Magnani as Lidia), Ernesto is once again out on the streets. He steals money from a card sharper, spots a streetwalker and follows her to her brothel. As the orchestral score strikes up, the tension mounts, and a close-up to her legs alternates with his journey down the street and past another street fire (fire having in the meantime been associated through Lidia with intense sexuality and avarice). Reaching the brothel, an old doorkeeper gives a lascivious wink, and Ernesto continues up the stairs of the working-class apartment block, where he waits his turn for several anxious minutes. At the end of his journey, on entering the boudoir, he notices a photograph, and the score, up to now increasing the tension almost unbearably, halts. The prostitute enters, exclaims 'beh?' and exposes the flesh of her leg. The whip pan of the earlier scene is repeated, for Ernesto's gaze to alight on whom he sees is his sister (played by Carla del Poggio). What follows is an overtly melodramatic outburst, in a studio set, with artificial dramatic lighting and extreme close-ups, as Ernesto flies into a rage and becomes a fugitive killer.

I have described one scene that is exemplary of realism, and another that is undoubtedly melodramatic. Whereas the near-360-degree pan in the first scene allows Bazin to mount a characteristic defence of the long take as spontaneously revealing the world as one continuous and ambiguous whole, the close-ups of the brothel scene exploit dramatic manipulation and break the integrity of the profilmic world. But why are the two scenes structured so similarly? What is the role of the location shooting, the sense of a journey, the shock of revelation? It is that realism lays the basis of the intolerable tensions that break out in melodrama, their combination drama-tizing the alienation of post-war reality to the 'man who can no longer fit in' (*'L'uomo che non riesce più a inserirsi'*, Villa, 2002, p. 83).

Although the revelation of the sister as a prostitute is a wrenching moment of melodramatic excess, it is formed by a fleshy realism that reveals the new social relationships. The corrupting reality of material privation sublimates the opening realist tensions into the melodrama of excessive sexual and criminal desire. The shocking revelation of the disorientation of post-war reality recalls but jumbles up the earlier long take, tracking and location shooting. The first scene, with the emphasis on the realism, is key to understanding the (according to Gledhill's stipulation) 'melodramatic' morality of the film; the second emphasizes melodrama *by being* under-pinned by the social decay that causes the moment of outburst. Melodrama and realism interact to root the drama in social reality with a vividness that increases the melodramatic development of the plot.

Il bandito involves a realism of subject matter, an older, sensational newspaper-realism of the shocking violence and squalid sex that really does occur in life, rather than the emphasis on the everyday that neoreal-ism itself helped introduce as a main strand of twentieth-century realism. This realism is in tune with the legacy of the American novelists of the 1930s – Ernest Hemingway and the crime writers Dashiell Hammett and James M. Cain (whose *The Postman Always Rings Twice* provided the basis for *Ossessione*). These writers provide another example of a realism that is not based on rationalist epistemology, but a direct vividness of communica-tion, a newsworthiness within environments that flesh out a wider social picture, and, like nineteenth-century verism, the realism of a non-idealized portrayal of reality.

Il bandito is an example of an obscured but prevalent strand of neoreal-ism, whose artistic innovation existed in a lively relationship with popular genre cinema. It encompasses the neorealist desire to incorporate the environment as an essential component instead of just a backdrop to the drama (see De Santis, 1978, and Visconti, 1978). The environment as actor is often realized in neorealism through crime stories that sexualize the urban or rural landscape, the desperate poverty of the situation's sleazy materiality encompassing both realist description and melodramatic excess.

Melodrama as neorealist innovation: *La terra trema*

Although it has proved controversial to determine what exactly constitutes neorealism, melodrama is one of its most genuinely consistent traits. Different manifestations of melodrama are repeatedly applied to neorealist films, yet often considered isolated idiosyncrasies. Marcus calls De Santis's melodrama 'heterodox' (Marcus, 1986, p. 76), but De Sica understands society through the excessive emotional reliance of the poor on material objects. Rossellini, in turn, links an emotionality of religious feeling to social documentation and domestic crisis, whereas Visconti uses an operatic formalism. Lattuada's breathtaking dramatics and popular neorealist cinema incorporate realist innovation into commercial melodrama.

What is more, neorealist revelation occurs frequently through the excessive melodramatic impact of social reality. Pina's fiancé is captured by soldiers and she is shot to death on their wedding day, in *Roma, città aperta*, in an emotive outburst of violent movement and one whose fast editing moves to long shot, achieving melodramatic climax and the realist sense of newsreel simultaneously. Antonio Ricci's (Lamberto Maggiorani) ultimate attempt to steal a bicycle in front of his son in *Bicycle Thieves* (*Ladri di biciclette*, Vittorio De Sica, 1948) and Silvana's rape intercut with the folk song of the rice pickers in *Riso amaro* can be added as some of the canonical exemplars of neorealism that combine realist and melodramatic strategies.

Rather than being separable in the way that colour is from black-and-white in *The Wizard of Oz* (Victor Fleming, 1939), realism blends into melodrama in these most memorable scenes. Is it realist accident or coincidental contrivance that shows the precariousness of the lives of the poor, when Ricci stumbles upon the thief who stole his bicycle in *Ladri di biciclette*? Where does social critique end and moralism begin, political engagement separate from Manichean ethical dilemmas, or material sensuousness become melodramatic sensuality?

As to whether melodrama inherently deflects the political mission of realism, we should consider Visconti's *The Earth Trembles* (*La terra trema*, Luchino Visconti, 1948). Set among the fishermen of Aci Trezza, Sicily, it is the most ostentatiously realist of all the neorealist films, its opening statement coming close to providing that elusive definition of neorealism:

A story of man's exploitation of man, set in Aci Trezza, Sicily. These are the houses, streets, boats and people of Aci Trezza. There are no actors;

these are the inhabitants of Aci Trezza. They speak in their dialect to express their suffering and hopes.

As implied in Raymond Williams's description of realism (Williams, 1976), *La terra trema* does not restrict itself to rational comprehension of social rebellion, but seeks to express the intangible animating hopes and pains of the fishermen and their families. Throughout the film, these are not scientifically measured but expressed in a flowery and poetic language, with highly composed imagery and stock character types that express class status (a realist function) while simultaneously using melodramatic cliché (cliché is not used here as an evaluative term, but refers to a dramatic shorthand fruitfully exploited in melodrama). As a whole, the film uses theatrical and even operatic expression, brought from Visconti's lifelong stage career. As for the political aspirations of the characters, they are expressed in the melodramatic fairytale realm of 'if only', dramatized as dreams and romantic ambitions restricted by social and natural boundaries which the protagonists are too small to beat.

Sick of their exploitation by the wholesalers, the Valastro family mortgage everything to buy a boat and go into business themselves. During one expedition, a storm brews, and Mara, a daughter of the family, expresses her distress throwing herself onto the bed of a local and collapsing in tears. These traditionally melodramatic histrionics are unconventionally shown in a static one-take mid-shot, before the film moves even further away from the conventions of mainstream melodramatic cinema. Visconti rejects any classical use of mise-en-scène as backdrop to the action, the landscape becoming instead the focus of activity while the expectation of climactic character action is denied and the protagonists simply stop. Long, slow shots of the sea, the sound of the waves crashing against the shore, follow before a series of shots of the still women on the rocks looking out to the waters that contain their distant men. Yet, although this is certainly not conventionally melodramatic, it is not any realist image of life caught unawares. What then does this highly composed tableau, the succession of images of the women in their environment from long shot to close-up of their resigned acceptance, achieve? (Figures 4.1–4.3).

The long shots reduce individual agency by presenting the women as a group, wholly dependent on their natural environment, the activity of which is instead the focus. Environmental determination is foregrounded, communicating the precariousness of the dependence on the clemency of the waves for the family's livelihood. However, although the cut from Mara's distress to the women in their wider environment is fundamental to the realism of the scene, it is not a distancing device, communicating instead the depths of emotion invested in the activity of the waves. The move towards dramatic climax is transferred from the histrionic activity of Mara not to the rest of the family, whose stillness curtails the build-up of activity in human

Figure 4.1   In *The Earth Trembles*, highly composed imagery...

Figure 4.2   ...and stock character types express class status (a realist function)...

terms, but onto the activity of the sea. The crashing waves thus become, through their elemental force, an instrument of mighty expressivity.

The construction of the scene is realist, and simultaneously excessively significant, the women's repressed turmoil finding expression in the earth's very elements. However, although the scene is highly unconventional, it creates climax through the use of tableau and stasis, generic devices in scenes of dramatic high points in Italian melodrama imported into cinema from theatrical opera. The film's overt theatricality expresses the family's troubles through highly emotionalized stylization. Although the absence of hysteria in this scene is a dislocating denial of individual psychological identification, catastrophe is not deflated but displaced onto the position of the women within the greater environment. The composition is operatically crafted into a highly expressive whole (Nowell-Smith, 2003, p. 43), the environment

Figure 4.3   ...while simultaneously reflecting melodramatic conventions.

a grand theatrical stage on which the doomed aspirations of the protagonists find a melodramatic expressivity that powers the social criticism.

Conclusion

Neorealism forever changed Italian cinema, which adopted many of its techniques in the popular cinema of the 1950s. Popular 1950s cinema typically used an increase in realism alongside an increase in melodrama when it sought to turn towards serious or emotive scenes. Despite this, it was not the presence of melodrama per se that created a watering down of neorealism, nor even just a popularization, nor for that matter does melodrama necessitate a concession to reactionary ideology, as the engaged melodrama of Visconti's neorealism shows.

Realism of necessity brings up the question of the relationship between artistic fiction and reality, a relationship that has been negotiated in various ways across the history of art. The naturalist aim was a scientific understanding of the passions through reproduction of surface details, whereas Bazin believed in cinema as a tool whose aesthetics could encompass reality in all its ambiguity. By the 1970s, realism was under attack as encouraging illusions that reality was a fixed, uncontradictory entity, hiding the problematic nature of the relationship between artistic signification and its referent as if reality can ever just 'appear' through fiction (Williams, 1973, p. 66). Melodrama was again set against realism, but for the first time in approving terms, because its excess ruptured the illusory unity created by the classic realist text (Gledhill, 1987, pp. 8–9, 1992, pp. 140–1, see also MacCabe, 1974, and MacArthur, 1975–6). Yet once again neorealism problematizes this opposition, as in neorealism it is realism that performs the expressive role of erupting from the inadequacies of the prevailing conventions of the classical cinematic text.

Nor can neorealism be dismissed as failing to be a realism. Not only is it one of the most important realist movements globally in any medium, but it is also an answer to the wider question of how dramatic construction can relate art to reality. One could consider here why throughout its history realism is so intermingled with melodrama. Is it mere coincidence that melodrama occupies a central place in the novels of Zola, in kitchen-sink drama, or contemporary realism as a glance at *Bullet Boy* (Saul Dibb, 2004) or *Tsotsi* (Gavin Hood, 2005) could show? Or is it because, as I have been claiming in regard to neorealism, melodrama has a deeper affinity to realism?

I started with the very general point that realism is a partial selection, by its nature constructed, a representation of reality that depends for its significance on cultural determination more than any inherent essence. Cinema is not reality in the sense that the outside world is. Nevertheless neorealism shows how the interaction of realism with melodrama is one way to reveal the suffering of ordinary people with vividness and authenticity, establishing the common realist concern to encourage empathy with the protagonists of a fiction, while maintaining a questioning focus on the reality outside of its frame.

Notes

I thank Richard Dyer for providing me with materials and comments on an earlier draft of this chapter.

1. I refer to the notion of dependence on enclosed domestic spaces as specified by Marcia Landy as melodramatic (1991, p. 575).
2. However, the *popolana* (woman of the people) image displayed by 'Anna Magnani shows that the realist values marked as positive by neorealism could also be marked as feminine (see Grignaffini, 1996).
3. Recognition and revelation being two terms between which realist theorists, including Williams, continually slip (see Williams, 1976).

References

Alicata, Mario and De Santis, Giuseppe (1978), 'Truth and Poetry: Verga and the Italian Cinema', in David Overbey (trans. and ed.), *Springtime in Italy: A Reader in Italian Neorealism*, pp. 131–8, first published as 'Verità e poesia: Verga e il cinema italiano', in *Cinema*, 127, 10 October 1941.

Antonioni, Michelangelo (1978), 'Concerning a Film about the River Po', in David Overbey (ed.), (1978), pp. 79–82, first published as 'Per un film sul fiume Po', in *Cinema*, 68, 25 April 1939.
Bazin, André (2004), *What is Cinema?*, vol 2, trans. by Hugh Gray. Berkeley/ Los Angeles/London: University of California Press.
Bondanella, Peter (1993), *The Films of Roberto Rossellini*. Cambridge: Cambridge University Press.
Brooks, Peter (1985), *The Melodramatic Imagination: Balzac, Henry James, Melodrama, and the Mode of Excess*. New York: Columbia University Press.
Castello, Giulio Cesare (1956), *Il Cinema neorealistico italiano*. Rome: Edizioni Radio Italia.
Chiarini, Luigi (1978a), 'A Discourse on Neorealism', in *Springtime in Italy: A Reader in Italian Neorealism*, pp.139–69, first published as 'Discorso sul neorealismo', in *Bianco e nero*, 12(7), July 1951.
Chiarini, Luigi (1978b), 'Neorealism Betrayed', in *Springtime in Italy: A Reader in Italian Neorealism*, pp. 207–13, first published as 'Tradisce il neorealismo', in *Cinema nuovo*, 55, 25 March 1955.
De Santis, Giuseppe (1978), 'Towards an Italian Landscape', in *Springtime in Italy: A Reader in Italian Neorealism*, pp. 125–30, first published as 'Per un paesaggio italiano', in *Cinema*, 116, 25 April 1941.
Gledhill, Christine (1987), 'The Melodramatic Field: An Investigation', in *Home Is Where the Heart Is: Studies in Melodrama and the Woman's Film*. London: British Film Institute, pp. 5–43.
Gledhill, Christine (1992), 'Between Melodrama and Realism: Anthony Asquith's *Underground* and King Vidor's *The Crowd*', in Jane Gaines (ed.), *Classical Hollywood Narrative: The Paradigm Wars*. Durham/London: Duke University Press, pp. 129–69.
Grignaffini, Giovanna (1996), 'Il femminile nel cinema italiano. Racconti di rinascita', in Gian Piero Brunetta (ed.), *Identitá europea nel cinema italiano dal 1945 al miracolo economico*. Torino: Edizione della Fondazione Giovanni Agnelli, pp. 357–89.
Hillier, Jim (ed.) (1985), *Cahiers du Cinéma vol 1 1950s: Neorealism, Hollywood, New Wave*. London: Routledge.
Landy, Marcia (1991), 'Family Melodrama in Italian Cinema, 1929–1943', in Marcia Landy (ed.), *Imitations of Life: A Reader on Film & Television Melodrama*. Detroit: Wayne State University Press, pp. 569–77.
Lovell, Terry (1980), *Pictures of Reality: Aesthetics, Politics, Pleasure*. London: British Film Institute.
Lukács, Georg (1970), 'Narrate or Describe?', in Arthur Kahn (ed. and trans.), *Writer and Critic, and Other Essays*. London: Merlin, pp. 110–40.
Lukács, Georg (1971), *Realism in Our Time: Literature and the Class Struggle*, trans. by John and Necke Mander. New York: Harper Torchbook.
MacCabe, Colin (1974), 'Realism and the Cinema: Notes on Some Brechtian Theses', in *Screen*, 15(2), pp. 7–27.
MacArthur, Colin (1975/6), 'Days of Hope', in *Screen*, 16(4), pp. 305–9.
Marcus, Millicent Joy (1986), *Italian Film in the Light of Neorealism*. Princeton, NJ: Princeton University Press.
Monticelli, Simona (1998), 'Italian Cinema and Neorealism', in John Hill and Pamela Church Gibson (eds), *The Oxford Guide to Film Studies*. Oxford: Oxford University Press, pp. 455–61.

Morlion, Felix A. (1978), 'The Philosophical Basis of Neorealism', in *Springtime in Italy: A Reader in Italian Neorealism*, pp. 115–25, first published as 'Le basi filosofiche del neorealismo cinematografico italiano', in *Bianco e nero*, 9(4), June 1948.

Nowell-Smith, Geoffrey (2003), *Visconti*. London: British Film Institute.

Overbey, David (trans. and ed.) (1978), *Springtime in Italy: A Reader in Italian Neorealism*. London: Talisman Books.

Rivette, Jacques (1978), 'Letter on Rossellini', in *Cahiers du Cinéma vol 1 1950s: Neorealism, Hollywood, New Wave*, pp. 192–205, first published as 'Lettre sur Rossellini', in *Cahiers du Cinéma*, 46, April 1955.

Tinazzi, Giorgio (1983), 'Un rapporto complesso', in Giorgio Tinazzi and Marina Zancan (eds), *Cinema e Letteratura Del Neorealismo*. Venice: Marsilio Editori, pp. 11–39.

Villa, Federica (2002), *Botteghe di Scrittura per il Cinema Italiano: Intorno a Il Bandito di Alberto Lattuada*. Torino: Fondazione Scuola Nazionale di Cinema.

Visconti, Luchino (1978), 'Anthropomorphic Cinema', in *Springtime in Italy: A Reader in Italian Neorealism*, pp. 83–5, first published as 'Cinema antropomorfico', *Cinema*, 173/4, 25 September 1943.

Williams, Christopher (1973), 'Bazin on Italian Neorealism', in *Screen*, 14(4), pp. 61–8.

Williams, Christopher (1980), *Realism and the Cinema*. London: Routledge.

Williams, Raymond (1976), 'A Lecture on Realism', in *Screen*, 18(1), pp. 61–74.

5
Scale and the Negotiation of 'Real' and 'Unreal' Space in the Cinema

Mary Ann Doane

I

The question of realism in the cinema has traditionally hinged on either the indexicality of the photographic image and sound (the approach of André Bazin) or generic or classical Hollywood conventions that produce an effect of the 'real' (characterizing the apparatus theory and so-called '*Screen* theory' of the 1970s). However, the issue of cinematic scale and its relation to a sense of either the real or the unreal has remained largely unexamined. This is curious because a significant event in the historical emergence of the cinema was the projection of the image – a projection that allowed a larger sized image as well as a transition from the individual spectator of the kinetoscope or optical toy to the community of spectators labelled an audience. And much of the discourse around issues of scale in the early cinema centred around an anxiety about preserving the 'life-size' qualities of projected bodies, as though a defence were necessary against the spectacular possibilities of the gigantic image. With cinema and the accomplished projection of the illusion of movement came an increase in abstraction as well as one of scale. Now untouchable, at a distance, the image had the potential to become gigantic, 'larger than life'. The viewer, who could dominate, manipulate the optical toy or kinetoscope, controlling the speed and timing of its production of movement, became dominated, overwhelmed and dispossessed in relation to an image that seemed to be liberated from the obligation of dimension.

Although the miniature appears completely intelligible and knowable, the gigantic, as Susan Stewart (1993) has argued, exceeds the viewer's grasp and incarnates the limited possibility of partial knowledge. The growth of capitalism and a consumer economy situate the subject as epistemologically inadequate, as incapable of ever actually mapping or understanding the totality of social forces that determine his or her position. As Guy Debord argues in *The Society of the Spectacle*, the giganticism of the spectacle is particularly in synchrony with the effects of capitalist production.

The success of this production [of the workers], that is, the abundance it generates, is experienced by its producers only as an *abundance of dispossession*. All time, all space, becomes foreign to them as their own alienated productions accumulate. The spectacle is a map of this new world – a map drawn to the scale of the territory itself.

(Debord, 1995, p. 23)

In cinematic projection, the distance of the image is a measure of this dispossession, its intangibility a sign of the increasing abstraction of a consumer economy.

Cinematic scale is thus imbricated, from the outset, with a dialectic of the real and the unreal (or spectacle, which in media studies is often invoked as the antonym of 'real'); the body and disembodiment; and possession and alienation. With the transition from the optical toy and the kinetoscope to the projected image came a new apparent guarantee of realism insofar as projected bodies more nearly mimicked the size of actual human beings. In 1895, Thomas Edison referred to projected kinetoscope images as 'life size' (Ramsaye, 1986, p. 130), and, as John Belton points out with respect to the Lumière Cinématographe projections in London in 1896, 'in comparison with peepshow images, a 5-to-6 foot projected image would clearly be perceived as "life-size", rendering human figures on a scale closer to their actual size' (Belton, 1992, p. 242). Jan Holmberg has extensively documented the demand for 'life-size' images and *grandeur naturelle* in early press commentary on moving pictures (Holmberg, 2000). The clearest violation of this norm was the close-up, an object of anxiety and hostility in much of the journalistic discourse of the early period. The close-up presented two threats to the norm of the mimetic body: first, it was perceived as aesthetically offensive in extreme ways – as monstrous or grotesque, an excessive display of disproportion in scale; and second, as an untenable fragmentation of the human body. One particularly adamant rejection of the close shot was written by an author with the pseudonym of Yhcam in a 1912 issue of *Ciné-Journal*:

Now we have reached what could be called *the age of the legless cripple*. For three-quarters of the time, the actors in a scene are projected in close shot, cut off at the knees; from the artistic point of view, the effect produced is highly disagreeable and shocking. ... I have seen a film where an actor and a horse, placed side by side, were both partially cut off at the knees; then when the man mounted the horse, he found himself suddenly decapitated. To pass instantaneously from being legless to being headless is really pushing things a bit far.

(Abel, 1988, p. 72)

Yhcam also strongly criticizes the 'unnatural grandeur' of the close shot and the tendency to move quickly between shots of different scales, disorienting the spectator.

Paradoxically, and despite the frequent claim, buttressed by his own propaganda, that D. W. Griffith invented the close-up, the technique was used extensively in the very earliest period of the cinema, particularly in those films described by Tom Gunning as the 'cinema of attractions' (1997). As a performance or display of the sheer capabilities of the new technology, the close-up was in itself an attraction, a demonstration of the cinema's potential for disproportion and the play of scale. Within the non-narrative cinema of attractions, the close-up is often the site of a hysterical performance of faciality, of exaggerated expressions and hyperbolic affects. The monstrosity of its scale is rationalized, in effect, by the monstrosity/grotesqueness of the facial expressions that exceed all expected norms, re-inscribing disproportion at a different level. Edison's (1902) *Facial Expressions* consists of a single close-up of a woman assuming a variety of expressions involving deliberate contortions of the eyes, mouth and nose, including crossing her eyes, scrunching her face and stretching her mouth. In *Goo Goo Eyes* (Edison, 1903), Gilbert Saroni, a well-known vaudeville performer and female impersonator, distorts his features in similar ways, playing on the iconography of the ugly old maid. And perhaps one of the most intriguing instances of this tendency is located in the opening shot of the 1906 AMBCO film, *The Village Cut-Up*, in which the title figure, in close-up, moves and fidgets, twisting his facial features, while posing for a photograph. Behind his head is an anachronistic photography brace, used to stabilize and offer support for the human body for the long duration required for the early daguerreotype – here, its function successfully evaded by the perpetual movement of the protagonist. In an extremely rare invocation of off-screen space, two hands emerge from the right of the frame, attempting to still or steady the village cut-up (Figure 5.1). The body of the film traces the pranks of a figure whose social marginality is marked, who cannot be contained. The obsessive attempt to still this figure in the introductory shot, to immobilize him for representation, is a reiteration of and response to the instability of scale embodied in the close-up.

In this example, the use of the close-up is emblematic, haunting the edges of the film body 'proper', evicted from the narrative space itself (another quite famous example would be the close-up of the outlaw firing a gun at the camera in Edwin Porter's *The Great Train Robbery*).[1] To segregate the close-up as an alien entity, as extra-diegetic and therefore more legible as a *sign*, is one way of attempting to contain the trauma of scale associated with it. Through this strategy, the close-up's legibility is no longer spatial; hence, the disturbance of excessive scale is reduced. The success of this tactic seems to be demonstrated by the fact that the avid criticism of the monstrosity of the close-up is most prevalent during the period in which narrative becomes the dominant cinematic mode and the close-up is incorporated within the diegesis – the years from 1907–13.

Another means of reducing the threat of the close-up as narrative takes hold might be seen as transitional. The close-up is integrated within

Figure 5.1   The Village Cut-Up (AMBCO, 1906).

the diegesis at the end of the film, but is associated with hysteria or the catastrophic, borrowing from the excessive faciality of the earlier films.[2] In *The Curtain Pole* (AMBCO, 1909), a man breaks his friend's curtain rod as he attempts to help hang it over the window. The body of the film traces his attempts to return with a new pole, which continually escapes his control, hitting passers-by and objects as he walks, then takes a carriage. By the time he returns, the friend has already replaced the pole and everyone in the gathering ignores the protagonist. His hysterical and seemingly irrational response is to bite into the pole in close-up. However, this close-up is incorporated within the diegesis when there is a cut back to a medium shot in which the protagonist ultimately throws the pole down on the floor. This shot is a final instance of the way in which the pole is used throughout the film as a humorous device to test the limits of the frame and film space, to work out, in comic form, the spatial possibilities of the screened image.

II

However, why is it historically necessary to contain or domesticate the anxiety associated with the close-up, which is initially read in terms of scale (giganticism) rather than distance (closeness or intimacy)? Why the emphatic insistence upon 'life-size' bodies and 'normal' scale? Where does the fear of disproportion or of a massive, overwhelming scale come from? No doubt it is overdetermined, for many critics and theorists, stemming from an initial compulsion to evaluate moving pictures in relation to what was seen to be their closest rival or point of comparison – the theatre, where scale was a constant and the close-up unthinkable. Perhaps it can be aligned with the agoraphobia theorized by Anthony Vidler as the most telling pathology of modernity in its production of an urban space of increasing complexity and illegibility. However, the desire for proportion takes many different forms and has a long history whose effects have lingered in an uneven development. The obsession with proportion in the human body is common to both the ancient Greeks and Romans, and, in modernity, Le Corbusier, but in strikingly different incarnations.

Vitruvius, for instance, proposed that the architecture of temples should be based on the imitation of the perfectly proportioned human body, in which all parts exist in harmony. Leonardo da Vinci's 'Vitruvian Man' (also known as the 'Canon of Proportions' or 'Proportions of Man') is an illustration of Vitruvius's rules of proportion – the height of a man is equal to the width of his outstretched arms creating a square enclosing the human body; the hands and feet in this configuration touch a circle whose centre is the navel; the body is divided in half at the groin and by the golden section at the navel (Figure 5.2) (Elam, 2001, pp. 12–17). What is at stake here is a mathematically pure ideal of proportion, incarnated by the male body, and used as the measure of a transcendental aesthetics. Architecture hence mimics the greatest work of art, the human body – but an ideal rather than a contingent or concrete body. Sergei Eisenstein's invocation of the golden section in relation to film is accompanied by a recognition of its fundamental value to the Greeks – as a method of generating a perfect unity between a whole and its parts, where each part maintains a mathematically precise relation to the whole (Eisenstein, 1987, pp. 18–22). Le Corbusier, on the other hand, although he invoked the mathematics of the golden section and the proportionality of the body, conceived architecture first and foremost as a space designed *for* the human body, one that humans must inhabit, and therefore, one whose proportions must accommodate that body.

In the 1942 treatise, 'The Modulor: A Harmonious Measure to the Human Scale Universally Applicable to Architecture and Mechanics', Le Corbusier embraced units of measure based on parts of the human body: elbow (cubit), finger (digit), thumb (inch), foot, pace and so on, and disdained the move to the metric system which was abstract and 'indifferent to the stature of man' (Le Corbusier, 1954, p. 20). These organic units were superior to the metric units because

they formed an integral part of the human body, and for that reason they were fit to serve as measures for the huts, the houses and the temples that had to be built. ... More than that: they were infinitely rich and subtle because they formed part of the mathematics of the human body, gracious, elegant and firm, the source of that harmony which moves us.
(Le Corbusier, 1954, p. 19)

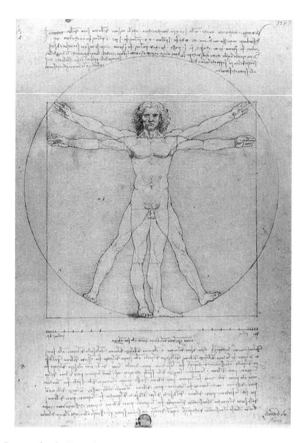

Figure 5.2   Leonardo da Vinci's 'Vitruvian Man', c. 1487.

Here, the body is no longer the Vitruvian ideal of an abstract mathematical purity but the generator of a mathematics of measurement that could guarantee the correct scale of the architecture that housed an empirical body. Scale moves from the realm of abstract and conceptual perfection (the fascination of mathematics) to the more clumsy or awkward, but livable, scale of the body and a form of rationalization and standardization designed to accommodate it. Each system generates its taboos in relation to a vision of corporeality that ultimately grounds an aesthetics of space. The dislocation and perversion of an architecture based on the metric system are, for Le Corbusier, a function of the fact that it loses sight of *man as measure*. In modernity, anxiety about 'man as measure' is linked to the incessant rationalization of time and space, its standardization and abstraction from the realm of lived time and space.

With respect to space, this rationalization is, in effect, an assault on the body and hence an assault on the experienced anchor of the real.

For knowledge of space is in close collusion with the body, its movements and gestures. Part of the threat of railway travel and its reduction of distance in the 19th century is the loss of the capacity of the body to gauge space in its relation to time and movement. Extrapolating from Leibniz's analysis of space, Henri Lefebvre argues that space must, above all, be occupied – occupied not by bodies in general or corporeality itself but by a quite specific body. This body's gestures and looks mark out space, indicating direction; it is a body that demarcates, orients, and demonstrates rotation, for instance, by turning around (Lefebvre, 1991, p. 170). As Lefebvre points out, for Leibniz space is 'absolutely relative' – it is both abstract (accessible to a mathematical mapping) and concrete (because bodies exist in space, manifesting their material existence there). According to Lefebvre,

> there is an immediate relationship between the body and its space, between the body's deployment in space and its occupation of space. Before *producing* effects in the material realm (tools and objects), before *producing itself* by drawing nourishment from that realm, and before *reproducing itself* by generating other bodies, each living body *is* space and *has* its space: it produces itself in space and also produces that space. This is a truly remarkable relationship: the body with the energies at its disposal, the living body, creates or produces its own space; conversely, the laws of space, which is to say the laws of discrimination in space, also govern the living body and the deployment of its energies.
>
> (Lefebvre, 1991, p. 170)

This is why space, for Lefebvre, cannot be *read* as a text. Both abstract and concrete, conceptual and material, or 'the perceived, the conceived and the lived' in his terms, it is inaccessible to a semiotic or post-structuralist interpretation whose foundational concept is a language that pre-exists and informs all signifying activity (Lefebvre, 1991, p. 39). Instead, space is a strange conjunction of abstractness and concreteness. Although space cannot be theorized as simply *there*, a container to be filled, but must be thought as produced, it is also concrete, material, real – in the sense that it is lived, the result of a practice.

III

Yet, in the context of the cinema, the spectator's body is incapacitated, rendered useless, deprived of its role of demarcating space through gesture and movement. As has so often been pointed out, the spectator must become immobilized, bodiless, his or her senses reduced to those characterized by distance – vision and hearing. Space is not lived – at least in the sense of the ordinary or everyday experience of space in its relation to the body – but abstracted, alienated. Perhaps this is why much of film theory attempts to resuscitate this body in some form. For Pascal Bonitzer, the cutting up of space effected by montage generates a filmic world that he compares to a labyrinth – the spectator wanders through corridors of shots, confronting limits and most especially the limits of vision and knowable space (Bonitzer, 1981, pp. 56–63). Famously, Walter Benjamin claimed in 'The Work of Art in the Age of Mechanical Reproduction' that, in contrast to the jail-like claustrophobia of urban spaces, the film 'burst this prison-world asunder by the dynamite of the tenth of a second, so that now, in the midst of its far-flung ruins and debris, we calmly and adventurously go traveling' (Benjamin, 1968, p. 236). Hugo Münsterberg's theory effects a displacement of gesture and bodily movement to filmic technique: a pan mimics the turning of the head; a close-up reincarnates attention (Münsterberg, 2002). And frequently, the body's bracketing is overcome by invoking the metaphors of inhabitation–the spectator figuratively inhabits the space of the mise-en-scène.

Space in cinema is delimited by the frame, which acts both as an edge or border (against the abyss outside it) and as an apparent container (of the plenitude of objects and people within it). This twofold function can be mapped onto a distinction inspired by the one Lefebvre sees in abstract space – film is both a representation of space and a representational space (although my deployment of the terms is quite different from Lefebvre's).[3] Given its indexicality, the cinematographic image appears to transparently inscribe the things, the buildings, the beings of 'real' space, which, as Lefebvre has extensively demonstrated, are already infused with ideological significance in lived space. It is as if everything in film were twice represented – as its already socially meaningful self and as the image of that social sign (as filmed). It is in this sense that the cinema is a representation *of* space – of landscape, of architecture, of fields and rooms and of the things and beings that, tellingly, 'take up' that space. Yet, it is also a representational space insofar as there are fairly strict spatial determinations – aspect ratio of the frame, size of the screen, scale of the shot (close-up, medium shot, long shot), focus, etc. – that signify, in themselves, cinema and its possibilities. There is the two-dimensional space of the screen as well as the edge that separates the image from absence, from darkness. It is the space of the screen – in the darkness of the movie theatre – that signifies, generating representation.

The space of narrative cinema, like social space, is inherently contradictory. On the one hand, cinema posits a space that is full of meaning if not symbolism, where each location and each object carry a significance that nevertheless is careful not to assert itself as such. Cary Scott's home in Douglas Sirk's *All That Heaven Allows* (1955) signifies class distinctions, notions of wealth, culture, bourgeois comfort and hierarchy. Yet, the spectator is invited to accept this naturalized space that does not announce its own meaning, that is simply *there*, the place where things happen. Space itself – the space of the frame, the space of the diegesis (which can be as large as the world or even universe) – is invoked simply as vacancy, as blankness, an emptiness to be filled. Hence, space is simultaneously both full, symbolic, meaningful – 'telling' – and empty, neutral – as Lefebvre points out, a space 'of insignificance, of semiological destitution, and of emptiness (or absence)', a container to be filled with contents (Lefebvre, 1991, p. 349).

This contradiction in the significance of space is accompanied by another – that of fragmentation versus unification/coherency, resolved only illusorily by a fragile activation of metonymy (a close shot, for instance, always indexing a larger space within which it is contained). Historically, film theorists have invested heavily in the coherence, legibility and transparency of space in the classical cinema. Its very classicism consists in its having attained these goals through the production of a homogeneous space, guaranteed above all by continuity editing. However, fragmentation – the discontinuity between shots – is of course the condition of the possibility of classical cinematic space and its economy. Yet, the legibility or rationale of that discontinuity with respect to scale – that is, the recognizable although imprecise differences between close-up, medium shot and long shot – invades the filmic space as a haunting reminder of difference. This is a contradiction not peculiar to film and characterizes what Lefebvre refers to as 'abstract space' in general:

> The fact is that abstract space contains contradictions, which the abstract form seems to resolve, but which are clearly revealed by analysis. How is this possible? How may a space be said to be at once homogeneous and divided, at once unified and fragmented? The answer lies first of all … in the fact that the 'logic of space', with its apparent significance and coherence, actually conceals the violence inherent in abstraction.
>
> (Lefebvre, 1991, p. 306)

In narrative film, the notion of a 'diegesis', a virtual space that binds together the fragments that are shots, their diversity and their inevitable exclusion of space beyond the frame, is the point of a fragile but effective coherence that denies the spatial violence of editing and framing. Its provision of an imaginary, unified space – a world, in effect, with its own spatial and temporal logic that mimes *the* world – holds at bay the violence of abstraction.[4] Bazin's frame as window on a world that extends beyond its borders, whose function of exclusion is only contingent, accidental, and does not destabilize the spectator's investment in that world, corroborates this reassuring spatial unity at the expense of a perception of the frame as cut or aggression. The frame is, in this theory, simply a necessary but benign impediment to vision.

Yet, the space of the diegesis, with its depth, its foreground and background, its horizontality and verticality, is only one aspect of the space of the cinema, although it is the one most often theorized. A consideration of cinematic scale must account for a different spectatorial experience of space, one that involves a recognition that the spectator is looking at a flat surface, of a certain height and width, at a certain distance, and a diegesis whose divisions are often those of the different scales of the shot, measured not only in relation to the contents of the narrative space but in relation to the spectator's body as well. In other words, cinematic scale can be measured in two ways: as the scale of the shot itself (close-up, medium or long shot); or as the scale of the image projected on the screen (height and width of the screen, aspect ratio of the image).

Within the conventional cinema, projection enables the 'bigger than life' scale of the image, a scale that can seem overwhelming – and certainly was in the earliest years of the cinema. However, scale as a problem is also internalized as the relation of the body of the spectator to the articulations of the image as close-up, medium shot and long shot. Suggestively, shot scale, whether it is conceptualized in terms of scale (largeness versus smallness) or distance (closeness versus remoteness), is generally defined in relation to the human body as its exemplary content. David Bordwell and Kristin Thompson define a close-up as 'a framing in which the scale of the object shown is relatively large; most commonly a person's head seen from the neck up, or an object of a comparable size that fills most of the screen' (Bordwell and Thompson, 2004, p. 501). A medium shot is 'a framing in which the scale of the object shown is of moderate size; a human figure seen from the waist up would fill most of the screen' (p. 504). Timothy Corrigan, who defines the close-up in terms of distance rather than scale, describes the close-up as 'an image in which the distance between the subject and the point of view is very short, as in a "close-up of a person's face"' (Corrigan, 2003, p. 177). The human body, as incarnated within the diegesis or in its spectatorial position, is the privileged exemplar.

Very early in the history of film theory, Jean Mitry conceptualized cinematic space as a kind of box, segmented into planes determined by distance and focus in relation to a human body (the French term for shot is *plan*) (Mitry, 1990, p. 59). For Mitry, that body was the character, but insofar as the spectator is situated at the place of the camera, the focus, distance and plane that define the shot are constituted as a reference to his or her body. For Mitry, then, scale becomes the primary measure of the cinema's ability to penetrate and organize space, through close-ups, medium shots and long shots (which are ultimately, entirely arbitrary as distinctions). From this point of view, scale becomes distinctive of the cinematic project not only in relation to the scale of the screen – the 'bigger than life' quality of the movies – but internally, as the regulator of the organization of space in relation to a body – both that of the character and the spectator.

In da Vinci's 'Vitruvian Man', the body is framed by both a circle and a square, the purest of geometric forms, and their geometrical precision is dictated by the ideal of the perfect proportionality of the human body.

For Le Corbusier, the geometry of architecture must be designed above all to accommodate the human body (admittedly a standardized body), to make it comfortable and secure – at home, in a 'machine for living' (Le Corbusier, 1931, p. 4). Idealism is displaced by rationalization. The historical fixity of the frame, that is, the aspect ratio, in the cinema (particularly in comparison with painting or drawing, even photography) is accompanied by the more apparently fluid division in the scale of shots. This variation allows for a management of distance, difference and the violation of a continuum effected by editing. There is a spatial ellipsis in a cut from long or medium shot to close-up – space is compressed much as time is compressed in a temporal ellipsis. This spatial violence that filmic abstraction entails is answered by continuity editing, which struggles to preserve the logic of a space that must be kept intact, homogeneous and continuous. Yet, it is the close-up that most frequently offers a resistance to this homogenization. The close-up always carries the threat of a certain monstrosity, a face or object filling the screen and annihilating all sense of scale. The inherent despatialization of the close-up, especially of the face, is a recurrent theme in film theory, surfacing in the work of Béla Balázs, Jacques Aumont and Gilles Deleuze, for whom the face is radically separable from the very notions of space and time. According to Deleuze, 'the close-up does *not* tear away its object from a set of which it would form part, of which it would be a part, but on the contrary, *it abstracts it from all spatio-temporal co-ordinates*, that is to say it raises it to the state of Entity' (Deleuze, 1986, pp. 95–6).

In the early cinema, with the emergence of narrative structure, and when the rhetoric of the spatial violence of the close-up is most intense, several filmmakers developed a formal technique for dealing with variations of scale that reduced the threat of the close-up. The technique also works to generate a sense of depth and a lengthened duration of the shot and is, in this sense, the inheritor of the repetitive form of the chase film. In it, a character appears initially in long shot or medium long shot and then moves towards the camera, traversing in his or her movement the various scales of the shot until finally emerging in close-up. This occurs, for instance, in *The Curtain Pole, The Ingrate* (AMBC, Griffith/Bitzer, 1908) and, most tellingly, in *Sweet and Twenty* (Griffith/Bitzer, 1909), where a couple meeting in a love tryst wander towards the camera, pausing at the points of the long shot, medium shot and close-up. These shots, in effect, enact the transition from long shot to medium shot or close-up while preserving the unity and homogeneity of space. Obsessively sustaining the integrity and coherence of space in the continuous long take, the perception of scale, that is calling attention to the size of the screen, that of the image, and aspect ratio (representational space), is transmuted into that of distance within the diegesis (represented space). This technique effects a displacement or amelioration of the threat of large scale, disproportion and a disturbing monumentality by translating scale (the logic of large and small) into distance (closer or further). It hence suppresses the structuring ambiguity of shot size in the cinema – is it close or is it large? The early reviewers of cinematic narrative, in and through their hysteria and diatribes against the close-up, saw it for what it was – a large picture.

The other aspect of scale – scale of the image projected on the screen (height and width of the screen, aspect ratio of the image) – is much more rarely discussed. In some sense, this could be called the 'real' space of the cinema, the concrete, material environment of the spectator's experience in the theatre, the scale of an image that is 'really' there, no matter how thoroughly and inevitably it is haunted by absence. And this space very rapidly became remarkably standardized. Until the early 1950s, the standard aspect ratio of 1.33:1 (set by Dickson in relation to the kinetoscope in 1889) remained one of the most rigid and unvarying rules of the cinema, despite several earlier and aborted attempts to promulgate a widescreen image. In the early 1950s, overdetermined by several reasons (including economic factors as well as cultural competition with television) outlined by John Belton, widescreen processes (CinemaScope, Cinerama, Todd-AO, Vistavision) were embraced, given their promise of an even greater plenitude of the visible and a denial of the frame as limit (Belton, 1992, p. 196). The discursive rationalization for widescreen promoted its relation not to any abstract mathematical purity but to the capacities of the human body. Widescreen processes were said effectively to duplicate the peripheral vision of the eyes and therefore to provide a more 'realistic' image. According to John Belton, 'Cinerama and CinemaScope, in particular, effectively transformed the notion of frame, expanding the horizontal angle of view to such an extent that there was, for all intents and purposes, no sense of any borders at the edges of the frame' (Belton, 1992, p. 196). For Belton, this 'illusion of limitless horizontal vision' intensified the spectator's sense of immersion or absorption in the space of the film (much of the advertising for these processes emphasized the spatial relocation of the spectator from his/her seat to the world provided by the cinema) (p. 197).

Widescreen processes allowed the accentuation of the fullness and presence of the image and the denial of its 'outside', of the alterity of off-screen space. They invoked the idea of an infinity of horizontal space, reinforcing the promise of infinite depth of the vanishing point. Whether crowded or expansive, the CinemaScope frame conveyed plenitude and the negation of all loss. Like the panorama of the 19th century, widescreen processes facilitated the transformation of time and history into space. The widescreen films of Otto Preminger at the historical moment of the emergence of this technology offer a particularly illuminating series of examples of the activation of diegetic space in relation to a frame whose horizontality greatly exceeds its vertical dimension. For Preminger, a long-take director, seems to accede to the notion of the frame as container of all cinematic meaning, as the instance of a fullness, presence and homogeneity that he is loath to mutilate. Everything is there, to be seen. Nothingness is kept at bay. The diegesis is not a labyrinth for Preminger, but instead a guarantee of wholeness, presence and continuity, a denial of contradiction – everything is there, all at once. This is a powerful resistance to abstraction – in particular, the *violence* of abstraction, to the notion of the frame as cut, as incision, as the poignant yet terrifying reminder of the absolute alterity of the space outside the frame (for Lefebvre, abstraction is the response to a certain terror of space). Preminger's cinema is the witness to a cinematic predilection for monumentality and infinity.

In *The Cardinal* (1963), the impressive architecture of the Vatican in the credit sequence infuses the narrative of one priest's memory with the immensity of historicity. The human body, wandering beside massive pillars, across seemingly limitless squares, and climbing endless steps, is dwarfed by an architecture signifying the solidity, institutionality and historical mandate of the Catholic Church. In *Exodus* (1960), the landscape itself becomes monumental, riddled with Biblical references, and indicating, above all, the historical authority of ownership, possession, right aligned with the Jewish return. Perhaps the guarantee that widescreen gives to an almost limitless sense of horizontality leads Preminger to mark continually the intense depth of the image, incessantly reiterating the vanishing point. This entails an architecture of the shot whose vertical lines of force lead back to the vanishing point, as in *Exodus*. Or quite commonly, a shot in which a character seems to emerge out of the vanishing point itself or conversely, to disappear into the seemingly infinite remoteness of space, centring the composition but also acting as a reassurance of the depth of the image. The insistence of perspective corroborates the regularity and rationality of a highly legible space and its seemingly endless, indeed infinite, coherence. Vidler refers to the centre of the horizon as the 'vanishing point of the spatial sublime' (Vidler, 2002, p. 175). However, why should a widescreen technology, defined by an exorbitant horizontality, emphasize the dimension of depth? Widescreen is paradoxically only a more intense demonstration of the aspiration of the cinema to represent, within a finite image, the sense of an infinite expanse of space, to affirm the inconsequentiality of the frame.

Perspective as a system calculates distance as a relation to scale. The large is close; the small, distant. The infinitely distant would be the infinitely small – the geometric point, without extension, in short, the vanishing point – the point that vanishes and can only be conceived mathematically. According to Hubert Damisch,

The question of infinity consistently preoccupied Renaissance culture, just as it has unceasingly preoccupied geometry, *from the origin*. Finding itself inscribed, within the perspective context, in a position marked by a hole in the centre of the prototype, this *original* feature (in all senses of the word) took on an emblematic value. For it is here, at this point that absented itself, so to speak, from its place, that was decided the destiny of a system that would have been unable to escape its own closure if it hadn't resorted to it.

(Damisch, 1995, p. 388)

In a discussion of Brunelleschi's first experiment, in which the viewer was placed behind the painting and looked out through a hole at the painting's reflection in a mirror, Damisch claims that it functioned as a self-reflexive demonstration of the very condition of perspectival representation – that the 'point we today call the "point of view" coincides, in terms of projection, with the one we call the "vanishing point": both are situated at the intersection of the perpendicular sight line and the picture plane' (Damisch, 1995, p. 120). The place from which a perspectival representation must be viewed has an echo within the field of the painting at the vanishing point. Nevertheless, the relation between the two is asymmetrical, for the vanishing point is not an image of the point of view, which if it were represented in the painting would have to be at a virtual distance equal to that of the viewer's distance from the painting. However, the vanishing point is an image of infinity and would put infinity at the back of this image of the point of view and therefore behind the viewer's head (Damisch cites Louis Marin's discussion of infinity as an 'idea of what is behind one's head') (Damisch, 1995, p. 121n.). Obsessed by infinity, classical perspective conceived it in relation to the subject.

In perspectival representation, infinity is the unseen within and beyond the seen. It is the point where vision fails, the unrepresentable but necessary premise of representation. Within film theory, the fact that the logic of classical perspective is built into the technology of the camera lens has occasioned an understanding of the spectatorial position as a point of mastery and coherency, ideologically informed by a notion of the unity and mastery of subjectivity. Perspective is hence stabilizing. Yet, Damisch takes issue with this interpretation. Although the subject gets its bearings through perspective, it is not 'any the more stable' for it (Damisch, 1995, p. 388). Instead, the allegedly dominant and masterful subject of perspective '*holds only by a thread*, however tightly stretched this might be' and Damisch compares that subject to a tightrope walker.

The subject interpellating the painting, and interpellated by it from the point marked at its center, this subject can only get its bearings within the configuration by being reabsorbed into it, by becoming lost in it. In the sense not of a walk through it, but rather of a *transversal* of it, manifested externally by a point or hole: in ideal terms, the one through which would pass a string, perpendicular to the painting, stretched from the observer's eye to the vanishing point. So it's not a point that perspective designates, but rather a line, one corresponding in projection to the plane marked as that of the eye, or the subject.

(Damisch, 1995, p. 389)

The line is that thread from which the viewer hangs, in a fragile, because incalculable, infinity of space. Nevertheless, whether point or line, this subject is still conceived as disembodied.

The cinema would seem to instantiate perfectly Lefebvre's notion of an abstract space 'that transforms the body by transporting it outside itself and into the ideal-visual realm' (Lefebvre, 1991, p. 309). For Lefebvre, with the advent of modernity there is an 'intense, aggressive, and repressive' visualization. Reducing all sensory perception to vision, this process diminishes the subject's apprehension of a lived space – that space becomes alienated, distanced. The spectator is *dispossessed* of space. For Lefebvre this is a regrettable, negative consequence of advanced capitalism, the corollary of an increasing quantification of space that results in the elimination of the human body as measure.

The overemphasis upon vision generated the distance of the metropolitan subject (analysed by Georg Simmel) as opposed to the intimacy and haptic quality of interaction in smaller, less technologically mediated, communities (Simmel, 1950, pp. 409–24). Although that distance is reinscribed and consistently re-evaluated in the cinema with the breakdown of shots into different scales – close-up, medium shot, long shot – it is also a distance whose threat must be reduced or denied. The notion of narrative cinema as a labyrinth within which the spectator is lost but simultaneously immersed and absorbed together with all the metaphors of inhabitation seeks to redress the distance and dispossession of spectacle. This is the oxymoron of a 'virtual real' space – one that is *more real* than that of the everyday – evoking the nostalgia for a past utopian space of closeness, intimacy and an immediacy of sensory experience. According to Simmel, 'spatial relations are only the condition, on the one hand, and the symbol, on the other, of human relations' (quoted in Vidler, 2002, p. 68).

However, because the cinema continually puts into play variations of scale that are given as relations of proximity and distance, it also allows for perturbation, dissonances within the structuration of space designed to the measure of rationalization. There are by-products, barely contained and unenvisaged effects. I will take as my examples here two very different kinds of film: a classical Hollywood narrative of the early widescreen era and a contemporary art film that deliberately cuts up space in its relation to the body differently. Even in a filmmaker like Preminger for whom the frame is a container characterized by fullness and presence, with no outside or alterity, loss and undecidability invade the shot, generating a disorientation of space, a momentary illegibility. In what is often referred to as Preminger's limit text, *Bunny Lake is Missing* (1965), whose narrative circles around an over-closeness, an excessive intimacy in the quasi-incestuous relationship between brother and sister, there is a scene in a doll hospital in which a regular, readable and orderly space gives way to one of uncertainty, even opacity. The protagonist, Ann Lake, enters the building and climbs the stairs to speak with the old man who fixes excessively 'loved' dolls. He tells her she will have to look for her daughter's doll herself, and when she descends the stairs (now dark and barely recognizable as the stairs she ascended) the space becomes uncanny, disorienting. Neon lights from the street intermittently illuminate and then darken the room, but it is the character's movement with respect to the camera that seems to warp the space and diminish its readability. The camera moves to follow her trajectory, but at points she approaches the camera so closely that the image becomes quasi-abstract (Figures 5.3–5.5).

Within the widescreen field, the immense shadowy close-up of Ann Lake suggests a dangerous over-closeness to the camera, hence the viewer, making it difficult to interpret the spatial field. It is an excessive proximity that produces at least a transitory illegibility and disorientation, witnessed by the broken dolls, fragmented simulacra of discarded human bodies. Not only does Ann's head block out space, but there is no compensation in the form of the easily legible expressivity of a face. Wong Kar-wai's *In the Mood for Love* (*Fa yeung nin wa*, 2000), on the other hand, does not so much produce a spatial disorientation as an acknowledgement of the violence of abstraction, of

Figure 5.3   Bunny Lake is Missing © 1965, renewed 1993 Otto Preminger Films, Ltd. All rights reserved. Courtesy of Columbia Pictures.

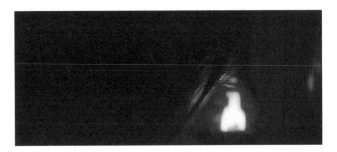

Figure 5.4   Bunny Lake is Missing © 1965, renewed 1993 Otto Preminger Films, Ltd. All rights reserved. Courtesy of Columbia Pictures.

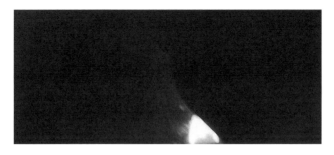

a frame that severs. What is most striking about the deployment of scale in this film is again an excessive and sustained proximity to bodies. However, in this case the film activates the close-up differently in relation to the body, frequently undermining the expectation that the face is the privileged content of the close-up. The possibility of expressivity and of legibility is shifted from the face to other parts of the body, resituating affect.

These instances of spatial destabilization are both the leakages and the critiques of a system that produces homogeneity through fragmentation, a logic of scale mapped as distance, and the virtual charting of a potentially navigable space. One could say that the space of the cinema simultaneously stabilizes – producing an illusory orientation of the spectator in his or her relation to an incomprehensible space (that of modernity, of urban space, of the ungraspability of totality in Jameson's terms, 1988, p. 349) – and destabilizes – placing a different inflection on Lefebvre's notion that abstract space 'transforms the body by transporting it outside itself'. These moments of destabilization are what Manfredo Tafuri has called the 'irremediable dissonances that escape the plan of advanced capital' (Tafuri, 1976, p. 137). Studies of the spaces of perspective, of modernity and of cinema are infused with the figures of a body beside itself, or a body fragilely suspended in its relation to space. Siegfried Giedion, in his study of the organization of space, line and architecture in modernity, characterizes the modern subject as 'a tightrope dancer who, by small adjustments, keeps a continuous balance between his being and empty space', echoing Damisch's subject of perspective as tightrope walker (quoted in Vidler, 2002, p. 50, originally in Giedion, 1941). Le Corbusier's concept of ineffable space displaces extreme affect – the cry, the terror – onto the space of architecture, transforming it into a body that is 'touched, wounded, dominated, or caressed'. ('The release of aesthetic emotion is a special function of space', quoted in Vidler, 2002, p. 54, originally in Le Corbusier, 1948, p. 8.) For Sergei Eisenstein, pathos in film also produces extreme affect, even ecstasy, in its etymological sense – *ex stasis*, out of a state, forcing the viewer to 'be beside himself' (Eisenstein, 1987, p. 27).

The disembodiment associated with a cinematic space that is said to absorb or immerse the spectator is hence double-edged. It has been both disdained and embraced enthusiastically. However, to the extent that the cinema is inevitably about scale in relation to a body – spectacular, monumental scale in its theatrical incarnation, shifting scales in its *découpage* – that body is never lost, never truly eliminated. It is simply led to find another way of finding its way.

Notes

I am grateful to Jan Holmberg for providing me with an English translation of Chapter 3 of his dissertation on the close-up, 'Large and Small' (Holmberg, 2000).

1. Similarly, in *The Widow and the Only Man* (AMBCO, 1904), the two protagonists are introduced at the beginning of the film in isolated close-ups.
2. For a discussion of the use of catastrophe as arbitrary ending in early silent films, see Burch (1990, pp. 191–3).
3. Lefebvre himself insists upon breaking the antagonistic relation of the binary opposition between 'representations of space' and 'representational space' by adding a third term – 'spatial practice', manifested in the competence and performance of users of specific spaces; spatial practice is a particular perception of space. Representations of space, for Lefebvre, are ways of conceiving space and are associated with architects, urban planners, and the use of such notions as the golden section. It is the representational space, in this schema, that is associated with art (but also with inhabitants and users of space) – it is the arena in which the imagination seeks to 'change and appropriate' socially dominated space. This is 'lived' space. Hence, my use of the opposition, which remains binary in my schema of film space, is only inspired by Lefebvre, because I am dealing only with space as represented and experienced in film, a representational system. Lefebvre's notion of representational space might be useful in thinking about individual filmmakers' spatial practices, but I am more concerned here with cinema as an apparatus. See Lefebvre (1991), especially pp. 38–40, for a fuller discussion of these categories.
4. One might well ask why abstraction is a form of 'violence' for Lefebvre. A clue can be found in the etymology of the word 'abstract', which stems from Latin *abs*, off, away, and *tractus*, past participle of *trahere*, to draw – hence, to 'draw away'. The term 'abstract' is associated with some form of subtraction (from an entity that would otherwise be 'whole'): to withdraw, remove, take away, extract. Early usage also associated it with theft – 'to take away secretly, slyly, or dishonestly; to purloin' (Oxford English Dictionary, http://dictionary.oed.com).

References

Abel, Richard (ed.) (1988), *French Film Theory and Criticism: A History/Anthology, 1907–1939, vol 1, 1907–1929*. Princeton, NJ: Princeton University Press.
Belton, John (1992), *Widescreen Cinema*. Cambridge, MA: Harvard University Press.
Benjamin, Walter (1968), 'The Work of Art in the Age of Mechanical Reproduction', in *Illuminations*, trans. by Harry Zohn, ed. and intro. by Hannah Arendt. NY: Schocken Books.

Bonitzer, Pascal (1981), 'Partial Vision: Film and the Labyrinth', trans. by Fabrice Ziolkowski, in *Wide Angle*, 4(4), pp. 56–63.

Bordwell, David and Kristin Thompson (2004), *Film Art: An Introduction*, 7th edn. NY: McGraw-Hill.

Burch, Noël (1990), *Life to Those Shadows*. Berkeley: University of California Press.

Corrigan, Timothy (2003), *A Short Guide to Writing about Film*, 5th edn NY: Longman, 2003.

Damisch, Hubert (1995), *The Origin of Perspective*, trans. by John Goodman. Cambridge, MA: MIT Press.

Debord, Guy (1995), *The Society of the Spectacle*, trans. by Donald Nicholson-Smith. New York: Zone Books.

Deleuze, Gilles (1986), *Cinema 1: The Movement-Image*, trans. by Hugh Tomlinson and Barbara Habberjam. Minneapolis: University of Minnesota Press.

Elam, Kimberly (2001), *Geometry of Design: Studies in Proportion and Composition*. New York: Princeton Architectural Press.

Eisenstein, Sergei (1987), *Nonindifferent Nature: Film and the Structure of Things*, trans. by Herbert Marshal. Cambridge: Cambridge University Press.

Giedion, Siegfried (1941), *Space, Time and Architecture: The Growth of a New Tradition*. Cambridge, MA: Harvard University Press.

Gunning, Tom (1997), 'The Cinema of Attractions: Early Film, Its Spectator and the Avant-Garde', in Thomas Elsaesser (ed.), *Early Cinema: Space, Frame, Narrative*. London: British Film Institute, pp. 56–62.

Holmberg, Jan (2000), 'Förtätade bilder: Filmens närbilder I historisk och teoretisk belysning'. Stockholm: Aura Förlag.

Jameson, Fredric (1988), 'Cognitive Mapping', in Cary Nelson and Grossberg (eds), *Marxism and the Interpretation of Culture*. Urbana: University of Illinois Press.

Le Corbusier (1954), *The Modulor: A Harmonious Measure to the Human Scale Universally Applicable to Architecture and Mechanics*. Cambridge, MA: Harvard University Press.

Le Corbusier (1931), *Towards a New Architecture*, trans. by Frederick Etchells. New York: Dover Publications, Inc.

Le Corbusier (1948), *New World of Space*. New York: Reynal and Hitchcock and Boston: The Institute of Contemporary Art.

Lefebvre, Henri (1991), *The Production of Space*, trans. by Donald Nicholson-Smith. Oxford: Blackwell.

Mitry, Jean (1990), *The Aesthetics and Psychology of the Cinema*, trans. by Christopher King. Bloomington: Indiana University Press.

Münsterberg, Hugo (2002), *The Photoplay: A Psychological Study and Other Writings*, Allan Langdale (ed.). New York/London: Routledge.

Ramsaye, Terry (1986), *A Million and One Nights: A History of the Motion Picture through 1925*. New York: Touchstone Books.

Simmel, Georg (1950), 'The Metropolis and Mental Life', in *The Sociology of Georg Simmel*, trans. and ed. by Kurt H. Wolff. London: Collier-Macmillan.

Stewart, Susan (1993), *On Longing: Narratives of the Miniature, the Gigantic, the Souvenir, the Collection*. Durham: Duke University Press.

Tafuri, Manfredo (1976), *Architecture and Utopia: Design and Capitalist Development*, trans. by BLL Penta. Cambridge, MA: MIT Press.

Vidler, Anthony (2002), *Warped Space: Art, Architecture, and Anxiety in Modern Culture*. Cambridge, MA: MIT Press.

Part II World Cinema and New Realisms

6
Realism and Gus Van Sant's *Elephant*

Anna Backman Rogers

Gus Van Sant's *Elephant* (2003) is based loosely on the real events of the 1999 Columbine High School killings. As the second part of a trilogy of films inspired by true stories about people who die young – the other two parts being *Gerry* (2001) and *Last Days* (2004) – the film's action is seemingly presented in a resolutely realistic manner in order to match the veracity of the events it portrays. Most of the film's time is concerned with the quotidian routine of the young protagonists. The camera, through a series of long takes, traces their movements very carefully to observe every nuance and gesture of the ordinary adolescent body.[1] The film is divided into eight sections, each of which is named after the particular adolescent or group of adolescents whose peregrinations the camera follows. The names of these teenagers are the real names of the actors, suggesting further the potentially indexical relation that the film has to actual events. In addition, their presence as non-professional actors and the fact that many of them improvised their dialogue confounds further the distinction between reality and fiction in the film.

Van Sant's characteristic long takes serve here to emphasize the impression of real time and existence as duration. Indeed, much of what the camera isolates seem to be rather inconsequential. The students do not engage in entertaining conversation and interesting activities designed to amuse the cinematic spectator. Rather, Van Sant forces the viewer to experience the sheer banality of their routines and idle chatter. Despite the common knowledge about the terrible events on which the film is based, the build-up to the tragedy is not presented in the expected, classical cinematic fashion. In particular, the viewer is not offered large sections of crosscutting between simultaneous places of action to increase sensations of tension and anticipation. Instead, Van Sant presents this outburst of violence as disquietingly and suddenly as it would have been experienced. Namely, as an intrusion into the mundane that, in retrospect, imbues these normal events preceding the massacre with an elegiac quality.

This persistent use of the long take, the use of non-professional actors, the location of the narrative in historical reality and the focus on the quotidian aspect of ordinary people's lives arguably allies *Elephant* with the kind of theory of realist filmmaking developed by André Bazin with relation to Italian neorealism, in particular the films of De Sica. Additionally, Van Sant's own admission that he was inspired in his visual approach by the documentaries of American filmmaker Frederick Wiseman, whose unabashed approach to examining controversial subject matter often makes for uncomfortable viewing, links him to the documentary tradition and, in particular, a certain observational and, arguably, non-manipulative or moralistic type of filmmaking.

However, many of the film's techniques undermine our common sense of reality in order to create an evocation of the experience of trauma and its aftershock instead. It is a complex psychological reality that Van Sant is showing in his film rather than an indexical one. In effect, despite his rejection of traditional cinematic techniques used to create narrative tension, the director manufactures a disquieting atmosphere within the diegetic world even before the appearance of anything overtly untoward in the film. Thus, although Van Sant may tantalize his viewers with a few visual cues as to the source of these violent events, such as Nazi documentary footage and scenes of bullying, he suggests that the reasons for this tragedy are at once more socially complex than these facile symptoms would suggest. There are several ways in which Van Sant undermines prosaic notions of reality and avoids accusations of moral didacticism: the use of time-looping and the interplay of actual and virtual elements, the creation of a mise-en-scène of threat that is reminiscent of Bonitzer's theory of de-framing (as I will explain below),[2] the use of defamiliarization techniques in the last section of the film, such as the use of shallow focus and enhanced colour, and the discrepancy between sound and visual tracks that is reminiscent of Deleuze's characterization of the 'thought of the outside' (Deleuze, 2005, p. 173). In doing this, Van Sant not only promotes the film medium as a resource through which society may confront its mass grief but also acknowledges the real, social complexity of his subject matter. By eschewing a more conventional approach towards the topic of violence among youth, particularly through his editing scheme, Van Sant does not dictate what the viewer must think. Furthermore, by adopting these techniques of defamiliarization, he forces the viewer to think beyond a simple and reactionary response to the tragedy. In direct contrast to the critics who excoriated *Elephant* with charges of irresponsibility and immorality, I will argue that this non-didactic approach to such an incendiary topic is actually a thoroughly responsible one and one that reflects the real complexity of our modern world.

The use of time-looping in *Elephant* is one of its most salient characteristics. The sparse use of cutting in the film initially suggests to the spectator that the film is composed of 'real time'. However, it soon becomes clear that, with the exception of one scene that takes place the day before the event, what we are seeing is, in fact, selected portions of the morning leading up to the massacre replayed from different perspectives. Thus, what would have happened in a relatively short time in reality is protracted into an onscreen time of an hour and a half. Amy Taubin comments pertinently on this cinematic device: '[t]he effect [of this repetition] is to transform what seems like "real" time into recorded time and the time of memory, which is the mode in which the reality of Columbine now exists. The reversals also suggest a longing to stop time, to prevent the inevitable tragedy from ever taking place' (Taubin, 2005, p. 18). The mental process that the spectator undergoes in trying to piece together the different segments of the film mirrors the process of actually trying to understand the event of 'Columbine'. In addition to this need to try to comprehend, which the film's form reflects, the use of repetition renders the seemingly mundane mournful and, thus, lends the whole body of the film a poignant atmosphere.

In conjunction with this, Van Sant occasionally films his protagonists in slow motion and juxtaposes Beethoven's melancholic Piano Sonata in C Sharp Minor with common scenes of high school activity, making these sequences emotionally affecting and contributing to the impending sense of inexorable tragedy the film possesses from the outset. The manner in which the protagonists are shot and framed suggests that they are doomed from the beginning as well. As Taubin reflects, the effect of this desire to pause moments before the tragedy is suggestive of a need to try to stop the inevitable from happening. This idea comes into distressing fruition in the scene where the camera cuts away from Michelle, the school geek and first victim, seconds before her death. Although we do not see Alex, who is one of the assassins, pointing a gun at her, we know she is fated to die because we hear the loading sound of a rifle. However, the stalling of a frame does not only signify a need to stop time but also, like the photograph, connotes death and stasis too, thus reflecting the liminal status many of the protagonists have as characters between life and death. Repetition is also a coping mechanism invoked by those who have suffered trauma. Freud famously noted in 'Beyond The Pleasure Principle' (Freud, 2003) that a patient's need to compulsively revisit the event of trauma is reflective of the need to come to terms with the fact of death and dissolution; in fact, it could even denote a death wish and the fact that the protagonists seem so devoid of authenticity and hope from the outset of the film becomes all the more alarming in light of this desire.

Indeed, in the final part of the film, I would argue that some of these students seem to allow themselves to be killed by remaining disturbingly passive. Arguably, then, Van Sant's repetitive structure in *Elephant* recalls the Freudian desire to assimilate the fact of death and bring about some level of comprehension while also possibly signalling a need to return to a state of non-being as a way of resisting progression into the adult world and rejecting its coterminous norms. Yet, importantly, such an effect is achieved in a way that is psychologically rather than cinematically realistic. In addition to this psychological element, Martine Beugnet (2006) has noted that a prevailing motif of the film's mise-en-scène, camera work and framing is that of virtual reality. This is initially suggested through the use of a graphic match between an earlier scene of a video game and a later scene from the massacre in which the protagonist's viewpoint echoes that of a player in a video game with a gun in the centre of the lower portion of the frame, and further emphasized through the film's overall aesthetics. This interplay of virtual and actual elements reminds one of Susan Sontag's description of 11 September 2001 in which she notes that the actual experience of trauma often seems like its virtual representation (Sontag, 2004, p. 19). Therefore, although the use of a mise-en-scène of virtual reality is not a staple of the realist tradition, its presence here suggests the reality of the experience of trauma and simultaneously foregrounds the fact that any filmic representation of an event is an inescapably virtual experience.

Elephant has an uncomfortable atmosphere from the outset. This is not simply to do with the problems the protagonists evidently have with interacting with their peer group and elders; it is also a function of the way in which they act and are framed in the film. These adolescents resemble automata in their movements and their lack of visible emotion. They wander through the school corridors like characters in a computer game, echoed by the smooth tracking shots of the camera, and often automatically respond to those around them or seem completely oblivious of their surroundings. In one telling scene, John, who is having problems at home, retreats into an empty classroom to be alone and cry. However, he registers little emotion and merely rubs his eyes as though feigning distress. This is more than bad acting. The emotional disconnection felt between the students, their peer group and the adult community is also apparent in the disjunction between the protagonists and their own emotions. Tellingly, when a fellow student asks John if 'something bad happened' to him, he just shrugs his shoulders and says 'I don't know' (Figure 6.1). In *Elephant* the protagonists are not presented as fully articulated characters, and the spectator is not given a great deal of information about their lives. Rather, they function as indirect symptoms of the wider social malaise that Van Sant is exploring. Thus, the detached characteristics of the protagonists that lend the film a surreal atmosphere are an integral part of the general mise-en-scène of impending harm that the director creates.

Another way in which the director renders this everyday situation strange is through unusual framing and camera angles that recall Bonitzer's theory of de-framing. Bonitzer characterizes a de-framing as a shot that unsettles the viewer's perception and visually places the protagonist in a position that suggests extinction as an ever-present possibility. These shots are often taken from oblique angles and points of view that are narratively unjustified and thus throw the viewer's gaze into crisis by de-centring it. The de-framed

Figure 6.1   Elephant: When a fellow student asks John if 'something bad happened' to him, he says, 'I don't know'. Courtesy HBO®.

image also plays on the notion of unassimilated off-screen space by offering images of characters who seem about to disintegrate into a void or who are surrounded by a vast space which seems to dwarf them, reducing them to vulnerable figures or potential victims. This sense of inevitable harm is most apparent in the scenes when the protagonists seem diminutive in comparison to their surroundings. In one particular scene, Michelle walks across the gymnasium but is only a shadowy figure picked out by patches of light in-between the surrounding darkness (Figure 6.2). She is placed towards the left-hand side of the frame, throwing the viewer's gaze off balance, and she eventually disappears into the left-hand side of the frame as though absorbed by something that the spectator does not see.

Van Sant also has a tendency to focus tightly on the back of his protagonists' heads as if some unknown body were observing them. By surrounding his characters with vast open spaces, or alternatively tightly framing them, Van Sant plays on the themes of surveillance and impending danger; thus, the fragility of the protagonists' social world is made apparent through the initially strange sense of apprehension that pervades the film's opening and is finally made manifest through the intrusion of horrific violence into this ordinary situation. In other words, the violence that breaks into the image in the final part of the film is seen to be latent within this everyday situation from the beginning, but this is very much to do with the way Van Sant has chosen to present the action and not something intrinsic to the film's setting.

Figure 6.2   Elephant: Michelle walks across the gym. Courtesy HBO®.

However, it is the last section of the film that demonstrates this effect of real-ity made strange most apparently and significantly. What were once brightly lit corridors turn into dark alleyways lit by fires, and the use of a shallow focus distances further this environment from both the protagonists and the cinematic spectator. The film's colours become more vivid in this part of the film too, in particular the bright red 'exit' signs that become a focal point in the blue darkness for the spectator but which do not aid the students to leave the building. Indeed, the pupils either run around manically as though they are trapped in a maze or, in the case of one student called Benny, continue to wander the corridors in the mode of a sleepwalker.

Furthermore, it is in this concluding part of the film that the discrepancy between the sound and visual tracks becomes most obvious. Significantly, Hildegaard Westerkamp's concrète score contains extracts of train departure announcements, sounds of nature and animals that not only suggest exit from the living world but also heighten the primordial mood of the film at this point. In his analysis of the modern time-image, Gilles Deleuze notes that one of the most prominent features of contemporary cinema is the separation of the soundtrack from the image. He writes: '[w]hat speech utters is also the invisible that sight sees only through clairvoyance; and what sight sees is the unutterable ... the visual image and the sound image are in a special relation-ship, a free indirect relationship' (Deleuze, 2005, p. 250). In other words, sound and image may seem autonomous but, in fact, they complement one another to show what cannot be said and to say what cannot be shown.

Echoing this, Van Sant is alluding to what cannot be simply addressed through focusing on what is generally held to be the causes of such violence in society. Indeed, he places elements such as the Nazi documentary footage, the video game or the website that easily facilitates the purchase of weapons into the film precisely to demonstrate to the viewer how facile and reactionary it is to isolate and identify these factors as the sole causes of such an incident as 'Columbine'. By using certain techniques that are reminiscent of Deleuze's time-image, then, Van Sant is counteracting our received ways of thinking. Indeed, Anna Powell has recently written of the time-image: '[r]ather than seeking to capture a pro-filmic, objective world in order to "tell" us a story, the time-image is more interested in foregrounding stylistic techniques to challenge familiar patterns of thought' (Powell, 2007, p. 147). This characterization of the time-image as one that counteracts and disperses received ways of thinking is reflective of the manner in which the images in *Elephant* are organized, in particular Deleuze's description of the modern cinematic 'spiritual automaton' (Deleuze, 2005, p. 164). Indeed, a Deleuzean reading of *Elephant* can account for the film's unusual aesthetic appeal and its profound connection to the modern world.

Taking his cue from Spinoza, Deleuze uses the term 'spiritual automaton' as a point of comparison between the classical and modern cinemas; whereas in the case of the former it is possible to form a comprehensive system of thought through association of images that correspond to logical cerebral patterns, finally uniting image, film viewer and world, the latter dissipates any such notion through the 'thought of the outside' (Deleuze, 2005, p. 161). In direct contrast to the classical regime of images and thought, the modern cinema is full of irrational cuts and literal insertions of moments of void such as white or black screens, whereas the scenes themselves are organized in such a way that it becomes impossible to predict a flow of narrative action – indeed, for Deleuze, predictable narratives are abandoned in the modern cinema of the time-image. According to him, this is as much a reflection of modern man's situation of alienation from the world as it is also, interestingly, the path back to *this* world. Deleuze writes of the modern protagonist that he or she is one who 'no longer' believes 'in this world' or even in the 'events which happen to us, love, death, as if they only half concerned us' (Deleuze, 2005, p. 166). As a result of this, he argues that it is modern cinema's duty to capture an absurd belief in this world, which is our 'only link' to it (Deleuze, 2005, p. 166). Yet this cannot be enacted under the terms of the classical cinematic regime, it must be done in a manner befitting its absurd task; this is the task of the modern cinematic spiritual automaton.

In *Elephant*, the protagonists seem detached from their environment, each other and themselves; their speech and movements appear to be automatic to the viewer, as though issuing from a site beyond themselves, whereas the mundane seems to be a mere veneer that camouflages an underlying sinister reality. Significantly, their journeying through the school corridors seems without end and they continually occupy liminal areas, a situation that places them literally in zones of indeterminacy and ambiguity. Unable to act, they merely stare as though registering something that they are powerless to react to or stop. This situation reflects Deleuze's description of that of the modern cinematic character. He writes of: 'the "psychic" situation which replaces all motor-sensory situations; the perpetual break of the link with the world, the perpetual hole in appearances, embodied in false continuity; the grasping of the intolerable even in the everyday and insignificant' (Deleuze, 2005, p. 165). Yet these very symptoms that are a manifestation of modern man's disillusionment also provide a visual and philosophical prescription for the resolution of this situation. In fact Deleuze, referencing film theorist Jean-Louis Schefer, states that the special case of thought in modern cinema is to be 'brought face to face with its own impossibility', all the while drawing from this 'a higher power of birth' (Deleuze, 2005, p. 163). Thus, what the modern cinema makes possible is a re-instatement of belief in this world but only through a process that forces us to see, hear and think anew. Deleuze writes:

> The spiritual automaton is the psychic situation of the seer, who sees better and further than he can react, that is, think. Which, then, is the subtle way out? To believe, not in a different world, but in a link between man and the world, in love or life, to believe in this as in the impossible, the unthinkable, which nonetheless cannot but be thought.
>
> (Deleuze, 2005, p. 164)

Elephant contains these elements of false continuity held within a quotidian carapace that allows the 'unbearable' to break through, while constantly challenging the viewer's modes of thought and logical deduction. Although the film, in part, visually conveys the inherent loneliness, cruelty and separation of the adolescent world, it also directs the viewer's attention back towards what is overlooked in the everyday, urging him or her to think and look beyond the obvious. Although the film offers prime examples of protagonists who are reflective of Deleuze's description of the modern cinematic character who 'acts and speaks himself as if his own gestures were already reported by a third party' (Deleuze, 2005, p. 177), these adolescents are, in fact, indirect manifestations of the Deleuzean spiritual automaton – a presence that is felt and shown more widely in the filmic images and its soundtrack and, as we shall see, has resounding repercussions for the way the film is *thought*.

The Deleuzean spiritual automaton is manifest in the cinematic spectator's experience of watching the film, but it is also contained within the images and soundtrack on screen; these processes connect to confound the boundaries between the viewer and the film in order to challenge and renew thought. To the extent that *Elephant* frustrates the viewer's attempt to think and understand the film through metaphorical association of the images and patterns of logical deduction, it prompts a way of thinking that challenges predetermined, structured answers to the tragedy of 'Columbine'. This is immediately notable in the lack of a cohesive and resolute conclusion to the film. Van Sant chooses to end his film by focusing on clouds rolling past in a blue sky as though to signal deliberately towards the openness of the very question the viewer has been asking since the film's opening: *why* did this happen? In turn, through his use of time-loops and the insertion of these literal moments of void, the cinematic spectator has had his or her thought directed towards the 'outside' (Deleuze, 2005, p. 161). In other words, the film has perturbed any attempt to understand it analytically or rationally; rather, the viewer has come up against the limitations of his or her own thinking. Yet, through the visceral experience of viewing the film, the spectator has been asked to think, see, hear and, thus, to understand it in a completely new manner.

Furthermore, this engagement with the cinematic world is, by extension, nothing less than an engagement with his or her own world. It is possible, then, to find a dialogue between Deleuze's own description of the modern time-image and Van Sant's idiosyncratic filmmaking. Deleuze notes that: 'this time-image puts thought into contact with an unthought, the unsummonable, the inexplicable, the undecidable, the incommensurable' (Deleuze, 2005, p. 206); reflecting this, Van Sant himself has spoken of his own technique in a manner that recalls Deleuzean thought:

> It is not psychology through character analysis, via dialogue and action. Rather, it's the psychology that happens as you, the viewer, are ruminating on these events that you're watching ... because of the layering of different visual and sound elements ... It almost impacts another part of the brain ... I am not cutting in a traditional manner. I am not trying to show a point of view.
>
> (Levy, 2005)[3]

Indeed, although the eight sections of *Elephant* have been allocated to particular members of the adolescent group, this does not seem to have been done to relate the event of 'Columbine' from different perspectives. In fact, the overall viewpoint is an anonymous, floating one that pervades every area of the school. This is different from the camera merely following particular students (which it certainly does) because it retains its own autonomy. This is to say, the camera effects an anonymous presence that undertakes journeys of its own accord for which the young protagonists are not catalysts. A perfect example of this is during the sequence entitled 'Brittany, Jordan and Nicole', in which the camera leaves the three girls choosing their lunch at the school canteen and travels into the kitchen, through its corridor, past the meat locker and captures two of the kitchen staff smoking drugs before picking up the three girls again. The result of this is that these images serve no readily identifiable purpose in the 'narrative' (if there can be said to be one in *Elephant*); rather, the wandering presence of the young protagonists is replicated in the peripatetic motion of the camera and the unpredictable thought-processes in the cinematic spectator.

Ronald Bogue, commenting on Deleuze, has noted of the stream of images in the modern cinema that they belong 'to no localizable or discretely identifiable mind; instead mind is ... immanent within the images, dispersed, acentered, multiple' (Bogue, 2003, p. 178). As such, then, this representation of 'Columbine' is a highly unusual one; yet this is not simply something that the viewer *sees*, it is also something that he or she *feels* and *thinks*. Indeed, these processes, for Deleuze, are not readily differentiated ones. The vision of the spiritual automaton is also its manner of 'speaking' and 'thinking' (Bogue, 2003, p. 178) and this is not only constitutive of the film itself but also of the way in which the spectator views the film.

According to Deleuze, if modern cinema at once notes the disconnection between man and his environment and his subsequent disillusionment with the world, it also provides the path back to believing in this world. The images seen in the most challenging films confront the cinematic spectator with what is not easily assimilated, understood and thus abandoned. These images haunt the spectator, compelling them to look and think in challenging and unforeseen ways. Following Deleuze, I argue that this kind of cinema restores us to the world by making us look beyond clichéd images and towards the reality from which we are often cushioned. In *Elephant*, reality breaks into the images even before any insurgence of onscreen violence as we are made to look at the minutiae of the everyday, while the very format of the film challenges passive and received ways of thinking. Although Van Sant uses several techniques that could be likened to a system of defamiliarization, the overall effect is one that makes us look at and think about the quotidian in a way that would not be prompted by a more traditional approach to such controversial material.

I have argued that by making *Elephant* a thoroughly unsettling experience for the viewer from the outset, even when focusing on mundane reality, Van Sant is forcing the viewer to think beyond the regimented, moralistic approach that is, arguably, common of other artistic responses to such a topic. By way of contrast, Van Sant suggests that the reasons for this violence are far more socially complex and embedded in what we may overlook in the everyday. To achieve this, he has to make us look at life itself but in such a way that it is made strange to us and we are forced to look, see and think anew. Indeed, the cinematic spectator can no longer stand outside this world from a place of judgment; instead, he or she is immersed in this world so that it impacts on both the body and brain in a visceral manner. The cinematic world becomes one that reflects and confronts our ways of interacting with and thinking about our own modern world. *Elephant* is a film that does not allow its viewer to be distanced from what it is showing; it plunges the spectator into the everyday but, as has been shown, in a manner that is not strictly synonymous with the tradition of Realism. By making banality sinister and strange, *Elephant* forces us to re-establish a link with our quotidian reality that has been broken due to our need to distance ourselves from, and thus morally 'explain away', any tragic event such as 'Columbine'. Arguably, if the film leaves us with a message, it is that it is not until we reunite ourselves with *this* world and recognize it as our own that we can really begin the infinite process of trying to understand it.

Notes

I thank Professor Martine Beugnet and Professor Jean Duffy for all the time and effort they put into reading drafts of this chapter.

1. The protagonists are played by non-professional actors who are notable precisely because they are ordinary teenagers and not preternaturally talented and attractive 'child stars'.
2. For a detailed explanation of Bonitzer's theory of de-framing, see Beugnet (2004, p. 169).
3. Although Van Sant said this in connection with his film *Last Days*, the aesthetic similarities between the two films have been noted. Indeed, his comments here are equally true of *Elephant*.

References

Beugnet, Martine (2004), *Claire Denis*. Manchester: Manchester University Press.
Beugnet, Martine (2006), 'Contemporary Cinema and Computer Games or the Poetics of the Virtual', paper given at The French Institute in Edinburgh, March, unpublished.
Bogue, Ronald (2003), *Deleuze on Cinema*. London: Routledge.
Deleuze, Gilles (2005), *Cinema-2: The Time-Image*, trans. by H. Tomlinson and R. Galeta. London/New York: Continuum.
Freud, Sigmund (2003), *Beyond the Pleasure Principle and Other Writings*, trans. by J. Reddick. London: Penguin Modern Classics.
Levy, Emmanuel (2005), 'Gus Van Sant on *Last Days*', available on http://www.emanuellevy.com/article.php?articleID=281, accessed on 15 October 2007.
Powell, Anna (2007), *Deleuze, Altered States and Film*. Edinburgh: Edinburgh University Press.
Sontag, Susan (2004), *Regarding the Pain of Others*. London: Penguin.
Taubin, Amy (2005), 'Blurred Exit', in *Sight and Sound*, 15(19), pp. 16–19.

7
Observational Realism in New Taiwan Cinema

Ming-yeh T. Rawnsley

This chapter explores a particular kind of realism in New Taiwan Cinema that is observational, self-reflexive and closely linked to Taiwan's cultural, social and political context. The case studies chosen for analysis include Hou Hsiao-hsien's *Dust in the Wind* (*Lianlian fengchen*, 1986), Edward Yang's *The Terrorizer* (*Kongbu fenzi*, 1986–7) and Tsai Ming-liang's *Vive l'amour* (*Aiqing wansui*, 1994).[1]

Cultural and film critics proclaimed the death of New Taiwan Cinema in 1987 (Mizou and Liang, 1991), the same year as martial law was lifted and society began to experience a new wave of cultural liberation and pluralism. However, the filmmakers of New Taiwan Cinema, such as Hou and Yang, not only continued to make films after 1987 but also to exercise a profound influence on future filmmakers in Taiwan including award-winning directors such as Tsai.

In this chapter, 'New Taiwan Cinema' is used in a broader sense to include films made after 1987, that is post-New Taiwan Cinema, in order to demonstrate the continuing thread of observational realism in these films. Moreover, it is important to situate these films within Taiwan film history to appreciate fully the uniqueness of New Taiwan Cinema in terms of its form, rhythm, subjects and how the element of realism is articulated.

Historical perspective

The film industry in Taiwan was commercially successful during the 1950s, 1960s and 1970s. After half a century of Japanese colonialism between 1895 and 1945, most of its inhabitants could only speak Taiwanese and a little Japanese when the island was returned to the Republic of China (ROC) after World War II. Owing to political sensitivity in the postcolonial period,[2] social realism was an approach avoided by local filmmakers who began to make Taiwanese-language films based on traditional folk opera (*gezai xi*) or modern melodrama to entertain the domestic audience. When they realized that there was a huge appetite for locally produced cinema, an increasing number of Taiwanese-language films were churned out. Over a thousand Taiwanese-language films were made between 1956 and 1970 (Lee, 1998, p. 17). The production time for many of these films was within ten days (Rawnsley, 2008b). As a result their quality was extremely uneven.

When the Kuomintang (KMT, or the Nationalist Party) fled to Taiwan after their defeat by the Communists in 1949, the government strongly promoted Mandarin, ROC's national language, on Taiwan in order to enhance national unity. Yet Mandarin-language cinema did not take off until the 1960s when a series of historical musical productions broke box-office records.[3] As the popularity of Mandarin-language cinema grew, the number of Taiwanese-language films dwindled. There were only ten Taiwanese-language films made in 1970, two in 1971–2 and another four in 1980. The last traditional Taiwanese-language film, an adaptation of a folk opera, *Chen san wu niang*, was made in 1981 (Lee, 1998, pp. 23–4).[4] It is noteworthy that many film-makers of New Taiwan Cinema returned to the use of Taiwanese language in their films. However, these are very different from the traditional Taiwanese-language cinema of the 1950s in terms of form and narrative strategies, as will be explained later.

In addition to historical musicals and dramas, the KMT-owned film studio, Central Motion Picture Corporation (CMPC), began championing a new style of films branded 'healthy realism' (*jiankang xieshi*) in the 1960s. Although being named 'realism', it is

> a didactic construction of romantic melodrama and civic virtue ... It mixes the interior/private mise-en-scène specific to family melodrama with the civil, public space to accommodate government policy, enabling a smooth integration with the state ideological apparatus.
>
> (Yeh, 2007, p. 206)

Hence the products of healthy realism are often seen today as part of KMT propaganda activity. Nevertheless many films of this genre enjoyed both commercial success and critical acclaim in the domestic market at the time. Prominent filmmakers of healthy realism, such as Li Xing and Bai Jing-rui, have influenced many younger generations of filmmakers in Taiwan, including Hou Hsiao-hsien.[5]

Although healthy realism gradually faded out, Taiwanese viewers embraced a variety of different genres in the 1970s. Examples are traditional martial arts films (*wuxia pian*), kung-fu films (*gongfu pian*) that exploded onto the international consciousness largely because of Bruce Lee, as well as military, political and campus dramas that enhanced the KMT-oriented worldview when the ROC lost its seat in the United Nations in 1971 and severed formal diplomatic ties with Japan in 1972 and the United States in 1979. Furthermore, a significant number of contemporary female romance novelists, most notably Qiong Yao, provided rich escapist materials for screen

adaptation. This genre is called *aiqing wenyi pian* (literally 'romance, literature and art movie') and was popular not only in Taiwan, but also in Hong
Kong and many Southeast Asian countries. As Emilie Yueh-yu Yeh (2007,
p. 206) has pointed out, 'the literary *wenyi* feature helped create a distinctive
reputation for Taiwan cinema abroad'.

Although the 1970s were regarded as the golden age of Taiwan film production (Yeh, 2007, p. 206), the challenges from the much more energetic and
commercially driven Hong Kong cinema also intensified during the same
period. Unfortunately the ROC government made several policies that were
damaging to the Taiwan film industry, including tax breaks for Hong Kong
film companies, and demonstrated its inability to manage bootleg videos.
Moreover Taiwanese filmmakers responded to fierce competition by repeti-
tively copying popular formats of Hong Kong cinema with a much smaller
production budget in the hope of earning a quick buck. Consequently both
the quality and quantity of commercial films produced in Taiwan began to
face a serious crisis by the beginning of the 1980s (Lu, 1998, pp. 196–254).

A new beginning

The starting point of New Taiwan Cinema is a contentious issue. It would
perhaps be fair to say that *In Our Time* (*Guangyin de gushi*, 1982), a collection
of four short films directed by four unknown filmmakers at the time,[6]
brought to the public's attention for the first time 'realistic images of contemporary Taiwan' (Yip, 2004, p. 56). The four segments are set between the
1960s and 1980s to reflect the process of modernization of the island, and
the film was hailed as a breakthrough in Taiwan film history. One year later,
Chen Kun-hou directed a feature film in a similar fashion, *Growing Up* (*Xibi
de gushi*, 1983), scripted by novelist Zhu Tian-wen,[7] which explores contemporary social issues faced by second marriages and marriages between
Taiwanese and mainlanders. The box office proved the financial appeal
of a 'new' cinema made by young filmmakers. Later in the same year *The
Sandwich Man* (*Erzi de da wan ou*), a collection of three short films based on
stories by a nativist novelist, Huang Chun-ming, was released. The three
segments, set in Taiwan's early period of industrialization, were respectively
directed by Hou Hsiao-hsien, Zeng Zhuang-xiang and Wan Ren.[8]

While *The Sandwich Man* was playing in theatres, another film consist-
ing of three integrated stories full of familiar film stars in Taiwan came
out: *The Wheel of Life* (*Ta lunhui*, 1983) told a reincarnation romance set in
ancient China, and was directed by three far more established filmmakers
at the time, Li Xing, Bai Jing-rui and King Hu (Hu Jin-chuan). Interestingly,
whereas Hou, Zeng and Wan of *The Sandwich Man* were either born or raised
in Taiwan, Li, Bai and Hu of *The Wheel of Life* all grew up in the mainland.
The latter failed both commercially and critically. In contrast, *The Sandwich
Man* not only became a surprise box-office hit but also attracted serious

attention from the media and cultural commentators. The success of *The Sandwich Man* formally confirmed the arrival of New Taiwan Cinema as a phenomenon (Berry and Lu, 2005, pp. 5–6).

Another element in *The Sandwich Man* that is important to the kind of 'realism' associated with New Taiwan Cinema is 'the use of dialogue in Taiwanese   the language used by the majority of the people but suppressed under the Mandarin-only policy in the post-war period' (Chiu, 2005, p. 18). As previously discussed, Taiwan became the retreat of the ROC government when the KMT lost the civil war to the Communists in China. Taiwan was seen as a temporary base for the eventual recovery of the motherland by many mainland immigrants who were forced to settle in Taiwan for several decades. Local languages and Taiwanese identity were suppressed for the sake of the KMT-interpreted Chinese ideology. The government made a series of policies to prohibit the use of local languages in films (Lu, 1998, pp. 162–6). Yet such suppression became a thorny issue after the process of democratization began on the island in the early 1980s. *The Sandwich Man* used the Taiwanese dialect in one-third of the film, going against the official policy. All the major press in Taiwan were united in supporting the film as it awaited the approval of the Government Information Office. Cultural and social elites appealed to the government to loosen the ban on local languages in films, and the government obliged. When Hou Hsiao-hsien made *Boys from Fenggui* (*Fenggui lai de ren*, 1983–4) with half of the dialogue spoken in Taiwanese, the Government Information Office also approved its release. Martial law was finally lifted in 1987 and there have been no restrictions on the use of local languages in films made in Taiwan since 1989.

I must point out that among the three chosen case studies, *Dust in the Wind* uses Taiwanese but *The Terrorizer* and *Vive l'amour* mainly use Mandarin. The truth is that Taiwan went through a very successful and vigorous Mandarin campaign in the 1960s until this language became embedded in daily lives of all parts of the society. The population today is generally said to comprise 73 per cent Taiwanese, 13 per cent mainlanders, 12 per cent Hakkas and 1.7 per cent Aboriginals (Scott and Tiun, 2007, p. 54). However, most Taiwanese people are equally fluent in Mandarin and one local language. Mandarin proficiency is especially widespread among those who received their school education after the late 1940s. For the generations that have been through the Mandarin campaign in the 1960s and for younger speakers, Mandarin has become their daily and most familiar language, even though many of them can also identify another local language as their mother tongue. In other words, Mandarin is widely used across ethnic boundaries in Taiwan today although the standard Mandarin widely spoken in Taiwan is somewhat different from the Mandarin spoken in mainland China in terms of accents, slangs and terminologies.

Therefore the freedom to use languages realistically in films as spoken by ordinary people in Taiwan, not just the dialects of Taiwanese or Hakka, but also Taiwan's own version of Mandarin, has been one of the major contributions of New Taiwan Cinema. This is one of the reasons why the rise of New Taiwan Cinema is often seen as closely related to the cultural, social and political democratization of the island and is regarded as 'an attempt by the young generation to render their vision of Taiwan on film' (Chiu, 2005, p. 18).

Literary cinema

Although New Taiwan Cinema was accepted as mainstream because of its early popularity, it is hard to deny its elitist agenda aiming at 'reforming unsophisticated artistic sensibilities' (Chang, 2005, p. 14). Indeed, many filmmakers of New Taiwan Cinema shared a similar sense of cultural elitism and literary *wenyi* idealism with their predecessors of the 1960s. The major difference is that whereas the masters of healthy realism looked at Taiwan from a KMT-oriented Chinese perspective, the directors of New Taiwan Cinema strove to reconnect 'with Taiwanese society by drawing inspiration from the realist tradition' (Chiu, 2007, pp. 17–8). Their preference to cast semi- or non-professional actors instead of movie stars is one of the common methods to capture their vision of realistic and contemporary Taiwan.

The pursuit of observational realism marks the fundamental departure of New Taiwan Cinema from previous cinematic works produced on the island. Firstly, the filmmakers began to avoid theatrical conflicts, meaningful characterization and purposeful dialogue. As Chris Berry and Feii Lu (2005, p. 6) have observed, New Taiwan Cinema 'abandoned the simplistic black-and-white storytelling methods of the past in favour of a more subtle and complex mode that was close to real life experience'. Hence in Hou Hsiao-hsien's *Dust in the Wind*, for example, the audience is not pre-warned of the eventual separation of the two young lovers by any dramatic plot development. There is no conflict or confrontation after the break-up to stimulate the spectators' emotions or curiosity either.

Dust in the Wind is set in the 1960s between the city of Taipei and a poor mountainous mining village outside it. The protagonists, Wan and Huen,[9] grew up together in the village. Wan gives up his education to work in Taipei to help support his family. Huen follows Wan to Taipei a couple of years later when she graduates from senior high school. Wan and Huen help and care for each other during their stay in Taipei. However, when Wan takes up his national military service far away from Taipei, he receives a letter from his younger brother one day saying that Huen is getting married to a postman. When the younger brother's monotone voiceover tells the episode of the newly-weds' home visit, the scene cuts from a medium shot of Wan first to a long take of the sky above the village and then to Wan's family members sitting or standing still in silence on the steps leading to their family home. A cut goes to Huen's mother, clearly in anger and shame, and

Wan's mother looking sorrowful. Both of them are motionless and quiet. Following Wan's mother's gaze, another cut takes us to Huen and her new husband standing outside Huen's family home. Once again, neither of them says a word or moves much. The next scene cuts to a scenic long shot of the offshore island where Wan takes up his military service. The following cut shows us Wan lying on his bed crying his heart out. However, this is the end of the love affair in the film. What follows is a long take in which the camera pans across trees and sky. As far as the narrative goes, when Wan finally completes his military service and returns to the village, he finds his grandfather out in the field near their home. The only thing the old man talks about is the potatoes he grows, and the chit-chat carries on for quite some time. The film ends here without further explaining what happens to Huen, Wan or anybody else.

The natural, realistic and minimum style of performance, weak plots and a slow pace of movement reflecting real-life events require 'an actively engaged audience rather than a passive one', which is an experience unfamiliar to and hard to be fully appreciated by 'an audience accustomed to commercial entertainment' (Berry and Lu, 2005, p. 6). Despite the commercial and critical success at its early stage, the movement subsequently loses the support of the domestic audience from the mid-1980s. As ticket sales diminish, producers and investors also turn their backs. Nevertheless New Taiwan Cinema filmmakers continue to seek opportunities to make low-budget cutting-edge work, and many of them have since earned international admiration in the art-house and film-festival circuits.

The international recognition of New Taiwan Cinema may be due to the second common feature among these filmmakers in terms of how they observe and accentuate reality in their work. Many of these filmmakers are much more interested in cinema as an art form than their predecessors, and often pay equally close attention to images, music and languages. Through the experiment of balancing and composing these filmic elements, they have uncovered hidden layers of meanings that are close to 'real'. As Tsai Ming-liang once said, he rarely uses background music in his films because the natural environment a person is situated in, as well as one's internal world, are almost always much more noisy and powerful than any extra music or sound he can add.[10] In *Vive l'amour*, for example, there is no music and even very little dialogue. In a film that portrays the loneliness and 'postmodern alienation' of urban dwellers (Martin, 2003, p. 175), the silence of the film heightens the noise of their surroundings – car horns, motorbike engines, shrieks of bicycles – and in turn exposes vividly the emptiness the characters feel inside. Moreover, the characters' mental state of isolation reflects and is reflected in the images on the screen such as dismal concrete, neon streetscapes, a desolate park and so on.

Vive l'amour is set in urban Taipei of a post-economic miracle era. Mei-mei is an estate agent who tries to sell a luxury apartment. A-rong is a stranger she meets on the street, and they go back to the empty apartment for a one-night stand. In the meantime there is another man, Xiao-kang, a salesman of funerary niches in a crematorium who steals the key to the apartment at the beginning of the film and who secretly lives in it. Neither Mei-mei nor A-rong is aware of Xiao-kang's presence. The three characters exist in the same confined space separately. Xiao-kang is so depressed that he tries to cut his wrists, until he hears Mei-mei and A-rong enter the apartment and listens in silence to their lovemaking. When Mei-mei leaves the apartment and A-rong is still asleep, Xiao-kang emerges and kisses A-rong's face. The final act before the film ends happens the day after Mei-mei's second one-night stand with A-rong. A long-take reveals her walking through an empty park, amidst the ugly urban landscape. When Mei-mei eventually sits down, we see 'an extremely long-take close-up of her face. She starts to cry, neither silently and elegantly nor in a distraught and melodramatic manner, but whining and sniffling. She stops, lights a cigarette, and then cries some more' (Berry, 2005, p. 94). As Berry (2005, p. 91) points out, Tsai intends to make films like real life and so the technique he uses 'performs realism so rigorously and thoroughly that it teeters back and forth at its limits. Just as drag does not simply negate gender but takes on an ambivalent stance toward it, so *Vive l'amour* engages in the same realist style that it exposes'.

Another shared attitude among New Taiwan Cinema filmmakers is that many of them prefer to keep the audience at an arm's length. They try to (re)present an observation or an experience objectively and then leave it to the audience to draw their own interpretation. For example, there is no real indication in which decade *Dust in the Wind* is set. However, there are some not-so-obvious clues. Firstly, Wan's father once mentions Wan's elementary school teacher who had strongly encouraged Wan to take the entrance examination for junior high school. As the system of six-year free and compulsory primary education was extended in 1968 in Taiwan to include three years of junior high school, the audience can figure out roughly when the film is set, but only if familiar with Taiwan history. Secondly, movie screens appear three times in the film. The first time is a blank outdoor movie screen set up in Wan and Huen's village. The second time is in an almost empty cinema in Taipei where Wan and Huen watch an exciting martial arts film together. The third time is back in the village where director Li Xing's healthy realism classic, *Beautiful Duckling* (*Yangya renjia*, 1964), attracts a large crowd in front of the outdoor movie screen.

Haden Guest (2005, p. 28) interprets the appearance of these movie screens as *Dust in the Wind* casting 'a retrospective gaze. It looks back at the "new wave", which was encouraged and sponsored by the CMPC and already drawing to a close by the end of the decade'. This may be true. However, more important is that the films shown in *Dust in the Wind* not only work as an indicator of chronology, but also offer a subtle and interesting contrast to Wan and Huen's reality. Although *Dust in the Wind* is a film itself, compared with films of healthy realism or the martial arts genre that the Taiwanese audience consumed in a large quantity in the 1960s as Wan and Huen seemingly do in the film, it sends out such a strong sense of realism that it feels real.

Another good example of how filmmakers keep observational distance in order to make their cultural commentary sharp is Edward Yang's *The Terrorizer*. Like *Vive l'amour*, *The Terrorizer* is set in urban Taipei. Although it satirizes middle-brow culture of the 1980s, it is also a chilling tale of art imitating life with disastrous consequences. Yang maintains throughout the film a calculated and precise structural form which prevents the complicated narratives from becoming melodramatic and the audience from sinking into sentimentality.

There are several parallels within the film. First, Yang casts a combination of middle-aged professional actors and young non-professional actors. Several of the professional actors come from the Little Theatre (*xiao juchang*), an art movement that flourished in the 1980s alongside New Taiwan Cinema. The second parallel lies between two characters: a middle-class wife who dreams of becoming a famous writer, and a rich boy who wants to be a professional photographer. The middle-class wife who is trapped in a loveless marriage is frustrated because the deadline for a major literary competition is approaching. She confines herself in her room to write a masterpiece, but the writing does not go well. Meanwhile the rich boy who loves photography accidentally comes across a teenage girl nicknamed 'White Chick' who is part of a gang. He becomes obsessed with her and leaves his own girlfriend to chase after 'White Chick'. However, 'White Chick' steals his cameras while he is asleep.

'White Chick' likes to make prank phone calls to amuse herself. One day she rings the novelist and makes the latter suspicious that her husband is having an affair. The misunderstanding prompts the novelist to leave her husband and move in with an old flame who offers her an office job. Moreover, she uses the episode of an anonymous caller in her plot and finally wins the top prize of the competition. In her novel the husband kills his wife and then commits suicide. When the rich boy reads the story in the newspapers, he understands what 'White Chick' did. Terrified of what may happen, the boy contacts the husband who then feels he may be able to save his marriage. Unfortunately, his wife does not think truth matters and asks for divorce.

The contrast between the two would-be artists is that the rich boy wakes up from his fascination both with 'White Chick' and with his artistic pursuit, while the wife's high-culture aspirations persist. She leaves her husband in pursuit of a literary dream. When she wins the competition, she is also prepared to leave her lover should he dare to limit her ambition. While Yang critiques the wife who values the pseudo-artistic activities more than the two men who love her, one begins to wonder if Yang is also critiquing the literary tendency of the Little Theatre and New Taiwan Cinema, both of which were then accused by many of not caring what the audience wants.

The third parallel is between fiction and non-fiction, dream and reality. The wife's novels are always autobiographical, but she constantly criticizes her husband for misunderstanding her by being unable to differentiate fiction from non-fiction. The long dream sequence towards the end of the film blurs the boundary between her novel and reality: when the husband realizes that his marriage is over, he steals a gun from his friend who is a policeman. He shoots his boss who overlooks him for a promotion. Afterwards he goes to her flat to kill her lover, and then points the gun at her. When a gunshot is fired, we see the wife is unhurt and the husband leaves the flat. He wanders the streets and meets 'White Chick'. He takes her to a hotel room while a member of the girl's gang is waiting to burst into the room to rob him. Policemen arrive nearby at this point and the husband goes into the bathroom and turns on the tap. When the husband's policeman friend kicks the door open, the bang coincides with a gunshot. While we see blood on the wall, a cut goes to the policeman friend who suddenly wakes up, and another cut shows the wife waking up from her nightmare at the same time. The policeman friend walks to his bathroom and discovers that the husband has shot himself. Next, we see the wife feel sick and turn her head to vomit. It is hard to tell if she feels sick about her own behaviour towards her husband or if she is finally pregnant.

In the film, one of the literary critics comments on the wife's award-winning novel as being 'dramatic yet very close to real life'. This is exactly how *The Terrorizer* should also be described. As Sung-sheng Yvonne Chang (2005, p. 25) has concluded, 'the modernistic device of self-reflexivity in *The Terrorizer* enables the film to maintain a critical distance from the objects it represents'. Edward Yang has demonstrated another dimension of observational realism that gives New Taiwan Cinema further depth.

Conclusion

From the discussion above, we can see why New Taiwan Cinema is an important movement. It is not only significant to the development of Taiwan cinema, but also an invaluable contribution to world cinema in terms of techniques, themes and how it articulates realism. Although New Taiwan Cinema is part of the cultural forces that pushed forward democratization in Taiwan, the process and the eventual lifting of the martial law in 1987 has enabled filmmakers to use cinema to reflect and rewrite Taiwan history from an individual's perspective.

Nevertheless, the identity of Taiwan is still contested. Democratization has allowed previously taboo subjects to be discussed openly and freely on the island, but the people on Taiwan have not yet established a consensus about their past or future. In addition to the various cinematic elements analysed above, which may explain the decline of New Cinema in Taiwan in terms of output numbers[11] and commercial circulation (Berry and Lu, 2005, p. 6), perhaps another reason is non-cinematic. There is no doubt that the images, subjects, languages of dialogue and the kind of observational realism in New Taiwan Cinema are all closely intertwined with Taiwan's cultural, social and political background. Yet until the people on Taiwan have finally come to terms with their local, regional, national and international realities, the representation of individual versions of reality on screen may prove difficult to be embraced by all.

Notes

1. Hou and Tsai are still active in filmmaking today and often work abroad with funding from international sources. Edward Yang (Yang De-chang), born in 1947, died of cancer in June 2007.
2. During the Japanese colonial period, Taiwan had very limited contact with mainland China. When Taiwan was returned to the ROC in 1945, there was a lot of cultural and social tension built up between the Taiwanese and new immigrants from the mainland. Moreover, people on Taiwan looked forward to more political autonomy after 51 years of colonial rule. However, they were soon disappointed by the conduct of the new government, which was seen by the islanders as corrupt with very limited local knowledge. On the other hand, the islanders were often viewed by the mainlanders at the time as Japanese collaborators. The political distrust and social unrest finally erupted and led to the infamous February 28 Incident, commonly known as '2–28' in Taiwan, when a random incident occurred on the streets of Taipei in February 1947. As a result of '2–28', more than 10,000 people died and a generation of Taiwanese local elites was killed, arrested and wiped out. The aftermath of '2–28' was intensified political oppression in Taiwan, known as the 'White Terror' of the 1950s. For more details see Lai, Myers and Wei (1991), and Rawnsley and Rawnsley (2001, pp. 77–106).
3. The Hong Kong film studio, Shaw Brothers, produced *Love Eterne (Liang shan-bo yu zhu ying-tai)* in 1963 as an Anhui opera (huangmei diao) film. It is an ancient Chinese story about a quest for formal education by an intelligent young lady, Zhu Ying-tai, and her subsequent love affair with a young man in her class, Liang Shan-bo. The film became a sensation in Taiwan and triggered a wave of Mandarin-language *huangmei diao* films and historical dramas on the island (Kam and Aw, 2003, pp. 137–43). Further, the director of *Love Eterne*, Li Han-xiang, went to Taipei to set up his own company, Guo-lian, in December 1963, which also contributed to the rise of Mandarin-language film industry in Taiwan.
4. There are many reasons that can explain the fall of traditional Taiwanese-language cinema. For example, the unpredictable quality mentioned earlier, and the repetitive themes, subjects and styles, disappointed viewers. More importantly, the policies of the KMT government discouraged the Taiwanese-language film industry. Finally, when three national television stations were established in Taiwan in 1962, 1968 and 1971, many talents from the Taiwanese-language film industry moved to the television sector. So television quickly became the biggest challenge and competition for Taiwanese-language cinema. More details can be found in Lee (1998), Chinese Taipei Film Archive Oral History Working Group (1994) and Rawnsley (2008a).

5. Hou used to work as an assistant to Li Xing within the CMPC. When Hou was promoted to the position of director in 1980, his earlier films were heavily influenced by Li's techniques and aesthetics. See Frodon (1999, pp. 13–31) and Yeh (2001, pp. 61–76).
6. The four segments are arranged in the following order: (1) *Little Dragon Head (Xiao longtou)*, directed by Tao De-chen, the main character of which is an alienated primary schoolboy; (2) *Expectation (Zhiwang)*, directed by Edward Yang, is about a teenage girl and her first love; (3) *Leap Frog (Tiao wa)*, directed by Ke Yi-zheng, tells a story of a frustrated university student; and (4) *Announce Your Name (Baoshang ming lai)*, directed by Zhang Yi, is a comic portray of a young married couple living in modern Taipei.
7. Zhu Tian-wen was born in 1956 in Taipei and is an important novelist in Taiwan. She adapted her award-winning novel, *Growing Up*, as a screenplay with Hou Hsiao-hsien in 1983. Since then, she has scripted almost all of Hou's films. Therefore Zhu's literary style has played a significant role in forming and shaping the development of New Taiwan Cinema.
8. The arrangement of the three segments are as follows: (1) *The Sandwich Man*, by Hou Hsiao-hsien, which depicts the difficulties faced by an illiterate young father in finding means to support his family; (2) *Xiao-qi's Hat (Xiao-qi de nading maozi)*, by Zeng Zhuang-xiang, which tells the story of two struggling salesmen and their friendship with a damaged little girl; and (3) *The Taste of Apples (Pingguo de ziwei)*, by Wan Ren, which is a tragic comedy about a poor Taiwanese labourer who has a road accident. Normally this would mean a total disaster for the family, their breadwinner being unable to work. However, because the labourer is hit by an American diplomat, the family receives a fortune in compensation and the tragedy becomes ironically, in the eyes of their friends, extremely good luck.
9. The names are pronounced in Taiwanese.
10. The British Film Institute and the Taipei Representative Office in the UK co-organized a Tsai Ming-liang retrospective in London in November 2007. There were a couple of public sessions in which Tsai answered questions from the audience. I was invited to chair one such session on 16 November 2007. Tsai made a comment about the noise of 'silence' during this session.
11. Between 1982 and 1986, the total number of films produced in Taiwan was 417, among which between 32 and 58 can be counted as New Cinema, depending on how the term is defined (Lu, 1998, p. 277). After 1987, however, the total number of films produced annually in Taiwan sharply decreased to 43 in 1992, 28 in 1994 (Lu, 1998, p. 433) and around or below ten after 2000.

References

Berry, Chris (2005), 'Where Is the Love? Hyperbolic Realism and Indulgence in *Vive l'amour*', in Chris Berry and Feii Lu (eds), pp. 89–100.
Berry, Chris and Lu, Feii (eds) (2005), *Island on the Edge: Taiwan New Cinema and After*. Hong Kong: Hong Kong University Press.
Chang, Sung-sheng Yvonne (2005), '*The Terrorizer* and the Great Divide in Contemporary Taiwan's Cultural Development', in Chris Berry and Feii Lu (eds), pp. 13–25.
Chinese Taipei Film Archive Oral History Working Group (1994), *The Era of Taiwanese-Language Films (I)* (*Taiyu pian shidai [I]*). Taipei: Taipei Film Archive (in Complex Chinese).

Chiu, Kuei-fen (2007), 'The Vision of Taiwan New Documentary', in Darrell William Davis and Ru-shou Robert Chen (eds), *Cinema Taiwan: Politics, Popularity and State of the Arts*. London/New York: Routledge, pp. 17–32.

Frodon, Jean-Michel (1999), 'On a Mango Tree in Fengshan, Feeling the Time and Space' (*Zai Fengshan de mangguo shushang, ganjue shenchu de shijian he kongjian*), in Chinese Taipei Film Archive (ed.), *Hou Hsiao-hsien*. Taipei: Chinese Taipei Film Archive (in Complex Chinese), pp. 13–31.

Guest, Haden (2005), 'Reflections on the Screen: Hou Hsiao-hsien's *Dust in the Wind* and the Rhythms of the Taiwan New Cinema', in Chris Berry and Feii Lu (eds), pp. 27–37.

Kam, Tan See and Aw, Annette (2003), '*Love Eterne:* Almost a (Heterosexual) Love Story', in Chris Berry (ed.), *Chinese Films in Focus: 25 New Takes*. Hong Kong: Hong Kong University Press, pp. 137–43.

Lai, Tse-han, Myers, Ramon H. and Wei, Wou (1991), *A Tragic Beginning: The Taiwan Uprising of February 28, 1947*. Stanford: Stanford University Press.

Lee, Yungchuan (1998), *Taiwanese Cinema: An Illustrated History* (*Taiwan dianying yuelan*). Taipei: Yushan she (in Complex Chinese).

Lu, Feii (1998), *Taiwan Cinema: Politics, Economics and Aesthetics, 1949–1994* (*Taiwan dianying: Zhengzhi, jingji, meixue, 1949–1994*). Taipei: Yuanliu (in Complex Chinese).

Martin, Fran (2003), '*Vive l'amour:* Eloquent Emptiness', in Chris Berry (ed.), *Chinese Films in Focus: 25 New Takes*. Hong Kong: Hong Kong University Press, pp. 175–82.

Mizou and Liang, Xin-hua (eds) (1991), *The Death of Taiwan New Cinema* (*Xin dianying zhi si*). Taipei: Tangshan (in Complex Chinese).

Mizou and Liang, Xin-hua (eds) (1994), *Beyong/After New Cinema* (*Xin dianying zhi wai/hou*). Taipei: Tangshan (in Complex Chinese).

Rawnsley, Ming-yeh T (2008a), 'Chapter One: How to Preserve Taiwan Cinema Culture' (*Diyi zhang: Ruhe baocun Taiwan dianying wenhua de zichan zuotanhui*), *EW Cross Road* (*Dongxi jiaocha kou*), *China Times* Blog (in Complex Chinese), 4 January, available on http://blog.chinatimes.com/mingyeh/archive/2008/01/04/232356. html, accessed on 10 November 2008.

Rawnsley, Ming-yeh T. (2008b), 'Chapter Two: Interview with Miss Chen Qiuyan' (*Dier zhang: Chen Qiuyan xiaojie fangtan lu*), *EW Cross Road* (*Dongxi jiaocha kou*), *China Times* Blog (in Complex Chinese), 6 January, available on http://blog.chinatimes. com/mingyeh/archive/2008/01/06/232933.html, accessed on 10 November 2008.

Rawnsley, Gary and Rawnsley, Ming-yeh T. (2001), 'Reassess Chiang Kai-shek and the 28th February Incident', in *Issues and Studies*, November/December, pp.77–106.

Scott, Mandy and Tiun, Hak-khiam (2007), 'Mandarin-only to Mandarin-plus: Taiwan', in *Language Policy*, 6(53), pp. 53–72.

Yeh, Emilie Yueh-yu (2001), 'Politics and Poetics of Hou Hsiao Hsien's Films', in *Post Script*, 20(2/3), pp. 61–76.

Yeh, Emilie Yueh-yu (2007), 'The Road Home: Stylistic Renovations of Chinese Mandarin Classics', in Darrell William Davis and Ru-Shou Robert Chen (eds), *Cinema Taiwan: Politics, Popularity and State of the Arts*. London/New York: Routledge, pp. 203–16.

Yip, June (2004), *Envisioning Taiwan: Fiction, Cinema, and the Nation in the Cultural Imaginary*. Durham/London: Duke University Press.

8
Realism and National Identity in *Y tu mamá también*: An Audience Perspective

Armida de la Garza

When referring to cinema and its emancipatory potential, realism, like Plato's *pharmakon*, has signified both illness and cure, poison and medicine. On the one hand, realism is regarded as the main feature of so-called classical cinema, inherently conservative and thoroughly ideological, its main raison d'être being to reify and make a particular version of the status quo believable and to pass it out as 'reality' (Burch, 1990; MacCabe, 1974). On the other, realism has also been interpreted as a quest for truth and social justice, as in the positivist ethos that informs documentary (Zavattini, 1953). Even in the latter sense, however, the extent to which realism has served colonizing ends when used to investigate the 'truth' of the Other has also been noted, rendering the form profoundly suspicious (Chow, 2007, p. 150). For realism has been a Western form of representation, one that can be traced back to the invention of perspective in painting and that peaked with the secular worldview brought about by the Enlightenment. And like realism, the nation state too is a product of the Enlightenment, nationalism being, as it were, a secular replacement for the religious – that is enchanted or fantastic – worldview. In this way, realism, cinema and nation are inextricably linked and equally strained under the current decline of the Enlightenment paradigm.

This chapter looks at *Y tu mamá también* by Alfonso Cuarón (2001), a highly successful road movie with documentary features, to explore the ways in which realism, cinema and nation interact with each other in the present conditions of 'globalization' as experienced in Mexico. The chapter compares and contrasts various interpretations of the role of realism in this film put forward by critics and scholars and other discourses about it circulating in the media with actual ways of audience engagement with it.

First, I give a brief summary of the plot. *Y tu mamá también* tells the story of a journey undertaken by Mexican teenage friends Julio and Tenoch with Luisa, an older woman from Spain they are hoping to seduce, to an as-yet unexplored beach in the south of Mexico. The journey turns out to be a decisive one in many ways, as it becomes a search for and discovery of identity. The film features many of the generic conventions of both the teenpic and a (Mexican) version of the road movie. A realist mode is often adopted – for instance in the film's foregrounding of local landscape, use of local language, indigenous actors, spatial specificity, hinting at local issues such as military men stopping travellers on their way to the beach and so on. In this sense, this particular rendition of a Hollywood-style genre film with a national inflection is in line with strategies often employed by filmmakers in a post-national era, when attempting to produce a 'crossover' that will successfully address a national audience as well as one beyond geographical boundaries and maximize profits (D'Lugo, 2004, p. 113). Realist conventions as featured in *Y tu mamá* can also be understood, in the same context, as part of 'the tradition of international art cinema … [of realist depictions] that became prominent in the global film festival and art house circuit by the late 1990s' and which has been central to the creation of the 'global literacy' of an incipient 'cosmopolitan citizenship' (McGrath, 2007, p. 82; Ezra and Rowden, 2006, pp. 3–4).

However, the film also features the off voice of a narrator providing additional information on the characters and situations the camera encounters, albeit not necessarily providing narrative closure by suturing over narrative gaps as is often the case in genre film, but underscoring the partial nature or version of the 'reality' the spectator faces. The camera itself at times seems to go astray of characters and scenes in the story to dwell on other people and places around, as if switching to an observational documentary mode (Figure 8.1). This in-built reflexivity results in an ambiguous, but highly successful hybrid form. Apart from receiving numerous awards and prizes and becoming a sort of cult movie in the New Mexican Cinema known as *Buena Onda*, it has been the object of some of the most interesting

Figure 8.1   The plight of peasants and workers in the face of globalization, captured by a documentary-like stray camera: This is where the 'realism' of *Y tu mamá también* resides, according to many critics. Reproduced with kind permission from Producciones Anhelo, S.A. de C.V.

debate and discussion on national identity and realism on film in what is often called a 'global era'.[1]

To Andrea Noble, for instance, apart from bringing 'modernity into dialogue with tradition' in its road movie guise, *Y tu mamá* is mainly a film on (still not) seeing the Other. That is to say, on the failure of one part of Mexico, namely the one that gained the most out of the construction of the nation-state and the revolution, represented by Julio and Tenoch, to acknowledge and address the disadvantaged situation of those Others left out of the nationalist revolutionary project of hybridization and *mestizaje*, incarnated by Indians and peasants in the film, characters they encounter, but do not see. Ascribing what John Mraz would call an anti-picturesque stance to the representation of the latter in the film, or what Noble herself calls 'eschewing folkloric spectacle à la Eisenstein, Figueroa and Fernández et al.', she contends 'the trappings of conventional documentary style' deployed in the film serve the function of 'exposing the human cost of advancing neoliberal reform' (Mraz in León, 2002; Noble, 2005, p. 144). In this interpretation, despite the conservative strand of *Y tu mamá* as road movie-cum-teenpic, its social-realist side still allows it to make a progressive intervention about the effects of economic reform on class and ethnicity, and a reflection on the nation state in Mexico today.

By contrast, María Josefina Saldaña-Portillo brings a psychoanalytic theoretical framework to bear on *Y tu mamá*, which to her is mainly an allegory on (the loss of) sovereignty in Mexico today, underpinned by a 'stereotypical oedipal narrative solved positively against a backdrop of an exotic and primitive Mexico', far removed from the anti-folkloric gaze Noble identifies (Saldaña-Portillo, 2005, p. 752). The very names of the characters, Saldaña contends, elicit a reading in which Tenoch Iturbide is to be understood as a PRI-father, whose power and authority the people, that is Julio Zapata, desire, manifested, among many other ways, by Julio's very desire of sleeping with Tenoch's mother as well – a desire which gives the film its name, *Y tu mamá también* – and by a need of both Tenoch and Julio to re-enact *mestizaje* 'in this new, neoliberal Mexico' by sleeping with Mum Spain, that is, with Luisa Cortés (who plays a Spanish character in the film), in a bid to incorporate 'an ideal imperial whiteness', to neutralize intervention (Saldaña-Portillo, 2005, p. 761).[2] This, however, will prove impossible. Julio and Tenoch attempt to restore the consensus that prevailed – if often through co-optation or corruption – under the corporatist but stable regime of the PRI, with its modicum of social redistribution. However, economic forces unleashed by globalization in the shape of North American Free Trade Agreement (NAFTA) render this an impossible task. In the end, viewers learn that after that fateful journey in which they slept with each other as well as with Luisa, their friendship ended and they never saw each other again. In this sense, 'realist' said of *Y tu mamá también* would have mimetic connotations, referring to its purported ability to render an accurate depiction of a historical moment in Mexico, a moment in which the transformative forces of capitalism that first fostered the nation state challenge it as it increasingly subordinates political – and aesthetic – autonomy to economic performance. In the words of Leonardo García Tsao, the film was successful, among other reasons, because of 'its ability to capture the Zeitgeist' (García-Tsao in Wood, 2006, p. 90). And, apart from plot, this is obvious in the very way the film was produced: outside the realm of Instituto Mexicano de Cinematografía (IMCINE), and of state-financed film production, and fully funded by private sources in Mexico (Smith, 2003).

Nuala Finnegan also sees *Y tu mamá* as being mainly about national identity, but is a lot more concerned with the way it is brought about structurally, by the interaction between the global and the local as played out in the film. Rather than providing a reading concentrating just on Mexican history, she points to the ways realism serves to situate Mexico in a global context, as with references made by the narrator to globalization, which will be the topic of the president's speech the following day; the juxtaposition of Tenoch and Julio's Mexican Spanish to that of Luisa's from Spain; and the diegetic, hybrid soundtrack (Finnegan, 2007, p. 32). She also takes the multiple references made to death, perhaps part of the realism of the mise-en-scène, to be a universal topic but also one deeply rooted in a specifically Mexican cultural understanding.

In short, all three accounts outlined above, and many others in the media in Mexico and abroad, acknowledge both a generic and a social-realist strand in *Y tu mamá también*, and generally conclude it is because of the latter that, even if in a rather lukewarm manner, the film can nonetheless be inscribed within the progressive, liberating side of the realist tradition of cinematic representation. Progressive meanings also continue to be attached to the film by means of the star persona of Gael García Bernal, who claimed Julio Zapata to be the character he most identifies with from among all those he has performed, in an interview that also foregrounds his credentials as a man who taught Huichol Indians to read and write, took part in the peaceful uprising in Chiapas in 1994 and took a public stance against the invasion of Iraq (Sullivan, 2006). As a producer, García Bernal continues to stand for indigenous causes, financing *Cochochi* (2007), a film by Laura Guzmán and Israel Cárdenas on the life of two brothers from the Tarahumara region in the north of Mexico (MacNab, 2007).

However, whatever progressive features the film would apparently derive and exhibit from its realism, as Julia Hallam and Margaret Marshment have persuasively argued, the main potentially emancipatory value of realism in popular film from a cognitivist perspective lies in its ability to cue spectators into questioning the status quo, that is, into altering received schemata for making sense of their social world. 'Our engagement with popular film is predicated on our experience of the world, but films themselves can alter the ways in which we understand and experience the world, potentially introducing alternative social and moral schemata' (Hallam and Marshment,

2000, p. 130). Was this the case with the young Mexican audiences *Y tu mamá también* was largely aimed at?

From interviews I conducted in Mexico in August 2007, it would certainly seem so.[3] Although a broad range of views was expressed about whether they had found the film, in their words, 'actually really very good', 'refreshing, innovative' and 'a pleasant surprise', or 'cheap, vulgar, and misleading to foreign audiences as to what Mexico is really like', there seemed to be consensus that the film had succeeded in cuing interrogation of what it means to be Mexican for a new generation, one growing up in the aftermath of NAFTA. The questioning, however, had nothing to do with the social issues that academic and media discourses had consistently ascribed to *Y tu mamá* as main concerns: the fate of peasants and indigenous populations both in Mexico and when forced into migration, the rupture of the – however minimal – welfare state anchored in the nationalist-revolutionary consensus that emerged from the revolution, the human cost of globalization and the imposition of a neoliberal worldview in Latin America. The only, overriding concern mentioned by all interviewees had to do with representations of gender and sexuality, the strand of the film that is taken to be the most formulaic and conservative in terms of its deployment of realist conventions but which was, in most cases, the feature identified by interviewees as 'very realistic'.[4]

Although many interviewees interpreted the homoerotic relation between Julio and Tenoch negatively, and indeed quoted this ending as the main cause of disappointment with the film, others viewed it as simply the product of the excess that otherwise characterized Julio and Tenoch's lives – an excess that on the other hand they regarded as 'natural' to the social class and age group the characters represent and in that sense not as 'excessive' as in a Bataillesque reading of it, signifying a surplus that would challenge the status quo. More interestingly, however, many more thought in fact the main point of the film was an exploration of the boundaries that sort, classify and seek to regulate relations of love and sexual desire, particularly an exploration of how and when these boundaries are raised in relationships between men (Figure 8.2). Many of the interviewees seemed to have derived a Foucauldian concept of homosexuality from the film, namely as a category not in the realm of 'essence' or being, and as such a deviation from the norm that allows 'heterosexuality' to hold together, but in the realm of doing, that is, in the realm of contingency, and from that point of view a position to be taken – or not – in a more fluid continuum of sexual behaviour (Foucault, 1991, p. 219). This was expressed in positive terms, as if the viewing of this particular behaviour on the part of the social – and Mexican – types Julio and Tenoch are supposed to represent had been interpreted as a liberatory experience. In one of the interviewee's own words:

> This story about the buddies, this sort of secret society they belong to, they are three or four guys these so-called *charolastras* and I think that is

Figure 8.2 Probing the boundaries of masculinity in contemporary Mexico: This is the most realist feature of *Y tu mamá también*, according to interviewees. Reproduced with kind permission from Producciones Anhelo, S.A. de C.V.

fine because I have a group of friends just like that, who are that close ... [others giggle] yes, they are close and I think that this matter of sex more than homosexuality, this communion that they have, this friendship that goes beyond body matters and brings them together to become one [is the most important aspect of the film, what makes it good].[5]

Moreover, when another interviewee expressed her disappointment with the film, saying she had been 'let down' by 'everything that went on, and just for them to turn out to be gay in the end', another male participant replied 'they were not gay'.[6] Yet another interviewee identified as the 'serious' or 'realistic' aspect of the film 'the feelings these two friends have for each other. That is the serious side, because *often you cannot tell the boundaries* of friendship'. Another thought the 'realistic' side was 'the friendship that is broken'.[7] From the discussion that ensued it was evident that the film had succeeded into cueing viewers to interrogate the meaning of categories such as 'homosexual' and 'heterosexual', and allowed for a more nuanced, ambiguous understanding of sexuality as a broad spectrum of multiple possible positions.

Moreover, drawing on Richard Dyer's seminal work on stars, in particular his argument that 'stars matter because they act out aspects of life that matter to us; and performers get to be stars when what they act out matters to enough people', I argue that it is in fact this alternative Mexican masculinity put forward by Gael García Bernal as Julio and Diego Luna as Tenoch that paved their way for becoming 'stars' (Dyer, 2005 [1986], p. 17).[8] Interviewees repeatedly identified García Bernal's ability to perform a variety of roles in which a contestation of received sexual behaviour took place as the main reason they admired him, among these roles his character as a lascivious priest in *The Crime of Father Amaro* (*El crimen del Padre Amaro*, Carlos Carrera, 2002) and a transvestite in *Bad Education* (*La mala educación*, Pedro Almodóvar, 2004). They also explicitly contrasted García Bernal with that earlier icon of Mexican masculinity enshrined in the national cinema, Pedro Infante, stating that whereas Infante earned his reputation and fame 'by always playing the same character, and playing himself at that', García Bernal had earned it by having no fixed identity, by being someone different every time, while always being a version of a male they read as 'Mexican'. That a 'commutation test' rendered Infante completely inconceivable in any of García Bernal's roles, but that both were acknowledged as 'very Mexican' by interviewees, is telling indeed about the extent to which constructions of gender have changed within the broader discourse of the nation and national belonging (Thompson, 1991, pp. 184–5).[9] Significantly, García Bernal's star image has been kept open to both female and male fan engagement with it, and although his career path has also been remarkably transnational so far, interpreting Spanish, Argentine and even Chicano characters, interviewees consistently cast him as 'Mexican' during the interviews.

Indeed, it is definitely true that *Y tu mamá* was made and shown in Mexico at a time when there was intense social debate on gender and sexuality issues, which must also be regarded as essentially a part of the upheaval caused by processes of 'globalization' or, as more accurately put by David Harvey, by the deep social and economic changes the passage from 'mass industrial production' to 'globalized regimes of flexible accumulation' has brought about, as these have entailed 'the emergence of entirely new sectors of production … new markets and, above all, greatly intensified rates of commercial … innovation' (Harvey, 1989, pp. 8–9). Some of these new markets include segments of the population previously marginalized on account of their sexual orientation, now re-conceptualized as primarily potential consumers, and all the more because they can be reached transnationally, as a niche market.[10] In 2000 the 'Ley de Sociedades de Convivencia' (law regulating co-habitation) was proposed for the first time, aiming at legalizing homosexual unions by granting them the same status ascribed to marriage. The law was passed in Mexico City only on 10 November 2006. Abortion too was legalized on 7 May 2007, and divorce is allowed on the grounds of domestic violence as of 21 February 2007.[11] However, all these regulations have been narrowly passed, as the conservative National Action Party (PAN) that won the general election in 2000 and 2006 with strong support from Catholic constituents has continued to oppose them. It nevertheless seems conservative positions have been losing ground, despite relative political victories.

Overall, the characters of Julio and Tenoch are best understood within a domestic social context in which the near-privatization of the film industry, the proliferation of the multiplex in the more privileged neighbourhoods of cities and price liberalization of tickets promoted a reconfiguration of the audience, who became decidedly more middle class, better educated and younger. On the other hand, the film must also be understood within the framework of trends to fragmentation and heterogenization within national boundaries that have characterized flexible accumulation, and moves towards the articulation of new markets have resulted in the – relative – em-powerment of a hitherto marginalized segment of the population.

In fact, returning to specific issues of realism, there are several similarities between the way this was used in Black Urban Cinema in the USA in the 1990s, 'one of those moments in the history of film when realism has been deployed progressively' as regards representation of a marginalized segment of the population – if on ethnic grounds – and the way it was *interpreted* by interviewed audiences of *Y tu mamá también* regardless of inherent features of the film itself (Hallam and Marshment, 2000, p. 52). It is true that, in both, 'the use of linear narrative time ... coincides with a coming of age thematic ... creating an overlap' as if both the characters and the nation were coming of age (Hallam and Marshment, 2000, p. 52). In both, too, the stories present, realistically, 'characters that change with the enfolding of the story line' (Diawara, 2000, p. 255). And like the New Black Urban Cinema, which was regarded as 'realist' by young audiences on account of its theme – that is, Black males' initiation into manhood – and its 'use of hip hop culture, which [was] the new Black youth culture', *Y tu mamá* too was described as realist on very similar grounds: 'The action takes place in Mexico and if you are Mexican it rings familiar when you go to see it, it brings back memories from our own experience, that is what made it popular here in Mexico, that all of us young people found some ground to identify ourselves with.'[12]

Further, Manthia Diawara has credited Black Urban Cinema with modifying the 'grammar book' provided by *The Birth of a Nation* (D. W. Griffith, 1915) for the cinematic representation of Black people. Before the Black Urban Cinema of the 1990s, Black people appeared on Hollywood screens as 'a problem' who existed 'primarily for White spectators whose comfort and understanding the films must seek ... [T]here are no simple stories about Black people ... without reference to the White world' (Diawara, 2000, p. 236). It would be somewhat exaggerated to describe *Y tu mamá* in the same terms for gender, but representations that called into question essentialist notions of sexuality were all but absent from Mexican mainstream cinema before this film.[13] Representations of gender that sought to portray the nation as a unified whole occurred within the framework of the family as a metaphor for the nation and were always hierarchical and mostly patriarchal, even if by the 1940s and 1950s some films successfully threatened the patriarchal ideology that was by then 'so contradictory that it could no longer manage to exert full control' (Hershfield, 2001, p. 151).

Be that as it may, what is clear is that *Y tu mamá también* was definitely a timely intervention on several debates about social change in Mexico, using realism in more than one way to address young audiences domestically and internationally, and which seems to have allowed for a slightly more progressive reading than would have seemed the case, despite – indeed, apparently thanks to – innovations made to its largely formulaic structure.

Notes

1. *Y tu mamá también* won the award for best screenplay in Venice in 2001, and Gael García Bernal and Diego Luna (actors in the film) were granted the Marcello Mastroianni award there. In addition, the film was nominated for the Golden Lion at Venice that year, and for both the Oscar and BAFTA in 2003. It also won the critics prize in Boston, Los Angeles and Australia (2002), Chicago, Florida and London (2003). The Fipresci prize in Havana in 2001 went to Alfonso Cuarón for 'the good melange of the comic and the tragic expressed in a very sophisticated style' (http://www.imdb.com/title/tt0245574/). In Mexico, it was awarded a special *Diosa de Plata* in 2002, an award granted each year by the Film Journalists Association in Mexico.

2. PRI stands for Partido Revolucionario Institucional (Institutional Revolutionary Party). Agustín de Iturbide ruled Mexico from 21 July 1822 to 19 March 1823. Emiliano Zapata was a revolutionary peasant leader fighting for 'land and freedom'.

3. This chapter is based on interviews conducted in August 2007 among students in higher education in Mexico as part of the research for a project entitled *Transnational Cinema in Globalizing Societies*, on audience reception of transnational films, funded by the University of Nottingham, UK.

4. Not that much academic and media discourse had not dealt with these aspects of the film as well. Baer and Long, for example, argued that the 'social realist interstitial scenes' and the male voiceover impose a sort of authoritarian narrative closure on the liberatory potential of the gender and sexual – homoerotic and liberated feminine – narrative that the central plot mainly addresses (Baer and Long, 2004, pp. 150–68). Others have also seen a conservative twist in Luisa's foreign status, ostensibly not representing a Mexican woman, and regard her death at the end of the film as punishment for her liberation. These examples come from work as yet unpublished: they were presentations I heard during the New Latin American Cinemas conference held at Leeds, UK, in June 2005.

5. *'Esta historia como de los cuates, esta como logia que tienen, que son como tres o cuatro los charolastras, creo que está bien porque así tengo un grupo de amigos así de cercanos* (others giggle) ... *si son cercanos, y yo siento que esta cuestión del sexo y eso mas que la homosexualidad, esta comunión que tienen, esta amistad que supera la cuestión corpórea y los lleva a ser uno mismo a ellos* [is the most important aspect of the film, what makes it good]' (EA, male, age 20). All translations are mine.

6. *'Todos los acontecimientos que desencadenan y que ellos resulta que eran gays, no'*, *'No eran gays'* (C, female, age 20 and A, male, age 22 respectively).

7. *'Los sentimientos que tienen estos dos amigos. Ese es el lado serio porque o sea, muchas veces no sabes cual es la barrera entre amigos o si sientes algo mas por ese amigo'* and *'la amistad que se rompe'*. (TC and S respectively, both female, age 20, emphasis mine).

8. Further, Dyer also argues that 'stars function in terms of their assertion of the irreducible core of inner individual reality', which also points at a crucial way in which realism is used in *Y tu mamá* through García Bernal star persona (Dyer, 2005 [1986], p. 10).

9. Indeed, it is no coincidence that at this time of reconfiguration of gender roles as part of the broader social reconfiguration of the national as – fragmented – markets, García Bernal's ability to impersonate was valued by respondents. As Barry King has argued, there is an authorial dimension to impersonation as opposed to personification or casting, as the latter relies more on mimesis or direct resemblance (King, 1991, p. 176). It is therefore more reassuring to believe in a kernel of truth that holds the star persona of García Bernal together, the ultimate – presumably *real* – source of all impersonations and the guarantor of a purported identity existing beyond performance, than on a star in which persona and characters overlap, as was the case with Infante.

10. B. Ruby Rich quotes the New Homosexual Film festivals in Mexico and Brazil as 'powerful seedbeds for local production in this regard' (Rich, 2006, p. 621).

11. Statistics also show profound changes taking place in marriage and divorce in Mexico: whereas in 1970 there were only three divorces for every 100 marriages, in 2005 there were 12 on average. And whereas 51 per cent of women married between the ages of 15–19 in 1950 the rate today is 26 per cent (INEGI, 2007).

12. '*Sucede en México y tú como mexicana vas y la ves y dices: "me acuerdo cuando no sé qué", no, entonces eso es lo que hizo que aquí en México gustara, no, que todos los chavos nos identificamos con ciertas cosas*' (TC, female student, age 20).

13. Even in the art realm, films have tended to put forward representations of either homoerotic desire, as in *Midaq Alley (El callejón de los milagros*, Jorge Fons, 1995), or transvestism, as in *The Place without Limits (El lugar sin límites*, Arturo Ripstein, 1978), or of homosexuality, as in almost the entirety of the work of Jaime Humberto Hermosillo. However, far from being interrogated, these categories were here reified.

References

Acevedo Muñoz, Ernesto (2004), 'Sex, Class and Mexico in Alfonso Cuarón's *Y tu mamá también*', in *Film and History*, 34(1), pp. 39–48.

Baer, Hester and Long, Ryan Fred (2004), 'Transnational Cinema and the Mexican State in Alfonso Cuarón's *Y tu mamá también*', in *South Central Review*, 21(3), Fall, pp. 150–68.

Burch, Noël (1990), *Life to Those Shadows*. Berkeley: University of California Press.

Chow, Rey (2007), *Sentimental Fabulations: Contemporary Chinese Films*. New York: Columbia University Press.

D'Lugo, Marvin (2004), 'Authorship, Globalization and the New Identity of Latin American Cinema: From the Mexican "ranchera" to Argentinian "exile"', in Anthony Guneratne and Wimal Dissanayake (eds), *Rethinking Third Cinema*. London: Routledge, pp. 103–25.

Diawara, Manthia (2000), 'Black American Cinema: The New Realism', in Robert Stam and Toby Miller (eds), *Film and Theory: An Anthology*. Oxford: Blackwell, pp. 236–56.

Dyer, Richard (2005 [1986]), *Heavenly Bodies*. London: Routledge.

Ezra, Elizabeth and Rowden, Terry (eds) (2006), *Transnational Cinema: The Film Reader*. London: Routledge.

Finnegan, Nuala (2007), 'So What's Mexico Really Like? Framing the Local, Negotiating the Global, in Alfonso Cuarón's "Y tu mamá también"', in Deborah Shaw (ed.), *Contemporary Latin American Cinema: Breaking into the Global Market*. New York: Rowman and Littlefield, pp. 29–50.

Foucault, Michel (1991), 'Complete and Austere Institutions', in Paul Rabinow (ed.), *The Foucault Reader*. London: Penguin, pp. 214–25.

Hallam, Julia and Marshment, Margaret (2000), *Realism and Popular Cinema*. Manchester: Manchester University Press.

Harvey, David (1989), *The Condition of Postmodernity*. Oxford: Blackwell.

Hershfield, Joanne (2001), 'La Mitad de la Pantalla: La Mujer en el Cine Mexicano de la Época de Oro', in Gustavo García and David R. Maciel (eds), *El Cine Mexicano a través de la crítica*. México: UNAM/ Instituto Mexicano de Cinematografía/ Universidad de Ciudad Juárez, pp. 127–51.

Instituto Nacional de Estadística, Geografía e Informática, INEGI website http://www. cuentame.inegi.gob.mx/poblacion/myd.aspx?tema=P, accessed on 6 December 2007.

King, Barry (1991), 'Articulating Stardom', in Christine Gledhill (ed.), *Stardom: Industry of Desire*. London: Routledge, pp. 167–82.

León, José (2002), 'John Mraz disertará sobre fotografía pintoresca y anti-pintoresca', in the Consejo Nacional para la Cultura y las Artes (CONACULTA) in Mexico, website http://www.conaculta.gob.mx/saladeprensa/2002/28may/johnmraz.htm, accessed on 6 December 2007.

MacCabe, Colin (1974), 'Realism and the Cinema: Notes on Some Brechtian Thesis', in *Screen*, 15(2), pp. 12–33.

MacNab, Geoffrey (2007), 'Why Latin Filmmaking is Ready to Set the Field Alight', in *The Independent*, 8 June. Available on http://www.independent.co.uk/ arts-entertainment/films/features/why-latin-filmaking-is-ready-to-set-the-field-alight-452160.html, accessed on 10 September 2008.

McGrath, Jason (2007), 'The Independent Cinema of Jia Zhangke: From Postsocialist Realism to a Transnational Aesthetic', in Zhen Zhang (ed.), *The Urban Generation*. London: Duke, pp. 81–114.

Noble, Andrea (2005), *Mexican National Cinema*. London: Routledge.

Rich, Ruby B. (2006), 'The New Homosexual Film Festivals', in *GLQ: A Journal of Lesbian and Gay Studies*, 21(4), pp. 620–5.

Saldaña-Portillo, María Josefina (2005), 'In the Shadow of NAFTA: *Y tu mamá también* Revisits the National Allegory of Mexican Sovereignty', in *American Quarterly*, 57(3), pp. 751–77.

Smith, Paul Julian (2003), 'Transatlantic Traffic in Recent Mexican Films', in *Journal of Latin American Cultural Studies*, 12(3), pp. 389–400.

Sullivan, Chris (2006), 'Gael García Bernal: Journeys of the Soul', in *The Independent*, May 8. Available on http://www.independent.co.uk/arts-entertainment/films/features/ gael-garcia-bernal-journeys-of-the-soul-477253.html, accessed on 10 September 2008.

Thompson, John O. (1991), 'Screen Acting and the Commutation Test', in Christine Gledhill (ed.), *Stardom: Industry of Desire*. London: Routledge, pp. 183–97.

Wood, Jason (2006), *The Faber Book of Mexican Cinema*. London: Faber and Faber.

Zavattini, Cesare (1953), 'Some Ideas on the Cinema', in *Sight and Sound*, 23(2), pp. 64–9.

9

A Journey through Time: Alexander Sokurov's *Russian Ark* and Theories of Mimesis

Vlad Strukov

In the mimeticist inheritance, film as a form of art stands out as a language of time. Temporal coherence and congruity construct − in a schematized structure − a response to a reality and a production of an imaginary world. It would be misleading to evaluate the quality of vraisemblance in a world-reflecting schema and maintain mimesis as a single, fixed reading of art and aesthetics. Rather mimesis presents a quest for meaning, whether that meaning is the issue of discovery or invention, or − most plausibly − both. Alexander Sokurov's *Russian Ark* (*Russkii kovcheg*, 2002) is a universally acclaimed production that questions interpretations based on mimetic dogmas, transcends film genre boundaries and celebrates illusion, visions and dreams. It is a cinematic text that draws on the whole material fabric of culture, including its visual and musical artefacts.

This chapter has two principal, overlapping aims. The first is to analyse Sokurov's unique mode of filmmaking. The second is to revisit some notions of mimesis and realism, which I will re-evaluate in the order relevant to my examination of *Russian Ark*. An underlying concern of my entire analysis is to demonstrate a complex − and sometimes paradoxical − relationship between mimetic art and the possibilities put forward by new digital forms of film production. To achieve my aims, I locate the film in the Russian cinematic tradition and identify the film's relation to Russian history and art, which enables me to examine *Russian Ark* as Sokurov's tour de force that transcends traditional perceptions of time and space. I use the myth of Orpheus to discuss the film's narrative structure, its cultural emblems and Sokurov's construction of the gaze. I enhance my argument by referring to theories of realistic representation, most notably Auerbach's theory of mimesis and Bazin's concepts of the long take.

In fact *Russian Ark* was filmed as one continuous take lasting 87 minutes, in a total runtime of 99 minutes including credits, which was possible thanks to a specially designed digital camera.[1] The camera glides through innumerable rooms of the State Hermitage in St Petersburg, presenting numerous extras in the museum's opulent interiors; the virtuoso camera work[2] creates a sense of perpetual mobility as the movement through the museum traverses 300 years of Russian history. Sokurov's film is grandiose in terms of the time extent covered by the narrative, its staging, performance and thematic concerns. The chosen location, subject matter and mise-en-scène allude to Sergei Eisenstein's *October* (*Oktiabr'*, 1927), which features a scene, 'The Storming of the Winter Palace', based on Nikolai Evreinov's re-enactments, on Dvortsovaia Square in 1918 and subsequent years, of the scene (invented by him) of the taking of the palace, a mass spectacle that involved at least 8000 participants and attracted over 100,000 spectators. The allusion provides evidence of both *October* and *Russian Ark* being inspired by theatre and presenting diluted versions of historical events, as a result in the former of the ideological necessities of the time and, in the latter, of the director's creative vision of Russia's past.

In Russia, Sokurov's film was premiered in St Petersburg in May 2003 as part of the festive celebrations of the city's 300th anniversary. Set entirely in the Hermitage museum, the film depicts modern Russia as a result of the revolutionary reforms introduced by Peter the Great (1672–1725), whereby the city he founded functions as a powerful symbol of Russia's conscious engagement with European thought, technology and artistic traditions. The film ends with the impressive scene of an aristocratic ball, after which the characters and the camera exit the museum. With this ending, the director says farewell to Europe in the year 1913 and signifies his detachment from the ensuing Russian history. *Russian Ark* presents the splendorous artefacts produced in or acquired by the Russian Empire before its demise and subsequent annihilation by Bolshevism in 1917. The Hermitage harbours vast collections of European, Russian and Asian art; however, Sokurov ignores the last collection, anchoring Russia's cultural identity within the European context. Thus, by letting the camera and the film's characters engage with the museum, the director excogitates over (Russian) history and the nature of time in relation to cultural objects, value and dialectics of vision.

After two days of preparation, the filming of *Russian Ark* took place on 23 December 2001, one of the shortest days in the year, with just over five hours of daylight. By choosing the time around the winter solstice as the temporal setting for his film, Sokurov suggests the transitory nature of the historical period brought into light and surrounded by the darkness of the pre-Petrine times and Soviet era. Most of the action takes place inside the museum: at times, when characters briefly leave the Hermitage, the camera captures the fading light of the Russian winter and collates it with the radiant lighting of the Winter Palace. The characters swiftly move from one room to another and from one historical period to a new one, with contemporary artists acting as figures from the Russian past, often distorting the chronology of historical events. Thus Sokurov explores and contrasts natural and artificial light, the exterior and interior of the museum, Western and Russian art, past and present, history and its reconstruction, the eternal and the ephemeral, art and reality. Similarly, the genre of *Russian Ark* blurs the boundaries between feature and documentary film, that is between the highly stylized performances and the production of a visual document of the events, between the subjective reading of history and the objective recording of such vision. With documentary generally being a problematic and often contested film genre, in *Russian Ark* Sokurov continues exploring the possibilities of the form and the use of the medium for its production, a trajectory that goes back to his earlier works, such as *Day of Eclipse* (*Dni Zatmeniia*, 1988) and *Moscow Elegy* (*Moskovskaia elegiia*, 1986–8), which maintained the contrast between genres, and later films, such as *Dolce ...* (*Nezhno*, 1999), in which this contrast fades.

Over 800 actors took part in the production of *Russian Ark*, creating an epic narrative that parallels Sergei Bondarchuk's monumental *War and Peace* (1968) and Andrei Tarkovsky's *Andrei Rublev* (1969). The actors' performances are carefully orchestrated as they simultaneously take place in different stately rooms of the Hermitage, constructing a concurring flow of action and, consequently, a synchronous perception of history. Individual scenes are often devoted to different historical periods and Russian prominent cultural figures; these scenes appear as discrete unrelated entities in the film's representational and narrative paradigm (Figure 9.1). The camera sails through the Palace as a means to connect disparate subplots and scenes, and conveys an overall sense of continuity. The museum – an assemblage of objects from different epochs taken out of their context – is used as a metaphor for the arbitrariness of time as a cultural construct. The actors' performances do not invoke the past to deploy its 'presentness' but rather to problematize it and to put forward the indeterminate nature of historical knowledge and execute the lucid nature of time. The artificiality of time subsisting on re-enacted actions is further demystified by the camera

Figure 9.1   Russian Ark: The camera enters the royal dining room where the family of Tsar Nicholas II are having a meal.

work, which registers events and occurrences in their actuality. Thus the film hints at André Bazin's understanding of the long take as a technique of film par excellence thanks to its ability to restore 'a fundamental quality of reality – its continuity' (Bazin, 1971, p. 28).

Russian Ark's complex temporal organization relies on a fusion of two styles of representation, as described by Erich Auerbach in his famous comparative study of the *Odyssey* and the Old Testament in the introductory chapter of his *Mimesis: The Representation of Reality in Western Literature*:

> On the one hand, fully externalised description, uniform illumination, uninterrupted connection, free expression, all events in the foreground ... on the other hand, certain parts brought in high relief, others left obscure, abruptness, suggestive influence of the unexpressed, 'background' quality.
>
> (Auerbach, 1953, p. 23)

Auerbach draws conclusions about the relationship between literature and the real world by showing the operation of mimesis as a form of historicism. In his view, the way reality is represented in the literature of various periods is intimately bound to social and intellectual conventions of the time in which they were written. *Russian Ark* evokes this argument on the thematic level by referencing Noah's ark and, on the formal level, by presenting an Odyssey-like journey. Indeed, both the film and the Greek epic depend on the non-linear plot, with the action beginning in the middle of the plot. That is, in *Russian Ark* the history of the Hermitage, St Petersburg and the Russian Empire is told in a non-sequential manner with the narrative point of entry being somewhere in the middle of the 19th century. Furthermore, as in the *Odyssey*, future events are described through flashbacks; for example, in the film, 18th century characters enter a room that depicts the events of World War II. In the world of the characters this is a leap forward; however, the viewer perceives this temporal anomaly as a flashback because both periods belong to the historical past. Finally, the film uses the metaphor of the ship and the portrayal of human – and national – existence as wandering across the sea of life, as they appear in the Biblical and Greek myths.

Auerbach's concept of mimesis is based on historical perspectivism. Bazin, in his understanding of cinematic realism, resorts to Plato, according to whom mimesis is as a way of showing through external action, rather than telling, a character's thoughts or inner processes. In the *Republic*, Plato's Socrates starts from the premise that all poetry is diegesis (narrative in a logical rather than formal sense), which differs from a narrative through mimesis which contains an element of time (Plato, 1953, p. 202). Furthermore, Plato's approach to the psychology of mimesis is grounded on the assumption that there is continuity, even equivalence and congruity, between a subject's relation to things in the real world and their representation in mimetic art. Thus Bazin's concept of realism rests on the assumption of the continuity of time and contingency of space articulated in the notion of the long take, which Bazin considers the cinematic device par excellence.

Paradoxically, the convention of the long take and the formally intact time of *Russian Ark* invariably draw attention to the organization behind the film. The steady flow of imagery, the constant dislocations, the sudden and unexplained appearances, and other disturbances that I will explore later on, force the spectator to notice the methodical marshalling and choreographing of events within the time frame of the film. The camera – meant to record the passing of time effortlessly – frequently stumbles upon the elements of a vast performance which disrupt the natural flow of the events. For example, in a scene towards the end, the camera enters the great hall of the Winter Palace where a full orchestra and hundreds of extras in spectacular period costumes await the camera's arrival. The ball goes into full swing once the camera has been favourably positioned to record it. The scene is a re-creation of a famous painting by Dmitrii Kardovskii, which itself is a re-construction of an historical event, a ball that took place in February 1913 to celebrate the tsar's prolonged visit to the capital. *Russian Ark* effects two simultaneous moves as it reinstalls historical contexts and moves away from a single, essentialized, transcendent concept of historicity. Thus, rather than intercepting the momentum of reality, *Russian Ark* deliberately engrosses a wealth of cultural allusions and second-tier referents held in the cultural memory of the nation.

This scene in *Russian* Ark gains extra symbolic meaning because it is Valery Gergiev – artistic director of the Mariinsky theatre from 1988 to 2005 and the current principal conductor of the London Symphony Orchestra – who conducts the orchestra. Among the Russian intelligentsia, he is something of a national hero for having kept alive the Mariinsky theatre after the dissolution of the USSR and for having maintained both the Imperial and Soviet traditions. Under his leadership, the Mariinsky 'has become one of the most celebrated – and recorded – opera companies in the world' (Ross, 1998, p. 86). Whereas in the Russian viewer's mind Gergiev functions as a symbolic link between the musical masters of the past and present, and a significant marker of national pride, his presence in *Russian Ark* deconstructs the carefully assembled illusion of historical reality. The use of the star disturbs the otherwise coherent sense of reality produced by non-professional actors, an advantage that – for Bazin – constitutes one of the features of realism in film (Bazin, 1971, pp. 22–3).

In addition to spatial and performance disturbances, *Russian Ark* uses temporal distortions to convey the director's complex understanding of history, which centres upon the notion of simultaneity of historical processes. For instance, in the scene in the coronation room, characters long deceased converse with the Hermitage's current director, Mikhail Piotrovskii, about the problems of conservation. Their discussion – the possibility of reconstructing and reproducing aging artefacts – informs Sokurov's agenda for the cinematic reconstruction of Russia's cultural past. Furthermore, Sokurov eschews temporal linearity by allowing some characters, for example Catherine the Great (1729–96), the German-born princess who began the Hermitage collection in the 1760s, to appear as young and old within the space of a few minutes, rupturing the chronology of the Romanov dynasty (Figure 9.2). To some extent, such shifts in time and narrative distortions are inevitable because the director cannot rely on the usual filmic signifiers of a cut, fade or dissolve. As a result, the chosen cinematic techniques of *Russian Ark* make apparent the edifice of the film's constructed reality.

The disorienting effect of the featured reality is supported by the reactions of the two protagonists. *Russian Ark's* grand tour through the Hermitage is presided over by a narrator who remains unseen to the spectator as well as to all the film's characters, with the exception of one, an eccentric man in a black costume (Sergei Dreiden) who later plausibly turns out to be Marquis de Custine (1790–1857), a French diplomat who is best known for his acidulous account of his travels through the Russian Empire in 1839. The narrator and de Custine are plunged into a different historical reality; their contemplative conversations and dreamy journey through the Hermitage establish the film's formal structure and thematics with the central idea of the museum as a national treasure and symbol of cultural heritage.

The identity of the narrator is never exposed; neither through dialogue nor through action is his persona demystified. Afraid to reveal its imminent presence – and the narrator's fictional status – the camera carefully avoids meeting any reflecting surfaces, which is not an easy task in a museum filled with glass, mirrors and various shiny objects. As the film starts, the narrator mumbles about an accident and the informed spectator recognizes the voice of Alexander Sokurov. This disembodied voice, the director's alter

Figure 9.2   Russian Ark: Catherine the Great and her companion stroll through the gardens of the Winter Palace.

ego, becomes the spectator's guide through the Hermitage and Russian history. Occasionally, the narrator reveals his views on Russian culture; for example, he adheres to the ideas of the Romanov dynasty as the vehicle of propagation of Enlightenment in Russia. He refers to the Bolshevik Revolution as a catastrophe which put an end to a specific aesthetic and spiritual tradition. So from an objective observer the narrator turns into a fully personified subjective character (I will refer to him as the museum visitor from now on) (Figure 9.3).

In this respect, the cinematographic narrative and the possibilities of the technique consummate *Russian Ark* – and, in general, cinema, according to Bazin – as an art form that is similar to the novel (Bazin, 1971, p. 26). To compare, in his theory of the novel, Bakhtin sustains the idea of an utterance being more than an element that helps the author represent reality but rather an object of representation itself. In his 1937–8 essay 'Forms of Time and of the Chronotope in the Novel', Bakhtin demonstrates how Dostoevsky's literary space – and, I propose, Sokurov's cinematic space, too – is governed by what he calls a 'chronotope of the threshold and of other related figures: the staircase, the corridor, the front hall'. It is a chronotope of crisis, of a break in life and in history; it is a time of the instantaneous and 'it has no duration and falls out of the normal course of biographical time' (Bakhtin, 1981, p. 248). Furthermore, Bakhtin argues that:

> heterogeneous stylistic unities, upon entering the novel, combine to form a structured artistic system, and are subordinated to the higher stylistic unity of the work as a whole, a unity that cannot be identified with any single one of the unities subordinated to it.
>
> (Bakhtin, 1981, p. 262)

Figure 9.3   Russian Ark: Marquis de Custine follows dancing children in the gallery of the Winter Palace.

In my view, in *Russian Ark*, the long take functions as the 'higher stylistic unity' and as an aggregate of the narrative voices. It also forces the spectator to be constantly aware of the visitor's presence who functions as both the subject of the narrative and the storyteller. In the film these functions are articulated through the visitor's interaction with de Custine: at some points, the visitor leads the Marquis through the labyrinth of the museum; at others, the visitor takes initiative and proceeds through the Hermitage of his own accord. The absence of editing which excludes, for example, the use of shot–reverse shot, causes the spectator always to remain – so to speak – behind the visitor, whereas the visitor is never able to look back. As a result, *Russian Ark* creates a type of fixed gaze that always looks forward, fearing to catch a glimpse of things behind, as in the Orphic myth.

The pair of interacting characters, de Custine and the visitor, also evokes Dante's *The Divine Comedy*, whereby Virgil guides Dante through Hell and Purgatory. The association with the Greek myth of Orpheus and the Renaissance poem suggest the interpretation of the world of *Russian Ark* as a type of inferno, an underworld. The opening remarks of the film enhance this impression: 'I open my eyes and I see nothing. I only remember there was some accident. Everyone ran for safety as best as they could. I just can't remember what happened to me.' The remark alludes to a historical apocalypse, whether the Biblical events or the Bolshevik revolution which put an end to monarchy in Russia, and presents the visitor as a post-mortem narrator fixated on his own condition of alterity.

In *The Gaze of Orpheus*, Maurice Blanchot suggests that it is concealment that reveals the truth because Orpheus can approach Euridyce only by turning away (Blanchot, 1981, pp. 99–100). The task of Orpheus is to bring light out of darkness; it is to bring Euridyce into the daylight, to make daylight more luminous through the visibility of Euridyce. The passage into the day is the movement of truth, the movement of negation that brings life out of death. The task of Orpheus is to clarify this movement, to give it form, to bring out its beauty, its harmony and fullness, which should result in the radiance of the real. However, it is not her beauty that Orpheus desires but Euridyce herself, Euridyce existing in darkness, as darkness.

The gaze of Orpheus relies on the duplicity of vision: the eye both desires to see and not to see, or to expose and to conceal what lies behind the visible. Blanchot elaborates on the paradox of the gaze by interpreting the artwork as the origin or cause of representation, whereby the autonomy of art entails the desire of the artwork to identify with its source (Blanchot, 1981, pp. 101–3). For Sokurov, such origins of representation – on one level – precipitate the visual structure of *Russian Ark*, and – on another – determine the relational quality of Russian art as a horizon of meaning, which substantiates itself through discursive relations with the complex of signifiers in Western art. In effect, Orpheus/the visitor yearns to see *the blind spot*, or the point of withdrawal, which makes cultural manifestations possible and visible. As Blanchot defines it, 'If he [Orpheus] had not looked at her, he would not have drawn her to him; and no doubt she is not there, but he himself is absent in this glance' (Blanchot, 1981, p. 100). Orpheus's desire for Eurydice becomes unlimited desire in *Russian Ark* by the use of the incessant, sustained and indefatigable gaze of the digital camera.

The story of Euridyce is the story of time, that is history, because she gives back to our gaze the non-coincidence, the endless interruption, which separates past and future. Euridyce's dying does not recede into the past; she vanishes into what Blanchot calls 'the terrifying ancient', which is an anarchic temporality, a siteless, limitless, interminable space of time (Blanchot, 1981, p. 103). Her disappearance causes the dismemberment of Orpheus; it shatters time and intimates the mosaic of history. Time in *Russian Ark* is not a totality made of linear events; it is multiple and fragmented in the sense that each event is between-time, which contains a promise of the eternal return through sacrifice. Orpheus immolates twice in one moment because in singing his lyric he yields the sovereignty of his 'I' and becomes a 'he': through his performative act, and to get closer to his Euridyce, he abandons his authority of the explorer and turns himself into the object of representation. Similarly, initially the visitor requires de Custine because it is through the Marquis that his identity is articulated, and as soon as the work of the gaze is completed, the visitor abandons de Custine, and the latter vanishes in the crowd descending the staircase of the Winter Palace. In the film, the movement of the camera is, thus, that of detour, errancy; it is the movement of the sacrifice because the characters abandon the Palace, which is the vehicle of history, to be devastated by the new Soviet regime, a concept prompted by the film's association with Eisenstein's *October* which depicts how the Hermitage is vandalized by Bolsheviks.

According to Blanchot, the gaze of Orpheus impels to comprehend oneself outside oneself, to achieve through a disjunction the continuity of perception. Lacan suggests that one can attain a goal only by stepping into the light, into language; it is there that appearance – the self as other, as sign – is forced into being (Lacan, 1977, pp. 50–97). In Lacan's conception of desire, the gaze is not the vehicle through which the subject masters the object but a point in the Other that resists the mastery of vision. It is a blank spot in the subject's look, a blank spot that threatens the subject's sense of mastery in looking because the subject cannot see it directly or successfully integrate it into the rest of the visual field. This is because, as Lacan points out, the gaze is 'what is lacking, is non-specular, is not graspable in the image' (Lacan, 1977, p. 53). de Custine, the visitor and the spectator form a Lacanian triad, whereby superimposed triangles depicting the path taken by Orpheus reveal the structure of desire. Rather than reached, the object of desire is always displaced; it is drawn from darkness to light, its absence or invisibility is re-articulated as a gap, a notion of loss, a signifier, within the frame of language and within a poem of lament. Alternatively, to put it in other terms, because the loss of the object is at once the moment of its emergence, desire can never achieve satisfaction by obtaining this lost object. Mimesis follows the trajectory of desire: Eurydice's absence lures Orpheus in his desire to possess her. This is the realm of the gaze, and the only place where interaction (through signifiers and codes) can occur. The reconstructed lure (unlike Orpheus's lyre), through mimesis, effects a shift from one type of dependence (Orpheus's dependence upon Eurydice) to another (his audience's dependence upon him, the poet).

The gaze of Orpheus produces a continuity effect, whereby in *Russian Ark*, as the camera moves around the museum, space becomes a fluid rather than fixed territorial reference. As the camera movements exaggerate motion and notions of space, the spectator begins to perceive the visitor's movement through the Hermitage as space navigation. The camera creates an illusion that the visitor has the freedom to choose the direction of his movements. However, it is not possible for the spectator to conceptualize the visitor's journey through the museum as a linear progression because the journey is spatially divided. Closed doors, dark unwelcoming spaces, people's interferences and other disturbances punctuate the visitor's advancement through the museum. In addition, each stage of his progression is spatially marked by the presence of historically and stylistically charged artefacts on display in the museum. These elements create visible paths of motion, reading and interpretation. They form a dynamic map of representation and knowledge and offer simultaneous alternative views of a single world.

Within this system, the visitor and the spectator are given complex reference systems for orientation. They include (a) action and characterization: the visitor and de Custine witness short performances being acted out in their presence and they recognize iconic faces of the Russian cultural milieu, such as Alexander Pushkin and Natalia Goncharova; (b) means of arranging and accessing knowledge: the setting/museum provides a platform for the reinterpretation of history, art and Russian national identity, whereby the navigation through the Hermitage actuates the structure of the museum and arranges it as discourse of knowledge; (c) retaining personal and social history and memory: the visitor and de Custine constantly struggle to recollect the past and often find themselves astonished by the realization of the misleading threads of history and perplexing qualities of the Winter Palace as the site of many historical events; and (d) obtaining a sense of security through familiarity: the visitor refers to a common experience and memory by prompting de Custine and the spectator to recognize cult figures from Russian history. Thus the visitor orients himself through the museum thanks to the systems of coordinates, familiar names, visual patterns and forms, which are the well-known elements constituting Russian history. The reference systems include external, fixed coordinates as well as internal, shifting referents associated primarily with the memory of the subject, and finally time-based systems that enable the visitor to follow lines of movement and the narrative sequence. These systems form a separate terrain of knowledge, a map that anchors the spectator's view of the world.

Sokurov uses a narrator who is out of time, out of place and who needs some time to adjust himself to a new reality of being. The director draws the camera – and with it the spectator – into action by the use of voiceover and specific camera movements, whereby the camera intervenes into the action (for example, the camera records how actors have to step aside to let it pass through) and thus marks its own presence. This technique enhances the sense of theatricality in *Russian Ark*; and it advocates the performative aspect of cinema, whose origins go back to pre-Chekhovian theatre of vaudeville and pantomime. The film features scenes that point directly to the aesthetics of theatre, such as the semi-improvised playacts between characters dressed in costumes à la *commedia dell'arte*, or the grand opening scene in the theatre of Catherine the Great. In the latter scene, as the camera glides across the stage and the auditorium, it adopts an inverted perspective on the spectator's experience. The scene begins with the display of the mechanics of a theatrical production, including acting, costumes, stage machines and so forth, and assembles these techniques for a full-scale impression as the onstage performance culminates. By exposing the apparatus of the period, Baroque theatre, Sokurov hints at the construction of his own cinematic creation operating as a multi-leveled multimedia edifice: the director shows contemporary Russian actors performing actors in the theatre of Catherine the Great, who in their turn are performing various roles on stage inside the museum presented as a grand piece of artifice (a representational strategy similar to Sokurov's earlier use of Dmitrii Kardovskii's painting as a point of reference). In other words, the director does not merely reconstruct reality but rather its reconstructions; that is, the film constantly operates on the level of second-tier referents, thus losing its power to connote. Consequently, Sokurov inverts the practices of early cinema, when, for instance, film projections were used in theatre performances, because he now includes theatrical performances into his film. Such an inversion, in fact, confirms the ontological parallel between *Russian Ark* and the experiences of early cinema as defined by Thomas Elsaesser:

Early cinema displays events and actions rather than narrates them; it addresses spectators directly, and as a physical collectivity; it has different kinds of closure, not all of which are textual; its unit is the autonomous shot or scene, where actions and events are continuous by virtue of some conceptual or narrational category, to which the autonomy of the shot becomes subordinated. These oppositions seem particularly fertile in a number of ways: they throw into relief the fact that one of the attractions of early cinema was the cinematic apparatus itself, quite apart from what it showed.

(Elsaesser, 1990, p. 14)

Indeed, *Russian Ark* lacks many formal means to narrate events; instead, it resorts to theatrical performances presented as singular sequences combined together by the consistent look of the camera and thus inverts the practices of early cinema. Frequently, the voiceover is used to explicate confusing moments or to point out the significance of certain characters or situations. The visitor either engages in debates with de Custine or indulges in melancholic monologues. The verbal exchanges between the visitor and de Custine serve the purpose of onscreen intertitles in silent films because they narrate passages of the story and elucidate the action for film audiences. Just as intertitles often were graphic elements themselves, featuring illustrations or abstract decorations that commented on the action, these dialogues – in accordance with the inversion principle – provide an acoustic frame for the cinematic narrative. Finally, listening to the voiceover renditions – just like reading intertitles – interrupts the rhythm of visual images, creating autonomous sequences. Progression from one separate scene to another is forced by external interferences rather than some inner logic (for instance, the museum keepers command de Custine and the visitor to leave a room, and thus a scene) and is demarcated spatially with the aim of designating a discrete scene to a discrete space.

In *Russian Ark*, the narrative closure refers back to the beginning (entering and leaving the Winter Palace). Such parallelism is a stylistic mark of early cinema, too: Marshall Deutelbaum shows that 'most Lumière films record action and events in which the end either rejoins or inversely mirrors the beginning ... thus providing a very effective narrative closure' (Deutelbaum, 1979, p. 30). Furthermore, Deutelbaum argues that the scope and duration of the actions are signalled in the films themselves, providing a form of narrative suspense and anticipation, which generates active spectatatorial involvement. In *Russian Ark*, de Custine signals to a beginning of an action or to its closure by such simple acts as opening the door to the next room or engaging in idle conversations with passers-by. He alienates the spectator into considering the arbitrariness of ritual aspects and theatrical limits of cinema. De Custine, in fact, makes no pretence of ignoring the presence of the cinematic apparatus and the audience it conceals. On the contrary, he crosses the proscenium and addresses the camera directly, or even playfully throws a snowball at it, which emphasizes the different dimensions of the worlds of the actor and spectator and creates an illusion of interaction. The spectator becomes an integrated onlooker, whose role is enshrined in the complexity of the shot, which moves fluidly from panorama to point of view, between sharing and observing an illusory nature of the experience. In fact, the visitor is alone in failing to perceive the construction of his own world: to everyone else, including the figure of de Custine, the artifice is not only transparent but heavily signalled at every turn. Illusion is not only a spectacle: the spectacular collusion in its construction and the spectacular innocence of the visitor who cannot perceive its artificiality combine in an

entirely artificial diegesis. Thus the qualities of vraisemblance and probabil-
ity are suspended in favour of the construction of a transparently artificial
script of algorithmic elegance.

In the concluding shot of *Russian Ark*, the camera leaves the Hermitage
and abandons Russian history; the digitally enhanced murky waters of the
Neva River allude to Euridyce, whose fate was to remain in the darkness of
afterlife forever. Her disappearance in the abyss correlates with the destiny
of Russian society as well as with the perception of time that comes to a halt.
In fact, the last few minutes of the film offer the continuous experience of
time, uninterrupted by vigorous staging and complex spatial organization.
Therefore, on the one hand, *Russian Ark* displays features – to borrow Bazin's
term – of 'the reconstituted reportage' (Bazin, 1971, p. 20). On the other,
the film abnegates the necessary adherence to reality by re-creating reality:
Sokurov presents his film as a collection of daydream materials, a colourful
fantasy that may not exist in reality. He triumphs over 300 years of Russian
history by eschewing chronology and causality; instead, Sokurov depicts
a mosaic of momentous events and an erratic gathering of historical figures
flaccidly arranged in a non-linear manner. His role as director becomes
synonymous to that of the museum curator who takes the responsibility
for the acquisition and exhibition of cultural objects intended to preserve
the momentum of historical reality. The absence of the cut is compensated
by spatial montage whereby acting and the museum settings function as
flashbacks and flashforwards. *Russian Ark* appears as constative, declarative
discourse, and the film requires from the spectator the knowledge of the
subject. At the same time, it departs from technical knowledge into the
realm of intuition and inspiration, thus desisting from the dichotomy of
present and past, reality and re-creation.

Notes

1. The information was recorded uncompressed onto a hard disk.
2. German cinematographer Tilman Büttner was also the steadicam operator in Tom
   Tykwer's *Run Lola Run* (Lola rennt, 1998), which incorporated unusually long takes.

References

Auerbach, Erich (1953), *Mimesis: The Representation of Reality in Western Literature*,
   trans. by Willard R. Task, with a new Introduction by Edward W. Said. Princeton/
   Oxford: Princeton University Press.
Bakhtin, Mikhail (1981), *The Dialogic Imagination: Four Essays by M. M. Bakhtin*,
   Michael Holquist (ed.). Austin: University of Texas Press.
Bakhtin, Mikhail (1973), *Problems of Dostoevsky's Poetics*, trans. by R. W. Rotsel. Ann
   Arbor, MI: Ardis.
Bazin, André (1971), *What is Cinema?, vol. 2*, trans. by Hugh Gray. Berkeley/
   Los Angeles/London: University of California Press.

Blanchot, Maurice (1981), *The Gaze of Orpheus and Other Literary Essays*, preface Geoffrey Hartman, trans. by Lydia Davis, P. Adams Sitney (ed.). New York: Station Hill Press.
Deutelbaum, Marshall (1979), 'Structuring Patterning in the Lumière Films', in *Wide Angle*, 3(1), pp. 30–46.
Elsaesser, Thomas (1990), 'Introduction', in Thomas Elsaesser and Adam Barker (eds), *Early Cinema: Space, Frame, Narrative*. London: British Film Institute.
Lacan, Jacques (1977), *The Four Fundamental Concepts of Psycho-Analysis*, Jacques-Alain Miller (ed.). London: Hogarth Press.
Plato (1953), *The Dialogues of Plato*, trans. by B. Jowett. Oxford: Clarendon Place.
Ross, Alex (1998), 'A Critic at Large, "The Maestro of Midnight"', in *The New Yorker*, 20 April 1998, p. 86.

Part III The Realism of the Medium

10
Realism, Real Sex and the Experimental Film: Mediating Eroticism in *Georges Bataille's Story of the Eye*

Beth Johnson

Andrew Repasky McElhinney's *Georges Bataille's Story of the Eye* (2003) begins with a grainy, close-up image of a woman giving birth. Over this image is narrated an account not of the life, but of the myth of Georges Bataille. It ends with his death in 1962, a year before the assassination of John F. Kennedy, as if there were something uncanny about the relative proximity between the two events. This deliberate 'uncanny' misconception is a signal that Bataille haunts McElhinney's scene, but is not part of it. As Freud notes: 'the uncanny is that class of the frightening which leads back to what is known of old and long familiar' (Freud, 1990, p. 340). Bataille is ob-scene (in the sense of being off screen), even though his life is referred to and the film takes the title of his most famous novella, *Story of the Eye* (Bataille, 2001b), the 'Ur'-text of a considerable portion of avant-garde pornography or intellectual erotica.

On screen, in full close-up, is the image of a real birth, re-edited from an old army documentary. McElhinney admits to 'de-humanizing the sequence by cutting all the reaction shots' (Kipp, 2003). This scene accordingly appears alien and must therefore be read in a different way. The birth can be read metaphorically: it is the birth of absolute obscenity, the absolutely explicit birth of absolute explicitness. The grainy scene presented denotes that this vision is not contemporary, but a re-presentation of older footage. This connection with the past both establishes an uncanny link between Bataille and McElhinney and further signifies the journey from Bataillean theories and images of the past to the present day. Recognizably, the scene indexes the in-between of intellectual literary theory and popular visual culture by way of similarity in representation to Gustave Courbet's painting 'The Origin of the World' ('L'Origine du monde', 1866): an explicit vision depicting a close-up image of female genitals that signify the origin of desire as well as, critically, the *obscene* in that: '[t]hrough the eyeholes of the door, the voyeur stares at the female "hole" at the centre of the scene, a vanishing point in which there is "nothing to see"' (Jay, 1994, p. 169).

McElhinney's appropriation of Bataille's novella indicates his own avant-garde status as an independent director who has chosen formally to revise serious sexual literature on screen in a non-titillating way. His film, like the literature it has emerged from, is marked by two inseparable movements: the move forward – the film's preoccupation with sex and the 'seen/scene' which, considering its explicit content, allows for a spectatorship of fascination and reflection; and secondly, the move backward – an enforced recoil by McElhinney (and potentially the audience) in order to express the serious avant-garde nature of his subject.

Notably, McElhinney dispenses (almost entirely) with conventions that differentiate film from visual and video art. Speech is purposefully sparse, relationships between characters are neither explained nor set against any recognizable moral/familial schema, and there is little narrative or plot. Interestingly, whereas McElhinney designates his work as film, conventionally the text appears to adhere to definitions of video art. McElhinney's choice of capturing the image – DV Cam that was transferred to DigiBeta for post-production work, thus interrogating the experience of spectatorship – reinforces a significant blurring of boundaries between video art and film. Defined in part by a lack of dialogue, unknown actors and the attack upon viewers' expectations (shaped by pornographic film convention), the work can be seen to traverse the borders between art film and video art, and between artistic beauty and pornography. The effect on the spectator can thus be perceived as a violent rocking motion, leaving the viewer with a feeling of disorientation, nausea and fascination. The close-ups of genitalia and the frequency of repetitive sexual and hardcore scenes do not serve to authenticate pleasure or arouse but to show and dispense displeasure.

McElhinney's real-sex production of *Story of the Eye* keys out the significance of unveiling desire, deferral, decay and death in our contemporary cultural visual field. Alongside immense amounts of real sex the film includes real footage of the assassination of John F. Kennedy: a Bataillean allusion, perhaps, to demonstrate the interrelation between sex and death, especially through Jackie Kennedy's proximity to death which could be figured as an erotic 'scene'. The importance of this scene lies in what it signifies: arguably an appropriation of (Bataillean) eroticism and horror equivalent to risking death. Alongside these elements, the film depicts what I argue to be real trauma experienced by one of the actors (Courtney Shea).

The inclusion of such scenes functions to unveil the process of metamorphosis of the 'obscene' in that the spectacle of eroticism, and death, pushes the experience of spectatorship beyond the gaze. The gaze is deterritorialized by the machine through which it is presented and restructures the viewer's amorous/erotic relationship to machines.

De-forming the kino-eye: Kitsch subculture

McElhinney's vision in *Georges Bataille's Story of Eye* is interesting in the way in which it combines avant-garde filmmaking and underground, trash, queer and explicit content. It also allusively sketches in the history of eroticism from the nineteenth century to the present including the boredom that Bataille finds in 'the pleasures of the flesh' that are served up for the delectation of decent people (Bataille, 2001b, pp. 42–3). The film draws attention to 'the present' of eroticism: the eroticism of the spectator through the digital, the eroticism of being filmed. This is sex primarily in relation to machines, not other people, and is demonstrated most spectacularly through two scenes: one of male masturbation where the sight of the actor's penis becomes interchanged with the image of a joy stick; and a second where, significantly, the aforementioned actor 'cums' onto the lens of the camera, occluding the vision of the viewer. Both of these scenes are analysed below.

Following the rebirth of eroticism as a digital experience, McElhinney presents a mechanical vision that is simultaneously a cliché of kitsch 1930s Berlin (as depicted by burlesque topless dancing girls) and post-1980s gay fetish subculture (indicated by the saturation of 'fetish' clothing, the use of a double ended dildo in a lesbian sex scene, and by heavily pierced, tattooed and leather-clad dominant and submissive, black and white, male actors who engage in anal sex before being murdered by a single bullet in an unclear shot). Through exhibiting naked references to specific underground styles and differing chronological points, McElhinney exposes his intentions to play with normative film conventions. His vision can thus be read from the opening as a deliberate attempt to display the shocking power of subculture.

The shock of the obscene takes place right at the beginning, with a dingy scene of two top-hatted topless dancing women being watched by a sole male viewer in a dark, small music hall. This scene plunges the viewer right back into the nineteenth century and the origins of modern pornography. The dark, heavy setting, music and theatrical mise-en-scène (including the ludic make-up of the dancers, their breasts painted as smiling faces while their actual faces are covered by over-sized hats) hark back to the illicit theatrical images of women captured by the camera from the 1850s onwards, most notably in Paris, Amsterdam and the US, where dance (the cancan and vaudeville) held a strong illicit sway. This scene also points to the male leisure pursuit of viewing stag films in the early twentieth century, particularly popular in the US, where McElhinney's film was made.

An uncanny assault is quickly materialized in the images after the dancing semi-naked women. The scene is now a dance hall, and attention is focused on a strange, seated male figure, who appears to be controlling the speed of the girls' dancing by a joystick which he jerks violently. As the shots cut back and forth, the image of the joystick becomes his erect penis. Essentially then, the figure is seen to control the scene through controlling the speed of the image that the spectator of the film sees. The fact that his penis doubles as a joystick again moves the viewer through time, bringing us right up to the present. The joystick is not that of a World War II pilot, but of a video-game player.

Although certain contemporary computer/video games directly acknowledge the link between technology and eroticism, they tend, in my view, to be focused towards appropriating a climax from a female animated character. As such, the scene is in line with mainstream pornographic models. The male 'gamer', in order to 'win', must prove his potency by pleasuring the animated female character and, as such, is positioned as both controller and voyeur. Writing of the computer game *Orgasm Girl*, in which the purpose of the 'gamer' is to stimulate an orgasm from a sleeping female character, Daniel Ashton notes that such a work 'questions the possibilities and potentials for how sex video games may present more pressing interventions and suggestions for our physical sex lives' (2006–7, p. 20). Such a statement serves to reiterate the point, of course, that the way we view and regulate the *image* of sex functions to infect the physical application of it. Such scenes, then, index an erotic renaissance in that while the pornographic scene is re-mediated, the implications of the repetition interpolate a binate questioning of the 'real' of sex, of the significance of desire, eroticism, horror and excess in light of new technologies. McElhinney's vision thus draws attention to 'the present' of eroticism: the eroticism of being filmed.

The interchange between the joystick and the penis operates to impregnate the scene with strangeness. The only 'known' for the spectator is that the male on screen appears to be manipulating the dancers as if they were a video game. The male can thus be seen to use his 'sex' as a weapon through which to control the women and the spectator. Significantly, however, the masturbatory spectacle calls into question the male viewer's control over his own body (or the lack of it). As Jorgen Lorentzen observes:

[M]en have been seen to embody the idea of rationality. [Yet,] one could argue that the male sexual organ is the only part of the male body that is not controlled by the will but instead governed by a complicated interaction between blood, nerves and muscles. Men cannot control the raising or lowering of the penis by force of will. ... Our culture, to a great extent, has made a taboo of the erect male member. ... That physicians, biologists and cultural fictions have caused men to turn this upside down, associating the experience of pleasure with the penis, and referring to their penises as their brains, has created the basis for misunderstandings, self-deceit, a lessening of the real brain's capability of pleasure, and the potential for sexual abuse. Sex becomes not just a weapon but a weapon that controls itself.

(Lorentzen, 2007, pp. 73–4)

Obscenity operates here then by an unveiling not of the genitals, but of other models of physical stimulation in connection with visual technology such as 'gaming'. The image of the hard penis refers, then, not to itself, but to something beyond the body. This scene sets up an immediate paradox: on the one hand we have pornography from vaudeville (a theatrical and risqué dance show) and on the other, topless *Tomb Raider*. This merging of the past and present exposes the sexual spectacle of the film with aesthetic and theoretical implications. The joystick/erect penis demonstrates the digital appropriation of eroticism. McElhinney uses an aesthetically 'obscene' image of the erect penis to make visible that which should remain hidden: man's lack of control over the penis and an abandonment to sexuality.

Through the fusion of differing media and generic distinctions, McElhinney makes visible a contemporary overlap that serves to remind the viewer that this film is a culmination of cultural, historical, theoretical and digital thought on the erotic. Generically, as well as demonstrating similarity to the 'stag' film, McElhinney's vision can equally be likened to earlier, non-erotic appropriations of the transgression of reality such as *The Never Ending Story* (*Die unendliche Geschichte*, Wolfgang Petersen, 1984), a film that shows the relay between reality and fantasy through the use of a joystick control, used to access other realms of/in space and time. Undoubtedly, however, McElhinney's scene is a masturbatory exhibition that operates on a micro-level as deliberately sensationalist in its sexual content. The control of sexuality is disrupted and positioned as (male) fantasy. Questioning gender positions in relation to power, Elizabeth Grosz asks:

> [C]ould men's refusal to acknowledge the effects and flows that move through various parts of the body and from the inside out, have to do with men's attempt to distance themselves from the very kind of corpore-ality – uncontrollable, irrational – they have attributed to women?
>
> (Grosz, 1994, p. 200)

McElhinney's vision arguably answers her challenge for men to acknowl-edge the uncontrollable. Deforming and defamiliarizing the fantasy model, he makes visible the irrational and uncontrollable aspects of male sexuality. Theorist Rosemary Jackson's definition of fantasy, then, is worth noting here: 'The "FANTASTIC" derives from the Latin, *phantasticus* ... meaning to make visible or manifest' (Jackson, 1981, p. 13).

Fetishising queer identity

The male couple McElhinney presents can be visibly pinpointed as belong-ing to the 1980s queer scene, judging by the males' outer appearance. The mise-en-scène, in part defined by the choice of male actors and costumes, is of relevance to notions of cultural obscenity and the underground 'scene'. The fact that McElhinney has chosen to focus on homosexual, rather than heterosexual, real sex, is another insight into his vision of generic and cultural deformations of desire. As the obscene is positioned purposefully outside the 'ordinary' cultural and visual arena, the choice of queer real sex can be seen as a tribute to underground, 'obscene' visions and versions of Bataillean desire. McElhinney's technical high-key lighting of this scene – rendering it overexposed – has symbolic resonance in line with Baudrillard's statement about contemporary obscenity in the realm of vision. Discussing virtual reality, in which 'signs seduce one another, beyond meaning' (as opposed to when the simulacrum was still a 'game on the fringes of the real'), he argues: 'The disappearance of this scene [of seduction] clears the way for a principle of obscenity, a pornographic materialization of every-thing' (Baudrillard, 2005, p. 69).

The male actors chosen to perform the real-sex scenes are, by extensive tattooing, body piercing and fetish costume, stylistically distinct. This differ-ence pertains to an underground movement that is connected to an abnor-mal identity relating to the sexual self. This idea is indexed by the physical honesty of the (male) body in the seen/scene. The appearance, style and dress of the males in this film (all taboo when placed against the accepted 'norms') thus highlight a movement towards otherness: a movement beyond the self. Similarly, in making visible a female queer couple (usually found in mainstream pornography to satisfy, through familiarity, a male demographic – the unseen male viewer), McElhinney reinforces the notion of abnormality. Both women appear bruised, battered, pallid and unsteady. One woman (Melissa Forgione) is seen to have an unexplained angry scar on her body, which she purposefully makes visible to the audience by run-ning her hands across it and weeping before beginning to masturbate. After reaching climax the woman stubs a cigarette out on her arm, further invok-ing the horror of erotic expectation.

It is essential, here, that the scar, the self-harming and the sexual act are seen. The body as a site of otherness is explored by the presence of the cam-era rather than the presence of another. By this, I mean that the practices of queer sex in the film are arguably connected to erotic desire by way of the intimacy of being filmed rather than being fucked.

The 'politics' of Queer Theory, as Pearce and Wisker point out, may be a source of illumination here: 'Queerness does not depend upon the sexu-ality of the practitioners per se, but rather the extent to which *any* liaison (straight or gay), exposes and makes visible hetero-normativity' (1998, p. 15). As with the male couple above, whereas the costumes of the actors posit difference, the actual sexual practices seen are transgressive in that they make visible the 'normal' conventions of the sexual scene. The sexual acts presented are notably 'normal' in terms of the known pornographic model: for the most part mechanical, lacking in intimacy and failing to dis-play emotional complexity convincingly. This pornographic style is further indexed by the fact that the actors change positions regularly, the sex is inconsequential and the camera is positioned to authenticate the reality of the penetration taking place. It is not therefore these explicit shots that con-vey obscenity, but rather the application of the strange/fetish object within these scenes and, significantly, the fact that these scenes arguably convey the contemporary significance and experience of *sex being filmed* that is of crucial interest here.

Traumatic re-play: Power and the cine-eye

Amid the very real sex we see, we are, as an audience, alienated from the desire (or the lack of it) that we witness. The extensive use of mirrors throughout the film points to the importance of self-reflexive spectatorship. This notion is reinforced by the fact that one of the dancers wakes, half-naked, to find her eyes bandaged as if she has been blinded (or had her vision castrated) (Figure 10.1).

The film invokes the notion of sight and the obscene by playing with the concept of temporal delay in terms of sexual fulfilment. The soundtrack audible at the beginning of the film, when McElhinney presents burlesque dancing women, is repeated in a later scene where one of the women is seen endlessly journeying, battered and bruised up the same flight of never-ending stairs. The staircase scene could be argued to depict an underground, art-house vision of hell where the woman is forced to repeat her painful journey up the staircase as, in line with the soundtrack, the audience is to imagine that someone unseen in the house is repeatedly watching a film with her in it. Accordingly, her body becomes an object of fetish

Figure 10.1 Georges Bataille's Story of the Eye: Melissa Forgione awakens wearing a bloody bandage over her eyes. Reproduced with kind permission from Andrew Repasky McElhinney.

to be manipulated at will by the use of a mechanical control: a joystick or remote control. This hellish scene demonstrates a folding back, through an 'imagined' vision of the girl as trapped in a time and space she is unable to control. This scene can, of course, be understood to signify the experience of eroticism itself.

This irrational vision is both perceived to be a traumatic experience for the character (cued by the slow movements indicating her body is on the verge of collapse) and a pleasurable/terrifying experience for the spectator who is, in part, positioned as rationally accountable, by way of watching and potentially controlling the vision (by moving the scene backwards/forwards), for inflicting pain and gaining pleasure from viewing the penetration of (and assault upon) the woman. The positioning of the spectator as both active (through the obscene spectator in the house forcing the woman to endlessly repeat an unseen act) and passive (the film spectator who potentially gains pleasure from submission unto the spectacle and the silent yet direct address unto him/her by way of spectatorial implication) functions to reduce the space between the imaginary and the real experience of eroticism. The repetition of the scene also serves to transform the spectator through a varying experience of emotional and psychological responses. This unexplained scene continues for exactly ten minutes, potentially enabling the spectator outside of the frame to experience fascination, desire, terror, frustration, boredom and trauma.

The compulsion to repeat arguably reflects the abnormal desire of the spectator to experience that which is not rational, and can accordingly be linked to both the psychoanalytic unconscious and the function of repression. Repression does not function to deny pleasure, but rather to avoid displeasure by way of: 'bring[ing] to light activities of repressed instinctual impulses' (Freud, 1991, p. 290). The experience of the erotic that cannot be rationalized (as it depends upon unknown animalistic impulses) is, however, dependent upon the penetration, but not the annihilation, of the Law of the Father (for example, the law that designates it is wrong to gain pleasure from witnessing/causing another's pain). As such, any erotic pleasure/displeasure attained is untranslatable and can never be considered as one's own, but exists only by way of spectral experience of the 'othered' self. The significance of this scene is, then, to be understood thus: the appropriation of transgression is grounded in the image by its revelation that we, the spectators, are *seen seeing*. What the text reveals is the dual positioning of the spectator. This duality allows for, and encourages, a saccadic split to take place: we are horrified and aroused by the sight of us seeing another's fear. As with any such duality, the simultaneous movement towards and away from the object of desire/horror can be experienced as a transformation of the self or a psychological trauma, a wound brought about by stress or shock.

This re-presentation of trauma is highlighted by the blurring of boundaries between actual real experience – real sex – and the mediation of the sexual act as a mere 'act'. However, McElhinney's work uses a third term for sanctioning the simultaneous artifice/reality of sex, which is 'perform-ance'. As noted by Linda Williams, performance is 'the art of opening the body of the performer up to the physical and emotional challenge of what is performed' (Williams, 2001, p. 22). The emotional challenge is seen, in this film, to elicit trauma. Peter Buse's definition of trauma is of relevance here: 'In its most general definition, trauma describes an overwhelming experience of sudden or catastrophic events in which the event occurs in the often delayed, uncontrolled repetitive experience of hallucinations and other intrusive phenomena' (Buse, 2001, cited in King, 2005, p. 67). The repetitive nature of this scene posits the register of art-house narrative as sovereign, yet, simultaneously, it echoes the repetitive nature of popular pornography.

The power of the spectator is further interrogated by the ambiguous reality of witnessing the female character/actor's trauma. After watching the woman endlessly climb the staircase, we see her finally reaching the top. The woman walks towards a window and witnesses (by the slicing of original footage) the murder of the former American President John F. Kennedy. As previously mentioned, this scene posits a Bataillean reference in that it demonstrates the visual spectacle of death and links it, in proxim-ity to the erotic image of woman by way of making visible the eroticism of Jackie Kennedy's proximity to (her lover's) death. As Bataille states in *Inner Experience*: 'There is in understanding a blind spot: which is reminiscent of the structure of the eye. The nature of understanding demands that the blind spot within it be more meaningful than understanding itself' (1988, p. 110). Thus, as Bataille explicates, the blind spot 'absorbs one's attention: it is no longer the spot which loses itself in knowledge, but knowledge which loses itself in it' (1988, p. 111).

Interrogating spectatorship

This scene also serves to interrogate the other 'other': the technological method of capturing images of terror, images upon which the specta-tor uses reason even where none exists. The very notion of the image, as well as the model of pornographic film, as a realm of spectacular abuse, is called into question. The spectator is shown explicitly the power they have over the production and reproduction of the image and the erotic object. The nightmarish control, drive and desire to see the obscene through the collaboration of eroticism and death – the matrix acknowledged by the actress/character within the film – are, in fact, all too 'real', with psychologi-cal implications that reach far beyond this chapter. Psychic reality is also explored through McElhinney's use of the fantasy scenes that can be read as dreams or nightmares.

This film, in presenting real sex and real death, questions the validity of technology truly to represent the real. This interrogation is, of course, a long-standing one that has been explored within the realms of academia many times, most notably by Roland Barthes who in the 1960s proclaimed that with the *effet de réel* the text makes us accept its fictional product as 'real' (Barthes, 1982, pp. 1–17). Most recently, the concept of 'reality' has been interrogated by theorist Slavoj Zizek. Although Zizek's discussion is actually focused on the image of the collapse of the World Trade Centre towers in the US, his theories are equally compelling when applied to McElhinney's choices:

> The Real which returns has the status of a(nother) semblance: *precisely because it is real, that is, on account of its traumatic/excessive character, we are unable to integrate it into (what we experience as) our reality, and are therefore compelled to experience it as a nightmarish apparition.* This is what the compelling image of the collapse of the WTC was: an image, a semblance, an 'effect', which, at the same time, delivered the 'thing itself'. The 'effect of the real' is not the same as what Roland Barthes ... called it: ... it is, rather, its exact opposite: *l'effet de l'irréel*. That is to say, ... the Real itself, in order to be sustained, has to be perceived as a nightmarish unreal spectre. Usually we say that we should not mistake fiction for reality. ... The lesson here is the opposite one: *we should not mistake reality for fiction.*
> (Zizek, 2002, p. 19)

Here, McElhinney keys out explicitly Bataille's theories upon desire and death as a final moment of enlightenment, of absolute recognition in its repetition, delivering, as Zizek notes, 'the thing itself': the reality and public control of real sex, real objectification. Through our technological control of the image in the form of a DVD remote control or a cinematic reel (mirrored in the film by the male in charge of the female dancers and one girl's repeated journey up the staircase) we, as viewers, not only deliver unto ourselves the fictive adaptation, but the 'real thing'.

Transgression, violence and the 'Thing': The unreturned gaze

The concept of spectatorship is further explored towards the close of the film. The scene can be divided into five sections: the first, a masturbatory positioning of the female viewer; secondly, a three-way sex scene between the main characters; thirdly, a woman looking directly at the camera (an assaulting gaze); fourthly, a shot in which the main actor cums onto the lens of the camera; and, lastly, a black, blank screen coupled with an ear-piercing high-pitched technological noise conveying extreme obscenity.

All five segments interrogate vision in slightly different ways. The first extensively uses the mirror image to depict the concept of self-reflexivity as well as employing the woman as erotic object. In this scene we see one of the nameless characters (woman 'a') from behind taking off her clothing and looking into a long mirror. This segment sets up an accepted pornographic convention in that the woman begins to masturbate and is positioned so that the (unseen male) viewer can read the image erotically. The woman's reflection in the mirror visible to the film audience is interestingly not the full-frontal of the woman's body, but the reflection of events in the hallway. This mirror image makes visible a heterosexual sex act between the other woman in the film (woman 'b') and the main male character. While watching the couple fuck, woman 'a' continues to masturbate. Again, this sight is shown partly as the camera is focused upon woman 'a's back as well as the reflection of the hallway 'action'.

Although McElhinney does not present a fully 'split' screen, the doubling of the images here creates tension. The tension in this scene operates because our vision is restricted. We see neither the close-up of the female spectator's masturbatory sequence or the close-up (and thus the authentication) of the couples' intercourse. This denotes the scene as one that plays with visibility in that the audience are torn between the two eroticized spaces presented. The lack of clarity of either vision serves to create a tension in which we are unsure of what we should be looking at and, more significantly, presents a tension that is exerted in the possibility of the unseen (obscene). Again, such a doubling of the image can be linked to the concept of the 'uncanny' by way of opening up a space where what is not shown serves to infect the seen with both fear and pleasure.

As previously mentioned, this scene mirrors the power relations usually presented in mainstream pornography in that it is a female who traditionally indexes the (represented) reader/viewer of pornography, so that for the (actual) male reader the process of reading/viewing is itself eroticized. This, however, points to a blind spot (perhaps infinitely regressed) in which the actual male viewer is not seen even as he looks, and does not see himself seeing himself in the image of the masturbating woman represented in the book or picture. As such, this segment makes visible the obscenity of the (male) look.

On relocating herself in proximity to the fucking couple, we see woman 'a' slump against a wall. Although she continues to masturbate, she does not look at the sexual spectacle before her, but rather looks off-screen into 'blind space'. This shot again makes visible the spectator's lack of complete vision. We do not know what she is looking at, as it exists beyond the boundaries of the screen frame. What is apparent, however, is that we see she is not experiencing pleasure through her spectatorship, but rather appears to be acting in a mechanical way. Continuing to masturbate she looks blank and appears mechanical in her movements. This action lays way for recognition of the contemporary amorous/erotic relationship to machines. Her appearance suggests she is to be viewed as a 'living doll' rather than an engaged participant. Her lack of pleasure operates to frame the spectator's own perception of this sight as one in which scopophilic pleasure is denied. Accordingly, a paradox is set up for both the failed gaze and fetishistic desire (Figure 10.2).

Figure 10.2   Georges Bataille's Story of the Eye: Courtney Shea 'looks away' from Melissa Forgione and Sean Timothy Sexton while mechanically masturbating. Reproduced with kind permission from Andrew Repasky McElhinney.

Potentially, this scene (and the paradox inherent) can be read in two ways. Firstly, woman 'a' could be seen to have withdrawn/retreated because she is sickened by her own loneliness compared with the couple. As such, the mechanical pleasure she can give herself can be read as the *only* pleasure she can have, and hence is a mark of failure. Secondly, the woman's lack of reaction – her reticence to look – positions her as a figure of monstrous perversity. Although her body is on show, she is not seen to be 'turned on'. Rather, her actions are focused towards the obscene, off-screen space that we as a film audience do not 'know'. One effect of this is that it positions woman 'a' as both an object of desire by the fact she is unable to challenge the situation she finds herself in, as well as a figure whose displeasure we are forced to confront.

As the scene continues, we see woman 'b' fellating the male. In a doubling up of aforementioned displeasure, woman 'b's face betrays no pleasure; she coughs extensively throughout the performance before finally withdrawing and curling up in a foetal position. This performance can be read psychoanalytically in that it explicitly links the physical to the psychological. Unlike pornography, in which the sexual act is disassociated from psychological consequence, woman 'b's actions mirror both the mechanical spectacle of woman 'a's movements and function to make visible the painful reality of such an act by way of distorting and re-appropriating 'the physical mechanics and rhythms of sexual performance' (Krzywinska, 2006, p. 225). This vision then points to a contradiction in that the mechanics of hardcore pornographic rhythm are repositioned in a site of visible displeasure.

McElhinney's refusal to cutaway from the scene means that the film-spectator is made complicit in the women's vulnerability. The framing of woman 'b' in a stream of bright light as well as the male's re-asserted dominance (his presence demands pleasure) functions to reintroduce the concept of the mirror. The mirror here is appropriated metaphorically in that this scene can be proposed to represent the economy of sex in a patriarchal field and, accordingly, make visible gender conflict beyond the dicgctic world of the film. In terms of regimes of looking, identification is split between an alignment with the power of the male gaze and identification with the object of the look.

Direct address

This dual positioning is indexed by the static status of the spectator who, unable to affect onscreen action, is forcibly positioned within a masochistic spectatorial experience. The appropriation of displeasure operates in terms of causing an assault upon the eye of the spectator. The seen displeasure is not expected from real-sex models and, as such, is shocking. This assault upon the audience continues in the third scene in which woman 'a' directly addresses the audience by staring at the spectator. This gaze both shocks and assaults as the woman has not, before this point, acknowledged the presence of the spectator directly. Her look essentially denotes that we, the audience, have been, and are currently seen, looking.

Her return of our gaze constitutes a shocking revelation in that she acknowledges, through our looking, the notion of sexual spectacle, and as such concedes the presence of the camera for the first time. For the politics of looking, specifically 'looking back', John Ellis observes: 'direct address makes explicit the relationship between viewer and the subject of the look' (Ellis, 1992, p. 60). This direct address further has the effect of making reference to early and silent cinema in that, as Johnathan Auerbach notes, it functioned 'mainly to shock, astonish, assault and/or delight its spectators rather than tell coherent stories to them' (Auerbach, 2000, cited in Peirse, 2006, p. 86). The woman's direct gaze at the audience lasts for 12 seconds, then cuts to a black screen with the words 'Arranging narrative is a bourgeois mania' in its centre.

This statement points to a further paradox. That is, putting things into a rational order of cause and effect, a structure of meaning, is evidence of *mania*: a pathology, an illness or a derangement. Such a quotation begs the question: What is a narrative if not a story? What is the *Story of the Eye* if not the story of bourgeois mania? All literature (though not necessarily all narrative) is bourgeois. That is to say, literature is a product of the bourgeois era, modernity from the nineteenth century to present day.

What is interesting about McElhinney's, and in fact all real-sex middle-brow, art films is that they attempt to mix narrative and pornography. Currently, in the West, mainstream pornography is not interested in narrative. Instead, a *series* of acts and practices is presented in the same order in every film.

The introduction of narrative, drama and subjectivity into the relentless mechanical utilitarianism of pornography is unquestionably a new thing.

'Cuming' on (the) camera

After this statement, we suddenly find ourselves looking up at the male who is positioned naked in front of the camera. In one single shot, the actor purposefully cums onto the lens of the camera.

As a background to the event, a gigantic eye can be seen to fill the screen. This two-second shot is significant for two reasons. Firstly, the cuming onto the camera makes visible *the presence of the camera itself*. Secondly, this imposition of the camera serves to displace the spectator. The erotic/sexual act ends here in ejaculation onto the camera, thus occluding the vision of the viewer and simultaneously establishing a new non-human relationship: an intimacy with the camera. The cum shot is directed at the gaze of the spectator and foregrounds the gaze as the camera (Figure 10.3).

This scene is significant as it connects the first masturbation scene to this final shot in the eye. The vision of the viewer is occluded through this act and therefore the shot draws attention to the act of viewing. In essence, the viewer has to become aware of (him)self. More importantly however, the occlusion draws attention to the *camera* itself and the means of viewing. The ob-scenity of the viewer, his position of off-screenness, is both disclosed and rendered redundant. As such, this act points to the last area of obscenity/eroticism in contemporary society which is the eroticism of being filmed: of being exposed to vision by vision machines.

Figure 10.3   Georges Bataille's Story of the Eye: Sean Timothy Sexton cums onto the lens of the camera, blinding the spectator. Reproduced with kind permission from Andrew Repasky McElhinney.

The question, the purpose of his work, is potentially brought to bear only once the vision has died. As Phil Hall of *Film Threat* notes, McElhinney poses, through the composition of this scene, certain questions: 'Is this not what you have been waiting for? Does this scene, this performance authenticate your experience? Can you understand my reasoning, my vision?' (Hall, 2004). To make 'sense' of the film the audience are required to respond to the act of being blinded. Such a response is formulated through language. Language thus acts as an instrument through which the importance of spectatorship becomes reinforced. Technicity is as important as maleness as it is the obscenity of the look that the camera exposes. The gaze and the voice are here bound up with machines that serve to change and render them uncanny. As Felix Guattari notes is *Chaosophy:* 'By opening the series of partial objects beyond the breast and the faeces, to the voice and gaze, Jacques Lacan signified his refusal to close them off and reduce them to the body. The voice and gaze escape the body ... by becoming more and more adjacent to audiovisual machines' (Guattari, 1995, p. 104).

McElhinney's final cut to a black screen is accompanied by a technical and high-pitched noise. The darkness of the screen image and the noise projected render visible the blind spot in which the gaze and the voice operate as obscene machines. As Bataille states: 'There is in understanding a blind spot: reminiscent of the structure of the eye. The nature of understanding demands that the blind spot within it be more meaningful than understanding itself. Thus, the blind spot "absorbs one's attention: it is no longer the spot which looses itself in knowledge, but knowledge which looses itself in it"' (Bataille, cited in Botting and Wilson, 2001, p. 91). McElhinney's blinding of his spectator can then, conclusively, be read as a sight that acknowledges the sovereign status of non-knowledge, of darkness and of death in the erotic body.

The re-presentation of sexual performance in terms of producing and purposefully evoking *displeasure* offers a contradistinction to common pornographic visions of sexual utopia, pleasure and titillation. The illumination of the uncanny and the 'abnormal' in association with eroticism also serves to disturb spectator expectations by way of making visible the blind spot in which the erotic can be perceived scientifically, while paradoxically 'undoing' science. The real sex on scene is not presented as spectacle but rather as a spectre of the unknown and the obscene, which, in connection with the erotic, signals death. Ultimately, McElhinney indicates that the camera itself, that is the spectacle of sexual performance to/for a camera, is a locus of non-knowledge and as such is profoundly erotic.

Note

I acknowledge and thank Andrew McElhinney, director of *Georges Bataille's Story of the Eye* (2003, www.ARMcinema25.com), for his permission to use the images.

References

Ashton, Daniel (2006–7), 'Design for an Orgasm', in *RevolveWire*, Winter–Spring, pp. 20–1.

Auerbach, Jonathan (2000), 'Chasing Film Narrative: Repetition, Recursion, and the Body in Early Cinema', in *Critical Enquiry*, 26(4), Summer, pp. 798–820.

Barthes, Roland (1982), 'The Reality Effect', in Tzvetan Todorov (ed.), *French Literary Theory Today: A Reader*, trans. by R. Carter. Cambridge: Cambridge University Press, pp. 1–17.

Bataille, Georges (2001a), *Eroticism*, trans. by Mary Dalwood. London: Penguin Books.

Bataille, Georges (1988), *Inner Experience*, trans. by Leslie-Anne Boldt. New York: SUNY Press.

Bataille, Georges (2001b), *Story of the Eye*, trans. by Joachim Neugroschal. London: Penguin Books.

Baudrillard, Jean (2005), *The Intelligence of Evil or the Lucidity Pact*, trans. by Chris Turner. Oxford: Berg.

Botting, Fred and Wilson, Scott (2001), *Bataille Transitions*. Basingstoke: Palgrave Macmillan.

Buse, Peter (2001), *Drama + Theory: Critical Approaches to Modern British Drama*. Manchester: Manchester University Press.

Eidos Interactive, *Tomb Raider* (1996), available on http://www.tombraider.com, accessed on 2 February 2007.

Ellis, John (1992), *Visible Fictions: Cinema, Television and Radio*, 2nd edn. London: Routledge.

Flash Games, *Orgasm Girl* (2005), available on http://2flashgames.com/f/f-738.htm, accessed on 21 November 2007.

Freud, Sigmund (1991), 'Repression', in Angela Richards (ed.), *Penguin Freud Library 11: On Metapsychology: The Theory of Psychoanalysis*. London: Penguin, pp. 139–58.

Freud, Sigmund (1990), 'The Uncanny', in Albert Dickson (ed.), *Penguin Freud Library 14: Art and Literature*. London: Penguin, pp. 335–76.

Grosz, Elizabeth (1994), *Volatile Bodies: Towards a Corporeal Feminism*. Sydney: Allen and Unwin.

Guattari, Félix (1995), *Chaosophy*, Sylvere Lotringer (ed.). New York: Semiotext[e].

Hall, Phil (2004), 'Review of *Georges Bataille's Story of the Eye*', available on http://www.ARMcinema25.com/GBSOTEfilmThreatMarch25_2004.html, accessed on 21 November 2007.

Jackson, Rosemary (1981), *Fantasy: The Literature of Subversion*. London: Routledge.

Jay, Martin (1994), *Downcast Eyes: The Denigration of Vision in Twentieth-Century French Thought*. London: University of California Press.

King, Geoff (ed.) (2005), *The Spectacle of the Real: From Hollywood to Reality TV and Beyond*. Bristol: Intellect.

Kipp, Jeremiah (2003), 'Blue Movie: Georges Bataille's Story of the Eye', in *Filmmaker: The Magazine of Independent Film*, 12(2), available on http://www.ARMcinema25.com/GBSOTEFilmmakerVol12No2.html, accessed on 25 January 2007.

Krzywinska, Tanya (2006), *Sex and the Cinema*. London: Wallflower.

Lorentzen, Jørgen (2007), 'Masculinities and the Phenomenology of Men's Orgasms', in *Men and Masculinities*, 10(1), pp. 73–4.

Pearce, Lynne and Wisker, Gina (1998), 'Rescripting Romance: An Introduction', in Lynne and Wisker (eds), *Fatal Attractions: Rescripting Romance in Contemporary Literature and Film*. London: Pluto Press, pp. 1–19.

Peirse, Alison (2006), 'The Destruction of the Male Body in Classic Horror Cinema' (unpublished doctoral thesis, Lancaster University).

Williams, Linda (2001), 'Cinema and the Sex Act', in *Cineaste*, 27(1), pp. 20–5.

Zizek, Slavoj (2002), *Welcome to the Desert of the Real: Five Essays on September 11 and Other Related Dates*. London: Verso.

11
Breath Control: The Sound and Sight of Respiration as Hyperrealist Corporeality in *Breaking the Waves*

Davina Quinlivan

In her book *Nothing Happens*, Ivone Margulies remarks on cinema's potential not only to reflect the social realism of the human condition but also to create a heightened sense of 'hyperreality' (Margulies, 1996, p. 45). For Margulies, hyperrealism, particularly in the case of Chantal Ackerman's cinema, fleshes out the otherwise discrete, liminal or even invisible moments that are normally untraceable, forgotten or lost within the cumulative cycle of the everyday. Above all, it is the resurfacing of such moments through the profilmic body or, rather, everything placed before the camera that is concretely visible, that affirms, for Margulies, a highly 'corporeal cinema' (Margulies, 1996, p. 19). Although Margulies is particularly concerned with the material representation and assertion of the everyday conveyed through the profilmic body, this paper focuses primarily on the filmed, embodied subject on screen in order to suggest the human body as itself a source of the banal and unremarkable that gains value through hyperrealism. In this respect, I explore one of the most mundane and overlooked, yet crucial, aspects of human corporeality that is charged with meaning when foregrounded: the sound and sight of the *breathing* body.

Engaging specifically with Margulies's definition of hyperrealism, I contemplate Lars von Trier's style of filmmaking, particularly in *Breaking the Waves* (1996), as it both reveals and restricts the body in a way that draws attention to respiration. To understand von Trier's evocation of the breathing body and, most importantly, its suggestion through *Breaking the Waves*'s lead protagonist, Bess (Emily Watson), I consider the philosophical thought of Luce Irigaray whose theoretical discussion of breathing offers a way in which to shed light on the significance of breath in the closing act of the film. Through discussion of both the visual and aural track, I suggest that breathing is not only hyperreal, but what I describe as an inner, and thus also immaterial, unravelling of the cinematic, corporeal subject. This will lead me to consider how breathing is a central aspect of Emily Watson's performance at the close of the film, while the film's audio track prompts me to consider the haptic implications of listening to a body that breathes.

Breaking the Waves is the first part of a trilogy of films made by von Trier to question the concept of goodness. Set on a remote coastal village in Scotland within a strict Calvinist community, the film opens with Bess confessing her love for Jann (Stellan Skarsgård), an outsider and non-believer whom she has come to know through his visits from the nearby oil rig where he is stationed as an engineer. Jann and Bess marry, but their happiness is abruptly compromised when Jann returns to work and is soon after involved in an accident which leaves him severely injured. Paralysed and doubting his virility and ability as a lover, Jann encourages Bess to leave him, but she refuses. Appealing to her childlike innocence, Jann lies to Bess, leading her to believe that if she takes a lover his condition will improve. Fatally, for Bess, Jann's condition does improve immediately after her first encounter with another man. Taking this as a sign from God, Bess continues to offer her body to other men, but when Jann's condition worsens, she convinces herself that only the sacrifice of her own life will truly save her husband from death.

Preceding *Dancer in the Dark* (2000) and *The Idiots* (*Idioterne*, 1998), *Breaking the Waves* is the first of von Trier's 'Gold Heart' triptych to submit to the ten rules of filmmaking of the 'Dogme Vow of Chastity'. This movement was established by von Trier and his Danish compatriot Thomas Vinterberg – *The Celebration* (*Festen*, 1998), *It's All About Love* (2003) – to challenge dominant modes of film production. The rules forbid artifice in the sense that props and sets are not allowed, as well as any allusion to genre. To further emphasize the importance of authenticity, both sound and location are also required to be real and therefore never fabricated or reproduced. Consequently, the Dogme rules inspire a fresh and energizing form of realism that is uniquely felt throughout *Breaking the Waves*.

Although I am interested in the way in which the Dogme rules lend to *Breaking the Waves* a particular kind of formal expression that foregrounds the breathing body, through sound as well as performance, I am also specifically concerned with the way the film addresses the breathing subject. The film's representation of the central female subject has prompted firm rejection by some critics on the grounds of its, seemingly, misogynistic and violent depiction of female suffering and self-sacrifice (see, for example, Collins, 1997). Yet, perversely, a considerable number of feminist and often psychoanalytic readings have supported a rather affirmative view of the film. Suzy Gordon's article, for example, emphasizes the importance of negativity as a 'constitutive condition of feminist film theory that puts at risk precisely the articulation of female subjectivity as it also compels' (Gordon, 2004, p. 225).

Gordon's interest in reclaiming the negativity of *Breaking the Waves* is also echoed in the work of Caroline Bainbridge, whose model of thought is especially informed by the philosophy of Irigaray. In her book *The Cinema of Lars von Trier: Authenticity and Artifice*, Bainbridge focuses on issues of trauma and the role of affect in order to understand the appeal of von Trier's 'unpleasurable' cinema, adopting an Irigarayan strategy that develops thought on the ethical positioning of the viewer. She writes:

> In the 'Gold Heart' trilogy, the narrative trauma, which is constructed through personal and intimate relationships, is paralleled by a trauma that is evoked in the spectator. Just as there is a shift away from the terrain of power toward the terrain of love, there is also a corresponding shift in the way trauma is motivated in the films and in their ethical investment in structures of feeling and affect rather than in structures of discourse and power.
>
> (Bainbridge, 2007, p. 119)

Elaborating on the 'Gold Heart' trilogy's foregrounding of female desire and pleasure, Bainbridge innovatively builds on Irigaray's assertion of a feminine consciousness to demonstrate how the film's subject matter exceeds, through von Trier's formal style, the limits of the contained world within the filmic diegesis and is inscribed upon the viewing experience. My discussion of the film is also concerned with issues of subjectivity from an Irigarayan perspective, but I aim to address more thoroughly the corporeal subject that is embodied by breath alone. Whereas Bainbridge's engagement with Irigaray draws on the ethical dimension of her theoretical discourse and her overarching concerns with sexual difference, my interest is with her most recent phenomenological line of enquiry, which contemplates the breathing body as well as air. This is not to say that Irigaray's later texts, such as 'A Breath that Touches in Words' (1996) or 'The Age of the Breath'(2004), should be viewed separately from Irigaray's other philosophical concerns; rather, that they form an important stage in her thinking that is most appropriate to my exploration of *Breaking the Waves*.

Phenomenological film theory, Irigaray and breath

Breathing is a fundamental aspect of human existence whose presence is rarely registered in film. In her book *The Address of the Eye*, Vivian Sobchack's phenomenological film theory draws a parallel between the cinematic apparatus and the human, breathing body, comparing film's intermittent flow of images into and out of the film projector to a respiratory process (Sobchack, 1992, p. 207). For Sobchack, the cinematic image is thus suggestive of oxygen or 'breath', whereas the apparatus is the body that breathes. However, despite an emergent trend within film studies privileging analyses of the body, corporeality and materiality, recent models of thought have yet to explore the significance of breathing. In the wider discipline of cultural studies, the current research objective pursued by the phenomenological, literary and media theorist Steven Connor explores the social and symbolic significance of air including an address of the radio (airwaves), architecture (spaces of air) and ventriloquism (pneumatics) (Connor, 2004). However, the visual source of air is, with the exception of Connor's essay on art and its abstract containment of air, predominantly absent. Curious about film's visual and aural suggestion of breathing and what it might mean in the context of analysing subjectivity and forms of being on screen, I synthesize Irigaray's concern not only with the significance of air as a metaphysical concept, but with the way in which air has been overlooked in criticism of Western cinema.

Although framed and contextualized by Irigaray's principal concerns with sexual difference as set out in her early work *Speculum of the Other Woman* (1985), her 'age' or culture of breathing, in many ways, stages a phenomenological encounter that moves towards a new culture of difference inclusive of a third space: air as fundamental mode of being. Air thus fulfils a mediatory role or, in simpler terms, it engenders a positive, inter-subjective space within which to live. Indeed, Irigaray's philosophy contends that the sharing of breath between men and women is more fundamental than the idea of exchangeable words, a language that is phenomenological as well as practical: a philosophical concept as well as a real, lived, subjective experience.

The thought of Irigaray provides a departure from Sobchack's analysis, theorizing breath not only in relation to the sexed body, but to the *elemental*, to the place of air as invisible dwelling and, more specifically, the relationship between breathing and sound, silence and music (see, in particular, Irigaray, 1999). It is this particular facet of Irigarayan thought, linking breath with a kind of aural, sensory experience (Irigaray, 1996), that most effectively illuminates my reading of Bess in *Breaking the Waves*. For Irigaray, breathing engenders a return to oneself, to the interior of what she describes as an embodied silence, and my concern is with how this materializes, as it were, through von Trier's hyperrealist aesthetic. Through my discussion of breath in *Breaking the Waves*, I not only challenge conceptions of the material, because this bodily act is usually understood as an invisible process, but also perceptions of the hyperreal, dominantly conceived of as a material inscription within the film.

Mise-en-scène, narrative and the breathing body

The breathing body is diegetically present in several ways in *Breaking the Waves*. For example, the microphone that Bess's sister-in-law Dodo (Katrin Cartledge) uses when giving a speech at Jann and Bess's wedding emphasizes an acute sense of onscreen sound which enables the viewer to hear her choked, anxious breaths fracturing her efforts to remain emotionally restrained. Also, when Jann and Bess make love, their energetic, overtly audible heavy breathing serves as a potent sign of the emancipatory nature of their sexual encounter, enunciating Bess's rapturous liberation from the joyless conditions of her patriarchal community. No doubt, these filmic moments where the breathing body is foregrounded contribute towards the film's fleshing out of its narrative discourse, but they offer limited scope for reflection beyond the analysis of their function within the diegesis. Breathing does, however, figure as a more central aspect of how we perceive the film's lead protagonist, Bess, as occupying a significant position both within the film's form and the viewing experience as a whole.

One of the most striking scenes where breath is foregrounded in *Breaking the Waves* takes place towards the end, when Bess is shown in close-up travelling on a boat towards a large ship. This is the last time we see her before she makes her ultimate sacrifice for Jann, and the subtle sound and image of her breathing serves as a measure not only of her fragile emotional state, but of the transient and fleeting nature of her mortal being. Bess knows she will be brought to her death by those on board the ship and is therefore deliberately voyaging towards her executioners, a passage towards death that also recalls *Dancer in the Dark*'s conclusion in the gallows. The passage also emphasizes the film's thematic hagiography, which often dwells on the procession or public display of the female martyr, subverted here by von Trier given the absence of a crowd or gathering in this scene.

A few seconds before Bess boards the boat, we see her in a medium shot framed with the mossy, Hebridean coast behind her on either side of the screen; she is clearly dishevelled and overwhelmed, but her patient resolve, the focal point of this scene, clearly reflects a determination to regain composure. There is very little movement in the frame except for a few strands of hair that sweep across Bess's face while the rest of her body is motionless. We hear nothing except the soaring cry of seagulls circling the harbour bay. Then, there is a small but significant movement: Bess inhales deeply and we view her mouth open a little, her head raises upwards, her shoulders move and her whole body lifts for the briefest of moments. Therefore, breath is suggested more through vision than sound as a bodily act that compels movement, and Bess's physical and emotional exertion are here matched by the co-ordinating image of her drawing breath.

Contrastingly, in the scene that follows, attention is drawn more to the prominent aurality of Bess's breathing, but here the visual representation of this expressive sigh is underpinned by a formal gesture: the image quivers and loses focus precisely when Bess inhales. Suddenly, the static framing of the image is affected by Bess's breathing: it slips slightly out of focus and then recovers composure. One might argue that this register of movement embodied through the film's form is simply characteristic of the lightweight handheld camera that von Trier uses. However, it seems that this perceptible instability conveyed through the film's form is rather more of a deliberate gesture by the filmmaker to provoke in the viewer similar feelings of disorientation that are felt by Bess and, given the timing of this formal affect, it appears to relate directly to Bess's breathing corporeality. If the momentary blurring of the image corresponds to the rush of oxygen entering Bess's body, then the image's switch back into sharp focus might be understood as a kind of exhaling. In other words, the 'body' of the film seems to suggest a movement of release or rather literal recomposure that is synchronous with the body in the film's diegesis.

Although we are unable to 'feel' Bess breathing, because screens cannot breathe, the image's loss of focal stability affects our bodily and conscious perception. Indeed, to a certain degree, the discrete change in focus creates an interval that evokes a sensation of relief, albeit visual, and therefore this freshly configured perspective echoes the 'feeling' that Bess's restorative breathing also grants her. In sum, Bess's emotive sigh is a fitting example of the way in which breath becomes an important element of the film and works to foster an interval of mutual, embodied experience between the viewer and the subject on screen.

Whereas breathing is visually alluded to in the scene I have just discussed, the next scene places emphasis on hearing rather than viewing. On screen, we see Bess's pale, almost translucent face, while in the background we view the coast and flat, silvery sheets of water. This image is crosscut with the distant view of the ship, underlined by thinning peaks of waves. What happens on the soundtrack, meanwhile, is reflective of earlier solitary scenes with Bess, her voice split into two as she asks questions to God and then answers them herself, in a mono/dialogue. The first line is hesitantly spoken: 'Father, why aren't you with me?'. Following this line, we cut to an image of the ship and then back again to Watson. Although this crosscutting plots a point of destination and emphasizes the narrowing path towards death, it also draws attention to the spaces of silence between the presence of speech. This also seems to act as a substitute for the body that the close cropping of Bess's face prevents us from viewing. Thus, what is heard on the soundtrack articulates an altered perception of corporeality, one that emphasizes the sound of breathing. For about eight seconds there is no speech. In this time we can clearly hear every fluctuation of Bess's breathing, softly, sharply, softly, and then a gasp (Figures 11.1, 11.2 and 11.3).

Accompanying these breaths on the imagetrack, the right side of the screen is immersed in sunlight, giving an impression of the sea as a shifting backdrop of whiteness. Almost glowing, the light illuminates one side of Bess's face and scatters highlights throughout the image, a constant reminder of her purity and transcendence, accentuated through her tentative breaths. In this respect, the most crucial difference between von Trier's cinematic depiction of the martyr and Carl Theodor Dreyer's in *The Passion of Joan of Arc* (*La Passion de Jeanne d'Arc*, 1928), one of the film's strongest formal influences, is the sound of breathing that von Trier originates in *Breaking the Waves*. Although von Trier is certainly inspired by Dreyer's tightly framed images of his martyr's face, the lack of sound in Dreyer's film denies the viewer the same kind of access to breath that von Trier offers

Figure 11.1   Breaking the Waves: The loss of sharpness of the image indicates that the film's 'body' breathes with the protagonist. Reproduced with kind permission from Trust Films and Emily Watson.

Figure 11.2   Breaking the Waves: Little breaths. Reproduced with kind permission from Trust Films and Emily Watson.

Figure 11.3   Breaking the Waves: 'Father, why aren't you with me?' Reproduced with kind permission from Trust Films and Emily Watson.

in *Breaking the Waves*. Although it might be argued that Dreyer effectively compensates for the lack of sound in his film through his formidable formal style and, in particular, the recurrent image of his martyr's open mouth and her almost palpable gasping breath, von Trier's inclusion of breath on his

soundtrack introduces a dual layer of meaning in relation to both the symbolic narrative of the film's diegesis and its role as an affective device. Breath
signifies another kind of vocalization of Bess's suffering within the diegesis,
which also has implications for the viewer who hears the sound of breathing. Ultimately, by offering the viewer this register of breath on the film's
soundtrack, von Trier pushes the limits of the diegesis from inside the film's
mise-en-scène, shifting its tone from the impressionistic and the mythical
to the real or, rather, the hyperreal.

Although Watson's breathing body suggestively evokes the realm of the
symbolic, the fantastic or the unreal, it must also be acknowledged that the
act of breathing itself is unexceptional, mundane, its sound is analogous to
the everyday. The hyperreal is thus effectuated through Watson's corporeal
performance. On the issue of performance in von Trier's cinema, Bainbridge
interestingly remarks on the staging of artifice that it 'has as its cause
a fascination with the possibility of authenticity' (Bainbridge, 2007, p. 166).
Such a paradoxical possibility of the authentic as the driving force behind
Watson's performance exists precisely through her breathing, which cannot
fully articulate artifice, because it marks her body's relationship with reality, that is, the immediate reality or 'truth' of that moment within which it
occurs. This kind of hyperrealist corporeality is not inscribed in a thoroughly
concrete way, as Margulies would argue, at least not in the *visible* sense of
materiality, but the haptic implications of hearing Bess's breathing body
suggest ways in which to analyse the matter of its 'invisible' presence.

Breath as affective device, audio haptics and the embodied viewer

Although Watson's performance tends to locate the viewer within a strong
position of identification, the specific act of *hearing* breath also draws attention to an embodied encounter between film and spectator that might
relate to a kind of aural form of haptics. The recent and most innovative
thinking of Laura Marks conceives the term 'haptic visuality' (Marks, 1999,
p. xi) to describe a mode of seeing that responds to the texture of the image.
Although Marks tends to privilege vision over sound in her analysis, her
thoughts on film hearing suggest a tantalizing engagement with breathing
that is brief, but richly suggestive. She writes: 'the aural boundaries between
body and world may feel indistinct: the rustle of trees may mingle with the
sound of my breathing, or conversely the booming music may inhabit my
chest and move my body from the inside' (Marks, 1999, p. 183). Marks's
underlining of breath is impressive given its minimal presence within
film theory, and her emphasis on the way it shares its sounds with other
noises recalls von Trier's deliberate enfolding of Watson's breath within the
elements where voice and body also become inseparable through sound.
However, whereas Marks develops a haptics that functions according to the

viewer's proximity to the image, breath reconfigures these issues in a way that, as Irigaray suggests, 'weaves a proximity' (Irigaray, 2004, p. 150), an invisible passage between the subject and the exterior world, as well as between viewer and film.

On the aural spaces between speech, Irigaray describes breath as a way in which we can return to ourselves, an interiority constituted through the flow of breath that is also comparable to what she terms a partial 'touching upon' and thus sensorial without ever reaching entirely outside of ourselves. She writes: 'breathing and speaking use breath in almost inverse proportion, at least in our tradition, at least for most of us, but *this touching upon* needs attentiveness to the sensible qualities of speech, to the modulation and rhythm of discourse, to the semantic and phonic choice of words' (Irigaray, 1996, p. 114). From a haptic perspective, Irigaray's thought might amount to a theorization of 'touching' with the ears rather than the eyes, as Marks has suggested through her concept of 'haptic visuality'. Irigaray's philosophy offers a way towards thinking about our aural perception of breath as a new form of hearing the materiality of the body. For Roland Barthes, the grain of the voice is the materiality of the body speaking its mother tongue (Barthes, 1977, p. 188). Barthes also considers breath as an aspect of vocality, but it is not included in his tangible notion of the voice. The recent article of Phil Powrie (2008) on François Ozon *5 X 2* (2004) makes a fascinating connection between the grain of the voice and an audible textuality which he suggests as an instance of haptic hearing. I share Powrie's interest in the aural possibilities of the haptic, but whereas his emphasis is on what he refers to as the 'gravelly' voice of the male singer featured on the soundtrack of Ozon's film and its signification of male melancholia, my engagement with Irigaray's theorization of breathing uncovers a different kind of hapticity in *Breaking the Waves*.

Von Trier uses sync sound throughout the film to produce a live or highly naturalistic effect and it is through this particular formal aspect of *Breaking the Waves* that breathing is most explicitly registered. Images of von Trier's visceral films are often noted for their graininess, but the audiotrack also produces something that is comparable to this impression of the visual field. Primarily, von Trier's use of sync sound in *Breaking the Waves* captures an aspect of Watson's performance that allows us to trace the relationship between speech and breath or what would normally be considered as the inaudible or silent pauses between dialogue. Von Trier's use of sync sound creates within these silences pockets of expression that are usually banished or minimized through the manipulation of sound levels. Furthermore, in *Breaking the Waves*, the level of breathing is recurrently as audible as the level of speech, a sound that contributes towards our impression of Bess as an embodied subject whose voice enunciates *through* and *with* her body.

Bess's 'bodily' enunciation of breath can be observed during the moment just after she asks, 'Father, why aren't you with me?', when we are able to detect both the visual and audio suggestion of her breathing body. This corporeal 'touching upon', as Irigaray suggests, draws attention to the immutable presence of breath that rests between language and words. On the imagetrack, we see Bess in close-up detail, her lips part, her nostrils contract, frown lines around her mouth crease, her eyes blink and she swallows the cold air. However, these delicate traces of emotion are more profoundly embodied through the soundtrack and therefore hearing is prioritized above vision. Although it is Bess's face that is physically close to us in its proximity to the camera, the dominance of breathing on the soundtrack penetrates beyond the surface of the skin and its suggestion of sensations, encouraging the viewer to experience the inner intensity of the body. On the soundtrack, the exasperation of Bess's body is felt through the sound of her quickening, laboured breaths; we hear the gently ascending and descending passage of air through the body, the shaft of breath escaping the mouth and its unsteady, uneven faltering and rising, we perceive the sensation of air against the back of the throat and the tightening of the chest as gasps rapidly increase. Attuned to this momentary rhythm, the sound of breathing creates another dimension of the lived body on screen for the viewer: it lends it volume and shape through the suggestion of a human physicality that can almost be felt and, as a kind of rough, sonic object, touched.

Concluding thoughts

This way of reading *Breaking the Waves*, both through Watson's performance and the sound of her breathing body as sonic texture within the film, asks the viewer to think again about their sensuous bodies and the rhythms, gestures and movements that respiration posits *between* the senses. Breathing is not a sense per se, but for Irigaray the act of breathing is itself sensuous in that we experience through breath a specific engagement with our bodies and with the world: a bodily movement constantly drawing away from and towards subjective being. In her book *Atlas of Emotion*, the film and contemporary visual arts theorist Giuliana Bruno describes a form of viewing as ingestion, an eye-mouth that maps a space where eating and knowing make for a 'gastric philosophy' (Bruno, 2002, p. 290). If Bruno's eye-mouth resembles a consumptive vision, then the *breathing-mouth* of *Breaking the Waves* seeks nourishment not from a contaminating closeness or appropriation. Breath is the preservation of the self, nourishing an inner vision that is forever unfolding and open to change; the breathing-mouth mediates a space between self and world and marks that moment in time through its cyclic rhythms.

The particularly dominant traces of breath in the sequence I have just described amplifies the tragic and immensely fragile nature of that particular moment in the film. However, breathing also effects a shift within the diegesis that reaches amplification through *Breaking the Waves'* formal expression. Thus both the filmed subject and the cinematic 'body' inform a different viewing experience that might, to borrow from Marks, relate to a *breathing visuality*. Above all, breath opens up a space for thinking about the everyday and the hyperreal not as a completely material presence, as Margulies has theorized, but as an (im)material or, rather, less visually perceptible aspect of *Breaking the Waves'* mise-en-scène. In conclusion, it would be possible to understand von Trier's hyperrealist aesthetic not in terms of what Margulies conceives of as a 'nothing happening', but rather something happening out of nothingness. Enabled by Irigaray's thought on breath as a fundamental aspect of human subjectivity, we glimpse an alternative mapping of Bess's interior consciousness in *Breaking the Waves*; we feel as if we have touched beneath the surface of her voyage in the flesh towards transcendence.

Note

I am grateful to Phil Powrie and to the editor of the special issue of *Paragraph: A Journal of Modern Critical Theory* (July 2008), Emma Wilson, for allowing me to view his article, 'The Haptic Moment: Sparring with Paolo Conte in Ozon's *5 X 2*', before its publication.

References

Bainbridge, Caroline (2007), *The Cinema of Lars von Trier: Authenticity and Artifice*. London: Wallflower Press.

Barthes, Roland (1977), *Image, Music, Text*, selected and trans. by Stephen Heath. London: Fontana.

Bruno, Giuliana (2002), *Atlas of Emotion: Journeys in Art, Architecture and Film*. London: Verso.

Chion, Michel (2004), *Audio-Vision: Sound on Screen*. New York/Chichester: Columbia University Press.

Collins, Noreen (1997), 'Counterpoint', in *Film West*, issue 72, February, p. 47.

Connor, Steven (2004), 'On the Air', transcript of his broadcast at 21.30 p.m. on BBC Radio 3 on 13 June, available on http://www.bbk.ac.uk/english/skc/onair/, accessed on 23 February 2007.

Gordon, Suzy (2004), '*Breaking the Waves* and the Negativity of Melanie Klein: Rethinking the Female Spectator', in *Screen*, 45(3), pp. 206–25.

Irigaray, Luce (1996), 'A Breath That Touches in Words', *I Love to You: A Sketch for a Felicity within History*. London/ New York: Routledge, pp. 121–8.

Irigaray, Luce (1999), *The Forgetting of Air in Martin Heidegger*. London/Austin: Athlone Press.

Irigaray, Luce (2004), 'Rebuilding the World', *The Way of Love*. London/New York: Continuum, pp. 137–66.

Irigaray, Luce (1985), *Speculum of the Other Woman*, trans. by Gillian C. Gill. Ithaca: Cornell University Press.

Margulies, Ivone (1996), *Nothing Happens: Chantal Ackerman's Hyperrealist Everyday*. Durham, NC: Duke University Press.

Marks, Laura U. (1999), *The Skin of the Film: Intercultural Cinema, Embodiment and the Senses*. Durham, NC: Duke University Press.

Powrie, Phil (2008), 'The Haptic Moment: Sparring with Paolo Conte in Ozon's 5 × 2', in *Paragraph: A Journal of Modern Critical Theory*, 31(2), pp. 206–22.

Sobchack, Vivian (1992), *The Address of the Eye: Phenomenology and the Film Experience*. Princeton: Princeton University Press.

Wilson, Emma (2004), 'Dogme Ghosts', *Cinema's Missing Children*. London: Wallflower Press.

12
Ontology, Film and the Case of Eric Rohmer

Jacob Leigh

In his 1945 essay, 'The Ontology of the Photographic Image', André Bazin compares photography to fingerprints and brass rubbing. In 1977, David Thomson echoes this when he writes 'the [photographic] image is accepted as a coin-like representation of the person' (Thomson, 1977, p. 240). Thomson argues that film actors are subjects of a film, the subjects almost of quasi-documentaries; even big-budget films with high-profile stars can appear like 'covert documentaries of a star, discreetly phrased as "stories"' (p. 242). For Bazin, whatever Enzo Staiola does as Bruno in *Bicycle Thieves* (*Ladri di Biciclette*, Vittorio De Sica, 1948), 'is never without meaning. On the contrary it is the phenomenology of the script' (Bazin, 1972, pp. 54–5). Most filmmakers would recognize this emphasis on the importance of the film actor to the meaning of a film. Eric Rohmer comments:

> In contrast to the theatre, the choice of an actor in cinema is a part of the film. It's Goethe who said 'Hamlet must be played by a flabby, indolent fat man, now that he is always played by a thin man'. In film, this discussion is not possible. One cannot replace one actor with another because the phrases are written to work for someone specific.
>
> (Villien, 1984, p. 53)

The credibility of a performance depends in large part upon the appropriate fit between an actor and the character they play.

Credibility and expressive significance are two things for which we often value films. Although actors are central to these achievements, so too are settings, whether studio sets or locations. V. F. Perkins writes of the use of locations and sets:

> Direction does not involve total freedom to locate actions or to design settings. Quite often a location is dictated by the plot and design controlled by the location. The director has to start from what is known or necessary or likely or, at the very least, possible. From this base he can go on

to organize the relationship between action, image and décor, to create meaning through pattern. But credibility remains the controlling factor.
(Perkins, 1978, p. 94)

Maintaining credibility, Perkins argues, disciplines directors. The camera is an impersonal recording instrument; it films what is before it; the director has to find a way of introducing his or her viewpoint and vision into that process. For Perkins, skilful direction involves the ability, as he writes, 'to annul the distinction between significant organization and objective recording' (Perkins, 1978, p. 97). The best directors find ways of introducing their viewpoints into films in ways that seem to be necessary, borne out of, as Perkins writes, the 'need to inform rather than the desire to comment' (p. 102).

Whereas for Perkins good directors annul the distinction between organization and recording, for art historian Ernst Gombrich, Raphael, in 'Madonna della Sedia', was able to satisfy the 'two mutually limiting demands of lifelikeness and arrangement' (Gombrich, 1993, p. 74). The ability to satisfy these two demands of lifelikeness and arrangement can be a mark of good film direction. Bazin writes, '[t]he great artists, of course, have always been able to combine the two tendencies. They have allotted to each its proper place in the hierarchy of things, holding reality at their command and moulding it at will into the fabric of their art' (Bazin, 1967, p. 11). Our demand for artistic realism becomes more urgent with film because, as Jean-Luc Godard has said, 'every film is a documentary of its actors'. Quoting this aphorism, Gilberto Perez suggests that

[a] fiction movie constructs the fiction of characters from the documentary of actors. It is the documentary of a fiction enacted before the camera; and it is the fiction of a documentary of characters merged in our minds with their incarnation in the actors.
(Perez, 1998, p. 343)

For Perez, as for Bazin, actors and their presence on film are part of film's ontology. Bazin (1967) starts his famous essay by referring to ancient religious beliefs that identify the representational model with the thing that it represents. Although he acknowledges that '[n]o one believes any longer in the ontological identity of model and image', Bazin insists that 'all are agreed that the image helps us to remember the subject and to preserve him from a second spiritual death' (p. 10). For Bazin, photographs resemble natural phenomena in that the 'vegetable or earthly origins are an inseparable part of their beauty' (p. 13). He compares photography with death masks by calling photography a 'moulding', 'the taking of an impression, by the manipulation of light' (p. 12). Bazin is not naïve, though; most readers will remember his essay's last sentence: 'On the other hand, of course, cinema is also a language' (p. 16). By this, Bazin does not mean that film is a language with a dictionary and rules of syntax, but that the medium of film has conventions, a system of rhetoric, which is influenced by technological, social and cultural factors.

In *The World Viewed* and *Pursuits of Happiness*, Stanley Cavell develops Bazin's insights about the ontological importance of actor or object to film and about the role of the original when sculpting the reproduction. Writing of *The Philadelphia Story* (George Cukor, 1940), Cavell asks 'who is this man, CK Dexter Haven/Cary Grant?' and then answers that he is, after all, Cary Grant (Cavell, 1981, p. 137). In doing so, Cavell affirms that the film character does not exist without the actor. Just as Enzo Staiola's particular gait affects our interpretation of *Bicycle Thieves*, so Katharine Hepburn's distinctive voice, gestures, postures and presence guide our understanding of *The Philadelphia Story*, and that film is built upon our recognizing this relationship between star and character, in that it addresses the transformation of Hepburn in the public eye.[1] Cavell notes of *The Lady Eve* (Preston Sturges, 1941) that it 'invites us to consider the source of romance' and then that 'we, as the audience of film, are fated, or anyway meant, to be gulled by film' (Cavell, 1981, p. 49). How can Hopsy (Henry Fonda) not notice that Jean and Eve are both Barbara Stanwyck? Marion Keane points out that Hopsy's dilemma relates to our own problem: Stanwyck is the same person as Stella Dallas, as Jean Harrington and as Naomi Murdoch in *All I Desire* (Douglas Sirk, 1953). Preston Sturges, Keane notes, exposes our 'willingness to be conned', our willingness to overlook what we know to be true: the same actor plays Stella, Jean, Eve and Naomi (Keane, 2001). If Henry Fonda does not recognize Jean as Eve, he is allowing himself to be duped as we allow ourselves to be duped when we do not acknowledge the significance of our knowing that Stella, Jean and Naomi are Barbara Stanwyck.

To acknowledge this is to reject arguments that seek to persuade us that film presents us with an illusion of reality; and, as Cavell notes, there are theories 'that assume that we do not know the difference between projections of things and real things' (Cavell, 1981, p. 62). These theories are sceptical because they doubt our ability to distinguish between illusion and reality. Bazin's emphasis on a boy's way of walking emphasizes film's capacity for showing us things. However, some accounts of fiction films describe film's capacity for transparency as an illusion, something that is sinister because it hides the means of representation, hides the way that what we see has been selected, arranged and organized; film apparently deceives us into thinking that we have a natural and neutral relationship with the world – what we see is what there is. To doubt the truth of what we see is to be a sceptic. J. L. Austin characterizes scepticism as follows: 'The general doctrine, generally stated, goes like this: we never see or otherwise perceive (or "sense"), or anyhow we never *directly* perceive or sense, material objects (or material things), but only sense-data (or our own ideas, impressions, sensa, sense-perceptions, percepts)' (Austin, 1962, p. 2). Austin argues that we should acknowledge what we ordinarily know:

> It is important to realize here how familiarity, so to speak, takes the edge off illusion. Is the cinema a case of illusion? Well, just possibly the first man who ever saw moving pictures may have felt inclined to say that here was a case of illusion. But in fact it's pretty unlikely that even he, even momentarily, was actually taken in; and by now the whole thing is so ordinary a part of our lives that it never occurs to us even to raise the question. One might as well ask whether producing a photograph is producing illusion – which would plainly be just silly.
>
> (pp. 26-7)

For Cavell, the refutation of scepticism only extends it; 'true recovery lies in reconceiving it, in finding skepticism's source' (Cavell, 1988, p. 80).

Film as a moving image of scepticism

In his study of 'undramatic achievement in narrative film', Andrew Klevan extends Cavell's ideas, while praising restraint in film style as a lack of assertiveness, a 'style of inconsequentiality' (Klevan, 2000, p. 183). Klevan links three related concepts. The first is a theory of value in film. He argues for the importance of films that do not assert their style or theme; he values integrated expressiveness rather than overt expressionism. We can find a productive combination of different elements in many works of art, but Klevan considers undramatic achievement in film as a test case for stressing the importance of expressiveness in films that do not assert style or theme, but allow audiences to discover them.

Klevan's second conceptual focus is on everyday topics rather than melodramatic events; he demonstrates how films by Bresson, Ozu, Rohmer and Forman express the rhythms of everyday interactions, rather than concentrating energies and tensions around big events. Klevan proposes that most films are organized around 'eventful change' (2000, p. 56). Undramatic films are all characterized by a focus on uneventful activity; they 'conform to transparency principles, obeying a spatial and temporal fluidity and continuity, but they are not tight and condensed with regard to events and actions' (p. 61). Eric Rohmer's films are examples of films that, Klevan writes, 'illustrate that cinema's unique narrational possibilities for combining photographic realism and patterned arrangement allow for an absorbing uncovering of the "fact of the visible" without relying upon *interesting* visuals (motivated by events, crisis or fundamental narrative change)' (p. 63). The crises of melodrama or spectacular catastrophes appeal to our interest in fiction that works through weighty vicissitudes in a high register, indirectly reflecting feelings we might have. Rohmer's films work through similar feelings, but do so openly: whereas melodramas exaggerate everyday feelings, Rohmer's films concentrate on uneasy longings, vague disappointments and nagging worries.

The third part of Klevan's thesis is his philosophical emphasis on the everyday and on ordinary language, with roots in Stanley Cavell's responses to scepticism. Klevan joins Cavell's concern with the ordinary and the everyday to a discussion of undramatic achievement in film and, quoting *Pursuits of Happiness*, Klevan summarizes Cavell's position:

> With the end of sureties provided by Christianity, and then the failure of a 'redemptive politics' or 'redemptive psychology', Cavell argues that there needs to be 'a new burden of faith in the authority of one's everyday experience, one's experience of the everyday, of earth not of heaven'.
>
> (Klevan, 2000, p. 25, quoting Cavell, 1981, p. 240)

Simon Critchley summarizes the problem of scepticism:

> The experience of religious disappointment provokes the following, potentially abyssal question: if the legitimating theological structures and religious belief systems in which people like us believed are no longer believable, if, to coin a phrase, God is dead, then what becomes of the question of the meaning of life?
>
> (Critchley, 2004, p. xix)

Critchely sees the new burden as a question of how to resist nihilism, and he writes of Cavell's response:

> [T]o acknowledge the truth of scepticism is not the same as admitting that scepticism is true, for this would constitute a further escape into a new inverted metaphysics of certainty, namely relativism. Rather Cavell is seeking to draw us into a position where we are denied *both* the possibility of an epistemological guarantee for our beliefs and the possibility of a sceptical escape from those beliefs.
>
> (Critchley, 2004, p. 155)

Film is connected to the problem of scepticism because, as Cavell argues, it offers a moving image of scepticism; it satisfies our requirements for the presence of a world and for people in it even though these things are absent. As Klevan puts it, film 'can consummately blur the distinction between fantasy, or the human desire to wish, and reality. It rests on the cinema combining an intimate relationship with reality with an ability to distort it' (2000, p. 19). Film, like photography, seems to reproduce reality mechanically; sceptics argue that the naturalness of photographic film's ontological relation to reality blinds us to the human intervention that helps construct that naturalness.

Cavell, however, resists theories that deny reality's role in film, not to deny scepticism's conclusion but, as he writes, 'to determine the place of skepticism's inspiration' (Cavell, 1979, pp. 165–6). He finds that film is unlike other forms of art because of the absence of what it causes to appear to us; this absence makes film a moving image of scepticism. His impatience with claims that photographs do not represent reality stems from his sense that a fake scepticism is used to deny human responsibility. Philosophers who propose that films offer an illusion of reality try to disguise a latent anxiety about 'what our conviction in reality turns upon' (p. 189). To acknowledge this lack of knowledge about what our conviction in reality turns upon is not to deny that we are convinced of reality's existence:

Film is a moving image of scepticism: not only is there a reasonable possibility, it is a fact that here our normal senses are satisfied of reality while reality does not exist – even, alarmingly, *because* it does not exist, because viewing it is all it takes.

(pp. 188–9)

For Cavell, film's capacity to project reality is the basis of its most profound dramas; as he writes, 'the basis of film's drama, or the latent anxiety in viewing its drama, lies in its persistent demonstration that we do not know what our conviction in reality turns upon' (p. 189). To talk about films as offering 'an illusion of reality' is for Cavell a way of disguising our anxieties about our belief in reality.[2] Klevan notes that for Cavell, 'the surrendering to the burden of scepticism is nothing less than a modern tragedy' (2000, p. 12). He argues that Cavell's analysis of the ontology of film shows why film is so suited to sceptical themes and to melodrama (p. 17); film shows us the dangers of scepticism.

Acknowledging the importance of the performer is a way of avoiding a surrender to scepticism. If we are able to remain involved with a film's fictional world while acknowledging the actor, then we cannot accept as accurate theories that oppose films that disrupt the means of representation against films that apparently do not. The fact that we allow ourselves to be conned into believing that Jean Harrinton in *The Lady Eve* is a different person from Stella Dallas means we are already ignoring one kind of disruption. As V. F. Perkins explains:

Because the world is created in our imaginations it need not suffer damage from any exposure of the devices that assist its construction. We can, if we will, glide over inconsistencies and absorb ruptures. It is not difficult to see the image on the screen simultaneously as a world and as a performance. We do it all the time.

(Perkins, 2005, p. 38)

Cavell develops a similar argument by comparing film with jazz, proposing that 'the tune is next to nothing; the performer – with just that temperament, that range, that attack, that line, that relation to the pulse of the rhythm – is next to everything' (Cavell, 1981, p. 52). For Robert Warshow, writing in 1954, the presence of different performers enables Hollywood genre movies to transcend their supposedly formulaic nature:

> The form can keep its freshness through endless repetitions only because of the special character of the film medium, where physical difference between one object and another – above all, between one actor and another – is of such enormous importance, serving the function that is served by the variety of language in the perpetuation of literary types. In this sense, the 'vocabulary' of films is much larger than that of literature and falls more readily into pleasing and significant arrangements.
>
> (Warshow, 1974, p. 55)

To conclude, I will briefly discuss Eric Rohmer, a filmmaker who profits from 'the special character of the film medium'.

The documentary of a fiction: Eric Rohmer's *A Summer's Tale*

Rohmer works within a small field, his own genre of Rohmerian comedy; but he is well aware of the importance of responding to the performers and settings available to him. In acknowledging the importance of film's ontological connection to reality, Rohmer follows the insights of his former editor at *Cahiers du Cinéma*, André Bazin. Before Rohmer finishes his scripts, he gets to know his actors and researches the area where he is going to film; he then incorporates features of both people and places into his films, aiming for maximum verisimilitude.[3] His film *A Summer's Tale* (*Conte d'été*, 1996) takes place during the summer in Dinard, a holiday resort in Brittany. The hero, Gaspard (Melvil Poupaud), comes to Dinard for four weeks. He stays at a friend's empty house and waits for a young woman, Léna (Aurélia Nolin), to arrive. While waiting for her, he meets two other young women, first Margot (Amanda Langlet), with whom he takes long walks, and then Solène (Gwenaëlle Simon). Gaspard thinks that he is attracted to all three women; the story depicts his attempts to choose one. His declared principle is to let luck 'provoke' him, but he is dim-sighted and passive, a chancer who shuns commitment and divides his allegiances between Margot, Léna and Solène, although the film indicates that his indecision comes from youthful folly rather than sneaky Don Juanism. The summer holiday of *Conte d'été* refers to both the time of year during which the film is set and the time of life experienced by Gaspard and Margot. With no work to do while waiting for Léna, Gaspard responds to whatever comes along; but he also feels that he is on holiday from adulthood. Holidays often offer opportunities for short sexual relationships, but *Conte d'été* indicates that these characters are experiencing their last moments of freedom before they settle down.

After casting Melvil Poupaud as Gaspard and discovering that he was a musician with his own band, Rohmer made the character of Gaspard into a musician and worked music into the story. This was one of two significant decisions Rohmer made while planning *Conte d'été*. The other was to film in Brittany, a place that is known for reviving its own folk music, both Celtic and sea shanties. Rohmer integrates music into the film further by making Margot an ethnographer specializing in Gallic culture in Brittany. The first piece of music we hear is a whistling over the opening credits. This is the song that Gaspard writes while staying in Dinard, 'Fille du Corsair', written by Eric Rohmer and his editor Mary Stephen. Even though he has promised to write a song for Léna, Gaspard writes his song after being inspired by the visit to the old sailor with Margot and hearing him sing. He ends up singing 'Fille du Corsair' with Solène and, in a moment of apparent spontaneity, giving it to her. Gaspard, Solène, her uncle and aunt, accompanied by an accordionist, then sing it on her uncle's boat when they are out sailing.

There is also music playing in the background when Gaspard dines in the *crêperie* on the evening of his first Tuesday. The background music may appear to serve credibility alone, but on their drive to the sailor's house, Margot tells Gaspard that she chose the sea shanties that were playing in the restaurant. He remarks on the difference between Celtic rock and rock inspired by sea shanties. He then adds that he would like to write a song like the traditional sea shanty 'Valparaiso'. In response, she starts singing it and he joins in. Singing together is an important part of their getting to know each other, yet all three women sing either with or to Gaspard. Margot's spontaneous singing of 'Valparaiso' indicates her willingness to open up to him; Solène's singing of 'Fille du Corsair' with Gaspard functions similarly; but Léna's singing of Hughes Aufray's 'Santiano', with its line about 'leaving Margot', makes him uneasy. When Gaspard finds himself trapped by his acquiescence to Léna and Solène, his music saves him from making a decision; a friend telephones him to tell him about the sale of an eight-track recorder. As he tells Margot, his music comes first. He meets Margot at Dinard's harbour, and on the soundtrack Rohmer includes Aufray singing the 'Santiano' verse about leaving Margot just as she walks up the jetty after seeing Gaspard sail away.

As well as Breton music, Rohmer makes Brittany's 1000-year-old sailing tradition part of the story, intertwining it with the music. The old sailor who sings for Margot and Gaspard is 'local colour', as the accordionist later says, and Rohmer films him like a documentary filmmaker would, using Langlet as an interviewer. In effect, the scene reproduces Rohmer's own activity in that he has researched the area, met local people (the sailor, the accordionist, the people playing Solène's aunt and uncle) and then integrated them into his film. Yet sailing also provides structural support for the story. Rohmer films *Conte d'été* as a modern-day sailor's story, with a romance between one mariner and another's wife. Gaspard sails into the port of Dinard at the start of the film and leaves by sea from the same place at the end of the film. Margot, as she jokes to Gaspard, waits like a sailor's wife for the return of her boyfriend, who is away in Polynesia, in the South Seas. Furthermore, as Rohmer remarks, 'each girl has her own location' (Amiel and Herpe, 1999, p. 16). Giving each woman her own location relates to Gaspard's exploits; he has a girl in every port along Brittany's Côte d'Emeraude: Margot in Dinard; Solène in Saint-Malo; and Léna in Saint-Lunaire. The film's evocation of Breton sailing traditions includes the three ports and the windswept island of Ouessant, west of mainland France in the Atlantic, near the entry to the English channel and famous for its shipwrecks. Gaspard promises to take all three women to this island. In the end, he takes none.

Much of the fascination in Rohmer's work resides in his elaboration of patterns and the relating of these to questions about characters' thoughts. Rohmer's films are about contemporary France, and they present us with credible fictional worlds. However, at the same time, they offer critical metaphorical versions of our world. They exhibit, in Gombrich's words, life-likeness and arrangement; in Bazin's terms, Rohmer is an artist who holds reality at his command and moulds it into the fabric of his art. He achieves this through planning and collaboration with his actors; and his method is based on an acknowledgement of the primacy of actor over character and location over setting. He researches settings and uses them to provide ideas for themes, metaphors and motifs, all of which relate to the characters in complex ways. Rohmer deploys place neither as touristic spectacle nor as generic background, but as a way of defining the fiction and its themes. Instead of starting with a story and looking for a setting, Rohmer starts with a location and then adapts his story to the place he has found. Rohmer's use of actors is similarly responsive; he adapts his stories to the people that he films. In other words, he uses film's ontological basis in photography to provide him with both a high level of credibility and the intricate story structures for which his films are renowned.

Notes

Andrew Klevan's chapter on Rohmer in *Disclosure of the Everyday* has been a source of inspiration. In addition, our regular conversations about Rohmer continue to stimulate my thinking and writing in provocative ways. Steven Marchant read an early draft of this essay. As always, his comments improved my work; no one could ask for a more supportive colleague. Lastly, Lúcia Nagib made several suggestions; these enabled me to clarify my argument, and my thanks go to her.

1. For full discussion of these matters, see Andrew Klevan's *Film Performance: From Achievement to Appreciation* (2005).
2. Cavell makes this argument during a discussion of the essence of the medium of film, in which he specifies the achievements of film art (Cavell, 1979, p. 164). The importance of thinking about reality is a logical next step; as he writes, 'since the objects of film I have seen which do strike me as having the force of art all

incontestably use moving pictures of live persons and real things in actual spaces, I began my investigation of film by asking what *role* reality plays in this art' (Cavell, 1979, p. 165). Cavell finds that there are two reasons for writing about what he calls 'the pressure of reality upon art' (Cavell, 1979, p. 165). The first is the intellectual fashion for accepting that 'we never really, and never really can, see reality as it is' (Cavell, 1979, p. 165). This view is sanctioned by the history of epistemology and the rise of modern science. The second reason for thinking about realism and film is that there is a history of the representative arts, especially the history of painting after the invention of photography, 'according to which art had been withdrawing from the representation of reality as from a hopeless, but always unnecessary task' (Cavell, 1979, p. 165). Painters after photography began to minimize the illusion of reality and real space. However, film finds its own relationship to painting's rejection of the illusion of three-dimensionality.

3. I explore this further in *Reading Rohmer, Close-Up 2* (2007), and in *The Cinema of Eric Rohmer* (forthcoming in 2010).

References

Amiel, Vincent and Herpe, Noël (1999), 'Eric Rohmer on *Conte d'été*', in Michel Ciment and Noël Herpe (eds), *Projections 9: French Film-Makers on Film-Making*, trans. by P. Hodgson. London/New York: Faber and Faber, pp. 13–7. First published in *Positif*, 424, June 1996.

Austin, J. L. (1962), *Sense and Sensibilia*, reconstructed by G. J. Warnock from the Manuscript Notes. Oxford: Clarendon Press.

Bazin, André (1967), 'The Ontology of the Photographic Image', in *What is Cinema, vol 1*, ed. and trans. by Hugh Gray. Berkeley/ Los Angeles/London: University of California Press, pp. 9–16. Essay first published in *Problèmes de la Peinture*, 1945.

Bazin, André (1972), '*Bicycle Thief*', in André Bazin, *What is Cinema, vol 2*, ed. and trans. by Hugh Gray. Berkeley/Los Angeles/London: University of California Press, pp. 47–60. Review first published in *Espirit*, 1949.

Cavell, Stanley (1979), *The World Viewed: Reflections on the Ontology of Film*, Enlarged Edition. Cambridge, MA/London: Harvard University Press.

Cavell, Stanley (1981), *Pursuits of Happiness: The Hollywood Comedy of Remarriage*. Cambridge, MA/London: Harvard University Press.

Cavell, Stanley (1988), 'Recounting Gains, Showing Losses (A Reading of *The Winter's Tale*)', *In Quest of the Ordinary: Lines of Skepticism and Romanticism*. Chicago/London: University of Chicago Press, pp. 76–101.

Critchley, Simon (2004), *Very Little … Almost Nothing*. London/New York: Routledge.

Gombrich, E. H. (1993), 'Raphael's *Madonna della Sedia*', in *Gombrich on the Renaissance, vol 1: Norm and Form*. London: Phaidon Press Ltd, pp. 64–80.

Keane, Marian (2001), Audio commentary included in *The Lady Eve* DVD. The Criterion Collection.

Klevan, Andrew (2000), *Disclosure of the Everyday: Undramatic Achievement in Narrative Film*. Trowbridge: Flicks Books.

Klevan, Andrew (2005), *Film Performance: From Achievement to Appreciation*. London: Wallflower Press.

Leigh, Jacob (2007), *Reading Rohmer, Close-Up 2*. London: Wallflower Press.

Leigh, Jacob (forthcoming), *The Cinema of Eric Rohmer*. London: Wallflower Press.

Perez, Gilberto (1998), *The Material Ghost: Films and Their Medium*. Baltimore/London: The Johns Hopkins University Press.

Perkins, Victor F. (1978), *Film as Film: Understanding and Judging Movies*. Harmondsworth: Penguin.
Perkins, Victor F. (2005), 'Where is the World? The Horizon of Events in Movie Fiction', in John Gibbs and Douglas Pye (eds), *Style and Meaning: Studies in the Detailed Analysis of Film*. Manchester: Manchester University Press, pp. 16–41.
Thomson, David (1977), 'The Look on an Actor's Face', in *Sight and Sound*, 46(4), pp. 240–4.
Villien, Bruno (1984), 'Rohmer Dans La Lune', in *Le Nouvel Observateur*, 24 August, pp. 52–3.
Warshow, Robert (1974), 'Movie Chronicle: The Westerner', in Jack Nachbar (ed.), *Focus on the Western*. Englewood Cliffs, NJ: Prentice-Hall, Inc., pp. 45–56. First published in 1954 and republished in Warshow (1962), *The Immediate Experience: Movies, Comics, Theatre, and Other Aspects of Popular Culture*. Garden City, NY: Doubleday and Company, Inc., 1962, pp. 135—54.

13

Up the Junction: Ken Loach and TV Realism

Cecília Mello

The years between 1956 and 1963 have been customarily regarded by studies of post-war English film as marked by a move towards realism. The first witnessed the start of the Free Cinema movement, as well as the 'official' launch of the populist trend of the plays and novels of the 'angry young men'. The last is seen as the year in which kitchen-sink realism and the whole post-war populist wave lost impact. A closer look reveals, however, that the spectrum of post-war innovation, closely linked to an aspiration to realism, should be enlarged, for cinematic realism was very much alive on television after the death of the kitchen-sink dramas.[1] As John Caughie crucially argues: 'The breach which was opened in 1956 and seemed to close in 1963 actually remained opened in a place that very few "serious" critics thought to look: in television, and specifically in BBC television drama after 1964' (2000, p. 58).

This chapter will be concerned with one television film, which in its innovative format both incorporated and negated the realist tradition of the post-war years. *Up the Junction*, directed by Ken Loach in 1965, showed that perhaps English cinema needed television finally to embrace the subversion of film language pioneered a few years earlier by various 'new waves' across the world. Usually overshadowed by Loach's best known work for television, *Cathy Come Home* (1966), *Up the Junction* was an innovative film not only in the context of television dramas but also in relation to English cinema, and established an important bridge between both worlds.

In the mid-1960s, television was still on the cusp of achieving the ubiquitous status it holds now, and it could be seen as a relatively new medium in its formative stages. 'Drama' was one of the many formats supported by the vehicle, and after an initial period of cementing conventions it began to be challenged by new possibilities in terms of subjects and languages. Caught in a tradition of theatricality, which meant most television plays were shot or transmitted live from the studio in the mode of a theatre play, the late 1950s and early 1960s saw an insurgence of voices questioning the constraints of such conventions and stressing the need for innovation. The new medium of television thus invited a new language in its search for specificity.

What distinguished television from film and theatre, alongside its production modes and the technology of reproduction, was its essential domesticity. Television was quotidian, everyday, and belonged to the 'unsanctified' space of the living room, deprived of the aura of the theatre (and of the film theatre). And in its domesticity it was an essentially demotic medium, having the potential to reach and 'speak to' the nation as a whole. Moreover, in 1965 the rise of commodity culture and of affluence meant that the working classes could afford to own television sets. This defining characteristic in some ways set the tone for television drama's specific challenge in the 1950s–60s. A rejection of theatricality involved a conscious attempt to introduce everyday life on television, and the search for new ways to address the everyday.

In a first instance, film technology played a crucial part in the development of a new language, but television drama was searching for something other than theatre or film, trying to find what could be specifically televisual. *Up the Junction* is a seminal work in that it embodies this search for specificity and for new ways to articulate everyday life. Its break with theatricality was immensely helped by the 16mm technology, which allowed not only for location shooting with synchronous sound, but also for the post-shoot editing, subverting the limitations of electronic studio and live shooting. It somehow brought to the 'unsanctified' space of television elements of the 'respected' art of film, benefitting from television's ephemerality and fragmentation and turning them into the very essence of its filmic language.

It is possible to detect an interesting paradox in the moment television drama incorporates film and with it the ability to record and edit. John Caughie has called this transitional moment television's 'Fall from innocence', in that it lost the immediacy of live transmission: 'A moment between the "pure" television drama of liveness and immediacy and a television drama which had begun the process of becoming film' (2000, p. 101). The innocence or 'purity' of live drama transmission, however, seemed too much like the 'purity' of theatre itself. *Up the Junction* and its moment epitomized not so much a distancing from a 'pure' or uncorrupted television drama, but rather a search for the specificity of television drama, or in other words for its 'purity'. And despite having assimilated film, television drama (or television film) knew it could never really be cinema. It had to move towards something televisual, and *Up the Junction* was particularly successful in absorbing influences and creating something fresh. It incorporated television's current-affairs format, and especially the direct address, to its mixture of 16mm and electronic images, thus bringing the old studio drama, film and the specific televisual style together for the first time. The paradox refers to the fact that the immediacy of live drama generally resulted in a still and stuffy style (the theatrical), while the incorporation of film (or the loss of immediacy) resulted in a vibrant and 'alive' style which – in aspiring to be cinema – occasionally found the televisual.

Up the Junction was the fruit of a realist impulse that contained an important subversion of the traditional conventions of film language. As a work of fiction, it invited the element of the 'document' into its diegesis. It is, in the words of Tony Garnett (2000, p. 18), 'a dramatic document', which set out to capture everyday life's fragmentary essence and the 1960s spirit of change, rejecting the coherence of illusionism and inaugurating a new form of realism in the English audiovisual landscape.

'A little closer to the modern scene'

Up the Junction was first shown on BBC1's third season of the *Wednesday Play*, on 3 November 1965, from 9.40 p.m. to 10.50 p.m. It was based on a series of short stories by Nell Dunn, first published in book form in 1963. Dunn wrote her stories from personal experience: bored with her comfortable life in wealthy Chelsea, she decided to move across the river to Battersea and, in the words of Pulp's singer/songwriter Jarvis Cocker, 'live like common people'. She got a job in a chocolate factory and became fascinated by the liveliness and warmth of the working-class community of that area. *Up the Junction* was mainly founded on observation, and the first story, 'Out with the Girls', firmly places the first person narrator as an outsider to the community being portrayed, as seen in the following dialogue:

-   You come from Battersea, don't yer?
-   Yeah, me and Sylvie do. She don't though. She's an heiress from Chelsea.

(Dunn, 1988, p. 13)

The short stories, despite not following a continuous narrative, mainly focus on episodes in the lives of Sylvie, Rube and the narrator – the heiress from Chelsea – who live in Battersea and work in the same factory. Extensively based on interviews, the stories are structured around dialogue written in the vernacular, increasing their observational character. Dunn's fiction has a straight dialogue with reality which brings it close to the world of the newspaper and journalism, and it is fitting that four of the 16 stories in *Up the Junction* first appeared on the pages of the *New Statesman* in the early 1960s.

Loach considers *Up the Junction* his first real film. It was produced by James MacTaggart but owes a lot to the collaboration with Tony Garnett, who worked as story editor before assuming the producer title in *Cathy Come Home*, marking the start of a collaborative process with Loach that would last many years. *Up the Junction* had an audience of almost ten million viewers, and its three main roles were played by Geraldine Sherman (Rube), whose only previous film experience had been an uncredited appearance in *A Hard Day's Night* (Richard Lester, 1964); Vickery Turner (Eileen), making her screen debut;

and Carol White (Sylvie), an experienced if not renowned actress who was to star in Loach's two following films, *Cathy Come Home* and *Poor Cow* (1967).

The production history of *Up the Junction* somehow matches the spirit of immediacy of the book. Loach recalls how 'there was a gap in the BBC schedule, and so we had six weeks to get something together. ... It was agreed that I would knock a script out of this little book and make a collage of events and mood pieces' (Fuller, 1998, p. 13). As mentioned before, television drama until the mid-1960s had mostly been transmitted live from a studio, with pre-recorded material being inserted on the spot. For the pre-recorded material, the shooting still operated as if during a live transmission, perpetuating the theatrical format. The use of film during production and post-production in television remained exclusive to the documentary and the news department. In a move that would deeply affect the whole production of *Up the Junction*, the BBC finally yielded to the pressures of Garnett and Loach and allowed a few days shooting on location with a 16mm camera. During this time, their cameraman Tony Imi played an essential part in making the most of the short time they had, and shot approximately half of the film on location.

Up the Junction's location sequences were shot on an Éclair, a small hand-held silent (self-blimped) 16mm camera with a separate sound recording system (an electrical battery powered tape recorder connected by cable to the camera, which emitted a synchronized pulse), developed by André Coutant in the beginning of the 1960s. The Éclair's manoeuvrability allowed for inconspicuous shooting on the streets, increasing the impression of authenticity and immediacy of the images. The other major breakthrough of the Éclair was the possibility of shooting on 16mm with synchronized sound, which increased the reality coefficient of the images and led to new definitions of realism. This move caused a shift of the creative input from the writer to the director during the process of production, since being on location with a 16mm camera allowed for a strong element of improvisation.

Up the Junction benefitted immensely from the new 16mm synch-sound technology, and from the sense of spontaneity of location shooting, of being in direct contact with the 'real'. This is noticeable in sequences that show Rube, Sylvie and Eileen almost as *flâneurs* in the streets of Battersea, echoing Jo's 'unmotivated' walks through Salford in *A Taste of Honey* (Tony Richardson, 1961).[2] The space of the city in the film is indeed dominated by the three girls: they are seen in a long tracking shot walking down the street and singing (in synch sound) 'I Should Have Known Better' by The Beatles. They go past piles of rubble, reinforcing the idea of the fluidity of space in the ever-changing 1960s London. Later in the film, Rube is seen walking aimlessly across the Common, in a series of shots displaying her in full body, close-up or profile, and always in a tracking movement. And the film ends with a sequence of shots of the girls walking down a busy street, looking at shop windows, playing pinball, talking and laughing among the hustle and bustle.

Perhaps the most famous location sequence in *Up the Junction* is the swimming pool sequence, in which the girls go for a night swim with three boys they had met in the pub earlier in the evening. The whole sequence is edited in jump-cuts of the six jumping in the water stripped to their underwear, playing with each other like kids and finally kissing and hugging. The closeness and the thrill of these more erotic than romantic encounters is conveyed by beautifully shot close-up images of the couples' embraces and kisses, captured by Tony Imi with the Éclair from inside the swimming pool.

As well as benefitting from the mobility of the Éclair, Loach made sure that the studio sequences in *Up the Junction* were shot in a way not dissimilar to the location sequences, privileging improvisation over a carefully planned structure. And because these sequences were shot less like television and more like a film, it became almost impossible to edit on tape, still a cumbersome and slow technique at the time. Loach explains:

> The only solution was to cut it on the 16mm back-up print that the BBC used at the time as a safety measure. This was greeted with absolute horror because they said it wasn't up to broadcast quality – it was very grey and misty. ... But they let us cut on 16mm in the end because it was the only way they could salvage the material.
>
> (Fuller, 1998, p. 14)

Up the Junction epitomized the search for a new language, but it was also the product of changes being felt in the world of television drama since the end of the 1950s, when new tendencies began to be embraced. Sydney Newman, the crucial figure behind two of the most important slots for the presentation of new drama on television at the time, first at ABC and later at the BBC, should be seen as a catalyser of the reactions against drama conventions rather than as the sole figure responsible for them. He did, however, foment innovation on more than one level, by encouraging the inclusion of topical issues and working-class themes – a move in tune with the populist vein of literature, theatre and cinema at the time – and by promoting television drama's break with the theatrical and welcoming the work of new writers and directors, as well as giving power to people such as James MacTaggart and Tony Garnett, great advocates of innovation.

Ken Loach was among the new team of directors working for the *Wednesday Play*, Newman's slot for drama at the BBC, which started to air on Wednesday evenings in October 1964. His first directorial opportunity came in early 1964 with three episodes of the popular police series *Z Cars*. At the end of the same year he directed Troy Kennedy Martin's and John McGrath's (the creators of *Z Cars*) six-part series *Diary of a Young Man*. This series already signalled a shift away from the more established conventions of television drama, as Stuart Laing points out: 'The style was explicitly non-naturalistic and self-regarding, using stills, voice-overs, fantasy sequences and time-shifts freely to disrupt the straightforward narrative' (1997, p. 15).

Earlier in 1964, Troy Kennedy Martin's article 'Nats Go Home: First Statement of a New Drama for Television' had been published in the theatre magazine *Encore*. An open attack on the theatricality of television dramas, the article called for the development of a new mode of production and a new language for television. The 'nats' in the article's title referred to the naturalism inherited from the theatre, defined by Martin as an over-reliance on dialogue and a dependence on 'a strict form of natural time', a consequence of plays being broadcast live from a studio. He believed that the 'dictatorship' of the text limited the camera to photographing dialogue, and the absence of pre-recorded material eliminated the creative possibilities of the editing. Moving away from the theatrical presupposed the erosion of the text as the spinal cord of the work. Martin advocated the use of voiceover narration to take the weight off the stage dialogue, consequently allowing for an increased use of the 'lost speech of everyday life' that is characteristic of cinema.

Martin's arguments are not as clear cut as they might seem, but what is important here is to place *Up the Junction* in the context of his crucial call for a demotic televisual language, 'a new idea of form, new punctuation and new style' and 'something which can be applied to mass audience viewing' (1964, p. 21). His article, which also echoed other calls against the theatricality of television drama at the time, set out to awaken the director to the stimulus of the contemporary:

> It is to be hoped that the great demands this kind of drama makes will stir some kind of response – and that their [the directors'] basic television thinking, which is reminiscent of Victor Sylvester's fox-trots being danced in the world of the Beatles, will be fragmented into something a little closer to the modern scene.
>
> (1964, p. 32)

The fragmentation of everyday life

Up the Junction was put together as a jigsaw of images and sounds, not strictly to 'tell a story' but to describe and comment on a world. As in the book, it is set around three main events: Rube's abortion, Terry's fatal motorcycle accident and the death of Mrs Hardy. These are, however, interwoven in the film's kaleidoscopic structure and only stand out for their nature and not for their treatment, happening naturally alongside sequences devoid of any strong narrative motivation. From the book, which in Loach's words 'was made up of little vignettes, like newspaper pieces or descriptions' (Fuller, 1998, p. 13), the film also incorporated the element of the document to its fiction, thus infusing it with the immediacy and direct contact with reality present in the world of the news. The document was brought into the film especially through the use of images and sounds directly addressed to the viewer (henceforth referred to as 'direct address').

Topicality plays a part in approximating *Up the Junction* to the journalistic practice, as exemplified by the inclusion of a powerful sequence on abortion, in tune with the debate on legalization which indeed came two years later in 1967. It is, however, in the film form where the dialogue between film and journalism is best observed. This was in tune with the subversion of film language carried out by the French *nouvelle vague* and other new waves in the early 1960s, a time when filmmakers seemed fascinated with the contemporary and ephemeral character of the newspaper and the radio.

Up the Junction's incorporation of the 'document' through the direct-address technique revealed Loach's intention partly to emulate the style of the news and current-affairs programmes on television:

> It was very much to do with our programming slot. For about forty weeks a year, the *Wednesday Play* aired every Wednesday at 9pm, after the late evening news. We were very anxious for our plays not to be considered dramas but as continuations of the news. The big investigative documentary programme at the time was *World in Action* ... and we tried to copy its techniques and cut with a rough, raw, edgy quality, which enabled us to deal with issues head on.
>
> (Fuller, 1998, p. 15)

World in Action was Granada's current-affairs programme, which ran from 1963 to 1998. Unlike *Panorama*, the studio-based BBC rival programme, *World in Action* avoided the 'guests-talking-to-the-anchor-who-talks-to-the-audience' format, and abandoned the studio in favour of the streets. It devoted each half-hour programme to a single issue and, making the most of the mobility of lightweight film equipment, pioneered a form of pictorial journalism on location. Innovative also was its use of the direct address, through which interviewees talked straight to the camera without the mediation of an anchorman, thus breaking the spatial divide between television and the living room.

Up the Junction, through Dunn's book, brought in from the television world the fragmented character of televisual news and especially of *World in Action*, incorporating its use of the direct address to bring in 'pieces' taken from reality with no apparent articulation, producing a different kind of realism from that achieved by means of illusionistic representations of reality. One eloquent example is the long sequence focusing exclusively on a tallyman, who is driving a car and directly addresses the camera as if he were talking to someone in the back seat. He explains the rules of his trade in detail, and the film gives no indication of whom he is seemingly speaking to. His voice thus becomes an unarticulated element within the film's fiction (Figure 13.1).

Figure 13.1   Direct address in *Up the Junction*: Who is the tallyman speaking to?
Reproduced with kind permission from BBC and Ken Loach.

The use of voiceovers in *Up the Junction* is perhaps the main means through which the 'document' is interwoven into the diegesis. Here it is important to point out that although Dunn's book was written in the first person, from the perspective of an outsider narrator, in the film the subject of enunciation is fragmented as a result of the elimination of the outsider character and of a single subjective point of view. This enabled the film to achieve a more democratic and demotic structure: it is the camera and the tape recorder that observes and registers, and the resulting vision does not need to be validated by that of an outsider/observer character.

This democratization of the subject of enunciation becomes explicit through the use of voiceovers in the film's soundtrack, which includes not only commentary by the three main characters but also by many other characters in the film, as well as unidentifiable voices speaking in the first person and relating an experience. This means that the episodes in the lives of the three girls are underpinned with comments introduced through the technique of the direct address. The effect is the social contextualization of the individual drama. Caughie makes an important point in relation to the hierarchy between what he calls 'the voice of the drama' and 'the voice of the documentary' in *Up the Junction*. In his view, 'the voice of the drama', for instance the diegetic dialogue between two characters, 'exists at the same level of banal "typicality" as the inserted monologues of the background voice-overs – the "voice of the documentary"' (2000, p. 116).

Up the Junction's use of the direct address in a variety of witness-style voiceovers is in tune with a Brechtian rejection of illusionism, as Raymond Williams explains in *Drama from Ibsen to Brecht*: 'What Brecht seized on was the exclusion, by particular conventions of verisimilitude, of all direct commentary, alternative consciousness, alternative points of view' (1973, p. 318). *Up the Junction* indeed privileges through the direct address the presentation of alternative points of view, and invites the active engagement of the spectator with the richness of what is heard and seen. Despite not clearly adopting the tableaux structure, the film is nevertheless composed of self-contained segments not linked by causal relationship, once again indicating the fragmentary essence of everyday life.

Up the Junction opens with a close-up image of a man looking straight at the camera – thus acknowledging the audience – and singing 'Oh, oh little girl, pretty little girl, you're such a good little girl, why don't you let me make you a bad girl?'. What follows is a montage of shots cut to this song ('Bad Girl'), which has words by Nell Dunn and alludes to teenage sex – a theme that runs through the film. This prelude sequence – entirely cut to music – contains a few important movements that relate to the film as a whole. It sways between inside and outside, the detail and the general, the old and the new. The sequence starts inside the club, moves outside to establish the location – the station sign and the chimneys of the power station leave no doubt that this is Battersea – and then moves back inside the club where the action takes place. The constant zooming in and out alternately highlights the detail and the general, a movement suggestive of the very structure of the film, based on the articulation between the individual and the collective. The zoom was commonly associated at the time with the new kind of film language derived from direct cinema and *cinéma vérité*, which privileged the 16mm handheld camera and the freedom it engendered. *Up the Junction*'s repeated use of the zoom also indicates a rejection of the conventions of both studio drama and classical narrative film associated with the 35mm gauge. Finally, old and new are juxtaposed in the same image as the tracking shot of a row of old terraced houses ends on a new tower block.

Rube, Sylvie and Eileen, first seen at the station platform, are now inside the club talking to three young men, Terry, Dave and Ron. Most of the dialogue heard is of the 'behavioural' type, the 'lost dialogue of everyday life' retrieved and spoken in the vernacular, and not conveying any essential narrative information. Rather than shot-reverse shot montage, with its customary reactive dialogue, the sequence is edited to present only fragments of conversations. The soundtrack is further complicated by pieces of other people's conversations, as well as the song in the background. The imagetrack is made of an abundance of close-up images of the three girls and boys and other people in the club, as well as extreme close-up shots of hands and mouths. It is therefore not only the speech but also the body that is fragmented by the editing and the camerawork.

A long sequence inside the chocolate factory is another example of fragmentation of the narrative voice in *Up the Junction*. The camera lingers on workers talking about their lives before revealing Sylvie and Eileen working in the production line (Figure 13.2). The soundtrack is once again very busy, with dialogue, factory noise and background music competing against one another. The montage principle dominates, dialogue only heard in

Figure 13.2   Up the Junction: The mechanical nature of work in the chocolate factory's production line. Reproduced with kind permission from BBC and Ken Loach.

fragments and never carried forward. The camera movement used to film a conversation between three women working at the conveyor belt is revealing of this democratic structure: the camera pans left from one close-up to the next, stopping to capture what each of them has to say, and finally tilts down to reveal the conveyor belt and the repetitive movement of hands putting chocolates in a box.

The montage principle of the factory sequence is exaggerated by the use of cutting to music, which results in a much faster editing, aimed at mimicking the repetitive and mechanical nature of the factory work. A close-up shot reveals a circular machinery structure going round and round to the beat of Johnny Kid & the Pirates' 1963 song 'Hungry for Love', and images of the workers alternate in rapid succession with a close-up shot of the loudspeaker, of the conveyor belt and of hands putting chocolates in a box. The pace of the editing is dictated by the song and the mechanical and fragmentary nature of the factory work.

This music-video structure, recurrent in *Up the Junction*, was pioneering at the time. Dunn had already used quotes from popular songs referring to specific passages in her book, and the film explores pop music's potential even further by using it intra- and extradiegetically in almost every sequence. Hits from the 1960s such as The Kinks' 'I Need You', Sonny & Cher's 'I Got You Babe' and The Searchers' 'Sugar and Spice' are essential to the creation of a contemporary atmosphere in the film, and frequently relate to sex and romance, establishing a contrast with the problematic relationships portrayed. *Up the Junction*'s link with pop music finds an echo in the 1978 release of an eponymous record by the band Squeeze, which reached number two on the UK singles chart that year. The song relates indirectly to the book and the film, offering a first-person description in the vernacular of the hardships of working-class life in Clapham, as well as dealing with the subject of an unexpected pregnancy. The disappointing cinema version of *Up the Junction* (Peter Collinson, 1968) also contained an eponymous song by Manfred Mann, which compares as unfavourably to Squeeze's song as Collinson's film to Loach's.[3]

Rube's backstreet abortion episode occupies the central part of the film. The subject is introduced by a series of images of pregnant women walking down the street, accompanied by unidentified voiceovers commenting on the hardships of motherhood, unwanted pregnancies and abortions. It starts with the following testimony:

> I never once lay down with him. I used to meet him in a back alley off the Latchmere. I never really knew what he was at. I never got no pleasure out of it. I didn't know I was carrying till I was five months. I couldn't believe it. I kept thinking it would pass off.

This initial part of the sequence operates in an asynchronous mode, in that the voices heard do not belong to the women seen on the imagetrack, despite relating to them through the subject of pregnancy. However, both tracks have the value of 'document', inserted as they are into the fiction's fabric with no articulation, and remain illustrative throughout, providing the backdrop context for Rube's abortion. This is introduced by an extreme close-up of Rube's face (Figure 13.3), and by the return of the synch sound. Gazing at the camera, she says in a fatalistic tone: 'When you love a boy, you want to give him the best thing in the world. And there's only one thing, isn't there?' This statement calls the film from the general back to the particular, from the document back to fiction, and next Rube is seen with Eileen looking for Winnie, the abortionist. Over a shot of the girls walking through the Common, new voiceovers are introduced, relating more stories of pregnancies and abortions. Also heard is the more authoritative voiceover of a doctor, who provides a 'scientific' take on the issue, in sharp contrast with the vernacular voices heard until this point:

> In my surgery I see at least one woman a week who is seriously contemplating an abortion. Quite apart from the 35 deaths per year that we know are directly attributable to the back street abortions, the most common and seriously disturbing result must be that this girl is unable to have any more babies. She may not be able to have any. She may be unable to have a family.

Rube sees Winnie, but it is later, once back in her room, that she has to endure the abortion process itself, suffering immense pain and sickness.

Figure 13.3   Up the Junction: Rube's matter-of-fact statement: 'When you love a boy, you want to give him the best thing in the world'. Reproduced with kind permission from BBC and Ken Loach.

Her wall is decorated with ripped up pictures and posters of Elizabeth Taylor, an allusion to cinema, pop culture and to her young age (she is just 17 years old). After a series of jump-cuts of extreme close-up images of her face, sweating and frantically shaking with pain, the voiceover of the doctor is reintroduced, silencing her screams: 'Take the lowest figure: 52,000 abortions a year. That's 1000 abortions a week. Something like five or six every hour of every day. And that's taking the minimum figure.' This state-ment is abruptly and unexpectedly followed by Ben E. King's 'Yes', a song about a woman giving in to sex (and which had been used by Dunn in the abortion chapter 'Bang on the Common'): 'Yes, you can hurt me / Yes, you can squeeze me / Yes, you can have my caress.'

This song relates directly to Rube's fatalistic statement ('when you love a boy'), and provides, in Brechtian style, a commentary to her present situ-ation, as well as a soothing counterpoint to the images of her pain and the sound of her screams. The song continues to play over a sequence of images of Rube in the Common, on the station platform and in the pub toilet. Here, it is perhaps worth noting the importance of Joan Littlewood and the Theatre Workshop, especially their 1963 production of *Oh What a Lovely War*, in the spread of Brecht's ideas within the English context. Heavily influenced by Brecht's epic theatre and drawing on music hall techniques (song and dance, the sketch structure), the widely acclaimed play about World War I had had a considerable impact on Loach and Garnett. Stephen Lacey recalls that in the play 'the newspanel announcement of losses of 85,000 men at Verdun was juxtaposed with the singing of "Goodbye-ee", an ironic song about a soldier leaving to go off to war' (Lacey, 1995, p. 160). *Up the Junction* uses exactly the same strategy by contrasting the doctor's statistics on abortions with the song's invitation to sex. The sequence finally ends with an abrupt cut from a close-up of Rube to one of Sylvie and the latter's voiceover: 'I was the youngest bride in Battersea.' It is her 'story' that will now be told, and her predominantly white image (she wears a white blouse and a white hair band, a probable reference to 'youngest bride') contrasts sharply with Rube's black hair, blouse and strong eye make-up.

Loach once claimed to have lost interest in Brechtian techniques towards the end of the 1960s, suggesting that they had lost their impact. Paradoxically, this rejection coincided with the gradual politicization of his filmmaking, suggesting that his interest in Brecht around the time of *Up the Junction*, *Cathy Come Home* and *Poor Cow* had not only been political but also, and sometimes to a greater extent, formal. Loach admitted that back in his university years as a law student 'Brecht was fashionable' (Fuller, 1998, p. 4) and that he was aware of his work. *Up the Junction* shows that Brecht was a decisive influence on him, both in terms of form (anti-illusionistic storytelling) and political content.

The ephemeral and fragmented quality of the real resulting from the narrative strategies adopted in *Up the Junction*, which draw directly from television news style, characterizes the film as essentially modern. In 1863 Charles Baudelaire, in a well-known phrase, described modernity as 'the transitory, the fugitive, the contingent' (1992, p. 355). Loach's filming style, marked by a 'distracted' camera that never lingers on the same character for too long, seems attracted precisely by what is fleeting and unstable, the urban fragmentary experience which characterizes modernity. A telling illustration is the film's third sequence, in which Eileen and Dave talk and have sex inside a derelict house, followed by a series of shots of derelict houses being demolished. This was a time of slum clearances, when old houses, and with them an old way of life, were being pulled down to be replaced by council estates. This transitory moment is reflected in both the demolition images and the film's fragmented structure (Figure 13.4).

Up the Junction is indeed about fluidity and movement. It captures the spirit of the time with its dynamic camera, jump-cuts and dense soundtrack. It is not by chance that the three main characters are first seen standing on a railway station platform and last seen walking around busy streets. They embody the fluidity of space and sense of transformation as experienced in the 1960s, bringing with them a breath of fresh air to English cinema and television.

A dramatic document

Up the Junction partly incorporated the realist tradition of the kitchen-sink dramas in its use of location shooting, unknown or non-professional actors, and

Figure 13.4   The fluidity of space in *Up the Junction*'s 1960s London. Reproduced with kind permission from BBC and Ken Loach.

its concern with topical issues and the everyday lives of the working classes. Ken Loach, however, declared that, despite following in the footsteps of the kitchen-sink dramas, 'we felt ... that we could take that sense of authenticity a few notches further' (Loach, 2003). As a director, he was moved by an impulse towards a greater realism, which related dialectically with the preceding form of realism, a move that is well explained by John Hill: 'Realist innovations ... take place in a kind of dialectic with what has gone before, underwriting their own appeal to be uncovering reality by exposing the artificiality and conventionality of what has passed for reality previously' (1986, p. 127).

Up the Junction's realism exposed the artificiality of what had previously passed for reality, namely the structured organization of the real of the kitchen-sink dramas. Loach's realist principle implied that, to convey immediacy and actuality, it was necessary to incorporate chaotic and fragmented aspects of reality as they presented themselves to the camera, rather than reorganize them according to a given set of rules. It also had to incorporate the document as a non-articulated element into the fabric of the fiction.

With *Cathy Come Home*, Loach assumes a more rigid position as the spokesperson for the plight of the homeless, and the film's 'realism' works as an act of denunciation, intended to instruct, sensitize and awaken the public to a specific issue. *Up the Junction* was conceived more as a celebration and was motivated by a feeling of empathy rather than the duty of protest, working as a platform for the voices of ordinary people. It represents a rejection not only of the theatricality of television drama but also of the conventionalities of cinema's illusionist grammar, and therefore stands as a seminal work within (and between) both worlds. It is a landmark in Loach's career as well as in the English audiovisual landscape.

Notes

I am grateful to Ken Loach and Eimhear McMahon of Sixteen Films, and Vicky Mitchell of the BBC, for granting me permission to use images from *Up the Junction* to illustrate this chapter. I also thank Laura Mulvey, who first encouraged me to write about *Up the Junction*. The original research for this chapter was sponsored by CAPES, Brazilian Ministry of Education.

1. My PhD thesis *Everyday Voices: The Demotic Impulse in English Post-war Film and Television* focuses on the aspiration to realism present in the post-war period of renewal, and redefines its boundaries to include the cycle of 'spiv films' (1945–51) and *Up the Junction* (1965).
2. Jo can also be seen as prefiguring the revelation of the working-class girl's voice as seen in *Up the Junction*.
3. In 1995 the band Pulp released the single 'Common People', which speaks of a girl who 'wants to live like common people', and thus rents a flat above a shop, cuts her hair, gets a job, smokes some cigarettes, plays some pool, pretending she never went to school. This is almost a checklist of the actions performed by the 'heiress from Chelsea' in the 1968 version of *Up the Junction*, which, unlike Loach's, kept the character of the outsider.

References

Baudelaire, Charles (1992), 'Le peintre de la vie moderne', in *Critique d'art: suivi de critique musicale*. Paris: Gallimard, pp. 343–84.
Caughie, John (2000), *Television Drama: Realism, Modernism, and British Culture*. Oxford: Oxford University Press.
Dunn, Nell (1988), *Up the Junction*. London: Virago Press.
Fuller, Graham (ed.) (1998), *Loach on Loach*. London: Faber and Faber.
Garnett, Tony (2000), 'Contexts', in Jonathan Bignell, Stephen Lacey and Madeleine Macmurraugh-Kavanagh (eds), *British Television Drama: Past, Present and Future*. Basingstoke: Palgrave Macmillan, pp. 11–23.
Hill, John (1986), *Sex, Class and Realism: British Cinema 1956–1963*. London: British Film Institute.
Lacey, Stephen (1995), *British Realist Theatre: The New Wave in Its Context 1956–1965*. London: Routledge.
Laing, Stuart (1997), 'Ken Loach: Histories and Contexts', in George McKnight (ed.), *Agent of Challenge and Defiance: The Films of Ken Loach*. Westport, CT: Greenwood Press, pp. 11–27.
Leigh, Jacob (2002), *The Cinema of Ken Loach: Art in the Service of the People*. London: Wallflower Press.
Loach, Ken (2003), 'Audio Commentary', *Cathy Come Home* DVD. London: BFI Video Publishing.
Martin, Troy Kennedy (1964), 'Nats Go Home: First Statement of a New Drama for Television', in *Encore*, 48, pp. 21–33.
Williams, Raymond (1973), *Drama from Ibsen to Brecht*. Harmondsworth: Pelican Books.

Part IV Documentary, Television and the Ethics of Representation

14
Filmmaking as the Production of Reality: A Study of Hara and Kobayashi's Documentaries

Lúcia Nagib

'Life is acting.'
Kazuo Hara

A victim of severe cerebral palsy slowly drags his tiny, lame body on all fours across the zebra crossing of a busy Tokyo avenue, while cars and motorbikes drive dangerously close by him. A woman gives birth to a child entirely by herself in front of a static camera in an uninterrupted sequence-shot. A former World War II soldier pays an impromptu visit to one of his comrades nearly 40 years later, now a frail old man, and assaults him while the camera carries on rolling. A popular novelist has three-quarters of his liver removed in front of the camera. These scenes, drawn respectively from *Goodbye CP* (*Sayonara CP*, 1972), *Extreme Private Eros: Love Song 1974* (*Gokushiteki erosu: renka 1974*, 1974), *The Emperor's Naked Army Marches On* (*Yuki yukite shingun*, 1987) and *A Dedicated Life* (*Zenshin shosetsuka*, 1994), exemplify the radical kind of realism embraced by director Kazuo Hara and his lifetime companion, collaborator and producer Sachiko Kobayashi.[1] Their films are so confrontational towards their characters, so intrusive into their private lives, so exposing of their intimacy, that one wonders how they could have possibly been made. The filmmakers' daring and uncompromising mode of address of the most explosive social issues is, on the other hand, undeniably effective. Rarely has cinema been as politically active, while refusing to send any straightforward political message. Hardly ever has it been so supportive of minorities of gender, race and disability, while remaining thoroughly averse to victimization.

In this chapter, I will examine the four films listed above, all of which have commonly been defined as 'documentaries' on the basis of their use of real characters and locations, but which have extended the frontiers of the genre to hitherto unknown realms. As I will endeavour to show, these films testify to an auteurist realist project based on physicality pushed to the 'extreme' – as expressed in the title of the duo's second feature – as a means to go beyond realism as style and turn the act of filmmaking into producing, as well as reproducing, reality.

Rather than establishing a teleological model based on a progression from film to film, I will first consider the extent to which they express and transcend their historical time, marked by the late developments and ramifications of the Japanese New Wave. I will then move to an examination of the films' phenomenological time, that is, the protracted periods they have taken to be produced as a means to adhere to a character's lifespan and allow for the emergence of the revelatory event. Finally, I will address the conflicting authorial subjectivities at work within each film, in order to evaluate the ethical imperative – as well as consequences – of this unique realist project.

Historical time

Hara and Kobayashi's career harks back to the late 1960s, a moment when Japanese cinematic aesthetics and modes of production were undergoing a revolution triggered in the early years of the decade by the emergence of the Japanese New Wave. Hara started as a still photographer in the mid-1960s, working for the *Asahi* newspaper from Yamaguchi, in the south of Japan, where he was born in 1945. In 1966, he moved to Tokyo to attend the Tokyo College of Photography, while making a living by working at a school for disabled children whom he also photographed. These pictures led to his first photographic exhibition, at the Nikon Salon, in Ginza, in 1969, where he met another photographer, Sachiko Kobayashi, herself a victim of disability caused by polio. Their relationship quickly progressed into their first collaborative motion picture, *Goodbye CP*, a film about a group of adult individuals affected by cerebral palsy, shot in the early 1970s and released in 1972, and to their marriage in 1973. From this very first film, Hara and Kobayashi set in motion a radical method of physical approach to reality which would remain practically unaltered through their subsequent films and become their distinctive auteurist signature. Let us examine how it relates to the cinematic new wave and realist tendencies of that time.

As John Hill, quoting Raymond Williams, observes with relation to the British New Wave films, 'it is usually a "revolt" against previous conventions which characterizes a "break towards realism" in the arts', as a means 'to communicate a new, and more fundamental, "underlying reality"' (Hill, 1986, p. 59). Such a 'break towards realism' certainly applies to most cinematic new waves and new cinemas in the world, starting with Italian neorealism and including the Japanese New Wave. This adds to a perception that representations of 'pain and deprivation are more real than pleasure' (Grodal, 2002, p. 87), meaning that many of these films have immersed themselves into the world of the dispossessed and underprivileged, especially in post-war periods.

The early revolutionary films of the Japanese New Wave were all about unveiling a deep and more real Japan, that is to say an underlying reality of poverty, illegal businesses, petty crimes and general amorality which thrived in the country in World War II's long-lasting aftermath. And this was in frank opposition to the conciliatory humanism until then prevailing in the films by studio directors, such as Kurosawa, Ozu and Naruse. However, this 'social realist' phase, together with its national agenda, was already receding and giving way to new developments by the time Hara and Kobayashi emerged on the cinematic scene. At least a decade older than the duo, most Japanese New Wave directors, such as Oshima, Shinoda, Yoshida, Imamura and Suzuki, had started within Japan's studio system in the mid-1950s and launched their groundbreaking works in the early 1960s. By the late 1960s, most of them had already abandoned their respective studios and gone out to the streets in search of a stronger indexical backing for their fiction films, many even turning to documentary filmmaking, an emerging genre in Japan which would climax at the turn of the decade.

Hara and Kobayashi's initial output is entirely in tune with the independent street film style of that time. If most of *Goodbye CP* is set in Tokyo's Shinjuku station area, where the cerebral palsy victim Hiroshi Yokota recites his poems, this follows the lead of someone like Oshima, who in the late 1960s also had his camera out in Shinjuku focusing on avant-garde theatre troupes and interventionist artists. Oshima's 1968 *Diary of a Shinjuku Thief* (*Shinjuku dorobo nikki*) stars the outrageous graphic designer Tadanori Yokoo in the role of a shoplifter in Sinjuku's famous Kinokuniya bookshop, in which, years later, Hara would meet the novelist Mitsuharu Inoue, the star of his 1994 film *A Dedicated Life*.

The immediate aesthetic result of this opening up for the contingent was a shift from a representational to a presentational regime, and from illusionistic voyeurism to self-reflexive exhibitionism, including the revelation of the cinematic apparatus within the scene. An example is *A Man Vanishes* (*Ningen Johatsu*, 1967), the first independent film directed by Hara's mentor, Shohei Imamura, after he left Nikkatsu, in which the walls of a stage are torn down to unmask fictional devices within a documentary film and expose the theatrical quality of real life. Building on such groundbreaking experiments, Hara and Kobayashi used the street film format to abolish any notions of a double-layered reality opposing inner and outer worlds, society and the individual, real life and acting. Thus, going public, for them, became equivalent to going extremely private. As Hara himself remarks: 'In the 1970s it became clear that we should question ourselves. ... My films are not intended to debunk the state power, but to expose this power structure within ourselves' (Nagib, 2007).

This project is first put to practice in *Goodbye CP*, a film that pushes presentational, exhibitionist realism through to its ultimate consequences. In order to simultaneously expose disability to the world and demonstrate what the experience of the street is for the disabled, the camera not only *focuses* on cerebral palsy victims, but *becomes* one of them. An example is the opening scene, in which the poet Hiroshi Yokota, the most severely affected cerebral palsy victim in the group in focus, rejects his wheelchair and crosses a wide avenue on all fours, struggling to control his movements and constantly losing his thick spectacles with his involuntary head jerks. The shaky, aleatory handheld camera meanwhile seems itself affected by cerebral palsy, as it follows Yokota at ground level, experiencing together with him the rough touch of the tarmac surface and the frightening closeness of the wheels of cars and motorbikes driving past him. Yokota's roaming of the pavements of Tokyo culminates in the recital of his poem 'Legs' at Shinjuku station, during which the low camera, sharing the character's impaired sight and limited visual field, captures the legs around him like bars in a prison (Figure 14.1). *Goodbye CP* has been described as a 'documentary focused on how cerebral palsy victims were generally ignored or disregarded in Japan' (Doll, 2007, p. 4). Whether this is the case or not in Japan, the fact remains that not a word or image in the whole film suggests it. The camera's unprivileged positioning and restricted view, combined with the discontinuous editing, prevent the formation of any objective verdicts on a country or its society. Instead, the horror of exclusion is conveyed from the inside of disability, without the need of identifying a baleful Other.

Hara and Kobayashi's rejection of oppositional schemes encompasses the search for a 'spiritual' or 'metaphysical' reality beyond the 'apparent reality', which Williams defines as a common realist impulse (1978, p. 533).

Figure 14.1   Goodbye CP: Yokota recites his poem 'Legs', while the camera captures the legs around him like bars in a prison. Copyright © by Shisso Production.

Goodbye CP is eminently physical, not only for its stress on the characters' sensory experiences, but also for its open address of sexual taboos, in this case, the sex lives of the physically disabled. The interviews conducted by the crew with the cerebral palsy group unveil the excruciating difficulties they experience to fulfil their needs, including one account of rape. Here again Hara and Kobayashi are building on the example of their immediate Japanese predecessors, whose realist repertoire, more than in any other world new waves, resorted to sex as a privileged vehicle for the physical and therefore 'real' experience of the world. Homosexuality, paedophilia, incest, rape and sadomasochism were among the practices insistently focused on by Imamura, Hani, Oshima, Matsumoto and others. Their method excluded any moral judgments on their subjects while often requiring from casts their bodily engagement in sexual representations, as epitomized by *The Realm of the Senses* (*Ai no koriida*, Nagisa Oshima, 1976), entirely based on real sex among the cast.

I once defined as 'corporeal realism' this tendency of fusing performance and real life, typical of the 1960s–70s in Japan, which often relied on modern, self-reflexive cinematic devices to give expression to Japanese traditions of the cult of the body and the physical environment (Nagib, 2006). Hara and Kobayashi's second film, *Extreme Private Eros: Love Song 1974*, released two years ahead of Oshima's erotic masterpiece, is a perfect example of this trend. Carrying the date it was made in its own title, the film reflects even more explicitly than *Goodbye CP* the libertarian atmosphere of the period as it documents the sex life of Hara's previous wife, Miyuki Takeda, together with that of Hara and Kobayashi themselves, as both feature in the film. Once again, the camera is a character in its own right, with its needs, desires, frustrations and pains. At one point, it even becomes apparent to the spectator, through a shaky, blurry sequence of images, that Hara is shooting his own lovemaking with his former wife (Figure 14.2). Takeda, in her turn, is the period's typical heroine, with her intuitive feminism, pan-sexual drive and rejection of family ties, all of which culminate in an extreme act of independence, when she gives birth, entirely by herself, in front of Hara's turning camera, to the child of a black American soldier. As well as exposing her own intimacy, wonderfully represented by the birth of her child, Takeda's sexual curiosity leads the camera on an exploration journey to the underworld of prostitution in Okinawa, including the revelation of a large contingent of black-Japanese children.

Both *Goodbye CP* and *Extreme Private Eros* resort to typical low-budget techniques, such as 16mm handheld camera, black-and-white stock, discontinuous editing, asynchronous sound and an interview-based narrative structure redolent of *cinéma vérité*. This Hara attributes to second-hand knowledge mediated by the Japanese television documentaries being produced at that time, including those by Tsuchimoto, Imamura, Oshima and Ogawa, who were themselves influenced by *vérité* and the French *nouvelle vague* (Nagib, 2007). New as a genre, within a television system that was just

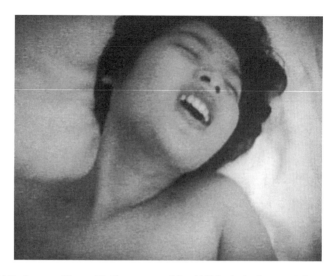

Figure 14.2 Lovemaking with the camera. Miyuki Takeda in *Extreme Private Eros: Love Song 1974*. Copyright © by Shisso Production.

completing a decade of existence, these documentaries became a privileged ground for political and artistic experiments at the turn of the 1960s to the 1970s. Despite the generation gap, Hara played a role in this movement, among others, as an assistant director to Imamura in some of his television documentaries.

It was Imamura who, in the late 1970s, first envisaged a television documentary on the protagonist of *The Emperor's Naked Army Marches On*, Kenzo Okuzaki, a former World War II soldier who had served more than 13 years in prison, three of them in solitary confinement, for having murdered an estate agent and shot steel *pachinko* balls with a sling at the Emperor. Imamura's project was finally scrapped by the television company because of its direct address of the taboo subject of the Emperor's responsibility for the war. Hara and Kobayashi then took it in hand and shot the film independently, with money borrowed from friends and Okuzaki himself. Even though here the camera is more stable and the editing more sutured than in the duo's previous *vérité* films, revelatory realism is again stretched to its limits through the film's unrestricted involvement in Okuzaki's obsession. His (and therefore the film's) mission is to extract from some of his former comrades the truth about the killing of two lower-rank Japanese soldiers in New Guinea, when the war had already ended. After repeated interviews with the veterans, in which Okuzaki often resorts to violence in front of a rolling camera, one by one they finally confess to the crime of cannibalism.

Jeffrey and Kenneth Ruoff (2007, p. 9) describe *The Emperor's Naked Army Marches On* as 'one of the most scathing and engaging indictments of Japan's Fifteen-Year War and of Emperor Hirohito's role in it'. If this is undoubtedly Okuzaki's message repeatedly hammered throughout the film, the film's own point of view is anything but an indictment of Japan. Instead, it is in Okuzaki's volatile behaviour, fuelled by dubious principles of selfless honour, that one is more likely to identify the nefarious elements of the war ideology.

Finally, *A Dedicated Life*, launched 22 years after *Goodbye CP*, in 1994, is very different from the artisanal *vérité* style adopted in the early Hara-Kobayashi films, with its sophisticated mixture of colour and black-and-white stock, including a plethora of materials, such as interviews, lectures, archival documents and even fictional inserts. Nevertheless, the radical revelatory drive of the early films is still very much at work here too. The film is a relentless investigation into the very nature of artistic fiction through a scrutiny of novelist Mitsuharu Inoue's life, including a physical search into the writer's own body, as he goes through liver surgery and finally dies. It is then revealed that most of Inoue's autobiographical data was sheer fabrication and his entire life nothing but acting.

Phenomenological time

Hara and Kobayashi's films seem to feed on the utopian search for the coincidence between lifespan and creative time. With a film career dating back to 1972, they have brought out no more than five features in 36 years of collaborative work so far.[2] All but one – *The Many Faces of Chika* (*Mata no hi no Chika*, 2004), a fiction film entirely conceived and written by Kobayashi and only directed by Hara – are character-based documentaries. Each of them has taken several years to complete for reasons unrelated to budgetary constraints, which have always been there of course, but derived from an uncompromising option for freedom of creation and unlimited shooting time. Time and freedom are the binomial that has regulated the duo's independent filmmaking so far and proved crucial to their intended aesthetic results. As Hara explains with relation to *The Emperor's Naked Army Marches On*:

> It was really a film that could only be made independently. I had no money, but I had time and freedom. Time and freedom were weapons to make a film about a taboo subject. The reason that lots of people came to see my film was that I used the power of time and freedom.
>
> (Ruoff, 1993, p. 107)

In keeping with this method, the shooting of *Goodbye CP* and *Extreme Private Eros* stretched, in each case, over a period of three years. *The Emperor's Naked Army Marches On* took longer, from 1982 to 1987, whereas the making of

A Dedicated Life, planned to last for a decade, was shortened to five years by the death of its protagonist.

In all cases, maximum adherence to a real lifespan was a condition for the films' existence, that is to say, shooting would continue for years if necessary, until a decisive event – wished for, but unpredictable – would take place which would become the film's raison d'être and draw the shooting to a close. This is the means through which one or more climaxes, as well as a coherent narrative structure, were secured in each of these films. Let us have a closer look at how these moments come to existence and how they function within the films.

In her remarkable book, *The Emergence of Cinematic Time*, Mary Ann Doane develops a concept of 'event', with relation to early cinema, which combines constructiveness with contingency. She explains:

> Insofar as the cinema presented itself as the indexical record of time, it allied itself with the event and the unfolding of events as aleatory, stochastic, contingent. It was capable of trapping events in all their unpredictability and pure factualness. However, the fact of its own finitude – the limits imposed by both the frame and the length of the reel – resulted in the necessity of conceiving the event simultaneously in terms of structure, as a unit of time, as not simply a happening, but a significant happening that nevertheless remained tinged by the contingent, by the unassimilable.
>
> (Doane, 2002, pp. 140–1)

Hara and Kobayashi's filmmaking seems to stand out precisely for the way it hinges on this 'significant happening', which is at the same time unpredictable and structural to the films. But how is this achieved? Raymond Williams, in his famous 'Lecture on Realism', refers to 'realist intentions' which are mediated through a specific ideology (Williams, 1977, p. 64). This is applicable to Hara and Kobayashi in that there is a clearly identifiable 'intention' – though not obviously mediated by ideology – which structures the unpredictable event in their films. This intention is actively exercised in the manner of a provocation, aimed at causing physical and psychological stress to its subjects, so that they are led or even constrained to open up and reveal their innermost motivations. The moment and content of this revelation, however, cannot be predicted, and so waiting is a condition for it to happen.

Take the case of *Goodbye CP*. The radically physical, exhibitionist shooting method used here results in mounting tension among the cerebral palsy group, leading to some of them wanting to quit the film. This finally comes to a head when Yokota's wife, another cerebral palsy victim, reacts furiously against what she considers the portrayal of her husband as a freak and orders an immediate halt to the shooting or she will divorce him. Rather than stopping, the camera keeps on rolling as the defining moment has not taken place as yet. At long last, however, the climactic and most exhibitionist scene of all is produced, in which Yokota, naked, in the middle of a Tokyo flyover, struggles to stay upright on his knees. After several minutes of his mute staring at the camera, we hear on the asynchronous soundtrack his impromptu speech, which reveals the shattering effect the film has had on him:

> We set out to make this film to show that we can't do anything. But I was hoping I could do something to make a different kind of film. That was what I thought. But while we went through the process of making the film, my hopes were completely shattered. How can I say, after all on many levels I require some form of protection. That's the only way I can survive. I could never be on my own. That realization made me feel totally empty. To be honest, I'm not sure how I can move on. That's how I feel.[3]

Yokota's naked, wobbling, mute figure, about to be run over by passing cars as he stares at the camera, has the effect of a Barthesian *punctum* with its inexplicable power of reality which pierces, hurts and mortifies the viewer, regardless of the latter's will (Barthes, 1982, pp. 26–7); or of a Lacanian *objet petit a* whose opaque formula indicates an irreducible remnant of the Real (Lacan, 2004). However, his final speech is a genuine event for its structuring intentionality combined with its unpredictable revelatory contingency (Figure 14.3).

The same applies to the other three documentaries. *Extreme Private Eros*'s several parts are demarcated by intertitles of dates – 1972, 1973, 1974 – which indicate several periods of waiting for events to take place. One of them is Takeda's pregnancy, and in fact one of the reasons for the film's existence was that she had expressed to Hara her wish to give birth

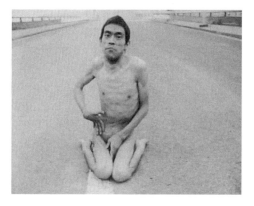

Figure 14.3 Yokota's naked, wobbling, mute figure, about to be run over by passing cars as he stares at the camera in *Goodbye CP*. Copyright © by Shisso Production.

in front of a rolling camera. The film must therefore wait for her to become pregnant, which finally happens when she has a three-week affair with a black-American soldier, Paul, stationed in Okinawa. Then another nine months must elapse until Takeda is ready to deliver. Although all this was intended and predictable, its outcome, her baby which pops out in a pool of blood right towards the camera, on the floor of Hara's tiny Tokyo apartment, without any help from third parties, has the *einmalig* quality of Benjamin's auratic events (Benjamin, 2007). It compares in all aspects to the uniqueness of death which, together with real sex, Bazin had deemed unrepresentable on screen (Bazin, 2003, pp. 27–31).

On the subject of representations of birth and death on screen, Sobchack states that:

> although birth and death are each processes and representations of liminal moments of bodily transformation and both threaten the stability of cultural codes and conventions with their radical originality, in our present culture death is the more subversive transformation of the two.
>
> (Sobchack, 2004, p. 233)

And indeed the representability of death is the sole limit Hara and Kobayashi have encountered and not surpassed in their two following films, not for lack of subversive will, of course, but because this would amount to concurring on the production of the liminal event.

In *The Emperor's Naked Army*, Okuzaki, who had already spent time in prison for murder, is clearly moved by an uncontrollable desire to kill again. This is certainly not the aim of the film, but it is one of its possible outcomes, as Okuzaki's increasingly violent behaviour suggests. He has an obsession with the figure of Koshimizu, the man who had ordered the execution of two lower-rank soldiers, from Okuzaki's own unit, both of whom were accused of desertion. Okuzaki did not participate in the firing, as he had been captured in the final months of the Pacific war in New Guinea, but he visits one by one his surviving comrades in different parts of Japan to interrogate them on the real reason for the killings, given that at that point the war had already ended. The process of finding out the current addresses of the veterans, visiting them, comparing answers, visiting them again, takes several years. However, all of them finally confess to the fact that, under the appalling conditions they were in, cannibalism had become the last available resort. As *kurobuta* ('black pork'), a euphemism for the natives, had become hard to catch, they had to turn to *shirobuta* ('white pork'), that is their own comrades. This is the startling, structural revelation of the film, but not yet its end. Koshimizu is visited twice by Okuzaki in the film, but at a certain point it is revealed, through captions, that Okuzaki has attempted to kill him, only managing to seriously injure his son. Okuzaki is again imprisoned and here the film ends, after reporting the death of his wife shortly thereafter.

It is not a secret that Okuzaki had invited Hara to shoot his killing of Koshimizu (Ruoff, 1993, pp. 109–10; Nagib, 2007). According to Hara, the murder attempt happened while he was taking advice from Imamura and a lawyer on how to deal with Okuzaki's frightening offer to kill in front of a rolling camera (Nagib, 2007), but it is also true that the camera never stopped rolling when Okuzaki physically assaulted the war veterans during his inter- rogations, sending one of them, who was recovering from an operation, back to hospital. The film thus leaves no doubt that all confessions (whose details were unknown to all, including Okuzaki) were obtained under duress, that is prolonged, intentional action, with unforeseeable consequences.

I will approach the ethical aspect of this method in the last section of this chapter, but let us first note the second case verging on the limits of representability, *A Dedicated Life*, which follows the daily life of the novelist Mitsuharu Inoue in his last years until his death from cancer. Inoue never bowed to Hara's coercive methods (Ruoff, 1993, p. 104), but welcomed the film crew during several years of his life and even allowed them to film the removal of most of his liver, though not his actual death. Almost by way of revenge, the shooting continues after he has passed away so as to uncover the sheer fabrication of his autobiography.

Conducive to the revelation of the unpredictable contingent as it may be, intention also entails manipulation, and Hara and Kobayashi have profited fully from 'the limits imposed by both the frame and the length of the reel', in Doane's words, to produce intended readings of their films, as in the case of *A Dedicated Life*. In contrast to their almost religious allegiance to phe- nomenological time as far as the creative process is concerned, the resulting product is nothing but montage and action cinema. The opening of *Extreme Private Eros* is an interesting and deliberate example of this manipulation, as it shows still photographs of Hara's former wife, Miyuki Takeda, and their little son, edited in the manner of a slideshow. Here, the film sends us back to the very origins of cinema (still photographs put side by side and set into motion) by accelerating the speed of the stills of the child, to give the impression that he is actually walking. More significantly, the discontinuous editing is constantly reminding the viewer that the intertitles and captions indicative of time progression, in both *Extreme Private Eros* and *The Emperor's Naked Army*, are no guarantee of a linear chronology.

Rather than on common people and their uneventful lives, as usually seen in realist films, Hara and Kobayashi focus on extraordinary characters engaged in transformative action, which defines the exclusion of non-action scenes in a film's final cut. If the filmmakers occasionally make use of the sequence-shot so cherished by Bazin, such as for the child birth in *Extreme Private Eros* or Yokota's crossing of a Tokyo avenue on all fours, in *Goodbye CP*, this is due to the exceptional character of the events in focus, which take a life of their own after being intentionally provoked. Hara and Kobayashi are foreign to what Cesare Zavattini once defined as the neorealists' drive to 'remain' in a scene that 'can contain so many echoes and reverberations, can even contain all the situations we may need' (Zavattini, 1966, p. 219). Zavattini's view was famously hailed by Bazin as the ultimate realist achievement in *Umberto D* (scripted by Zavattini and directed by Vittorio De Sica in 1952), exemplified by the scene of the maid grinding coffee, in which 'nothing happens' (Bazin, 1972, pp. 79–82). The revelatory power of this kind of empty moments became the distinctive trait of such epitomes of modern cinema as Antonioni (MacCann, 1966, p. 216) and the principle behind the work of a documentarist such as Frederick Wiseman, who seems entirely averse to the cut. However, dead time, or the patient waiting for epiphanic revelations that do not depend on the filmmakers' will and intention, does not feature in Hara and Kobayashi's films. Unlike Wiseman, Antonioni or Rossellini, Hara and Kobayashi are not interested in spontaneous happenings, because their aim is to produce reality.

Active subjects

Hara and Kobayashi's working system is basically collaborative, starting with the way both of them interact. This is how Kobayashi replied, when I asked her about her interest in directing films:

> From the very beginning I was interested in directing but at the same time I love collaborating as a team. And when it comes to shooting the film, Hara has the tendency of stepping forward and I have the tendency of stepping backward. Hara can be a strong presence and a strong signature in a film, which probably I am not. But when we decide to shoot a film, we discuss, I get involved in the scriptwriting and all other aspects of the film. I'm not interested in actually directing, but I am involved in the whole process of making the film.
>
> (Nagib, 2007)

This collaborative system was very much in vogue when they started as filmmakers. Nornes, in his book on the collective Ogawa Pro (2007), gives a full account of the revolutionary output resulting from such collaborative method as seen in the famous Sanrizuka series, which between 1968 and the mid-1970s documented as well as stirred mass demonstrations against the construction of Tokyo's Narita Airport. Hara was close to Ogawa's collective and even considered entering it at a certain point (Nornes, 2007, p. 132; 2003, p. 153).

Hara and Kobayashi's documentaries have drawn on this collective mode of production also with relation to the cast involved. All four of them have been in a way 'co-authored' by their stars, who are not only interesting personalities, but also either accomplished or amateur artists: Yokota is a poet; Takeda is an aspiring visual artist, actress and dancer; Inoue is a famous novelist; and Okuzaki, though not by profession, is perhaps the best actor of all. What really matters here is that all of them suggested and agreed to perform the most daring acts of their lives before the camera.

This shared authorship between crew and cast, however, eschews any idea of a harmonious conviviality, resembling much rather a battle of egos on a filming arena. *Goodbye CP* was partly conceived and financed by The Green Lawn Association, formed by the cerebral palsy group, who therefore felt entitled to decide about the directions the film should take. This is one of the reasons for the conflicts among the cast, and between these and the crew described above. However, another evidence of their authorial competitiveness is the fact that most members of the cerebral palsy group, in the film, are carrying photographic cameras, which they point at passers-by as well as at the crew members themselves, thus constantly swapping places between subjects and objects in the film.

As for *The Emperor's Naked Army Marches On*, the main problem faced during the shoot, according to Hara (Nagib, 2007), was Okuzaki's insistence on directing the film himself, which he had co-financed, arriving at a point where he threatened to destroy all footage shot thus far. *A Dedicated Life*, in its turn, can be seen as two overlapping films, one relating to Inoue's biography as he sees it, and another, corresponding to Hara and Kobayashi's contrasting view of it.

However, it is in *Extreme Private Eros: Love Song 1974* where the battle of authorial egos becomes most apparent. As his voiceover commentary reveals, Hara decides to make the film because he cannot come to terms with the fact that Takeda has left him and moved with their son to Okinawa. The film then develops in four stages, over three years: two trips by Hara to Okinawa; a third trip, in which he is accompanied by his current companion, Kobayashi; and a fourth phase when Takeda returns to Tokyo to give birth to her child. In his first visit, Hara finds Takeda living with a female lover, Sugako. They are fighting, and he films the fights. After a few days in these circumstances, Hara concludes, in voiceover commentary, that it is his presence in their apartment that is causing them to fight. The conflict, which is real, is, however, not only provoked by the director, but also performed by Takeda as a public display of her love for Sugako, which is certain to hurt Hara.

Takeda is no naïve character. She had artistic ambitions of her own. The stills edited at the beginning of the film show her next to some of her paintings, and she was active as a photographer and film actress (Nornes, 2003, pp. 145–6). In *Extreme Private Eros*, she is living for the film, making a film out of her own life and obviously delighting in it. This is, however, not readily accepted by the filmmakers. If she defies Hara by getting together with Sugako and then Paul, the American soldier, to the point of bringing Hara to tears in his sole appearance before the camera, he makes sure to bring his current companion, Kobayashi, to Okinawa to help him with the film and to drive Takeda mad with jealousy. And if Takeda delivers a baby by someone else in front of his camera, Kobayashi does the same, shortly after, and this time to a child by Hara himself (Figure 14.4).

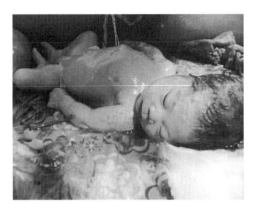

Figure 14.4   Birth equals death in its originality. *Extreme Private Eros: Love Song 1974.* Copyright © by Shisso Production.

Hara refers to this film as 'self-documentary', and he is known in Japan as the pioneer of the 'private film' (Nornes, 2007, p. 131), a first-person documentary genre that has its followers in the country up to this day. Commenting on the recent development of first-person documentaries or 'I-Movies' in the USA, Patricia Aufderheide observes that 'the first-person saga has become a feature of venues once identified as feisty bastions of left-wing perspectives' (Aufderheide, 1997). Indeed, the end of the socialist era in the early 1990s caused documentary filmmaking, to a considerable extent, to retreat from the public to the private sphere, making room for the identification between the personal and the political (Aufderheide, 1997). *Extreme Private Eros* precedes this trend by nearly two decades, also as concerns typical I-Movie journeys of discovery of one's own identity, as noted by Renov (2005, p. 243), who describes the genre as the 'stage for claims from ethnic, gay, lesbian and disabled minorities'. The fact is that the fight for individual expression has a particular meaning in Japan, a homogenous society marked by long military traditions. In the cinema, it had started in the early years of the Japanese New Wave and was entirely politically motivated.

As early as 1960, Oshima had proclaimed that 'new films must, first and foremost, express the filmmaker's active involvement as an individual' (Oshima, 1992, p. 47). The word used by Oshima to signify this is *shutaiteki*, a term very much in vogue at the time, which means an 'active subjectivity'. An individual endowed with an 'active subjectivity' is one in direct opposition to a uniformized society, who rejects victimization and takes full responsibility for the social consequences of his/her acts. An 'active subjectivity' is actually a merging of subject and object, an individual's intimacy turned into the stage for social happenings, on which the boundaries between public and private spheres cease to exist.

Thus what may sound like a purely narcissistic exercise in Hara and Kobayashi's films would perhaps be more accurately described as the crumbling of the usual filming hierarchy (the subject above the object, the director above the crew and the cast) through the productive clashing of active subjectivities behind and before the camera. It is a process of general empowerment and emancipation that frontally opposes the 'romance of victimization', which according to Aufderheide, quoting Baxter, derives from first-person narratives in current American storytelling, not just on television, but in literature and politics (Aufderheide, 1997). It is impossible to say who are victims and villains in the Hara and Kobayashi films, which also means that the filmmakers are exposed to the same stresses and risks as their characters.

In *Goodbye CP*, the crew is stopped by the police in the streets, their camera seized while still shooting, as one can tell by its aleatory focus on an empty sky for a few moments. In *Extreme Private Eros*, Hara is beaten up by thugs who are not happy with the feminist pamphlets Takeda is distributing in the streets of Goza, Okinawa, which also brings the shooting to an abrupt halt. Finally, in *The Emperor's Naked Army*, the crew is not only facing threats from the police and from extreme-right activists for filming a man who publicly announces his hatred for the Emperor, but is also at risk from working with Okuzaki himself, a murderer who intends to carry on killing.

The multiple authorships and exhibitionist methods applied to both casts and crews thus make it difficult, if not impossible, to identify an ethics of the documentary gaze, as classified by Vivian Sobchack (2004, pp. 226–57 [1984, pp. 283–300]), Bill Nichols (1991, pp. 84–5) and commented on by Linda Williams (1999, pp. 176–89), as this would presuppose a single-subject positioning represented by the camera. The exposing scenes in the films are all shot in full accordance with, and often on the suggestion of, their adult actors, even the most radical ones, such as the child birth in *Extreme Private Eros* and Yokota's naked pose on the road in *Goodbye CP*. It could be argued, of course, that if Okuzaki has agreed to and is steering the ways he is being filmed in *The Emperor's Naked Army*, the camera is not, for this reason, entitled to observe passively as he goes about making justice with his own hands. Even here, however, it must be said that in all cases where violence took place in front of the camera, help was immediately asked for from the police, by the crew and often by Okuzaki himself, in his theatrical stunts of bravery.

I will conclude by suggesting that Hara and Kobayashi's films are thoroughly and consistently ethical for their commitment to truth. This they exercise through what Rancière termed 'the inherent honesty of the film medium' (2006, p. 2), that is to say film's indexical property. This resonates with what Alain Badiou calls 'an ethic of singular truths', which is 'relative to a particular situation' (2002, p. lvi). Badiou's 'regime of truths' is also governed by the notion of event. He says: 'to be faithful to an event is to move within the situation that this event has supplemented, by *thinking* the situation "according to" the event' (2002, p. 41) This makes room for the uncertain, the unexpected and the contingent, as well as for intention, the combination of which accounts for the realism of Hara and Kobayashi's films. Theirs is therefore, I believe, an ethics of realism.

Notes

I thank Alex King for making available the recording of the questions and answers with Kazuo Hara and Sachiko Kobayashi, led by me, at the Leeds International Film Festival, on 10 November 2007. My thanks also go to Mika Ko who acted as interpreter of the questions and answers. I am grateful to Sachiko Kobayashi, Kazuo Hara and Shisso Production for their help and support.

1. It is common knowledge among critics that Kobayashi has been a partner in the making of all of her husband's films so far. Hara himself refers to his films as collaborative works with her. This notwithstanding, the authorship of their films continues to be attributed exclusively to him. This is probably because Hara is the public face of the duo, endowed as he is with a charismatic personality and the power to articulate his creative ideas with impressive clarity in his interviews. Kobayashi is, however, an intellectual herself and, as much as Hara, makes a living partly out of teaching film. In this chapter, I have chosen to attribute authorial responsibility for their films to both of them.
2. I have not included on this list *My Mishima* (*Watashi no Mishima*, 1999), as it is a collaborative work between Hara and a group of students from Cinema Juku, a filmmaking cooperative he founded, and would not therefore fit into the auteurist Hara-Kobayashi lineage I am analysing here. In the intervals between his films, Hara also worked as a television documentarist and assistant director in several important films, such as *Vengeance Is Mine* (*Fukushu suru wa sare ni ari*, Shohei Imamura, 1979) and *Sea and Poison* (*Umi to dokuyaku*, Kei Kumai, 1986).
3. The viewer is not given the means to certify whether this event is produced before or after the divorce threat, within the profilmic chronology. It seems, however, to have taken place at the end of the shoot, as Yokota's final speech sums up his experience with the film – although again the asynchronous soundtrack brings a doubt about the simultaneous occurrence of image and sound.

References

Aufderheide, Patricia (1997), 'Public Intimacy: The Development of First-person Documentary', in *Afterimage*, July–August, available on http://findarticles.com/ p/articles/mi_m2479/is_n1_v25/ai_20198552/print?tag=artBody;%20col%201, accessed on 14 August 2008.

Alain Badiou (2002), *Ethics: An Essay on the Understanding of Evil*. London/New York: Verso.

Barthes, Roland (1982), *Camera Lucida*. London: Vintage.

Bazin, André (2003), 'Death Every Afternoon', in Ivone Margulies (ed.), *Rites of Realism: Essays on Corporeal Cinema*. Durham/London: Duke University Press, pp. 27–31.

Bazin, André (1972), '*Umberto D*: A Great Work', in André Bazin, *What Is Cinema?*, vol. 2, ed. and trans. by Hugh Gray. Berkeley/Los Angeles/London: University of California Press, pp. 79–82.

Benjamin, Walter (2007), 'The Work of Art in the Age of Mechanical Reproduction', in Hannah Arendt (ed.), *Illuminations:Walter Benjamin*. London: Pimlico, pp. 211–44.

Doane, Mary Ann (2002), *The Emergence of Cinematic Time: Modernity, Contingency, the Archive*. Cambridge, MA/London: Harvard University Press.

Doll, Susan, 'Kazuo Hara' (2007), in the leaflet included in the DVD case of *Goodbye CP*. Chicago: Facets Video.

Grodal, Torben (2002), 'The Experience of Realism in Audiovisual Representation', in Anne Jerslev (ed.), *Realism and 'Reality' in Film and Media*. Copenhagen: Museum Tusculanum Press/University of Copenhagen, pp. 67–91.

Hill, John (1986), *Sex, Class and Realism: British Cinema 1956–1963*. London: BFI.

Lacan, Jacques (2004), *Le séminaire de Jacques Lacan. Livre 10, L'angoisse*, Jacques-Alain Miller (ed.). Paris: Seuil.

MacCann, Richard A. (ed.) (1966), *Film: A Montage of Theories*. New York: EP Sutton.

Nagib, Lúcia (2007), Q&A with Kazuo Hara and Sachiko Kobayashi, translated by Mika Ko, 10 November. Leeds: Leeds International Film Festival, unpublished.

Nagib, Lúcia (2006), 'Teoria experimental do realismo corpóreo baseada nos filmes de Nagisa Oshima e da nouvelle vague japonesa', in Christine Greiner and Claudia Amorim (eds), *Leituras do Sexo*. São Paulo: Annablume.

Nichols, Bill (1991), *Representing Reality: Issues and Concepts in Documentary*. Bloomington/Indianapolis: Indiana University Press.

Nornes, Abé Mark (2007), *Forest of Pressure: Ogawa Shinsuke and Postwar Japanese Documentary*. Minneapolis/London: University of Minnesota Press.

Nornes, Abé Mark (2003), 'Private Reality: Hara Kazuo's Films', in Ivone Margulies (ed.), *Rites of Realism: Essays on Corporeal Cinema*. Berkeley/Los Angeles/London: University of California Press, pp. 144–63.

Oshima, Nagisa (1992), 'Beyond Endless Self-Negation: The Attitude of the New Filmmakers', in *Cinema, Censorship, and the State: The Writings of Nagisa Oshima*, ed. by Annette Michelson, trans. by Dawn Lawson. Cambridge, MA/London: MIT, pp. 47–8.

Rancière, Jacques (2006), *Film Fables*. Oxford/New York: Berg.

Renov, Michael (2005), 'Investigando o sujeito: uma introdução', in Maria Dora Mourão and Amir Labaki (eds), *O cinema do Real*. São Paulo: Cosac & Naify, pp. 234–46.

Ruoff, Jeffrey and Ruoff, Kenneth (2007), 'Reception History: Japanese Memories of the War', in the leaflet included in the DVD case of *The Emperor's Naked Army Marches On*. Chicago: Facets Video.

Ruoff, Kenneth (1993), 'Japan's Outlaw Filmmaker: An Interview with Hara Kazuo', in *Iris: A Journal of Theory on Image and Sound*, 16, Spring, pp. 103–13.

Sobchack, Vivian (2004), *Carnal Thoughts: Embodiment and Moving Image Culture*. Berkeley/Los Angeles/London: University of California Press.

Sobchack, Vivian (1984), 'Inscribing Ethical Space: Ten Propositions on Death, Representation, and Documentary', in *Quarterly Review of Film Studies* 9(4), pp. 283–300. Reprinted in Sobchack, Vivian (2004).

Williams, Linda (1999), 'The Ethics of Intervention: Dennis O'Rourke's *The Good Woman of Bangkok*', in Jan M. Gaines and Michael Renov (eds), *Collecting Visible Evidence*. Minneapolis/London: University of Minnesota Press, pp. 176–89.

Williams, Raymond (1977), 'A Lecture on Realism', in *Screen* 18(1), Spring, pp. 61–74.

Williams, Raymond (1978), 'Recent English Drama', in Boris Ford (ed.), *The Pelican Guide to English Literature 7:The Modern Age*. Harmondsworth: Penguin.

Zavattini, Cesare (1966), 'Some Ideas on the Cinema', in Richard A. MacCann (ed.), *Film: A Montage of Theories*. New York: EP Sutton, pp. 216–29. Originally published in *Sight and Sound*, October 1953, pp. 64–9, edited from a recorded interview published in *La Revista del Cinema Italiano*, December 1952.

15
Character Construction in Brazilian Documentary Films: Modern Cinema, Classical Narrative and Micro-Realism

Ismail Xavier

My proposal is to compare two different ways of conceiving character construction and realism in Brazilian documentary films today. One way can be found in Eduardo Coutinho's *Master Building* (*Edifício Master*, 2002) and *The Mighty Spirit* (*Santo forte*, 1999); the other in José Padilha and Felipe Lacerda's *Bus 174* (*Ônibus 174*, 2002).

Coutinho became a major reference in Brazilian documentary in 1984 with his seminal film *Twenty Years Later* (*Cabra marcado para morrer*), which condenses 20 years of military dictatorship. In March 1964, he set out to make a film about the murder of a peasant and political leader from Brazil's arid northeast, but the military coup forced him to interrupt the project. In the early 1980s, he was able to resume his unfinished work thanks to the new political context ushered in with the decline of the military regime. He went back to the northeast to contact the peasants who had acted in the film and show them the footage he had kept hidden. *Twenty Years Later* starts with the public screening of the old images to the peasants, which triggers among the audience memories of a collective past of militancy and illuminates a significant part of Brazilian history. Alongside its portrait of the dictatorship years, the film presents a lucid view of the early 1980s, a political juncture of hope but also of dispersed political forces. *Twenty Years Later* is thus an essay-film that raises questions about the country's future, while avoiding any celebratory tone.

Padilha, in his turn, is a filmmaker from the 1990s generation, involved in the conception of several documentaries, such as *The Charcoal People* (*Os carvoeiros*, Nigel Noble, 1999) and *Estamira* (Marcos Prado, 2004). *Bus 174* is his first feature film, made in collaboration with Felipe Lacerda, an experienced editor who had worked with Walter Salles in *Foreign Land* (*Terra estrangeira*, 1995) and other Salles fiction films, as well as with João Moreira Salles in *Nelson Freire* (2003).[1]

The late 1990s saw documentary filmmakers facing new changes in the Brazilian public sphere, caused not by censorship or political constraints, but by the hegemony of television as a provider of social identities and a regulator of political voices. In response, they developed a new kind of audiovisual counter-discourse concerned with unveiling personal and social experiences usually reduced to clichés in media representations. Generally speaking, Coutinho's films and *Bus 174* share a common concern for realism understood as a process of image-making and profilmic performance that goes beyond social prejudices and class stereotypes as conveyed by conserva-tive or even intellectualist discourses on the poor and the populace. Despite this common impulse, both filmmakers resort to contrasting strategies when proposing alternatives to the realist traditions in a contemporary context.

Coutinho has developed a minimalist version of the interview-based documentary in order to give a new meaning to the sense of performance and role-playing implied in the interaction between camera, filmmaker and interviewed subjects. He is engaged in the systematic exploration of what is medium-specific in the cinematic representation of time, using long takes to capture revealing and unexpected moments of self-enactments hinging on the combination of planning and spontaneity. *The Mighty Spirit* and *Master Building* do not provide any comments on the subjects invited to talk about themselves, as their aim is to develop a new approach to the performative gesture based on parataxis and juxtaposition of interviewees.

In contrast to Coutinho's films, Padilha and Lacerda's *Bus 174* incorpo-rates classic narrative strategies to account for the life story of a young man, Sandro, who became famous when he hijacked a bus in Rio. Television cameras registered his dramatic confrontation with the police, who besieged the bus for several hours while Sandro held the passengers at gunpoint. Interviews and flashbacks are interwoven with images captured by the tel-evision live coverage and CCTV cameras, creating a kind of documentary thriller drawing on a detailed retrospective of the facts leading to the final tragic shoot-out. To show the exact chain of minimal displacements per-formed by Sandro, whose final decision has fatal consequences in the given circumstances, the film relies on the indexicality specific to the medium, so as to reveal dimensions inaccessible to other forms of representation.

Coutinho's character construction and modern cinema

A variety of modes of character construction can be observed in contem-porary documentary cinema. An example is Errol Morris's *The Fog of War* (2003), in which a character's profile is drawn by means of a long interview occupying the entire film, in this case Robert Macnamara's biographical account, concentrating on his actions as American Secretary of State during the 1960s. Another mode can be illustrated by Nicolas Philibert's *To Be and to Have* (*Être et avoir*, 2002), in which a single protagonist is seen performing the kind of action the film intends to discuss and praise, in this case the protagonist's teaching methods and interaction with children in a French provincial school. Here, a mixed strategy of interviews and action scenes is used to compose a character's profile. However, in both cases, the film is centred on single protagonists, who can express themselves at length about their (off or onscreen) social practices.

Examples of similar practices can also be found in contemporary Brazilian cinema, such as the documentary on samba composer and singer Paulinho da Viola, *Paulinho da Viola: meu tempo é hoje* (Izabel Jaguaribe, 2003) and *Nelson Freire*, João Salles's remarkable film, which combines the recording of Freire's performances as a world famous pianist with a biographical account based on interviews and other materials. João Salles's *Santiago* (2007) is a more complex case, owing to its reflexive dimension as a film about an unfinished film, but it can also be seen as a work in which the construction of a single character is based on the protagonist's long and fascinating account given to the filmmaker.

Whether combined with other cinematic narrative devices or not, interviews are the dominant strategy in current Brazilian documentaries. Examples of observational cinema, in the style of a Frederick Wiseman, or of classical documentary based on voiceover commentary, are extremely rare. Brazil has become the land of 'interactive' filmmakers (Nichols, 1991) who cautiously avoid provoking or pressurizing their interviewed subjects, whoever they are. Ironic interventions or aggressive modes of framing someone invited to testify – as typically found in Michael Moore's films – are normally regarded as manipulative and devoid of ethical rigour, even as 'anti-documentary' devices.

Within this national context, Eduardo Coutinho epitomizes a film practice exclusively based on interviews, according to those principles of rigorous respect for the subjects placed in front of the camera. *The Mighty Spirit* and *Master Building* can be taken as cultural and political statements embodying Coutinho's particular style around the year 2000. In them, his method revolves around a mosaic of interview scenes in which particular subjects talk about their own experiences leading to 'moments of truth'. Rather than concentrating on single characters, the films focus on different groups made of ordinary individuals who expose themselves during their encounters with the filmmaker. The series of juxtaposed interviews is the exclusive dramatic form used and the only source of information about each of the interviewees. Characters do not interact with each other, but only with the camera, which they confront in challenging moments. All effects must derive from the ways in which the interview scene is set and shot.

In both films, the encounter, with a few exceptions, takes place in the subject's house after an appointment has been made. The filmmaker pays a visit to the individual whom he is seeing for the first time, because the contact and preparation for the scene are in charge of his assistants. What follows is the performance of a ritual that separates the subject from his/her everyday life.

In *The Mighty Spirit*, there is a specific topic of conversation: religion. This is, however, not approached from an institutional perspective, as there is no intention to draw an 'objective' picture of a social practice as systematized by a researcher for whom popular utterances would be mere illustrations of a thesis. Instead, religion is taken as a lived experience. The filmmaker acts as a listener who follows a Socratic principle, functioning exclusively as a 'midwife' who helps interviewees express their thoughts. From among the poor inhabitants of the Santa Marta favela, Coutinho selected for interview those individuals deemed capable of going beyond the obvious clichés of their class, profession and ethnicity. He aimed at performances that could bring to the fore a subject's singular features and make room for their narrative skills at moments of self-assertion. Thus interviewees are given time to become the effective centre of the scene, defining its rhythm and tone, regardless of their interaction with the filmmaker, whose interventions are explicit and staged. The interviews are often lengthy, because the filmmaker knows that his subjects need time to gain control over their performances and get to the point in which their own pace and psychological investment can create the instant of a surprising revelation. This can happen through a detail, a felicitous word, a hesitation, a sudden gesture. A typical example of this exploration of protracted time is the testimony given by Dona Teresa, an old housemaid. She sees her courtyard as inhabited by ghostly, invisible entities who play a significant role in her life, as she firmly believes in reincarnation and has a matter-of-fact relation to it. Without trying to push her point, she just takes her time talking in a constant, enchanting flow of words, describing things around her as well as her feelings and faith. The resulting profile is that of a self-assured person endowed with great wisdom about life and death. She dominates the scene by acknowledging and respecting, but not bowing to the cinematic apparatus.

Coutinho's documentary-making is a dramatic form made of this kind of personal confrontation between subject and filmmaker, and inflected by the camera-effect, that is, the presence of the cinematic look through which every image becomes theatrical. Coutinho's method is meant to enhance this effect by exposing a mixture of spontaneity and theatre, of authenticity and exhibitionism, the moment between 'being real' and 'becoming an image'. These features become more explicit in *Master Building*, a film in which there is no specific topic of conversation. Coutinho interviews a group of lower-middle-class individuals living in a Copacabana apartment building. The choice of conversation topics is left for each individual, given that they live in an environment that is not regulated by the problems and demands common to a favela community. As a result, the binary relation between authenticity and exhibitionism is placed on an exclusively personal level, on which subjects are expected to express their own minds about the film's narrative direction. Subjects thus become the judges of their own false and true utterances. This paradox is illustrated by the interview with Alessandra, a call girl endowed with a remarkable intuitive feeling for what is implied by the camera-effect. She talks about herself very openly but, at a certain point,

Figure 15.1   'I am a truthful liar': Alessandra replays Diderot's 'paradox of acting' in *Master Building*. Reproduced with kind permission from VideoFilmes.

switches to a self-commentary, in which she considers whether it is possible to lie when telling the truth or conversely to be truthful when lying. She ends by saying: 'I am a truthful liar,' thus unwittingly replaying Diderot's famous 'paradox of acting' (Figure 15.1).

Coutinho is not alone in recognizing documentary as role-playing, but he knows like few others how to work within this premise to compose a scenario of empathy and inclusion, hinging on a 'philosophy of the encounter'. Often the object of theory, this philosophy is rarely put into practice, as it requires an effective opening towards dialogue, talent and experience. Only this can make room for the emergence of that which would not be possible without the presence of the camera, changed into a catalyst of self-expression.

Coutinho's method of character construction, based on the momentous self-expression through speech and body language, is in many ways attuned to that found in modern fiction cinema. He does not subscribe to linear narrative or to the idea that the truth about a subject requires the causal concatenation of successive moments to be revealed. Instead of drawing on the premise that things happen in a certain order as conveyed by a narrative discourse, Coutinho commits himself to the revelation of what empirically happens at a certain time and place, unlikely or extraordinary though it may be. His films emphasize the power of each episode resulting from the combination of planning and chance, thus drawing attention to the fragment, what is sketched but never completed, the instant in its radical contingency (Doane, 2002).

The subjects' performances neither follow a fixed script nor are entirely free, for the pressures to attain verisimilitude and an appearance of truth still remain. In this sense, Coutinho resists the interviewees' tendency to conceive their speech according to what they believe is their interlocutor's opinion – that of the filmmaker as well as the 'public opinion' represented by the camera. In his films, this is a basic challenge, and the staging of the interview as a ritual – a relatively isolated ritual, away from any sense of live television – enhances its tension as a dramatic form. Much of the viewer's interest is drawn by the interviewee's 'agony', which derives not from suffering, but from competition, from the challenge posed by the camera-effect. If the power of the instant and the very density of a moment in life are to be emphasized, it is best to let the camera explicitly take part in the situation and to acknowledge the asymmetry of powers which separates the filmmaker from his subject. There is the editing, the whole production context and the mise-en-scène (settings, lighting, space construction, framing, body positions), all of which condition the register of the speech.

Let us consider two examples. In Alessandra's case, the shot is tight, with nothing too noticeable around her, and full focus on her facial expression: she has to endure the close-up. Something different happens with Henrique, whose interview is the longest in *Master Building*. He talks about his past life and present loneliness, while the camera moves around and reveals more of the surrounding space: an image of Christ on the wall, the modesty of the scarce furniture, the stereo from which Frank Sinatra's voice singing 'My Way' will later resound. Henrique identifies with this song as a kind of redeeming hymn, which provides him with rare moments of self-assertion within his otherwise resentful mindframe. Henrique's communication with his neighbours has actually been reduced to this: every Saturday morning he plays Sinatra's record and sings (almost shouts) along with his beloved celebrity. While he performs this weekly ritual, the camera suddenly turns away from him to capture a second camera that is the source of the previous, closer view of his cathartic ritual. The director insists on registering the entire performance but refuses the unmediated enjoyment of it. Henrique, on his part, lives his catharsis as if he were an actor unaware of the camera. To show both him and the other camera closer to him is a way of exposing the process of representation, of warning that empathy has its laws and coordinates (Figure 15.2).

The interview, as a public speech, reveals one's intimacy and transforms the person who speaks into a 'character' in the etymological sense of the word: a 'public figure'. The filmmaker is neither the father nor the boss, as remarked in *Master Building* by the shy girl who finds it hard to face him. Despite being a stranger, he is an anticipated visitor, but there is an observance of decorum on both parts, marking a difference between a filmmaker's and a psychoanalyst's mode of listening. The catalysing power of the camera, which encourages subjects to confess, is a pillar of Coutinho's documentaries, but does not sanction the belief in 'objectivity', neutrality or the impression that all we see is therapy. The effort is to foreground how people are better than they seem and not worse, and how they can attract an unsuspected interest for what they say and do, and not only for what they represent or illustrate in a given social scale and cultural context (see Lins, 2002).

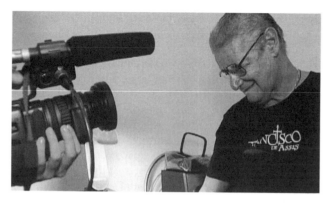

Figure 15.2   The camera focuses on a second camera focusing on Henrique, in *Master Building*: The laws of empathy are exposed. Reproduced with kind permission from VideoFilmes.

If Coutinho's refusal of aprioristic thought is reminiscent of the tendency to 'give voice' to the Other, typical of the 1960s–70s, his empirical investigation draws on different principles, as it is not restricted to politically relevant themes. He does not conform to the clichés of fragmentation, the crisis of the subject and the impoverishment of subjective perception. Quite the contrary, he encourages subjective affirmation and radicalizes the value of the Word in cinema. His plunge into orality is a way of fighting against the limits imposed to speech through manipulation, typical of television.

The encounter itself is the centrepiece. Conversation develops as an open theatre in which the filmmaker explores the indexicality of the moving image in order to capture a character's accidental words, looks, gestures. Here, realism means the friendly though challenging interaction involving a performing subject and the cinematic apparatus. In other words, the idea of realism is linked to the production of the personal encounter as a kind of *happening* made possible by the presence of the camera. The long duration of each interview and the way they are staged result in a particular mode of looking and listening compatible with a phenomenological description. Rather than drawing on pre-established conceptual frameworks, the intersubjective relation remains open to the unpredictable event.

Coutinho's particular realism in a way resonates with a seminal work on realism in visual arts, Ernst Gombrich's *Art and Illusion* (1969), which provides the context for a modern notion of realism in the cinema. Gombrich contends that illusion is produced when our eyes encounter an image that does not correspond to an existing concept of the object or human type represented. The image thus creates, through form and style, a sense of revelation. For Gombrich, to perceive is to 'notice relationships', and he emphasizes the 'interplay between expectation and observation' in our contact with images: 'To those used to the style we call "Cimabue" and expecting to be presented with a similar notation, the paintings of Giotto came with a shock of incredible lifelikeness' (1969, p. 61).

Likewise, in Coutinho's films, new aspects of the object are made visible because they do not correspond to an established view of them, as opposed to narratives inscribed in a coded verisimilitude that confirms our expectations and understanding of a 'known world'. Along the same lines, Christian Metz opposes classical narrative films, belonging to a coded genre with their own rules about what is acceptable and not acceptable, to modern films of the 1960s whose new way of presenting human experience produces a sense of freshness and unveiling understood as a sign of realism. For him, modern films are closer to the real because they break away from established conventions seen as obstacles to a clearer perception of life (Metz, 1974).

Classical narrative and micro-realism in *Bus 174*

In *Bus 174*, the interviews have a completely different function, and the process of character construction evolves through other audiovisual channels and procedures. They hinge on a carefully woven narrative based on a single dramatic event: the degradation of the police force and penitentiary system in Brazil. The film focuses on a *fait divers* in Rio de Janeiro that became a huge media event at the time. As mentioned, Sandro tried to rob the passengers on a bus, things went wrong and the police besieged the bus for hours until he decided to come out, taking one of the hostages with him. As he stepped out of the bus a policemen fired a shot at him and in the confusion the hostage, a young woman called Geisa, was killed. After Sandro's arrest onlookers started to shout, 'Kill him!', in a sort of lynching impulse not rare on such occasions in Brazil. The police shoved him into the van and left the scene, but ended up killing him on the way to the police station.

The film's account of Sandro's life story as someone 'doomed to die young' informs about his experience as an abandoned street kid and occasional prisoner. This had provided him with a sense of the value of public performance which he resorted to that afternoon. At a certain point during the negotiation with the police, he sticks his head outside the bus and, showing his face with no concern for his security, stages a kind of press conference for the television cameras and onlookers, revealing his awareness of the role played by the media in guaranteeing his survival (away from the cameras he would have been killed by the police, as indeed happens that same evening).

Part of what we see in the film comes from images produced by a television network as live coverage of the sensational event. Another part comes from images recorded by traffic control cameras placed at each corner of the road. They give us the detailed evidence of what happened, how it happened and at what time of the day. The time code display of the traffic control cameras was used by Padilha to create a sense of dramatic delay and suspense during the film. The editing does not avoid, but much rather incorporates all the effects typical of a thriller to engage the audience in gripping, highly emotional images, whose power is enhanced by the fact that they 'happened in reality'.

The on-site occurrences, accompanied by an ominous music soundtrack, are interspersed with three series of interviews. The first series focuses on people who had known Sandro as a child or had been in contact with him not long before that fateful afternoon. The second involves the young women who were taken as hostages and threatened by Sandro inside the bus. The third series focuses on policemen who comment on the questions of strategy and method, as they try to explain why things went wrong on that occasion.

The first series renders a narrative of Sandro's life story, emphasizing his social and family predicaments which had turned him into a victim of society. A fatherless child, he saw his mother being killed in front of their house; later, he became a street kid involved in misdemeanours and was sent more than once to reformatories. During his time in the streets he was part of the group of children who lived in the Candelária Cathedral surroundings, in Rio's city centre, and were massacred by hired gunmen one night while sleeping on the pavement next to the cathedral. He was not there at that moment and survived. He grew up to become an outlaw, taken to prison more than once, where he mixed with dangerous criminals and suffered the terrible conditions of the life typical of the packed and violent prisons turned into deposits of people awaiting trial. All the interviews give the same sense of a young man who could have become a better person, had he not been so inexorably exposed to violence from childhood. The narrative centrepiece is the description, in two scenes shot in real prisons, of the horrific conditions faced by the prisoners. Some of them even address the camera to denounce the inhuman treatment and lack of resources they are exposed to. These scenes illustrate the film's central thesis: an outlaw would do anything to avoid prison, would rather kill and die than be caught and sent to those hellish places where he would be treated like a beast, risking being raped or killed. This explains Sandro's despair when things go wrong in his robbery attempt, a despair heightened by other factors (it is suggested that he committed the assault under the influence of drugs, but this hypothesis becomes weaker in the course of the events). Essentially, he acted according to his worst expectations. He would rather attempt to escape, take hostages and create a scene than give himself up to the police and be taken to jail. Thus, the first series of interviews and its interpolations help create a context that turns Sandro's life story into an explanation of his fears and violent behaviour, suggesting he is a victim of a social dynamics marked by injustice and oppression.

The second series of interviews consolidates the image of Sandro conveyed in the first one. The hostages' accounts stress his ambiguous behaviour on the bus. They all talk about the kind of theatrical performance he staged to give the impression that he was more dangerous and mean than he actually was. He had told one of the girls to pretend that she was dead after he had fired his gun, just to make people think he was killing hostages. This is one instance, among others on that afternoon, of the mixture of reality and make-believe in which Sandro – with a certain degree of deliberation that does not exclude the ambivalent embodiment of the stereotype – performs the 'bad guy' as if saying, 'you all want me to act like this, and I will not disappoint you'. The paradox is verbally expressed when he looks at the people, the police and the cameras on the street and shouts: 'This is not yesterday's film; this is real' (Figure 15.3). His speech to such a large audience again has a double meaning: it shows his awareness of being on the verge of becoming an icon, his citizenship in the realm of images regulated by the audiovisual media; at the same time, his performance is part of a calculated strategy of survival. Once made visible and endowed with a public identity, he will have a chance to escape death in the hands of the police. For the viewer, the question remains whether Sandro is just staging his supposed identity as defined by the Other (media, police), or venting his resented self who, given his life story, emerges with full power in this extreme situation.

To complete the picture composed by different points of view, the film-maker interviews a young criminal who covers his face to conceal his identity, composing an image that bestows an aura of expertise to his words. Commenting on Sandro's performance, he highlights his incompetence and lack of experience in the execution of an erratic line of action. Thus the film brings about the suggestion that the dramatic situation resulted from Sandro's limitations and poor skills in the role of a bad man.

Figure 15.3 'This is not yesterday's film; this is real': Sandro and a hostage in *Bus 174*. Copyright © by Globo Comunicação e Participações SA.

The variety of statements presented to configure Sandro's identity is reminiscent of the strategy used in realist fiction, when the writer or filmmaker connects the opening scene with a long retrospect of the protagonist's past in order to situate and explain a decisive moment in their life. Here, Sandro's past is composed by means of distinct narratives in the form of a mosaic, where the pieces fit together most of the time. Although those pieces leave gaps, which provide him with a degree of ambiguity, this is similar to what happens in classical realist narratives, which play with verisimilitude and establish a larger context in which to appreciate a character's performance in extreme circumstances. The difference derives from the fact that *Bus 174* is a documentary, whose starting point is the video footage of Sandro's confrontation with the police. The film's rhetoric includes these images as 'visible evidence' of a real that Padilha and Lacerda wish to discuss during the film through the interspersed editing of interviews and other information. This editing work implies cognitive operations that are inscribed in a narrative paradigm borrowed from fiction cinema, and implies emotional effects created by strategies borrowed from classical cinema. The suggestive picture deriving from the interviews functions not exactly as a cause–effect explanation, but as the configuration of a life story bound to end with Sandro's tragic death. In this sense, the film provides a reading of the television images as the unfolding of a meaningful event that should be taken as the accomplishment of a certain promise already imbedded in Sandro's past life. This careful process of character construction suggests that, in the confrontation, Sandro's decisions were consistent with what he could expect from the police as a poor young man bearing the marks of previous confrontations with the social order.

Combining different strategies aimed at rendering the best explanation for what happened that afternoon, the film offers the representation of a social context and its effect on Sandro, who thus becomes a typical character. This is *classical realism* understood in the sense of the nineteenth century realist novel tradition in which both 'critical realism' and Naturalism, though in different ways, were concerned with social determinations in the unfolding of a life story. This is radically opposed to Coutinho's phenomenological, medium-specific *modern realism*, which shuns the construction of the subject as a social type. There is, however, something else. *Bus 174* also resorts to medium-specific devices to collect small details used as 'visible evidence', particularly towards the end of the film, in which we find a combination of cross-cutting and slow-motion that results in a kind of *micro-realism*.

In the kind of assemblage produced by the editing process, many voices interfere to comment on what we see on the screen. In the third series of interviews, the policemen who took part in the event are worried about their mistakes and the specific decisions taken by other Rio authorities. They release a central piece of information: the Governor, concerned with the shocking effect on audiences of a shoot-out on television, had ordered the police not to shoot Sandro in front of the cameras. That is the reason given by the policemen for not shooting him when he stuck his head out of the window to give his long speech. For them, the problems derived from the duration of the drama, the tension involved and the mistakes that paralysed the police until Sandro came out of the bus using Geisa as human shield. At that point, the police took effective action, profiting from the confusion created by Sandro's move to precipitate the shoot-out in which Geisa became the only victim. Amid all these mistakes and confusion, the final sequence of *Bus 174* concentrates on the question of who was responsible for Geisa's death. Was it Sandro or the police sniper who decided to shoot him in the head when he was within target, from a distance of three to four yards?

Further police investigation established that the two bullets that killed Geisa came from Sandro's gun, which was triggered when the sniper missed his shots. This information does not answer the question about the shared responsibility of the police, whose previous flaws and precipitate action at the crucial moment led Sandro to fire his gun. Padilha and Lacerda's way of dealing with this question of shared responsibility suggests that the complex combination of small details in the final stages of the drama makes it impossible to capture a clear decision-making process in Sandro's mind. Multiple factors and agents contributed to the denouement, and Geisa's death should be taken as a tragic fact in the full sense of the word.

Padilha and Lacerda compose this tragic view of the decisive moment very carefully. Firstly, they emphasize the sense of tension and instability, the increasing lack of control as it is described by the police and Sandro's female hostages on the bus. In their interviews, the women were unanimous in stating that their fear derived from a perception that the final outcome had been left to chance. To build suspense, the film shows the progression of chronological time using the time code display on the television screens, creating a sense of accumulation and dramatic flow of time.

As time evolves, our sense that each special moment can be the decisive one escalates. It becomes increasingly difficult to predict and judge decisions made in a fraction of a second. In its configuration of the climactic moment of shooting and death, the film emphasizes the crucial role played by minor details, the minimal lapses of time within which a small gesture can have fatal consequences. To reach these effects, the last scenes including the shoot-out are shown in progressive slow motion so as to render a clearer view of the small gestures that formed the chain leading to the disaster. The decisive moment is even replayed, because the television cameras had captured images from different angles. Only cinema – and video – thanks to its indexical property, could make visible the micro-fabric of tragedy as it is done in *Bus 174*. This is what constitutes the film's *micro-realism.*

Geisa's life was decided in that specific juncture in which the accidental was given plenty of room to emerge. This is what the *micro-realism* of the instant tries to unveil. At the same time, the film's back-and-forth movement narrates Sandro's past to emphasize the role played by the social context in the events of that afternoon. This is a typical strategy of *classical realism*, which is based on the macro-reality of the plot (*syuzhet*), or a narrative discourse that is not medium specific, but common to literature and drama, as described by Bordwell (1985).

There is surely a tension between macro- and micro-realisms, because the former points towards social determination and the latter towards the importance of the accidental and the contingent to the drama's final result. The former is concerned with the responsibility of the agents and with the construction of Sandro as a character whose actions can be explained by his social condition and appalling previous experiences. The latter is concerned with the multiplication of factors, forces and actions that compose an instant as the complex intersection of many lines of causality and contingent meetings, so as to suggest the idea of the tragic which can be linked to that of destiny, or to the supposed presence of a transcendental order that governs the facts, a capricious, highly ironic order.

Although different or even opposed, both realisms contribute to the defence of a central thesis in the film: given the (micro- and macro-) complexities they involve, Sandro is far from being the only person to blame. Forget the stereotype of the dangerous criminal and look at the structure of Brazilian society, a society that ended up murdering him when he was already under state custody, in a police vehicle. At the same time, see how the details, 'made visibly evident', can show how difficult it is to judge someone's gesture performed in those specific circumstances, on the spur of the moment.

Note

1. Padilha drew international attention more recently with his first fiction film, *Elite Squad* (*Tropa de elite*, 2007), which was awarded the Golden Bear at the Berlin Film Festival, after its strong impact on Brazilian audiences. This is a very controversial work, which confirms Padilha's talent for dramatic and violent cinematic representations.

References

Bordwell, David (1985), 'Fabula, Syuzhet, and Style', *Narration in the Fiction Film*. Madison: The University of Wisconsin Press.
Doane, Mary Ann (2002), *The Emergence of Cinematic Time: Modernity, Contingency, the Archive*. Cambridge, MA: Harvard University Press.
Gombrich, E.H. (1969), *Art and Illusion: A Study in the Psychology of Pictorial Representation*. Princeton: Princeton University Press.
Lins, Consuelo (2002), 'Coutinho encontra as fissuras do *Edifício Master*', in *Sinopse*, 4(9), August, pp. 30–2.

Metz, Christian (1974), 'The *Saying* and the *Said*: Towards the Decline of Plausibility in the Cinema?', *Film Language: A Semiotics of the Cinema*. New York: Oxford University Press.

Nichols, Bill (1991), *Representing Reality: Issues and Concepts in Documentary*. Bloomington: Indiana University Press.

16
The Difficulty with Documentary: A Filmmaker's View

João Moreira Salles

A book on documentary published several years ago by a prestigious British university press began thus: 'The nature of non-fiction and the non-fiction film has proven to be utterly baffling to generations of filmmakers and scholars' (Plantinga, 1997, p. 2). Hardly an encouraging beginning. It is highly unlikely that a book on culinary arts or mammal physiology would begin like this. There must not be many pedagogical books whose opening lines announce that they have an 'utterly baffling' object ahead of them. In our case, however (and unfortunately), similar descriptions can be found by anyone who is willing to search the genre's literature. Such statements almost always appear in the opening pages, but more recently they have started to appear at the end, as if we were fated not to know who we are.

What is the nature of this difficulty?

The first thing that strikes us about the documentary is that it is not one single thing, but many. We do not work with a fixed menu of techniques, nor do we display a set number of styles. Of course, the same can be said of fiction film, but in our case the instability is incomparably greater. As one critic observed, unlike classical fiction cinema, documentary has never relied on the stabilizing force of the industry to impose stylistic conventions and relatively homogeneous narrative patterns (Plantinga, 1997, p. 106).

This polymorphism is only the visible side of our difficulty. It is the symptom. What actually counts is what is (or is not) behind such variety. In other words, is there a common denominator between the workers leaving the factory in Lumière's *La Sortie des usine Lumière* (1895), the scenes Major Reis shot in the backlands of Brazil in *Across Brazil* (*Através do Brasil*, 1932), the film *Nanook of the North* by Robert Flaherty (1922), *Night and Fog* (*Nuit et brouillard*, 1955) by Alain Resnais, or *Twenty Years Later* (*Cabra marcado para morrer*, 1985), by Eduardo Coutinho?

Yes and no.

Yes, because the five examples relate to facts which took place in the world. With these films, filmmakers and spectators establish a contract by which they agree that these people existed, that they said such-and-such

things, that they did this and that. They are statements about the historical world, not about the fictional world. In order for documentary to exist, it is crucial that spectators do not lose faith in this contract.
How could they lose such faith?

The following is a dialogue between Flaherty and Nanook just before he started shooting one of the most important scenes in *Nanook of the North*, considered by historians as the inaugural film of the documentary genre:

> 'Do you and your men realize that you may have to refrain from killing the animal if this interferes with the film? Will you remember that what I want are scenes of you hunting the walrus? That the meat from the slaughtered animal is secondary?' 'Yes. The filming comes first', Nanook assured me in all sincerity. 'No man will move, no harpoon will be hurled, until you give the signal. You have my word'. We shook hands and agreed to begin the next day.
>
> (Calder-Marshall, 1963, p. 80)

This dialogue is not available to viewers of *Nanook of the North*. It is not part of the film. It can only be found in Flaherty's wife's memoirs, quoted in Calder-Marshall's book. But what if a grouch whispered the story to the viewer? The viewer might interpret the revelation as a breach of contract – if not of the entire contract, at least of some of its clauses. And if the grouch went on to explain that Nanook and his men no longer lived by hunting seals, that since the arrival of firearms they no longer used harpoons, to the point that they had to spend several days relearning how to handle them, it is very likely that the viewer, now certain that he or she had been fooled, would stalk out of the cinema.

Still, *Nanook of the North* is undoubtedly the first documentary in film history. Before attempting to explain why, it is important to note that ever since the beginning the question had been posed: What is a documentary? Is staging for the camera a betrayal? What is real? Should we have a commitment to truth? What sort of commitment, and which truth? Obviously, the fact that the questions are raised does not mean that they have been answered. After all, truth is not a trivial concept. Philosophy has dealt with it for at least 25 centuries. We documentarians have only been around for 80 years. Our answers are still, at best, mediocre.

I will now comment on some of the more recent answers to these questions. Let us leave aside the more canonical definitions of documentary, which may also be the most naïve, with their emphasis on objectivity, on uncontaminated access to reality, on the film as a mirror held up to the world. It is important to emphasize that such concepts have rarely been defended by documentarians themselves. They are primarily the result of received wisdom, of a certain kind of journalistic approach, of misinformed reviewers who are alien to the painstaking process of choosing lenses, defining framing and especially selecting, discarding and splicing hours and hours of raw footage.

Fiction/non-fiction

According to one school, documentaries are the product of companies and institutions devoted to the business.

This is the tautological explanation, but it is not as foolish as it may sound. The point of departure for the scholars who use it is the principle that the institutional framework in which films are exhibited is determinant. Documentary is context. If the BBC, the Discovery Channel or Eduardo Coutinho call their films and programmes documentaries, then such work is labelled as such long before the viewer's decoding process begins (Nichols, 2001, p. 21). They will be viewed as documentaries because they have been defined as such by those in charge.

The first few minutes of a non-fiction film play an important role in this process of contextualization. Before introducing Nanook to viewers, Flaherty uses three captions and two maps. With these resources he is stating: in a real place dwells a real man, Nanook. The point is to anchor the film in history. 'Here is Nanook, he exists.' Eighty years later, the device continues to be used, even though the captions have given way to other resources such as voiceover narration. This is the case of *Master Building* (*Edifício Master*, 2002), by Eduardo Coutinho, in which the initial voiceover commentary by the director himself ascertains the veracity of what the spectator is about to see:

> An apartment building in Copacabana, one block from the beach. 276 conjugated apartments. Around 500 residents. 12 floors. 23 apartments per floor. We rented an apartment in this building for a month. With three different teams, we filmed life in the building for a week.

A second concept is the following: documentary is the way the viewer sees the film. Here the emphasis rests not on the film itself, but on how it is perceived. Documentary is a way of seeing. In 2004 the Brazilian weekly magazine *Veja* published a review of the film *Collateral*, starring Tom Cruise in the role of a killer, with the following title: 'Now his hair has turned grey' (Boscov, 2004). The reviewer is obviously *not* referring to the film's character, but to the actor Tom Cruise, a man of flesh, blood, voice and hair. Instead of fiction, the reviewer chose to highlight the information regarding the historical world: the salt-and-pepper, middle-aged actor. For a moment, reality imposed itself on fiction, that is the customary suspension of disbelief failed to occur and the thriller became a document which conveyed the passage of time on a man's face.

I used the word *document*, not *documentary*, because there is in fact an important difference between the two. A document is contiguous to reality. Tom Cruise's image on the screen is an undeniable affirmation that Tom Cruise exists in the real world. When he speaks on the screen, 'the grain of his voice', as Nichols has noted (2001, p. 36), is a direct consequence of his having opened his mouth and uttered some sound in the past.

Very well, every film, whether fiction or non-fiction, is a document, and can be read as such. On the basis of this assumption, one could easily take a step further and see every fiction film as a documentary.

In one of his essays, documentary editor Dai Vaughan tells an interesting story about a Laurel and Hardy film he had seen on television with added commentary (Vaughan, 1999, p. 84). The film is a minor classic from 1929 in which the two comedians play the role of door-to-door Christmas tree salesmen. They come to the door of a grouch who hates salesmen and slams the door on their faces. They ring the bell again, the man reopens the door, this time even more furious, and the story is replayed until the bad humour escalates to a paroxysm of violence that brings down the house. The commentator then explained to the viewers that a serious mistake had been made during the shoot: the house rented by the film production to be destroyed was actually on the other side of the road, so what we see is the wrong house. Vaughan concludes that this information is enough to turn a fiction comedy into a documentary – in this case, a documentary on film actors who unwittingly destroy, with great voluptuousness, the house of a hapless, absent homeowner.

Alongside the indices of reality, we see the process through which a house is destroyed. It is a plot, a rhetorical organization that evolves according to the demands of a solid narrative structure. Whether the story of the 'serious mistake' is trustworthy or not, the key is that, according to the school of context and reception, much more than content or narrative strategy, what makes a film a documentary is the way we view it; in principle, anything may or may not be a documentary, depending on the spectator's point of view.

But of course this explanation is not satisfactory. As noted by another critic, a film such as *The Wizard of Oz* (Victor Fleming, 1939) can also be viewed as a documentary – in this case, a documentary on Judy Garland's 1939 acting style (Plantinga, 1997, p. 19). However, we know intuitively that there is a profound difference between *The Wizard of Oz* and, say, *The Sorrow and the Pity* (*Le Chagrin et la pitié*, Marcel Ophüls, 1969) – so profound a difference that it makes each of these films irreducible to the other.

It is useful to make a distinction between non-fictional understanding and non-fiction artefact. Non-fictional understanding allows us to perceive grains of reality in all images, even those belonging to the field of fiction. Conversely, the non-fiction artefact (of which documentary is certainly an example) does not depend on the individual uses made of it. It is a convention, a social phenomenon. It is possible that in a course on the vocal techniques of American actresses during the golden years of American musicals, *The Wizard of Oz* could be analysed as a documentary, but it would be a conceptual error to classify it as such (Plantinga, 1997, p. 20). It is, and always will be, a fiction film in which people sing. The history of cinema says so. In turn, *Nanook of the North* will never cease to be a documentary.

We thus return to the question: why is *Nanook of the North* a documentary? Further: why is it considered the first documentary, if the history of cinema was born with a clearly non-fictional scene, Lumière's workers leaving the factory?

We could answer as follows: because Flaherty's film is not merely the record of Nanook, the Eskimo. It is a story crafted from crises and resolutions, with a strong backbone which takes the viewer by the hand through the story until its conclusion. It is first and foremost this narrative structure which defines documentary and prevents it from becoming a variety film such as those produced before Flaherty. As once noted by John Grierson (1979), Flaherty understood cinema not as a branch of anthropology or archaeology, but as an act of imagination. This very narrative imagination – which Flaherty certainly possessed, and some would say excessively – is what makes him the pioneer of documentary. He does not describe, he constructs.

Other pioneers such as Major Reis, for example, lacked this intuition. His film *Across Brazil* (*Através do Brasil*), made of scenes shot between 1912 and 1917 – thus before *Nanook* – is an important record of the wondrous things he saw, but it is only this: a record. The images follow one another without any internal necessity. Unlike Flaherty, Reis did not realize that, for a documentarian, the relevant reality is the one which is crafted by the author's imagination and expressed both during the shoot and the editing process. As I have remarked elsewhere (Salles, 2003, pp. 154–8), perhaps that is why his films are more admired by anthropologists than by documentarians.

Flaherty understood the grammar of fictional cinema and wrote his film with it. As noted by Brazilian scholar Silvio Da-Rin, 'by choosing to concentrate on the life of an Eskimo and his family, [Flaherty] started from a principle close to that of cinematographic fiction' (Da-Rin, 2004, p. 47). His filming takes into account the value of the sequence, as well as of the image. Rather then relying exclusively on the record, he crafts the scene by resorting to point-of-view shots, crosscutting, reverse shots, eyeline and direction matches, pans, in short: the entire arsenal of classical cinematography perfected by Griffith and used in a story 'without actors, without a studio, without a script', in the words of Flaherty's wife (Flaherty, 1960, p. 17).

As Jean-Luc Godard famously said, 'all great films tend towards documentary, just like all great documentaries tend towards fiction … and whoever delves deeply into one necessarily encounters the other along the way' (quoted in Da-Rin, 2004, p. 17). This is certainly true of the first documentary in history. The boundaries between fiction and documentary were blurry right from the beginning.

In general, since Flaherty, we can say that every documentary has two distinct characteristics. On the one hand, it is the record of something that took place in the world; on the other, it is a narrative, a rhetoric drawing on recorded data. No film is complete as a mere record. There is always the additional ambition of being a well-told story. The rhetorical layer superimposed on the raw material, the way of recounting the subject matter, the oscillation between document and representation constitute the true problem of documentary. Our identity is intimately linked to the complex coexistence of these two characteristics (Plantinga, 1997, p. 32; Nichols, 2001, p. 38).

Over 60 years ago John Grierson formulated the classical definition that documentary is the 'creative treatment of reality' (quoted in Barsam, 1973, p. 2).[1] *Treatment*, as we know, entails *transformation*, a meaning that is further enhanced by the use of the adjective *creative* rather than *mimetic*.

A manner of speaking

According to Dai Vaughan, the difference between cinema and reality is that every film is about *something*, but reality is not (Vaughan, 1999). Historically, the critical tradition has sought the meaning of documentary in this *thing* of which the film speaks. My position, in keeping with some more recent trends, is that we should not look to the noun, but to the preposition, to the *about*, that is to say, not to the subject matter, but to the way the film approaches the subject matter. In other words, documentary is not a consequence of the theme, but a way of relating to it.

According to some scholars, this specific relationship is limited to the discourse, to the way of speaking; documentaries are primarily a type of rhetoric. The difference between fiction and documentary (and the question 'What is documentary?' refers precisely to that) lies in the documentary mode of address, which tells the viewer that what is being shown on the screen actually occurred in the historical world.

This position does not necessarily associate documentary with any kind of realism. For example, nature films often include slow-motion sequences, an unreal way of moving, yet they are still recognized as documentaries. The same can be said of soundtrack, non-chronological editing and even animation. These are not fiction techniques, but *cinematic* techniques. They are available not only to both classical and experimental films, but also to documentary (Plantinga, 1997, pp. 97 and 215).

The point of departure for those who deny an essential difference between fiction and documentary is generally based on the premise that documentary (if it exists) should offer direct, uncontaminated access to the thing itself. Because this is impossible, they prefer to claim that all film is fictional (Plantinga, 1997, p. 11). They are mistaken. To manipulate the material does not necessarily push a documentary towards fiction.

'Expression, Not Imitation; Rhetoric, Not Representation' is the subheading of an essay defending the notion of documentary-as-rhetoric (Plantinga, 1997, p. 37). This is a succinct way of saying that documentaries do not intended to reproduce reality, but to speak about it. On the one hand the mirror, on the other the hammer. In John Grierson's words: 'The idea of a mirror held up to nature is not as important … as that of a hammer helping to shape it. As a hammer, not as a mirror, I have sought to use the medium that fell into my restless hands' (quoted in Da-Rin, 2004, p. 62). The problem with the hammer is that it is a tool of fictionists. As for the somewhat solemn statement that the facts portrayed relate to events that have occurred in the historical world, it appears to be a necessary but insufficient criterion for distinguishing between fiction and non-fiction. No one would take the film *JFK* (Oliver Stone, 1991) for a documentary, and we know very well why, at least intuitively.

But what can we say of films such as *The Battle of Algiers* (*La Battaglia di Algeri*, 1966), by Gillo Pontecorvo? Whoever enters the cinema two minutes late and misses the opening captions, advising viewers that the film does not use archival images – in other words, that everything they are about to see is staged – will not be able to tell whether they are watching documentary or fiction. The fact that *The Battle of Algiers* states that the events portrayed occurred in the historical world, as in fact they did, does not qualify it automatically as non-fiction. A documentary needs something else.

Because answers to the usual question 'What is documentary?' have proved unsatisfactory, I will attempt to take a different path.

The ethical question

The traditional formula for documentary can be summed up as '*I* speak about *you* to *them*'. The documentarian, *I*, the character, *you*, and the viewer, *them*. However, this formula usually means '*I* speak about *them* to *us*', because viewers of documentaries tend to come from a similar environment to that of the documentarian rather than that of the street kid, the Northeastern migrant fleeing the drought in Brazil, the folk artist, the African villager or the Inuit, who form the genre's basic cast. The great documentarian and ethnographer Jean Rouch once wrote: 'Cinema is the only tool I possess to show the other how I view him' (quoted in MacDougall, 1998, p. 26). One perceives that documentaries are not exactly about others, but about *how* documentarians portray others. The representation of any thing is the creation of another thing. In the case of documentary, *this other creation is a character*.

We are approaching what for me constitutes the very core of documentary. Anthropologist and documentarian David MacDougall provides the following description of the successive metamorphosis undergone by the person filmed, in the course of their transformation from a person into a character in the film:

> A person filmed by me is a set of split images: first, the person viewed, within touch, smell, hearing; a face perceived in the darkness of the viewfinder; a recollection, sometimes fleeting, sometimes with lapidary clarity; a set of photograms in an editing studio; several photographs; and finally the figure moving on the movie screen.
>
> (MacDougall, 1998, p. 25)

MacDougall states that, once ready, the film represents everything for the viewer, whereas for the director it represents reality minus something. For the director – who had the character in front of him or her, who breathed the same air in the room in which they met, who felt the cold with them if it was cold, or the heat if it was hot, who laughed if they were interesting or yawned if they were boring – the film is the reduction of a complex situation, a decreased experience. Or, at the very least, a construction of another experience. In this construction, the real person in focus is pushed farther and farther away to make room for someone else, someone closer: the character.

In the course of a person's transformation into a character, information inevitably gets lost. The absence in the film of the sincere handshake when we arrived subtracts the information that the character was kind to us, and the same applies to the glass of water offered or the coffee fetched from the kitchen. Every director, when viewing their own films, feels compelled to say things like: 'Right after this cut, he looked at me and said'; 'This happened just as we arrived'; 'A plane flew over just then, and we had to stop shooting'; 'Right here he began to realize that we had to stop'; 'She welcomed us just like that, in her Sunday best.'

We know that the person can only define him or herself during the few minutes in which the camera is rolling. But *he or she* does not.

After a few weeks in the editing room, the director becomes hostage to the film. The theme imposes its priorities, and the structure leads the narrative along paths that allow no diversions. It is with pity that the documentarian abandons so many other hypothetical films. They are unfulfilled possibilities, defeated by the film's own logic and structural demands. The paradox is this: potentially, the characters are many, though only one person was filmed. In my opinion, herein lies the true issue of documentary. Its nature is neither aesthetic nor epistemological. It is ethical.

One characteristic of cinema is to set the characters into what MacDougall calls dramatic constellations. These constellations appear as pairs of opposites – the oppressor and the oppressed, the lover and the beloved, the hunter and the hunted, the victor and the vanquished. Inevitably all characters end up falling victim to this dialectics. I will take as an example an interview I filmed with the father of Iranildo, a football player, for the television series *Futebol* (1998), co-directed by Arthur Fontes. In this sequence, Mr Ivanildo (Iranildo's father) explains to us how he manages his son's income:

– Savings, savings, savings, I keep track of all the money he makes. I only tell him how much he has spent, you see. This is so he doesn't lose control, so let's say he makes 10,000 *reais*, I tell him he's made 4000, so then he will only spend 1000.
– Do you keep all his wages?
– Yes, sure. I transfer it to my account. It's as I say: I leave him 1000, the other 3000 are for expenses, but I tell him I have spent it all. Why?

Because he didn't have time to learn how to manage what he earns. So I couldn't just say 'Here Iran, have your money, you are earning 20,000'. That would mess his head up. So I have to keep it for him for a while. These days I explain things to him, 'Hey, this is how much you earn, you are spending this much, you are spending a bit too much'. When he comes home he says 'dad, I'm going out' and I say 'that's fine, how much do you need?'. 'This much.' 'There you go.' No cheque books, I keep them myself, I say 'Did you get any money out, did you write any cheques', everything is controlled. These days I give him, or he earns, what I couldn't afford to give him in the past, you see? He also gives me things I couldn't have before, things my father couldn't afford. These cars, this house. I own a house now, bigger than this one, in Pernambuco. I already have 15 plots of land near the beach. Everything is shared, so if I buy six plots, two are mine, two are his and two are his brother's. We have to make the most of this moment. His salary is a good salary to live off, but it's not enough to make us rich, these things take time. But if in the future we get an offer from abroad, if this really happens, then we can really become independent. So let's say, if he is sold by 6 million, he's entitled to 15 per cent of his transfer fee plus his wages.

The first press review on this documentary praised the ability of the series' directors to show the ways in which many athletes were exploited by their families. The example given was precisely this scene. It had not occurred to the film critic that perhaps the father was right – that the son was incapable of handling his own money, that, if left to his own devices, he would probably have wasted all his earnings in no time. Furthermore, the critic overlooked the sacrifices the father had made for his son: he had migrated from impoverished Northeast Brazil to Rio, hitching on the back of a truck, had lived in a violent slum, had slaved day and night to raise his family while the son went through countless tryouts that the father tirelessly took him to on his days off, always in the name of a sort of contract by which the present had to be endured in all its harshness in exchange for the future: if the son were successful, the family could finally rest easy.

Some of this information is in the film, whereas some or perhaps most of it is not. But even if it were, the father would almost inevitably be seen as reduced to the role of an opportunist, and herein resides the danger. Because the father may be precisely this, or perhaps not; maybe, who knows, he is a little of each, both the father who cares and the father who exploits.

What we documentarians must always remember is that the person filmed has a life of their own, regardless of the film. That is what makes the ethical issue central for us. If I were to express this in a synthetic formula, a film, provided with narrative structure, is a documentary when the director has an ethical obligation towards his/her character. The nature of our narrative structure differentiates it from other non-fiction narratives, such as journalism. And ethical responsibility towards the filmed subject distinguishes our films from fiction.

One of the benefits of this definition is that it rejects any ideological formalism: that is, it does not contend that some narrative models are inherently superior to others. If the ultimate proof is the nature of the relationship between the documentarian and the documented, every school will produce its specific challenges.

However, an important observation is needed on this point: in recent years, perhaps taking the cue from Jean Rouch, documentary cinema has been attempting to discover narrative strategies that reveal right from the beginning the nature of this relationship. They are films about encounters. Not all these films are good, but the best ones attempt to transform the formula 'I speak about him/her to us' into '*He/she* and *I* speak about *us* to *you*'. Such films do not intend to speak about the other, but about an encounter with the other. They are open films, hesitant in relation to categorical conclusions on the essence of others. They do not abandon the pursuit of knowledge, but merely do not aspire to know everything.

Consuelo Lins, an academic, documentarian and Eduardo Coutinho's collaborator, observes this healthy reticence in the final scene of *Master Building*:

> The young student who gives the last interview asks Coutinho: 'Who are you?', and goes on to say that it is difficult for her to think about what she's going to become in life. She says: 'I can't really imagine myself as anything.' With this, she produces a final line that fits fully into the trajectory of all of [Coutinho's] films. Hers is an apparently offhand remark, which resonates with the director's conviction that it is impossible to conclude, in the sense of providing a 'closing', not only for the documentary, but also for a character.
>
> (Lins, 2004, p. 156)

The argument I quoted at the beginning of this chapter closes as follows:

> Non-fiction films and videos bear great power in Western culture. They play a bardic role. They negotiate cultural values and meanings, disseminate information (and misinformation), provoke social change, and generate fundamental cultural debates.
>
> (Plantinga, 1997, p. 191)

This – unfounded – belief in the strength of documentary as an important instrument for social transformation explains to a great extent the ethical problems in which we become enmeshed. Given the occasional wholesale gains, the minor retail sins are automatically justified – to show this street kid sniffing glue, this woman eating food scraps from the garbage, that man weeping over his dead child. Auden famously said: 'For poetry makes nothing happen.' To paraphrase him, it would be good to convince ourselves that documentary does not make anything happen, that is, it does not have any measurable social use. For a long time it was thought that documentary could be instrumental in implementing various agendas. This idea has still some validity. For many people, documentary is supposed to play a social, political or pedagogical role. Documentary has uses. My argument is that we do not succeed in defining the genre by its outward duties, but rather by its inward obligations. It is not what can be done with the world, but what cannot be done to the character.

Note

1. For more details see John Grierson, 'First Principles of Documentary' (Aitken, 1998, p. 83).

References

Aitken, Ian (ed.) (1998), *The Documentary Film Movement: An Anthology*. Edinburgh: Edinburgh University Press.
Barsam, Richard Meran (1973), *Non-fiction Film: A Critical History*. New York: E. P. Dutton.
Boscov, Isabela, 'O cabelo dele mudou ... ... e a carreira de Tom Cruise também não vai ser a mesma depois do intenso *Colateral*', in *Veja on-line*, 25 August 2004, no. 1868, available on http://veja.abril.com.br/250804/p_122.html, accessed on 10 July 2008.
Calder-Marshall, Arthur (1963), *The Innocent Eye: The Life of Robert J. Flaherty*. NY: Harcourt, Brace & World.
Da-Rin, Silvio (2004), *Espelho partido: tradição e transformação no documentário*. São Paulo: Azougue.
Flaherty, Frances Hubbard (1960), *The Odyssey of a Film-maker: Robert Flaherty's Story*. Urbana, IL: Beta Phi Mu.
Grierson, John (1979), *On Documentary*. London: Faber and Faber.
Lins, Consuelo (2004), *O documentário de Eduardo Coutinho: televisão, cinema e vídeo*. Rio de Janeiro: Jorge Zahar.
MacDougall, David (1998), *Transcultural Cinema*. Princeton: Princeton University Press.
Nichols, Bill (2001), *Introduction to Documentary*. Bloomington: Indiana University Press.
Plantinga, Carl R. (1997), *Rhetoric and Representation in Non-fiction Film*. Cambridge/ New York: Cambridge University Press.
Salles, João Moreira (2003), 'João Moreira Salles', in Agnaldo Farias, Amir Labaki, Bernardo Carvalho, Inácio Araújo, Isa Grinspun Ferraz, João Moreira Salles and Ugo Giorgetti, *Ilha deserta: filmes*. São Paulo: Publifolha, pp. 151–96.
Vaughan, Dai (1999), *For Documentary*. Berkeley: University of California Press.

17
Losing Grip on Reality: A Reflection on British Factual Television

Diane Myers

Television has never been so real ... and so unreal. The rise of reality is relentless. The boundaries between game show and documentary, reality and artifice, are becoming increasingly blurred. Now no factual programme is safe from the formatting process. Yet the recent debate about breach of public trust in British broadcasting may have shown that this process is ending. The uncovering of unpalatable television untruths has ripped a tear in the fabric of television reality, allowing the public to probe more deeply into the making of factual programmes and ask pertinent questions about the methods used. The current situation might be likened in fictional terms to the part in *The Truman Show* (Peter Weir, 1998) when Truman finds the scenery at the end of the storm: suddenly reality has lost its familiar way; no one is likely to believe that anything on television anymore is real.

For at least a generation, commissioning editors and producers have been congratulating themselves on their efforts to create ever more watchable programming, and audiences have clamoured for more and more ratings-driven fodder. Yet in July 2007, the independent producer RDF Media found itself at the centre of a huge controversy when it showed footage to journalists from the BBC documentary series, *A Year with the Queen* (BBC1, 2007). It appeared to depict the Queen storming out of a photoshoot with photographer Annie Leibovitz, but it later emerged she was actually walk-ing *into* the room, not out. Stephen Lambert, RDF's Chief Creative Officer, admitted he was personally responsible for making the deceptive edit and resigned. The subsequent resignation three months later of BBC1 controller Peter Fincham illustrated only too well the assertion by Jeremy Paxman, in his 2007 MacTaggart lecture, that the industry was beginning to suffer from 'a catastrophic, collective loss of nerve' (Paxman, 2007).

As a senior television figure, Paxman was able to point out the lack of emperor's clothes from a position within the BBC court rather than outside it. His impassioned plea for the soul of television was made with an insider's knowledge and authority, and was all the more powerful for being so. In the lecture, he asserted:

> There is a problem. Potentially, it is a very big problem. It has the capacity to change utterly what we do, and in the process to betray the people we ought to be serving. Once people start believing we're playing fast and loose with them routinely, we've had it.
>
> (Paxman, 2007)

Indeed, the recent reality breaches come at a time when the relationship between viewer and broadcaster has already been seriously fragmented by the burgeoning multi-channel, multi-platform environment, placing enormous pressure on revenue streams, both within the BBC, linked to the setting of the licence fee, and in the commercial broadcasters through advertising revenue. However, unlike the questionable docusoap practices of the 1990s, the difference now is that the public has for the first time questioned not just individual programme-makers, but the whole way in which programmes are made – and unlike the phone-in furore that has accompanied the latest reality crisis, the situation is essentially not a matter for the regulator, but one of industry self-regulation.

The British television watchdog, The Office of Communications (Ofcom), is an effective deterrent in dealing with programmes that perpetrate out and out fraud, but an extremely unsubtle tool for dealing with distortions of reality. The BBC report on 'Crowngate' (as the controversy over *A Year with the Queen* became known) concluded that although the broadcaster did not intend to deceive, it had not done enough to ensure its presentation was truthful (Wyatt, 2007). Since this sorry saga, most channels have now pledged to be truthful, but truth is not the same as reality, and reality is an entirely different thing from veracity. Indeed, in television circles, a quip from an anonymous producer is often quoted: 'There's reality, and then there's television reality.'

Film and programme-makers have always used a combination of artifice and guile in their attempts to engineer a sense of reality. However, in their search for yet more compelling formats, yet more ways to make the ordinary extraordinary, provide programmes that (in common commissioner parlance) were 'big enough to punch through the schedules' and increase international sales, it is arguable that British broadcasters overestimated the public's ability to differentiate between the real and the unreal. In a leap from the 1990s, where programme-makers and contributors perpetrated out-and-out fraud, television reality has far extended beyond the boundaries of what we traditionally know as 'reality television' to a cosy mesh of collusion between audience, broadcaster, contributor and producer to agree about what could be construed and constructed to represent reality. What constitutes reality in television terms, its content – the language, visual and verbal grammar of reality, if you like – is created out of a compact between audience and programme-maker.

A single word, 'access', had always clearly differentiated documentary from drama, but in the 1990s the situation became decidedly more confusing. The language of fact was changing subtly into the language of fiction; observational documentary series were becoming docusoaps, contributors characters. As in the case of Maureen in *Driving School* (BBC1, 1997) these characters frequently became larger than the programmes themselves. Collectively contributors came to be referred to as 'cast' and the ubiquitous term 'jeopardy' first made its presence known on the lips of commissioning editors. Documentary began to clothe itself in the garments of drama, using the simple mechanics of entertainment to engage.

Corner (1995) argues that a defining feature of reality television is the capacity to let viewers see for themselves. During the birth pangs of the docusoaps, this was a key attraction to audiences, leading them, as Annette Hill describes in *Reality Television*, to judge the reality of situations on a 'fact/ fiction continuum' – docusoaps at one end and formatted reality game shows at the other (Hill, 2005, p. 54). However, it appears that at both ends of the television spectrum neither the providers, in the form of commissioning editors, nor the consumers, in the form of audiences, now seem to recognize the difference between the two. Simon Ford, Executive Producer of BBC Documentaries, says he believes former RDF Chief Creative Officer Stephen Lambert unwittingly played a role in increasing demands for drama in documentary. After programmes like Channel 4's *Wife Swap* (2003–), says Ford, where conflicts are engineered, 'commissioners are asking, "Where is my conflict" ... [Lambert] has inadvertently created a culture where filmmakers are much more interventionist. There has to be a moment of conflict and reconciliation' (Ford quoted in Esposito, 2007).

In 1995 Brian Winston wrote: 'claiming the real' is a common device of reality programming. In *Lies, Damn Lies and Documentaries* (Winston, 2000, p. 1) he maintains that the exposure and condemnation of dubious footage must depend on a proper acknowledgement of the complexities of filmmaking: 'It cannot rest on the basis of a naïve belief that screen truth equates with non-mediation, or that the latter is even possible in any meaningful way.' Audiences are certainly aware of how television 'puts reality together' (Schlesinger, 1978), but how many of us actually thought that in *Top Gear* (BBC2, 2006) Jeremy Clarkson accidentally set fire to that caravan? Broadcasters and programme-makers have always found it comparatively easy to assume that the audience knows certain things cannot possibly be 'real'. Clarkson himself argued in his column in the *Sunday Times* (2007) that 'having total transparency from every show means lots of foreplay and a withered ending'.

Lisa Campbell, Editor of *Broadcast*, maintains that television is all about the creative use of illusion and artifice to entertain. 'If it wasn't for editors and authorship, it's arguable that most television would be unwatchable' (Campbell, 2007). However, the new constructs of reality are certainly not

simply inspired by a mission to alleviate boredom. They owe their existence to avaricious television executives, impecunious producers and terror
of falling ratings. In postmodern television the engine of production is
being driven by two simple motivators: fear and greed. And these motivators are externalized in the power play evident at all levels of the industry– in the relationships between audience and contributor, contributor and
programme-maker, programme-maker and commissioner and commissioner
and broadcaster.

We're off to see the wizard

In 2004 former BBC chairman Michael Grade (now chairman of ITV)
highlighted the market dynamic that was pushing broadcasting towards
commodity programming, and partly blamed the casualization of the
industry for the direction in which it was heading. 'Casualisation is leading to derivative ideas. You give the commissioners what you think they
want, not what you are passionately dying to make and believe in' (Grade,
2004). Indeed the power of the commissioners and the budgets over which
they hold sway is now critical in determining how programmes are made.
Simon Ford says: 'These days budgets have been cut so far that people are
hoping to get a proper access film from a couple of days' filming.' He adds,
'Commissioners think they can commission these programmes on the
cheap. People get out there and it's not happening in front of them and they
start to cheat, or construct false narratives. Access is about filming people for
an enormous amount of time for them to lower their guard and for stories
to bloom' (Ford quoted in Esposito, 2007). However, behind the scenes it
appears very little even remotely organic, let alone blooming, remains. The
fraud and fakery debates of 2007 exposed the entrails of British television
and found them not to be warm, alive and pulsating, but merely a system
of cogs, levers and pulleys, entirely bereft of the very emotions they were
trying to stimulate in their audiences; and behind this engine of production, pulling the levers, oiling the cogs, ratcheting up the tension, conflict
and drama, the Oz-like operators, the commissioning editors and channel
controllers were weak, cowardly and desperately afraid.

The mantra of ratings, ratings, ratings, and the protection and promotion of the programme brand have become a constant feature of British
television at the beginning of the twenty-first century. Channel 4's Chief
Executive Andy Duncan argued in his 'New Statesman' Media Lecture in
2006 that it was brand value that made the station. Yet, as Channel 4 vies
for ratings against what Duncan describes as 'the institutional baggage of
the BBC' and the unashamedly tabloid appeal of ITV, it is curious to note
that it is the terrestrial channels' similarities rather than their differences
which unite them in the quest for reality, and these similarities have begun
to mirror the very state of the industry itself. The increasing feudalization of

the British television industry, where commissioners adopt an omnipotent stance in their relationship with their suppliers (the independent production companies), is ubiquitously reflected in the producers' relationship with their contributors. From *How Clean is your House* (Channel 4, 2003–), *The Secret Millionaire* (Channel 4, 2006–) and *Supernanny* (Channel 4, 2004–) to *The Apprentice* (BBC1, 2005–) and *Dragons' Den* (BBC2, 2005–), many of today's programme formats reflect television's feudal structure, often featuring God-like figures at the heart of the programme, either present or, as in the form of *Big Brother*, omnipresent. In a chilling parallel with *The Truman Show*, whether it be *Big Brother* or the *X Factor* judges reducing hapless contestants to tears, these figures position themselves on all facets of the moral spectrum – directing operations:

> Truman [*to an unseen Christof*]: Who are you?
> Christof [*on a speaker*]: I am the Creator – of a television show that gives hope and joy and inspiration to millions.
> Truman: Then who am I?
> Christof: You're the star.

> (*The Truman Show*)

The return of the native?

This is not the first time television has lost its moral compass; indeed the furore over faked scenes in Carlton Television's 1996 discredited documentary about drug trafficking, *The Connection*, might have led us to believe that the soul of television was in tatters more than a decade ago. Eight years later, in 2004, John Humphrys took the title of his MacTaggart lecture from the Hippocratic oath that instructs doctors to 'first, do no harm' (Humphrys, 2004).

One might legitimately argue that 'doing harm' was not something that formed a major stumbling block, even to the early filmmakers, in their attempts to exploit reality within the documentary format. Robert Flaherty is perhaps best known for his 1922 film *Nanook of the North* (in which a half igloo was constructed to film interior shots); however, in his later film about the Samoans entitled *Moana* (1926), one of the contributors had to spend six weeks being tattooed and another two recovering from the process, although tattooing had long died out from Samoan society. The noble savage Ta'Avale would never have been tattooed had not Flaherty requested it. The sequence was, however, heralded by Flaherty as 'the rite every Polynesian must pass through to win the right to call himself a man' (cited in Barsam, 1992, p. 51).

Spool forward nearly a hundred years: one look at recent terrestrial schedules tells you everything has come full circle; tribes like Ta'Avale's have become the new celebrities of reality television. Nearly a century after Flaherty made his first films, the questions of ethics and reality are as pertinent now as they ever were. In *Medicine Men Go Wild* (Channel 4, 2007) a pair of dashing twin medics literally test the boundaries of their Hippocratic oath as they leave no stone unturned or tapeworm-infested monkey uneaten in their exploration of the efficacy of native remedies. Their jungle forays come hard on the heels of BBC2's *Tribe* (2007) which, in its programme on the Matis, even dealt with the tribe's previous experiences with documentary makers, who, unhappy with the reality of their existence, urged them to conform to native stereotypes. Channel 4's *Meet the Natives* (2007) is made by Keo Films, the same production company who made *Medicine Men*. And in *Meet the Natives* the company takes the conceit of the noble savage still further, by persuading them to turn the tables (and cameras) on us.

This gentle documentary series encourages us to reflect on what Western society has lost: friendship, family, community, respect for the dignity of the land and the animals that supply us with our food. The natives in question hail from the undisturbed South Pacific island of Tanna. Far from being an exploitation of the native people themselves, it is a poignant reflection of what we have become. In that, it could genuinely be said to be real.

Yet tellingly also, in the framework of the modern-day production process that has delivered such a gem, you can still see the wires; and these elements are very important in showing how the current production process is shaped and what is driving the engine of production. In its journey into the counter-intuitive territory so beloved of Channel 4, three major factors are influential in shaping this documentary: formatting, jeopardy and a relentlessly tight production schedule.

Meet the Natives, like many of its counterparts, is 'lightly formatted'. The sub-format is the division of the three sectors of British society into tribes – middle, lower and upper class – and the premise to take the natives on a metaphorical and literal journey through Britain and the British class system. The 'jeopardy' is created by the bizarre belief among the tribe that Prince Philip is the Son of God and hinges on whether they will be granted an audience with him. The fact that the audience does occur but Prince Philip refuses to admit the cameras is perhaps the masterstroke; it leaves something to our imagination.

As the natives are transported wearily on to their next makeshift home, the stock six-week production schedule is beginning to take its toll on their exhausted, but still smiling faces. It is arguable that one could make a much stronger documentary by observing the natives for longer, but quite apart from the cost, ah, then you have the problem of them actually going native.

At times the series appears to be a spoof, at others its profound wisdom is stark and haunting. A few questions are left unanswered: for example, the sweltering native emissaries are shown returning to Tanna in suits and ties and one wonders, perhaps, whether this was the idea of the producers or the natives. However, these minor visual incongruities never disturb the perceived truths to be gleaned from the programme itself. Its warmth, humanity and trust between programme-makers and contributors are evident. This is a story with a happy-ever-after ending. All are glad to return to their island, take off the trappings of 'civilization' and don again their penis sheaths. Everyone whose lives are touched by the natives benefits from the experience. This is a cathartic journey, rather than one filled with conflict, shame, fear or greed, which allows the subjects and the audience to take time out and reflect. A documentary like this is real in that it is able to touch something deep and meaningful. However, how would the natives have reacted if they had been asked for their comments on so-called reality television – *Big Brother, Celebrity Love Island*? They had enough to say about the iniquity of artificial insemination on farms and how it compromises animals' natural dignity. What would they have made of Rebecca Loos in Channel Five's hastily truncated series *The Farm* (2004–5) and her engagement in celebrity pig masturbation? Faced with such unappetizing viewing, it is unsurprising that Jeremy Paxman should have devoted his MacTaggart lecture to 'a plea for the soul of television', yet he might have been forced to admit that despite the manipulated and formatted reality of *Meet the Natives*, this programme still retained its soul.

It is arguable that if the soul of the programme, or indeed the soul of television, is pure, that we should be able to see, despite the constraints of the production schedule and formatting, that programme-makers have acted with integrity. 'Access is about building a reciprocal relationship', says filmmaker Paul Watson; 'I tell them things about me, they tell me things about them' (Watson, 2007). Watson says of filmmaking that those who hold the cameras will be like 'painters and craftspeople. They will make things they can be proud of till the day they die, because it has an innate truth' (2007). Watson indeed might be seen to be emulating in his filmmaking the sentiments in Keats's 'Ode on a Grecian Urn':

'Beauty is truth, truth beauty', – that is all
Ye know on earth, and all ye need to know

Well, not necessarily. There was nothing beautiful about Watson's ITV documentary *Malcolm and Barbara – A Love's Farewell* (2007). There was no formatting, no jeopardy, the production schedule spanned 11 years and the contributor's death from Alzheimer's disease was inevitable. Yet it too became caught up in the debate about truth or, more correctly, a visual lie– whether or not Watson actually filmed Malcolm Pointon's death.

Truth or dare?

'Deathgate' followed 'Crowngate'. The man whose BBC 1974 series *The Family* was heralded as the first reality documentary on television had found himself firmly handcuffed by the reality police. A report by media lawyers Olswang, commissioned by ITV, concluded that Watson alone was to blame for the ambiguity over the death of Malcolm Pointon. It said he was the 'primary source of the misunderstanding about what was shown in the film' and exonerated the ITV press and publicity department (Conlan, 2007). In his defence Watson said: 'I don't expect to employ the politics of semantics when talking about the death of the only man she [Barbara] has ever loved in her life' (Gibson, 2007). The ending was subsequently re-edited.

There can be no doubt that the integrity of Watson's programme was a victim of the quest for ratings, which had previously got RDF's Stephen Lambert into so much trouble. However, documentary is by its very nature a constructed reality. The structural integrity of a programme is driven by the stitching together of events. In *The Daily Telegraph* Gerard O'Donovan said: 'there was nothing faked about Malcolm's catastrophic decline into mental illness. Nor was there anything essentially false in the portrayal of how a not-so-old man suffered and died in a way many people die in this country every day' (O'Donovan, 2007).

In the same way as it probably does not matter that *Wife Swap* is filmed in less than a week, did it really matter that we were denied the last moments of a man's life? Without this frisson, however, just as we hear Grierson (1947) abhor shapeless reproduction and Campbell (2007) decry the unwatchability of television without editors and authorship, here is an almost unwatchable film, but not for Campbell's reasons, that the material is not shaped and edited; this film is literally too raw and painful to be watchable. It is quite simply too *real*. To make it watchable, to make us hang in to the bitter end, what could alleviate the harrowing process of watching a man's journey towards death through hell on earth? Of course, the promise of a television 'first', which we as voyeurs can say we have witnessed – the moment of a man's *real* death. Watson's documentary was, by its very nature, true, but it got hung up on the real, and, as the media ravelled in the complexities of the debate about its visual truth – its veracity – the documentary lost public perception of and support for its undeniable universal truths.

Contrast this with another programme about dying (well, about corpses to be more precise), *In God's Waiting Room* (Century North, 2007), a documentary for Channel 4 about a Muslim funeral parlour. It might have brought us face to face with our own mortality. It could have elicited a gamut of emotions – anger, grief, sorrow, resignation – and taken us on a journey with those saying farewell to their dead. Instead, 'jeopardy' intervened. As Muslim funerals should occur as soon after death as possible, the body of a Muslim woman who had died abroad needed to be defrosted immediately after the plane bearing the body had landed. All the funeral arrangements had been made. The mourners were about to arrive. The central tension of this half-hour film was therefore based on an unbelievably shallow premise – will she or will she not defrost?

No painterly treatment here, setting death as the final brushstroke on the canvas of an individual's life. It was possible to watch the dead hands of the defrosting corpse with impassivity, without emotion, because we knew nothing of the former person to whom they were attached. Was this real? Yes, in that it presented us with veracity – a visual reality. Was it true? Some might say it was, in the sense that this was the undertakers' reality, not that of the bereaved families. Though the undertakers were depicted going about their work with sensitivity and care, here was a view of death at its most prosaic, delineated simply as a process of swift dispatch. The film's detachment from emotion perhaps also allowed us better to understand the time pressures inherent in a Muslim funeral and observe how the trappings of an alien country's bureaucracy hampered the dictates of Islamic tradition. However, if it were true, it was a truth almost entirely leached of emotion. Even prolonged scenes of keening relatives failed to elicit a cathartic tear.

Perhaps we no longer need to go through the pain of Paul Watson's documentary, when we can confront death on more manageable terms by merely experiencing the 'jeopardy' of a defrosting corpse in its race against time. In the world of television reality, as Zizek (2004) notes in his essay on canned laughter, as we go about 'our frenetic endless activity' there is no time for real emotion. It must be manufactured for us, packaged, formatted and boxed.

Where game shows and reality television lead, documentary often follows and confessional chatshows have already established new parameters for conflict. In describing *The Jeremy Kyle Show* (ITV1, 2005–the present) as 'human bear-baiting' and 'a morbid and depressing display of dysfunctional people who are in some kind of turmoil', Judge Alan Berg imposed a £300 fine on a contributor who headbutted the lodger who had had an affair with his wife (Bunyan, 2007). The case revealed that the incident was fuelled by the fact that the show's producers had contacted the defendant six times before he agreed to appear.

Conflict and reality television go hand in hand. Yet we have now begun to see programme-makers deliberately imbuing the principles that first embodied reality television – the drama of the police, fire and ambulance chases – 'car crash television', into the banality of the everyday. Why bother to observe genuine emotion triggered by real situations when we can quickly and cheaply engineer constructed scenarios to create a load of false ones, irrelevant to the linear experience of real life? *Wife Swap* is a key example, where the generation of conflict at intense levels in a domestic environment becomes the raison d'être of the show. Strangely, also, no one ever seems to question the effect on the children of the families involved. Though there is no doubt that *Wife Swap* at times elicits heart-warming changes and lessons are learned, the programme also simultaneously displays the qualities of some horrifying genetically modified crop, something akin to injecting scorpion venom into inert wheat – a dark and dangerous fusion of elements, which were never meant to be combined.

If one peruses the international programme market, the outlook is even more disturbing. In Endemol's *The Big Donor Show* (BNN, 2007) transmitted in the Netherlands, Lisa, a 37-year-old terminally ill woman, solicited advice from the studio audience and viewers as to which of three contestants should receive her kidneys. Here, perhaps for the first time, is a multifaceted demonstration of how real and false emotion might be simultaneously generated in audiences, contributors and cast alike. It was later revealed that although the woman was an actor, the three would-be transplant recipients were real patients. Laurens Drillich, the then chairman of BNN, now head of Endemol USA Latino, argued that the network deliberately wanted to shock people and draw attention to the shortage of organ donors. 'We very much agree that it's bad taste but we also believe that reality is even worse taste' (Lewin, 2007). Since the show was transmitted in June 2007, 12,000 people have registered as new donors. The revelation of the hoax was voted 'Best Moment on Dutch Television' (Source: BNN). It is unlikely, however, that Dutch audiences will be so easily spoofed again. The trauma of viewing the programme left many discomforted. The potentially damaging long-term effects on BNN's credibility as a broadcaster still remain to be seen.

The Big Donor Show was television with a moral purpose, despite its attempts to warp audiences' perceptions of the real and unreal, but television is full of programmes with an amoral purpose, or devoid of purpose entirely. In recent years, British producers have used audience demand to justify the inclusion of dubious scenes such as the *Big Brother* race row. Abuse and humiliation were deemed to be particularly ratings-friendly. British television's increasing reliance on a series of false constructs to entertain has removed human dignity, introduced shame, provoked conflict and literally and metaphorically created jeopardy. Yet, programmes that detach audiences from morality, distance them from any humanity within a scene and inject contributors and audiences alike with manufactured hyper-emotion are bound to produce a dysfunctional perception of reality. There is little discernable difference between programmes like these and a phone video of happy slapping. With telling irony, one of the contestants ejected from the faux hysteria of the *X Factor* (ITV, 2004–) was the perpetrator of just such a crime.

The return of the real?

Devoid of appropriate human emotion, television simply becomes exhibition. In an extraordinary reflection of art and artifice, an exhibition in London, *The Return of the Real* (Victoria Miro Gallery, 6–10 November 2007), by Turner Prize winner Phil Collins, did exactly that. Collins even set up Shady Lane Productions with an office in Tate Britain and invited those who alleged their lives had been ruined by reality television to share their experiences. In Collins's words, the exhibition 'underlines the complex and unpredictable transferences that occur between reality and its mediation in television, film, or, indeed, art' (Collins, 2007). Tellingly paraded as an art-form, the obsession with reality has now filled every crack in British television, embracing everything from high-end documentary to trailer trash game show. Collins's exhibition represents an uncomfortable reflection of that obsession in its representation of images of anonymous television professionals, describing the tricks of their trade juxtaposed against interviews with contributors who claim to have been exploited by the reality makers. The exhibition's publicity literature says it describes 'the post-documentary culture which reality television has come to epitomize, and the accompanying issues of authenticity and illusion, intimacy and inaccuracy, expectation and betrayal' (Collins, 2007). There is little doubt that audiences, broadcasters and producers are losing their grip on reality. We have become obsessed with reality – at the expense of truth. In producing a version of reality that they deemed audiences wanted, many programme-makers have masked and distorted the essential integrity of their programmes. As Paxman (2007) says, 'It's not that the television industry doesn't have a compass. It's that too often it doesn't even seem sure any longer that North exists'.

Critics of British television might argue that if the industry is to survive and prosper, its moral compass must be embedded into the language, grammar and portrayal of television reality. Yet although broadcasters, commissioners, producers and researchers may be seen to be collectively and individually responsible for the misalignment of television truth, many industry professionals believe the current crisis is an inevitable and obvious consequence of a culture that stems from the top. The industry itself is now beginning to recognize that responsibility for mending the tears in the fabric of television reality must rest with its senior executives, who need to demonstrate a stronger sense of purpose and integrity in the commissioning process, a clearer delineation of the boundaries between fact and fiction and a closer examination of the mechanics of production in which somehow television's soul has been misplaced. Unless this occurs, even if it weathers the current reality storm, British television may be left to drift rudderless into an artificial sunset.

References

Barsam, Richard M. (1992), *Non Fiction Film: A Critical History*. Bloomington: Indiana University Press.

The Big Donor Show, available on http://www.bnn.nl/page/donorshow, accessed on 2 December 2007.

Bunyan, Nigel (2007), 'Jeremy Kyle Show "Is Human Bear-baiting"', in *Daily Telegraph*, 26 September, available on http://www.telegraph.co.uk/news/worldnews/1564177/Jeremy-Kyle-show-%27is-human-bear-baiting%27.html, accessed on 3 October 2007.

Campbell, Lisa (2007), Leader column, *Broadcast* online, 20 June, available on http://www.broadcastnow.co.uk, accessed on 3 October 2007.

Clarkson, Jeremy (2007), 'It's Lies That Make TV Interesting', in *Sunday Times*, 28 October, available on http://www.timesonline.co.uk/tol/comment/columnists/jeremy_clarkson/article2752154.ece, accessed on 4 November 2007.

Collins, Phil (2007), exhibition guide to *The Return of the Real*, Victoria Miro Gallery, London, 6–10 November.
Conlan, Tara (2007), 'Alzheimers Row:Watson Blamed', in *MediaGuardian* online, 21 September, available on http://www.guardian.co.uk/media/2007/sep/21/ITV.television2, accessed on 10 November 2007.
Corner, John (1995), *Television Form and Public Address*. London: Edward Arnold.
Duncan, Andy (2006), 'New Statesman Media Lecture', in *New Statesman* online, 26 June, available on http://www.newstatesman.com/200606260065, accessed on 6 November 2007.
Endemol Nederland (2007), *De Grote Donor Show: No Donor in Big Show*. Press release, 2 June.
Esposito, Maria (2007), '"Docs" Reality Check', in *Broadcast* online, 30 October, available on http://www.broadcastnow.co.uk/technology/indepth/docs_reality_check.html, accessed on 5 November 2007.
Gibson, Owen (2007), 'ITV under Pressure after Revealing Truth about Alzheimer's Death Documentary', in *MediaGuardian* online, 1 August, available on http://www.guardian.co.uk/print/0,,330308208-110418,00.htm, accessed on 12 November 2007.
Grade, Michael (2004), *Building Public Value*. London: BBC Press Office, 29 June, available on http://www.bbc.co.uk/pressoffice/speeches/stories/bpv_grade.shtml, accessed on 12 November 2007.
Grierson, John (1947), *Grierson on Documentary*. New York: Harcourt Brace.
Higgins, Charlotte (2007), 'Artist Gives Voice to Daytime Reality Show Guests', in *The Guardian*, 5 October, available on http://www.guardian.co.uk/uk/2007/oct/05/artnews.media, accessed on 12 November 2007.
Hill, Annette (2005), *Reality TV – Audiences and Popular Factual Television*. Abingdon, Oxon: Routledge.
Humphrys, John (2004), *The James MacTaggart Memorial Lecture*, MediaGuardian Edinburgh International Television Festival, Edinburgh, 24 August. (A copy of the lecture is available on http://www.mgeitf.co.uk/home/news.aspx/John_Humphrys_Delivers_the_2004_MacTagga.)
Jack, Ian (2007), 'The Documentary Has Always Been a Confection Based on Lies', in *The Guardian*, 21 July, available on http://www.guardian.co.uk/media/2007/jul/21/broadcastingethics.bbc, accessed on 8 November 2007.
Keats, John (1978), *Ode on a Grecian Urn: Keats Poetical Works*, W. H. Garrod (ed.). London: Oxford University Press.
Lewin, Tamar (2007), 'A Television Audition for a Part in and of Life', in *New York Times* online, June 3, available on http://www.nytimes.com/2007/06/03/weekinreview/03lewin.html?ex=1338523200&en=0ec639c7fc5b2139&ei=5090&partner=rssuserland&emc=rss, accessed on 8 November 2007.
O'Donovan, Gerard (2007), 'Last Night on Television', in *Daily Telegraph*, 9 August, available on http://www.telegraph.co.uk/culture/tvandradio/3667105/Last-night-on-television.html, accessed on 10 November 2007.
Paxman, Jeremy (2007), *The James MacTaggart Memorial Lecture*, MediaGuardian Edinburgh International Television Festival, Edinburgh, 24 August. (A copy of the lecture is available on http://www.guardian.co.uk/media/2007/aug/24/bbc.edinburghtvfestival2007.)
Schlesinger, Philip (1978), *Putting 'Reality' Together: BBC News*. London: Constable.
Thompson, Mark (2007), 'Comment – The BBC Has Squandered Trust. But We Will Win It Back', in *The Guardian*, August 24, available on http://www.guardian.co.uk/

commentisfree/2007/aug/24/television.edinburghtvfestival2007, accessed on 10 November 2007.

Topper, James (2007), 'BBC Admit Top Gear Caravan Blaze Was a Fake', in *Daily Mail* online, August 3, available on http://www.dailymail.co.uk/tvshowbiz/article-471541/ BBC-admit-Top-Gear-caravan-blaze-fake.html, accessed on 6 November 2007.

Watson, Paul (2007), 'Four Docs, Archive: People', available on http://www.channel4.com/fourdocs/people/paul_watson_player.html, accessed on 10 November 2007.

Winston, Brian (1995), *Claiming the Real: The Documentary Film Revisited*. London: British Film Institute.

Winston, Brian (2000), *Lies, Damn Lies and Documentaries*. London: British Film Institute.

Wyatt, Will (2007), *An Investigation into a Year with the Queen*. London: BBC Press Office, 5 October.

Zizek, Slavoj (2004), 'Will You Laugh for Me, Please', available on http://www.lacan.com/zizeklaugh.htm, accessed on 10 November 2007.

Index